# The Manga Artist's Guide to
# Digital Color & Lighting

## Learn to Use Light, Color and Shadows to Achieve Professional Results

NAOTO DATE

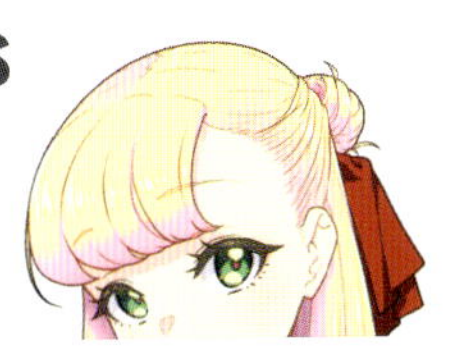

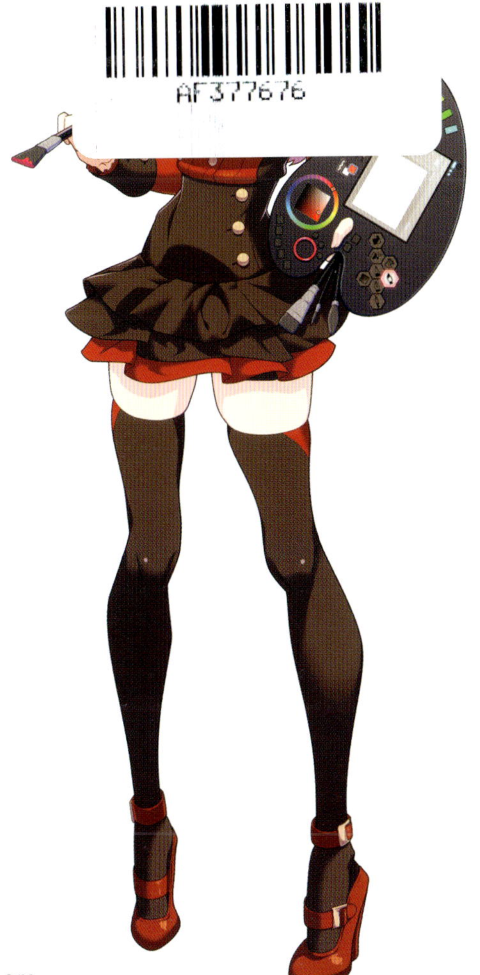

TUTTLE Publishing

Tokyo | Rutland, Vermont | Singapore

# Contents

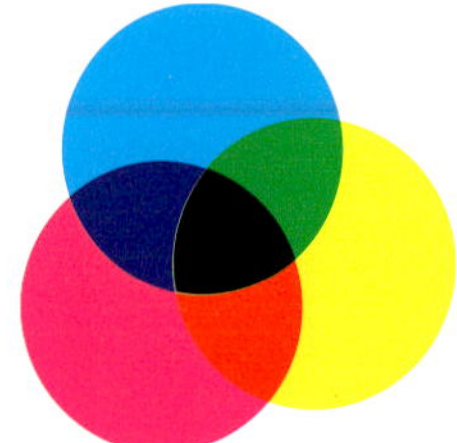

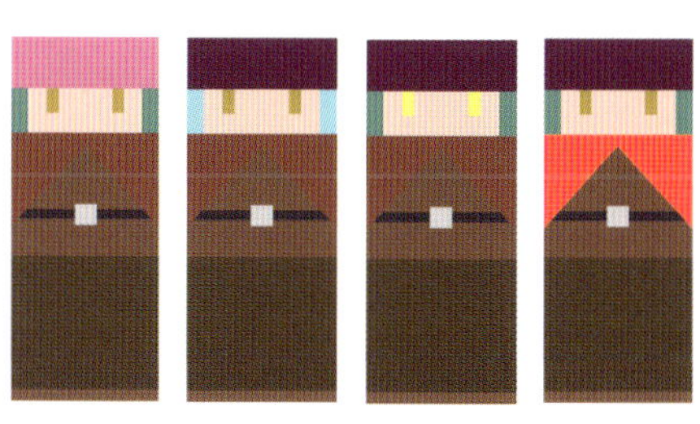

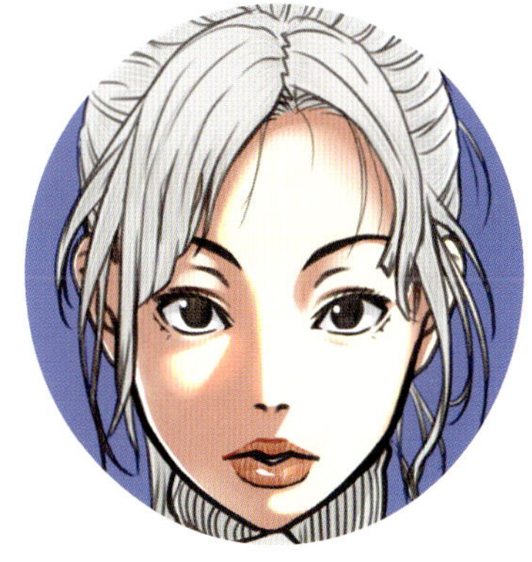



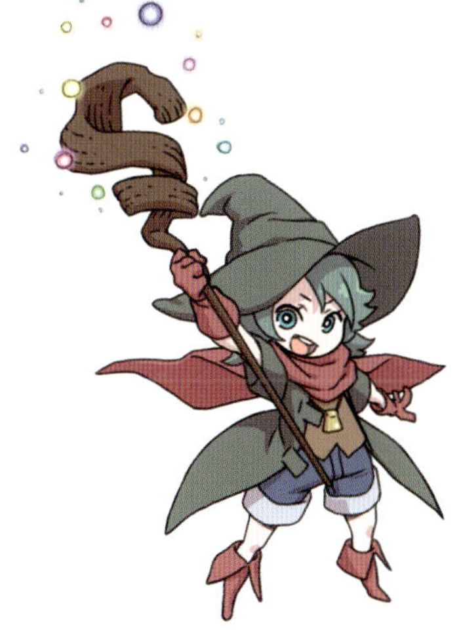

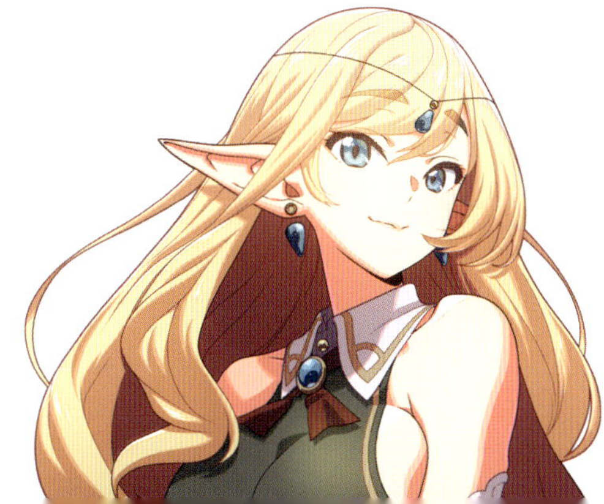

# Why I Wrote This Book

Many people think that coloring is difficult. It's true that it presents its own set of challenges and techniques altogether different from the previous stages: drawing, sketching and blocking in. Many artists prefer these preliminary stages, when you're responding to your initial inspirations and impulses, when your worlds and the characters that inhabit them are just coming into focus.

However, color is the first visual information we typically receive when looking at an illustration. Therefore, in the case of color illustrations, your viewer's first impressions are shaped by these key choices.

So let's look at some of the topics and themes to consider when infusing your creations with color and light. First is the degree of saturation you've chosen for your color scheme. If the saturation is too high or too intense, some viewers might find it offputting, so make sure the colorization isn't completely finished when you're separating the layers. It's a good idea to lower the saturation and to complete the finished image using shadows and finishing effects (see page 22 for the details).

Do you have a wide range of colors present, or is your illustration highlighting a limited number of hues? When you're using a larger number of colors, avoid creating contrast between them by using tones with low saturation and high brightness overall. When the colors present are limited, create contrast and increase the overall saturation while lowering the general brightness.

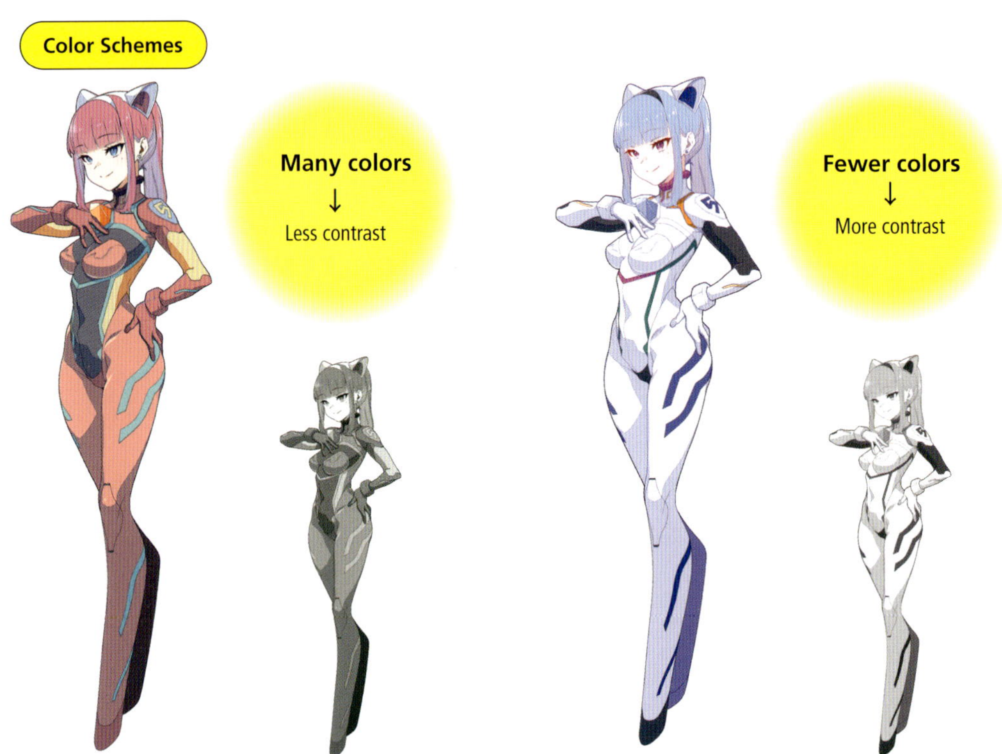

The real joy in coloring comes in the interplay of light and shadow, the surface contrast created between the skin tone and the costume or garment being worn. Color helps to distinguish and discriminate, while imparting key visual data to the viewer.

This type of coloration may be sufficient if the line drawing is already accomplished, but if you want to heighten or enhance its three-dimensional qualities, light and shadow effects are introduced. Light (in the form of highlights) has the effect of making objects appear to be in flux. Many painters tend to focus on shadows instead. In the end, finishing is everything when it comes to painting, shading and coloration. There are various methods and techniques you can use: aerial perspective, color correction and depth of field are just a few at your disposal. If you master these various techniques, you'll elevate your characters and scenes and create indelibly original images.

Follow the introductory explanations and try your hand at your own coloration and shadow techniques. Watch as your own illustrations come to life before your eyes!

—Naoto Date



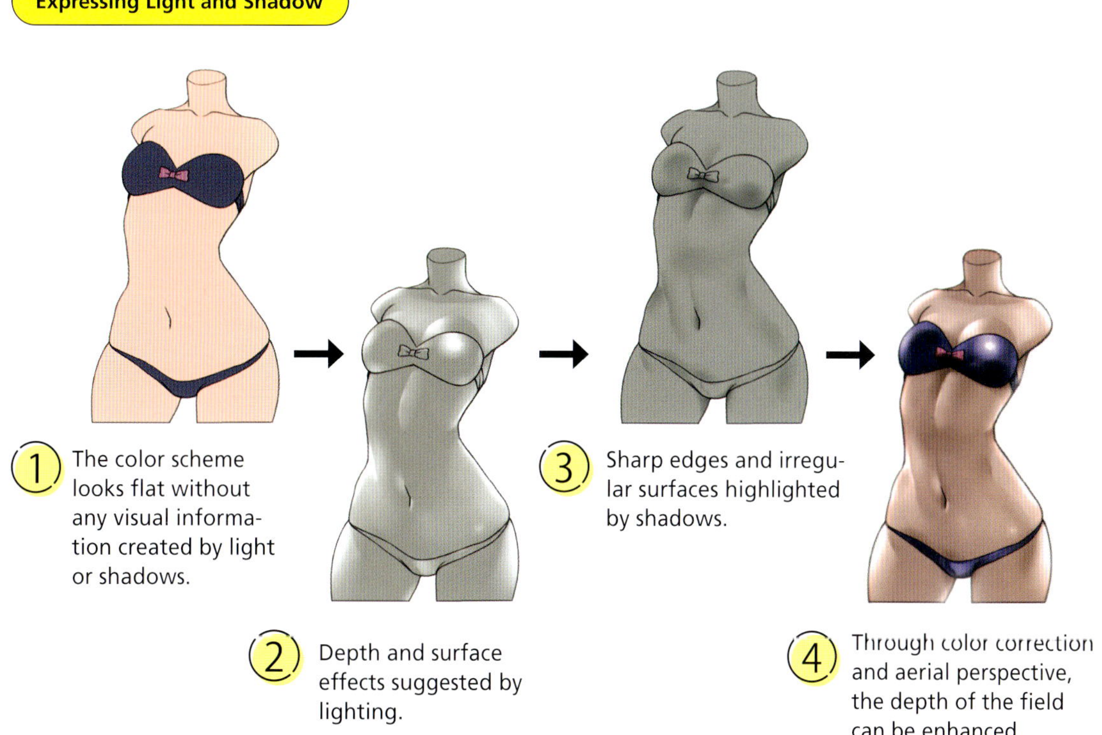

1. The color scheme looks flat without any visual information created by light or shadows.

2. Depth and surface effects suggested by lighting.

3. Sharp edges and irregular surfaces highlighted by shadows.

4. Through color correction and aerial perspective, the depth of the field can be enhanced.

# How to Use This Book

So you can create and illustrate characters but are having difficulties when it comes to coloring them in? Choose your colors with confidence. Analyze the results. Why didn't the color scheme come together? Why are the colors flashy and garish? Questions like these and so many more will be answered. Just follow the tips and techniques throughout, concluding with a summary of the basics of color selection and application.

Questions are asked at the beginning of each section followed by answers, hints and related information.

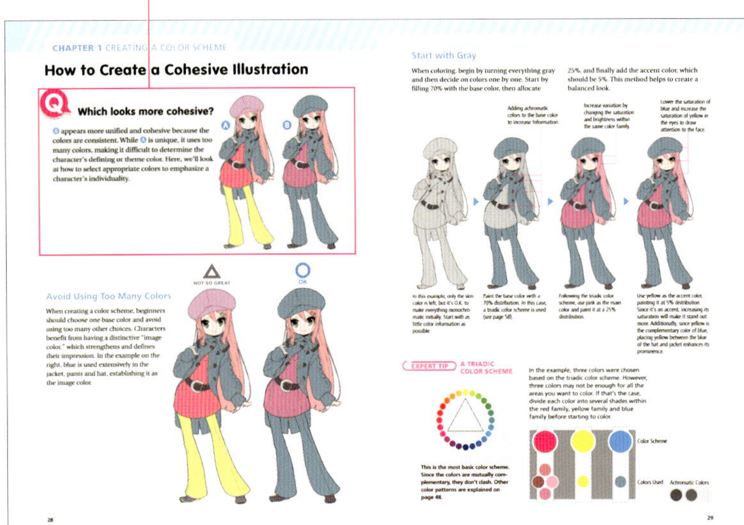

## — A CLOSER LOOK —

Key topics and ideas are explored with these in-depth explanations.

## EXPERT TIP

Special pointers offer additional information.

## GETTING STARTED

This section explains and compiles the operations and techniques necessary for drawing.

## HOW TO CREATE A COLOR SCHEME

**CHAPTER 1** Creating a Color Scheme
**CHAPTER 2** Color Selection Patterns
**CHAPTER 3** Color Controls the Reader's Gaze

Basics of colors and color schemes and how to choose schemes

## LIGHT AND SHADOW

**CHAPTER 4** Expressing Light and Shadow

Examines the relationship between light, shadow and color.

## TIPS AND TECHNIQUES

**CHAPTER 5** Finishing Techniques
**CHAPTER 5** Common Pitfalls & Errors

Techniques to improve illustrations and what to do when you're stuck.

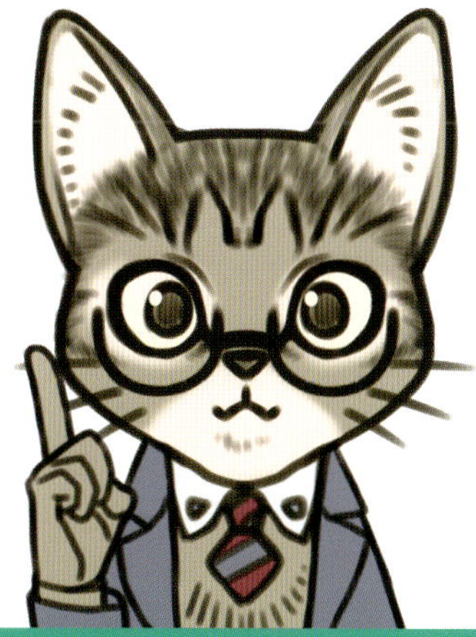

# GETTING STARTED

Let's begin with some basic tips and techniques. Complete the blueprint of your illustration and then the real fun begins, as the right colors start to add life and luster!

# Some Basic Tips & Concepts

## How Do I Know When The Illustration Is Done?

You've put on the finishing touches and have achieved that enviable point: you're done! But what does it exactly mean to complete a drawing or an illustration? Is there one right answer, one ideal finished state? Here are four concluded works, each complete in and of itself. Let's look at the differences and the placement of the rough colors starting with one on the left.

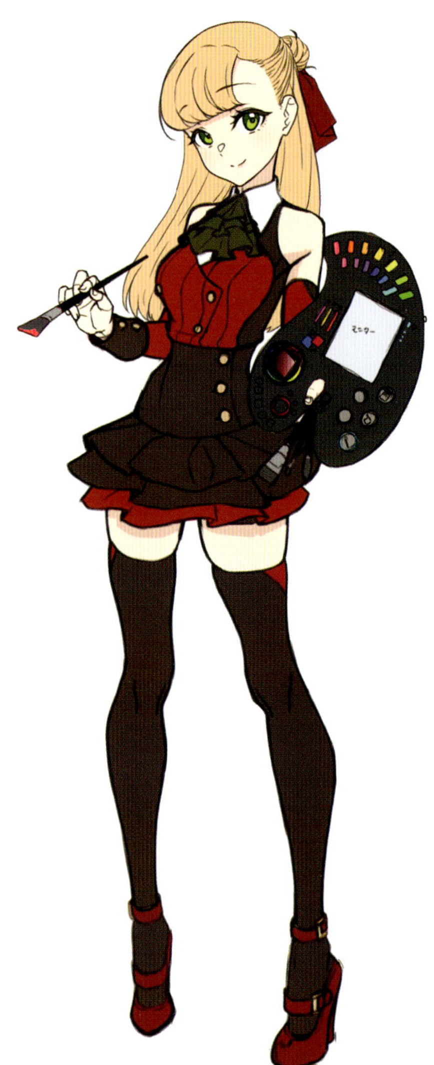

**Rough Color**
The completed line drawing is roughly colored in.

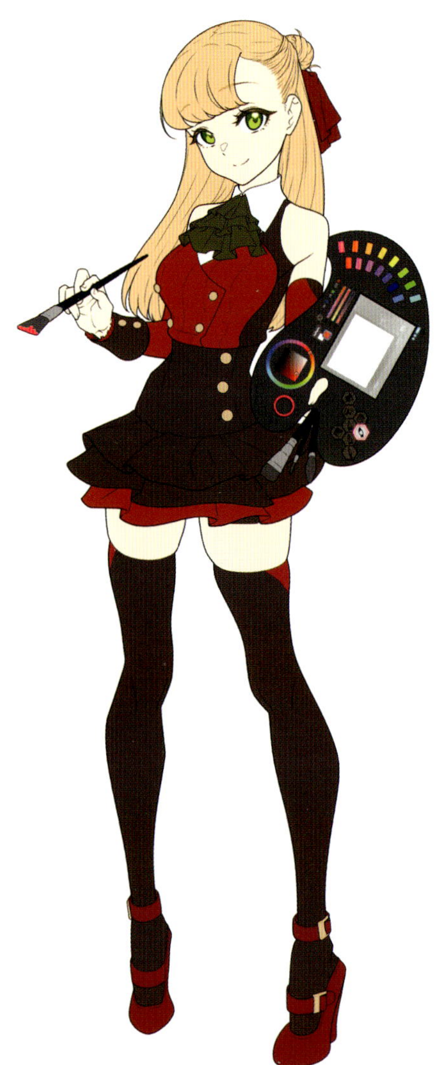

**Undercoat**
Colors are then arranged based on the roughed-in version. Paint the figure, being sure not to leave any unpainted parts and paying attention to layer composition.

Next comes the primer, when the basic colors are placed based on the rough painting. Then the character-painting stage adds shadows and reflections. The final step is to finish the painting by adding lighting and processing effects, taking into account the surrounding environment and other factors. In this guide, the rightmost or final version is the finished illustration.

Coloring techniques are the focus here, tips related to coloring illustrations that have been finished up to the line-drawing stage. Of course, the style varies from person to person. Some prefer a more simplified or less adorned style. If that approach more closely reflects your style, you can leave your work as completed at the halfway point.

When it comes to coloring, if you can't seem to get it right, this is the guide for you. This book is designed to help those who can produce line drawings but have trouble with the next steps and stages, the coloring. With a little expert guidance, you'll understand how to color in a more attractive way that will lead to that indelibly unique final result.

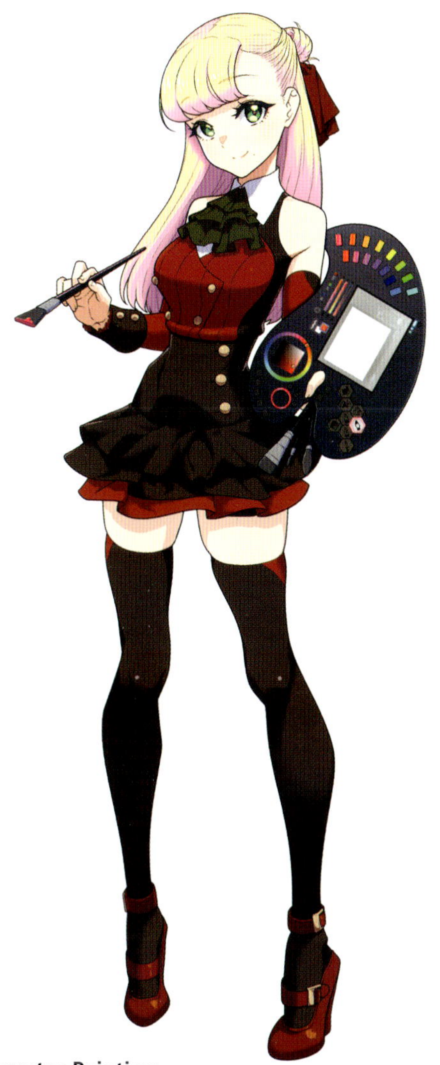

**Character Painting**
Shadows and highlights have been added, and the character painting is complete. The coloration now has a three-dimensional effect.

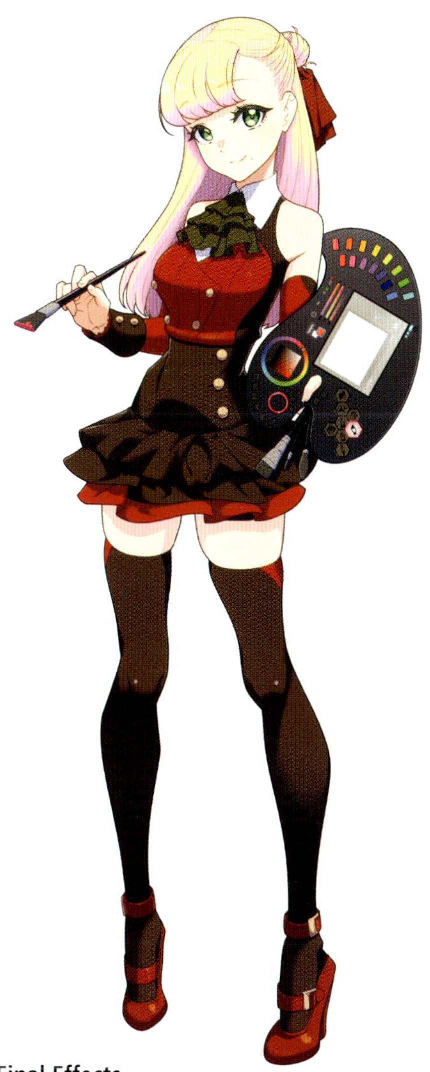

**Final Effects**
Lighting and shading have been added to match the background, and finishing touches have been applied.

## Using a Light Gray Canvas

Many beginners say that a blank canvas confuses them when they start working. More advanced artists and colorists tend to fill the canvas with one color as soon as they start working on a painting. There are many advantages to this, but one of the most important is that it makes it easier to detect leftover paint. The color you choose is based on your personal preferences and the goal of the illustration, but here we recommend light gray. Of course, you can change the fill color at any time according to your preferences.

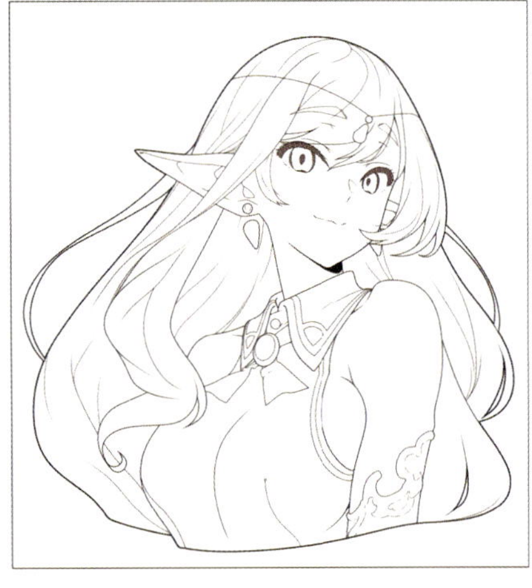

White Canvas

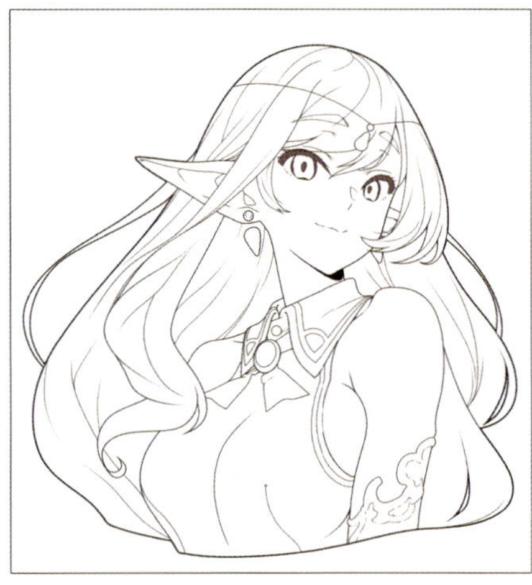

Light Gray Canvas

## Color Flow

This diagram shows the process from line drawing to color application and completion. The process of creating the line drawings and arranging the unique colors at the bottom of the pyramid requires more work than the later stages of finishing and adding color values. It's common for beginners to put the same amount of effort into all tasks until you become more familiar with the entire process. It's better to understand that there's a difference in the amount of effort required for each process so that you can allocate it appropriately and complete the finished illustration more easily.

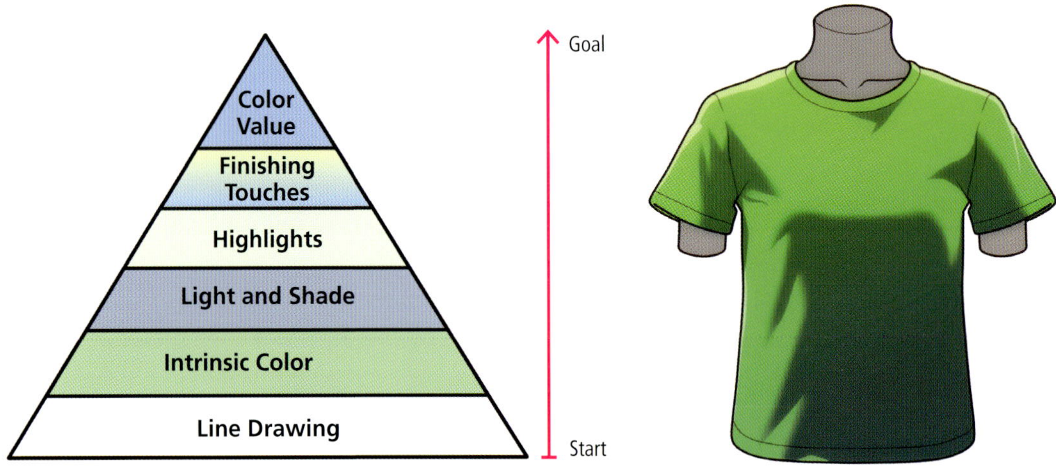

## ① Line Drawings and Silhouettes

Line drawings should be drawn thicker in silhouettes and front-to-back areas, and thinner in areas of high detail and line density.

| Main Primary Layer |
| --- |
| Normal |

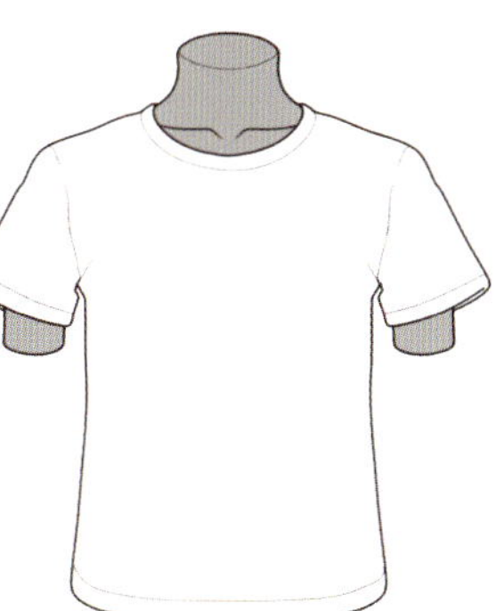

## ② Intrinsic Color

The intrinsic color is the base color. When deciding, be careful not to increase saturation too much or decrease lightness too much. Be aware that shadows should be added after this stage.

| Main Primary Layer |
| --- |
| Normal |

→ See page 18

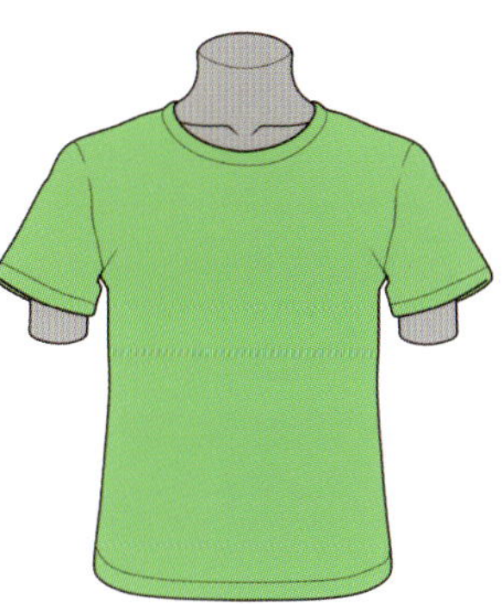

## ③ Light & Darkness

In the case of shadows, be aware of how to make them look three-dimensional while considering the direction of the light source.

| Main Screen |
| --- |
| Normal, Multiply |

→ See page 62

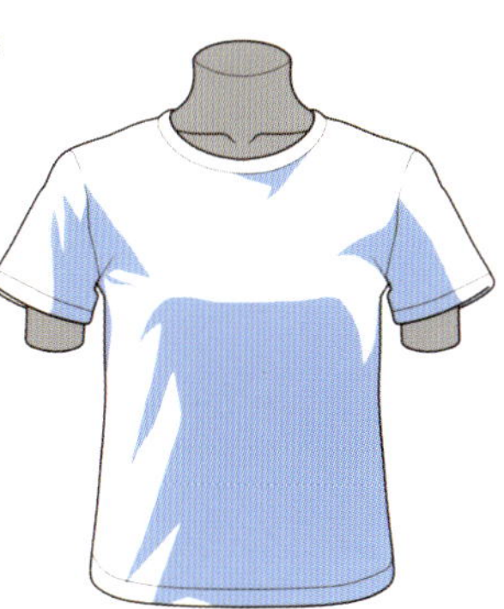

## ④ Highlights

These areas are singled out by a light source. Be aware that highlights also show surfaces. Avoid pure white highlights unless they're light in intrinsic color.

| Main Layer |
| --- |
| Luminous Screen |

→ See page 62

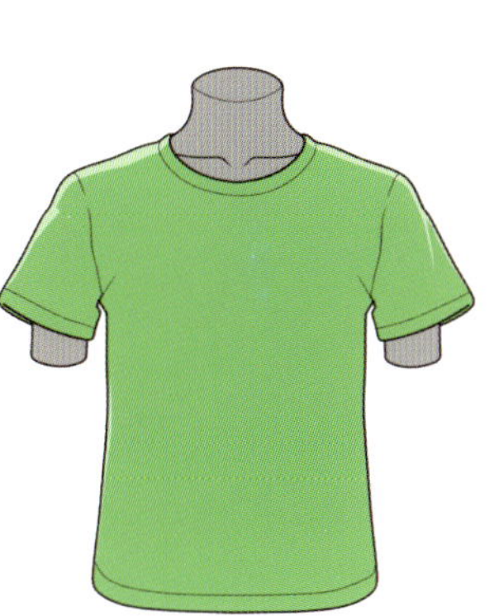

## ⑤ Finishing Touches

There are many different types of finishes. Finishing can greatly enhance the final level of a painting.

| Main Screen |
| --- |
| Overlays |
| Overlay, etc. |

→ See page 90

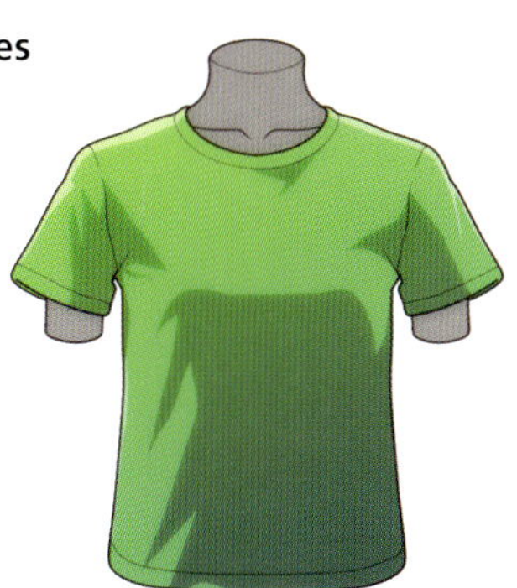

## ⑥ Color Value

Daytime and nighttime are associated with different tones. If you understand color values, you can freely change the same illustration from day to evening and from night to day.

| Main Layer |
| --- |
| Layer Opacity |
| Adjustment |

→ See page 120

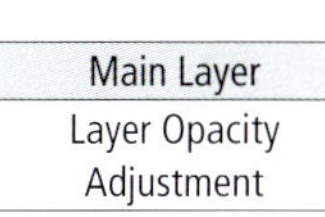

---

**EXPERT TIP** — **CREATING CHIBI-STYLE CHARACTERS**

There are various painting methods, such as the grisaille painting method, which involves painting in the following order: ❶ Rough ❷ Shading (grayscale) ❸ Line drawing ❹ Specific color (overlay) ❺ Finishing ❻ Color value.

# What Is a Color Scheme?

Look at the following two illustrations. They use the same line art, but the coloring is entirely different. The left one uses more anime-style coloring, which involves little to no blurring, while the right one uses a thicker painting style, layering colors while leaving the brush strokes visible. At first glance, these two styles seem entirely different, but the color scheme, which involves deciding what colors to place where, is the same for both. The final appearance varies greatly depending on what color shadows are used and what kind of brushstrokes are applied. This book focuses on the fundamental concept of color schemes, explaining how to choose shadow colors and how to think about lighting, regardless of the coloring method.

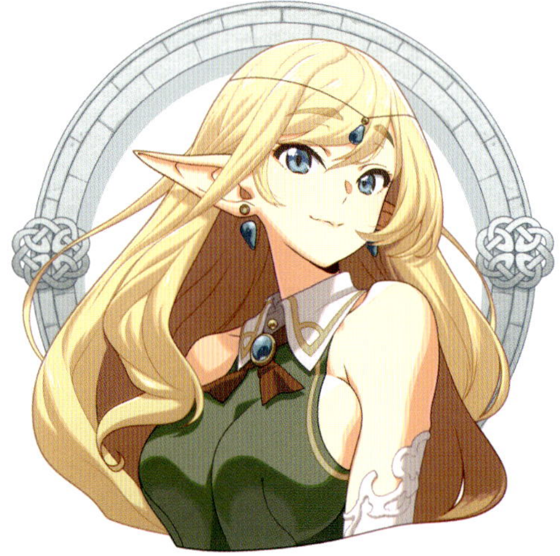

Anime Coloring

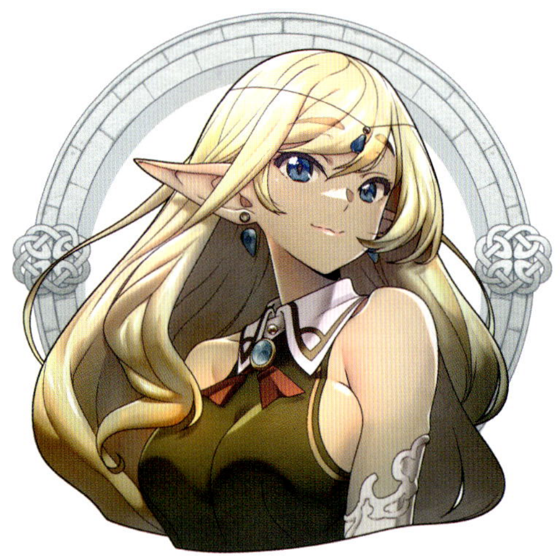

Thick Painting

# Basic Coloring Methods

There are several ways to apply color. The base color is typically applied using large brushes or fill tools to paint the primary color. Be careful not to color outside the intended areas or leave unpainted spots. Once the base color is done, proceed to add the shadow colors to the darker areas. There are several methods for applying shadows, with the most basic being simply placing them, a technique commonly used in anime coloring. However, this alone can make the illustration seem lacking in detail, so adding realistic effects and details through blurring and layering is often necessary. Finally, any excess color or areas that went beyond the lines can be cleaned up or erased. Depending on the finishing techniques and methods used, these steps may vary, but most illustrations follow these general processes for coloring.

This book primarily focuses on these four coloring methods, but feel free to adapt them to your own coloring style, using brushes with texture or gradients if preferred.

**Base Color**

A solid fill applied with fill tools or large brushes without texture.

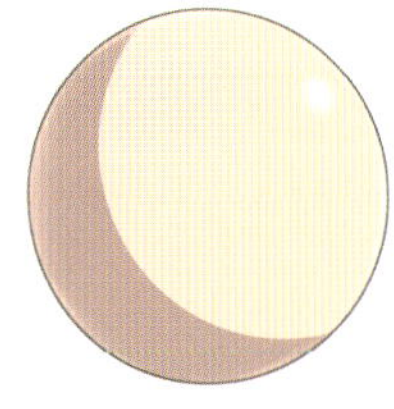

**Placing**

Applying shadow colors or highlights with a brush that doesn't blur.

**Blurring**

Using a blur brush to soften the edges of applied colors.

**Layering**

Adding more colors on top of the base color.

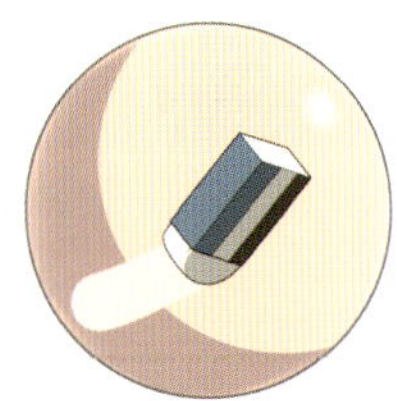

**Erasing**

Using an eraser to clean up or refine the edges of the applied colors.

# Layer Composition

Managing layers can be challenging. However, for professional illustrations, it's common to need revisions or color changes later on. To prepare for such situations, it's important to properly separate the layers. A recommended method for managing layers is using Layer Folders. Manage each Line Art, Coloring and Background with a layer folder. Properly naming each layer helps avoid confusion later. As you gain experience, gradually decide on a layer structure that works best for your workflow.

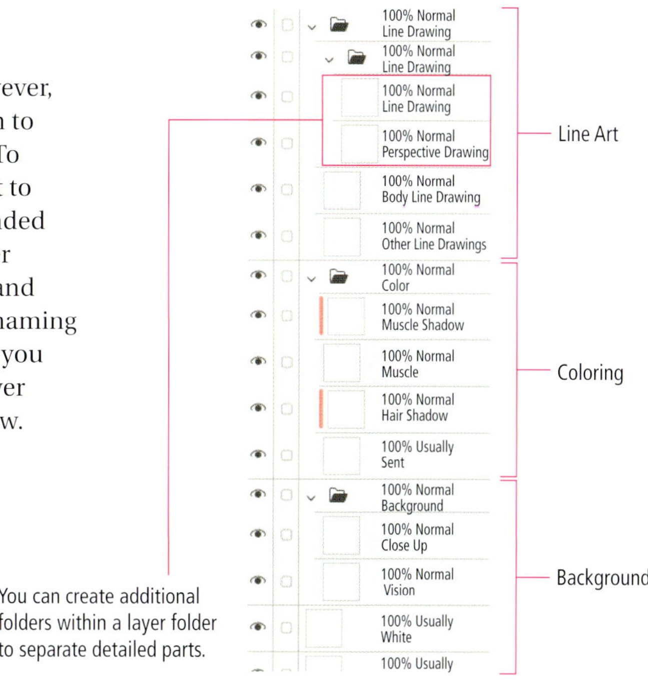


You can create additional folders within a layer folder to separate detailed parts.

# Layer Blend Modes

Layer blend modes allow you to set how the colors on one layer blend with the colors on the layer below it. This can create color harmony, change colors and achieve various effects.

Blend modes have effects as shown in the diagram to the right. This is a general summary, and the following pages will introduce the blend modes frequently used in this book.

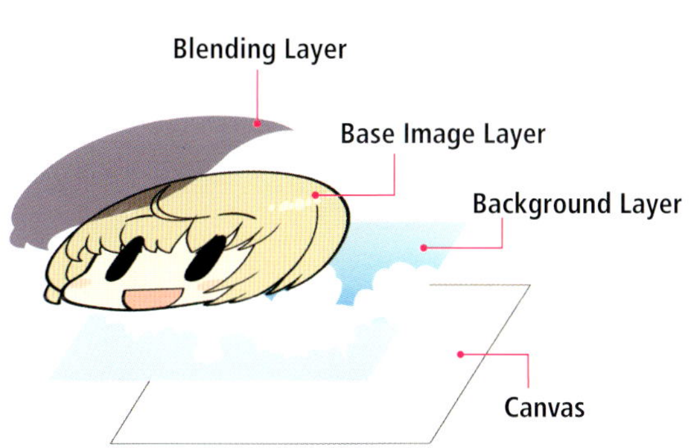


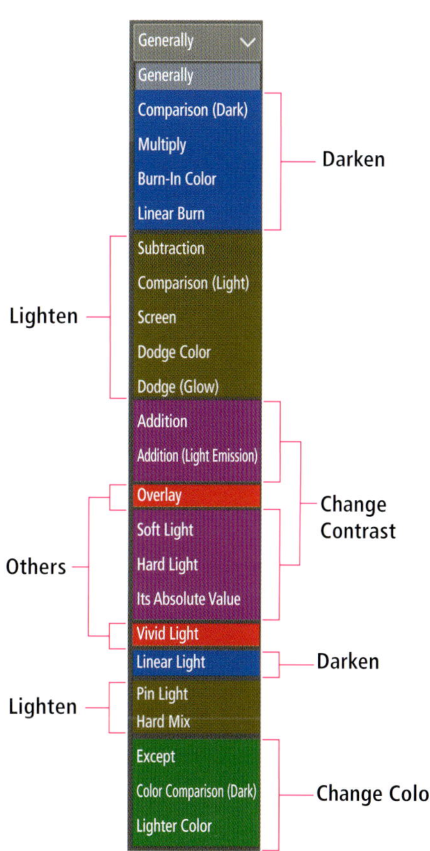

# Synthesis Modes

Here are the composite modes you'll frequently come across. The color in the lower left corner of each is the color applied to the particular layer.

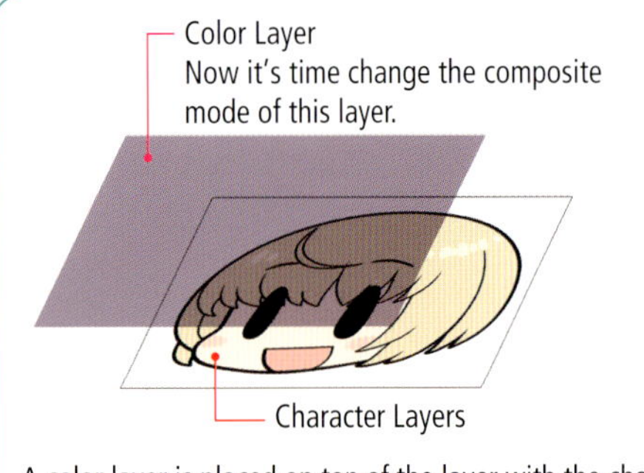



A color layer is placed on top of the layer with the character. The composite mode of the color layer is changed.

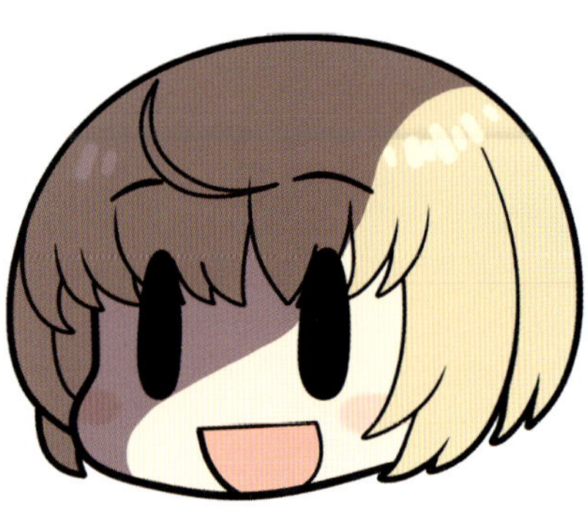

###  Multiplication

The colors (each RGB value) of the layers below the set layer are multiplied and combined. The result is a color darker than the original color. Often used to add a layer of colors such as shadows.

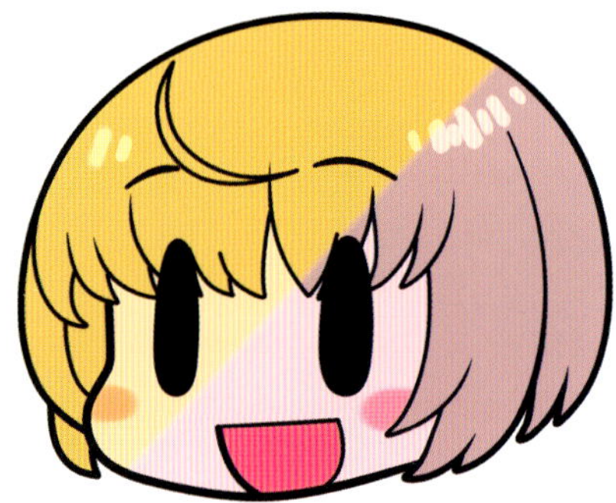

### 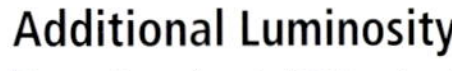 Burn-In Color

It produces an effect similar to the burn-in effect of film photography. The colors of the layer below are darkened and the contrast is strengthened, then the colors of the layer you set are combined. Often used when you want to increase the contrast during processing.

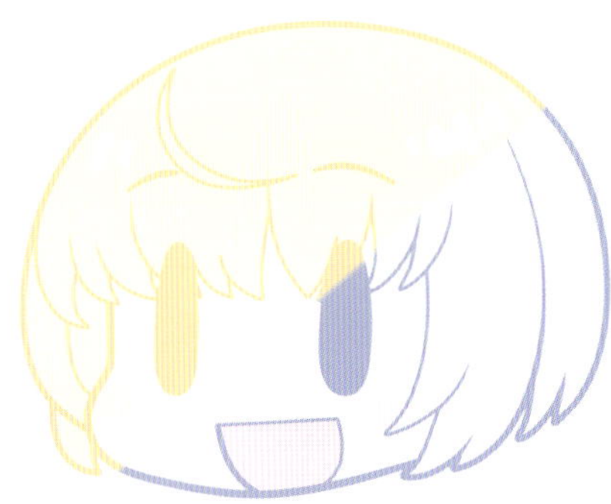

### 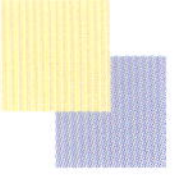 Screen

Inverts the color of the layer below and multiplies the color of the set layer to create a composite. The result is a color brighter than the original color. Often used to express light or to create a sense of airiness.

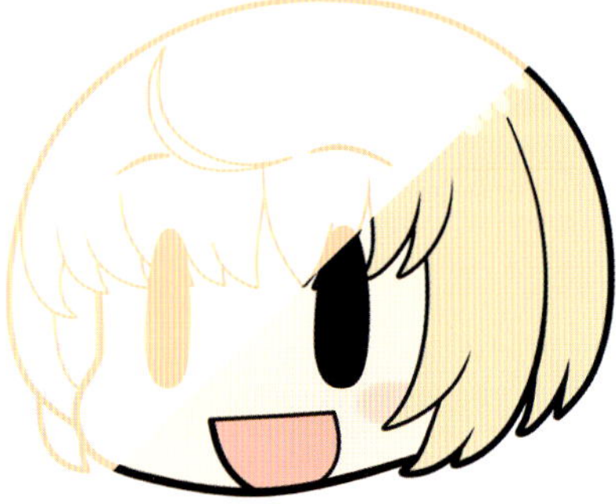

### Additional Luminosity

The colors (each RGB value) of the layers below the set layer are added and combined. The result is a color brighter than the original color. This is effective when you want to create a luminous effect. "Add (Luminous)" produces a stronger effect on transparent areas.

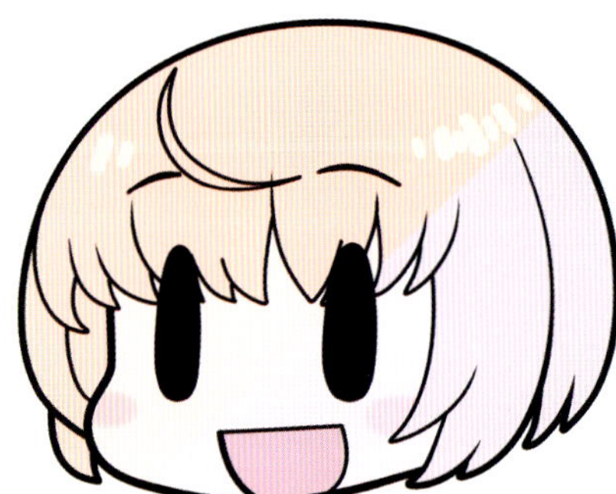

### 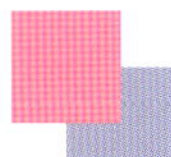 Overlays

Based on the color of the layer below, "Multiply" and "Screen" are determined and combined. After compositing, light areas become lighter colors and dark areas become darker colors. This function is often used to create a sense of color unity or cohesiveness.

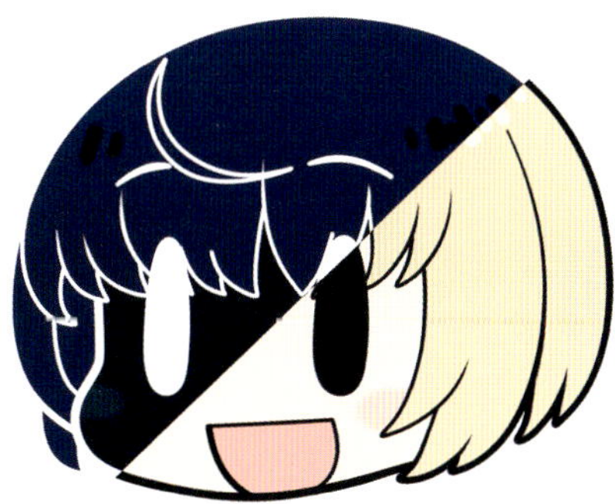

### Absolute Value of Difference

Subtracts the color (each RGB value) of the set layer from the layer below and displays the color that is the absolute value of the two. Often used to invert colors.

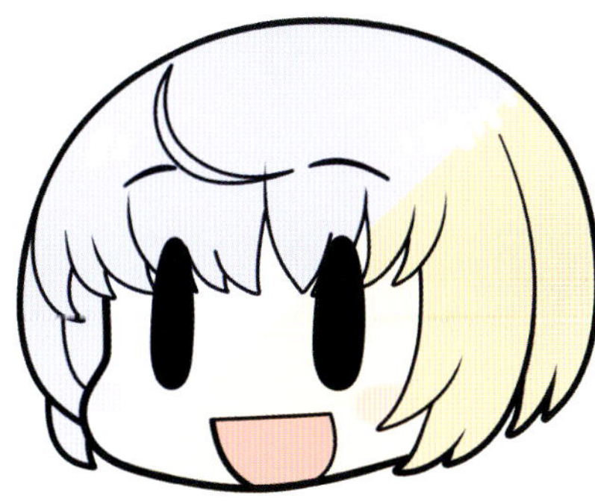

### Color

Applies the hue and saturation of the set layer. The luminance values of the layer below will be retained.

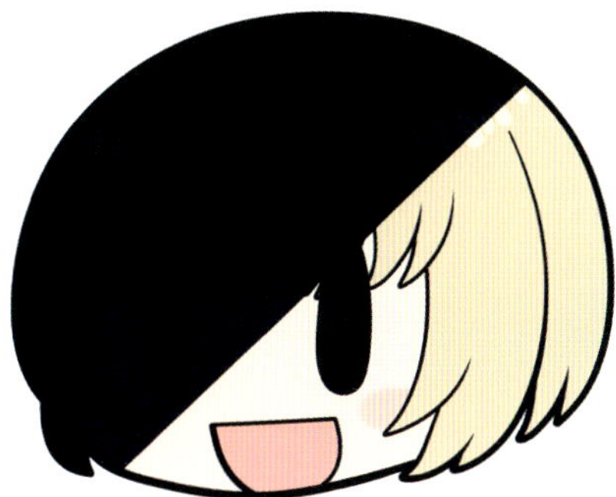

### Subtraction

Subtracts and combines the colors (each RGB value) of the set layer and the layer below. The result is a darker color than in the "Multiply" mode.

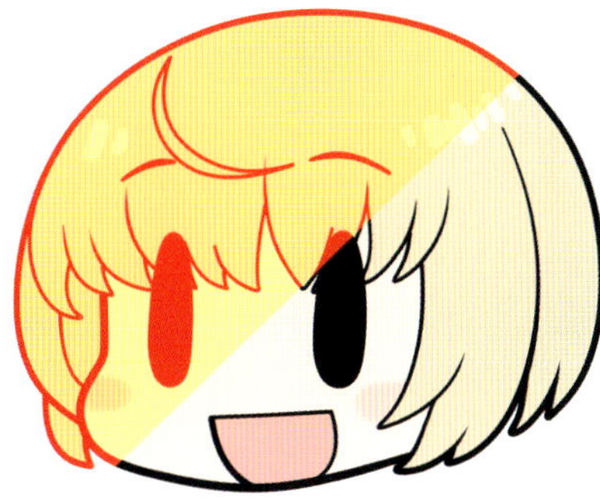

### Hard Light

Overlaying a color lighter than gray with 50% luminosity results in a lighter color. Overlaying a color darker than gray with a luminosity of 50% will result in a darker color closer to "Multiply"; overlaying a gray with a luminosity of 50% will result in the color of the layer below being displayed as is. Drawing without overlaying on a color area will result in white for a color lighter than 50% gray, and that color for a color darker than 50% gray.

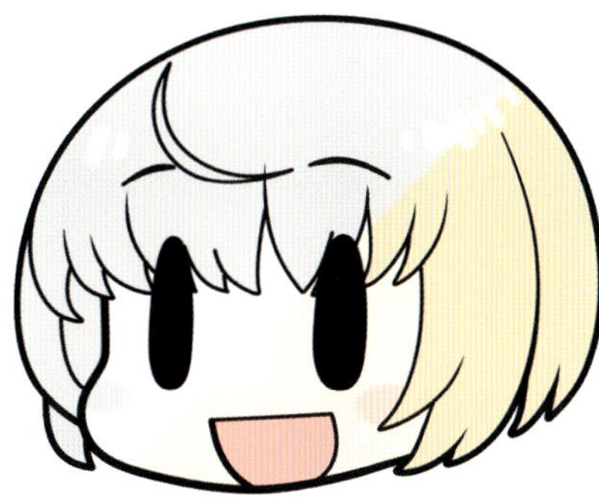

### Color Saturation

Applies the saturation of the set layer. The luminosity and hue values of the layer below are retained. Since black can be added to make the image monochromatic while maintaining luminosity, it's often used to check the image in monochrome.

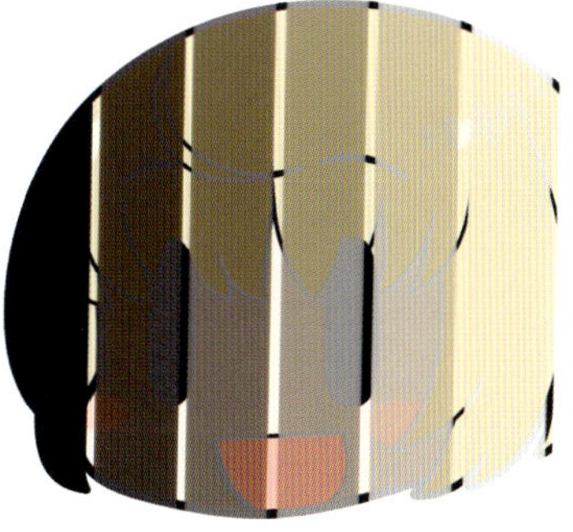

### Brightness

Applies the luminosity of the layer you set. The hue and saturation values of the layer below will be retained.

# Grayscale Conversion

Often you'll need to check or review an illustration by converting to grayscale. Here's a method to check without having to change modes or export in grayscale. Simply change the blending mode of a layer filled with white to [Color], and you can easily check the grayscale. You can achieve the same effect by setting the blend mode to [Hue] or [Saturation].

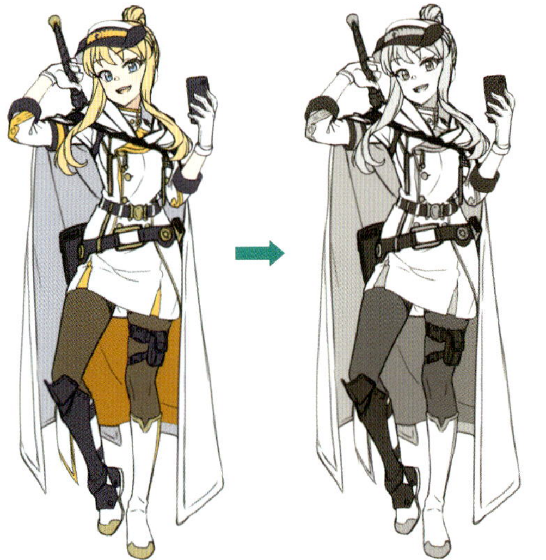

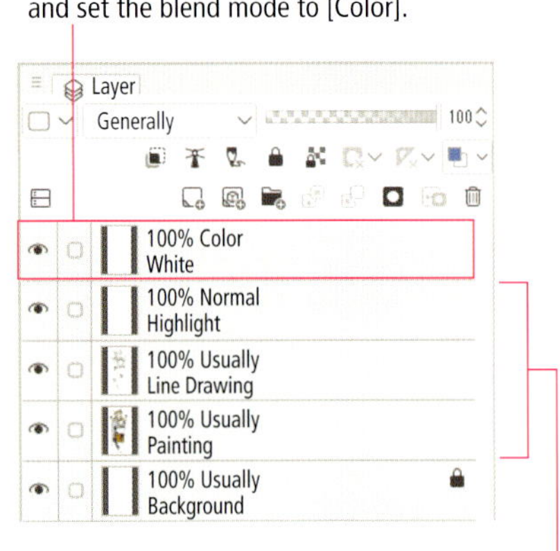

Place a white-filled layer at the top and set the blend mode to [Color].



It's O.K. if the layers for coloring, line art and highlights are separated.

# Basics of Changing Hue, Lightness and Saturation

When painting and coloring illustrations, terms like increase saturation or decrease lightness are often used. Here, we'll take a closer look at how changing the hue, lightness and saturation affects the colors.

It's easy to change colors in drawing apps, but knowing how these changes affect colors can help you paint faster and make corrections more easily.

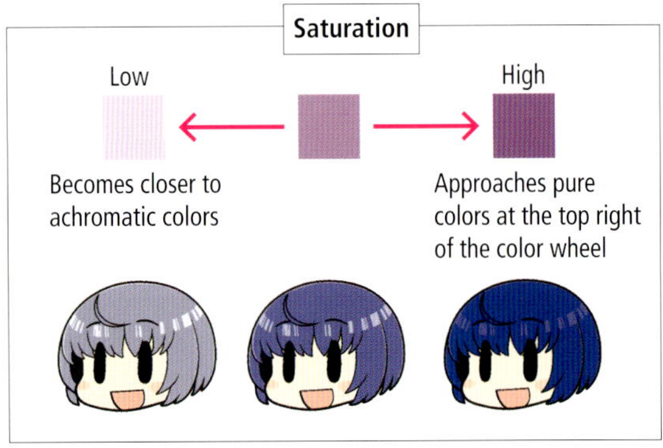


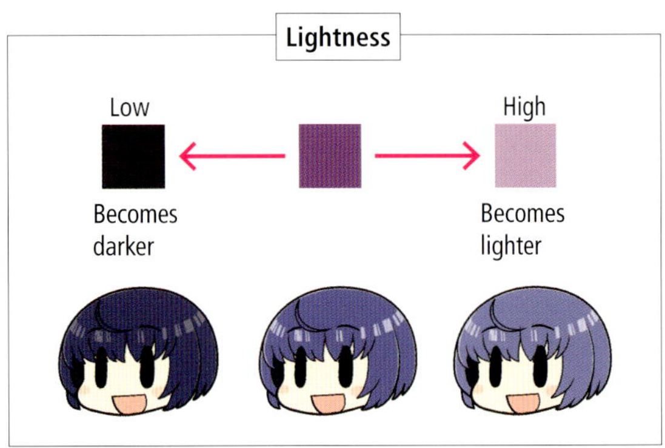


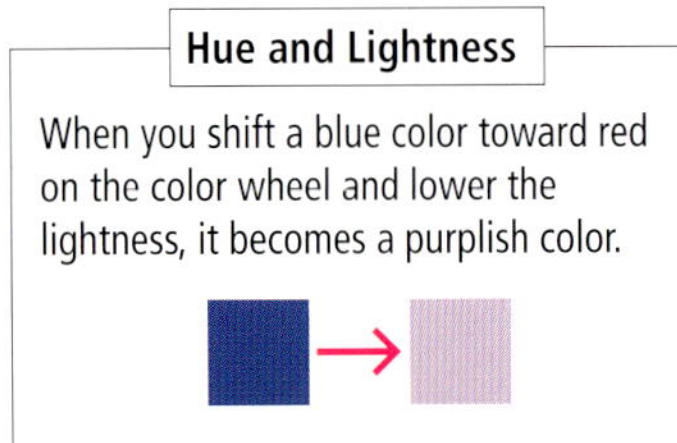




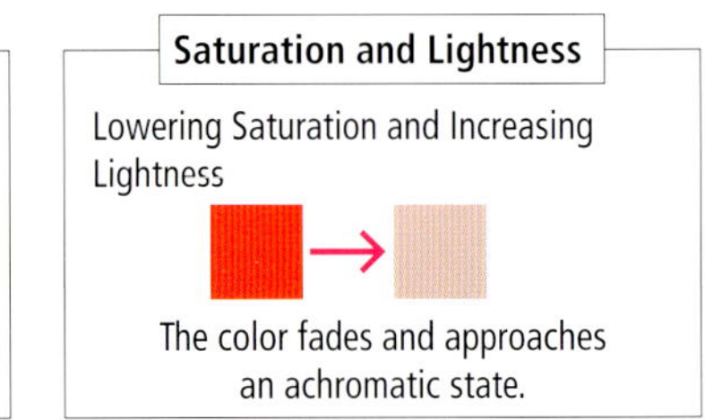

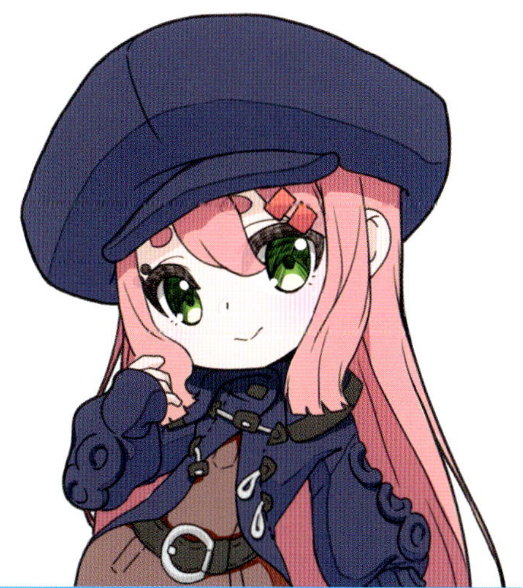

# HOW TO CREATE A COLOR SCHEME

This section explains the basics of color selection and arrangement, as well as how to effectively use color to guide the viewer's gaze.

# Balance Is the Deciding Factor

## Which is more balanced?

Which looks better balanced, **A** or **B**? **A** looks more balanced, don't you think? **A** is a color scheme that follows the basic balance, while **B** seems out of balance. You can see that balance is important when creating a color scheme.

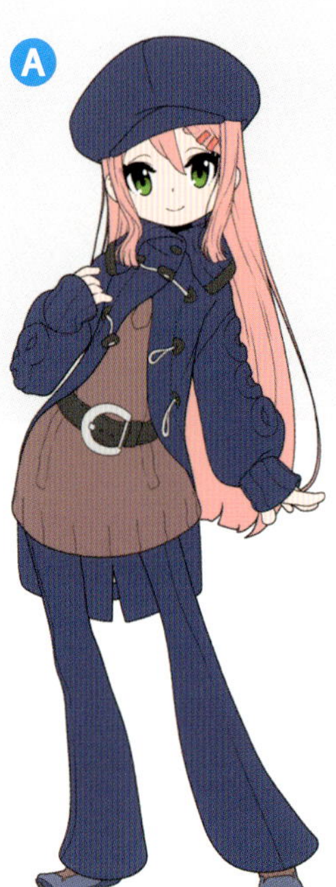

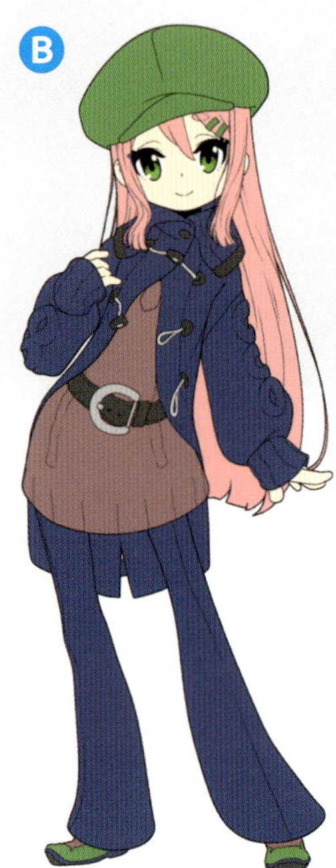

## Consider Color Proportions

Balance is key when it comes to color schemes. In general, the color you want to emphasize the most is set at 70%. Next is 25%. Last, the accent color should be placed at a ratio of about 5% to achieve a well-balanced look.

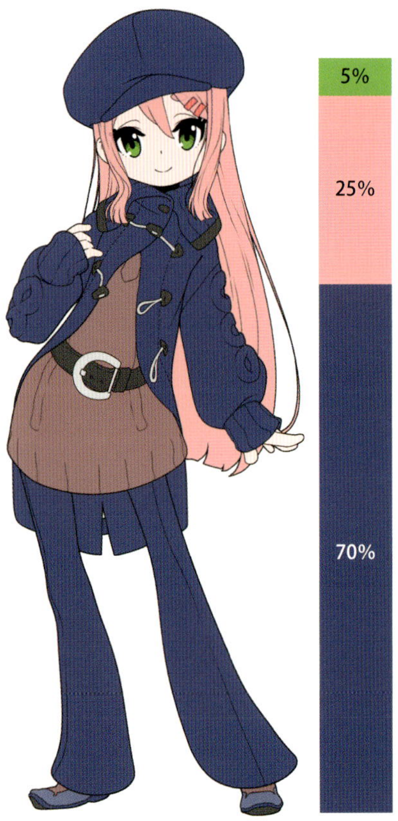

# The Relationship Between Light and Saturation

The same saturation doesn't necessarily translate to the same brightness when considering colors. The figure below shows six colors of the same saturation, converted to grayscale and arranged side by side. This phenomenon is caused by the difference in brightness of each color. When creating a color scheme, consider lightness as the basis of the color scheme. Especially when various colors are mixed, think of the color scheme in terms of lightness rather than saturation to achieve a better balance. However, colors expressed in the manner described here are for computer and smartphone displays, and the principle is a little different when printing on paper.

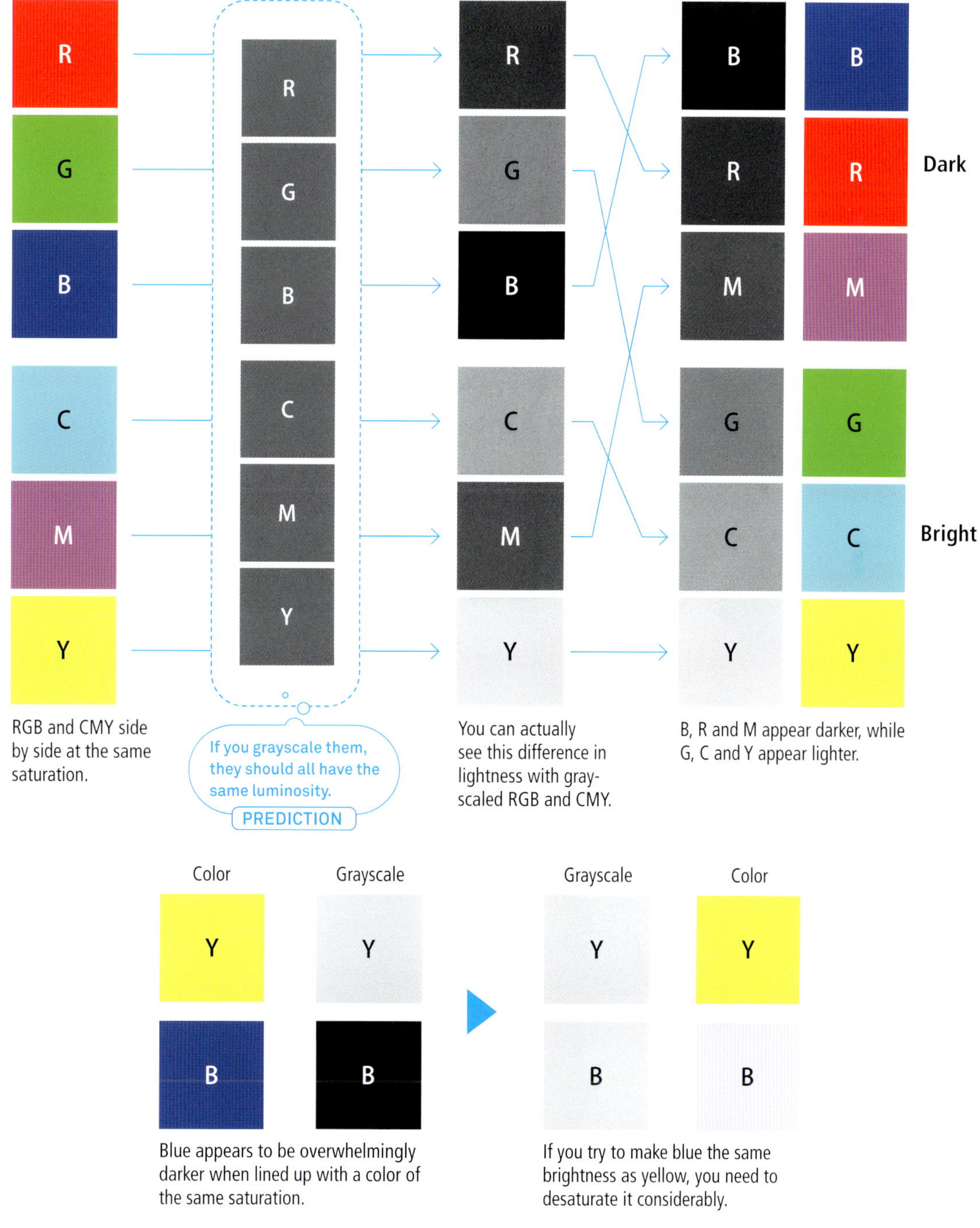


RGB and CMY side by side at the same saturation.

You can actually see this difference in lightness with grayscaled RGB and CMY.

B, R and M appear darker, while G, C and Y appear lighter.

Blue appears to be overwhelmingly darker when lined up with a color of the same saturation.

If you try to make blue the same brightness as yellow, you need to desaturate it considerably.

# Three-Color Schemes

This illustration uses the triad or three-color scheme. Dark blue (blue) is the most common color, accounting for 70% of the total. The next most common color is pink for the hair, which is about 25% of the total. Finally, if we keep the rest of the colors at about 5% and use only three colors for the entire image, a well-balanced color scheme is achieved. If you're not familiar with this color scheme, limit the number of colors to three. Other color schemes are explained in detail on page 48.

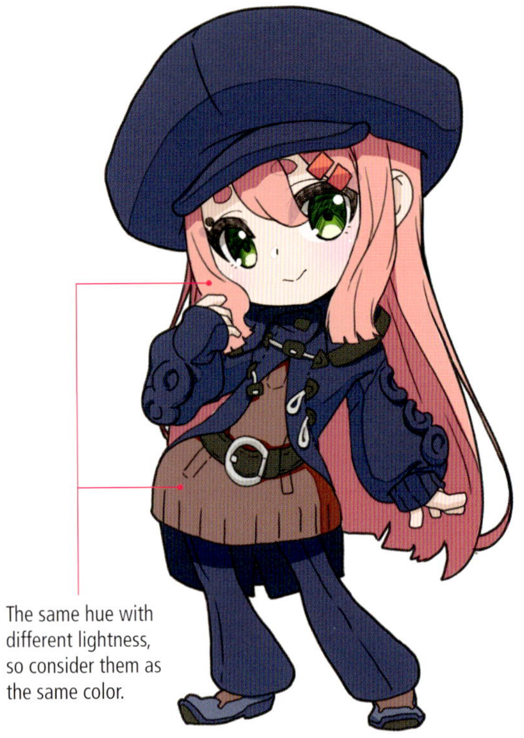

The same hue with different lightness, so consider them as the same color.

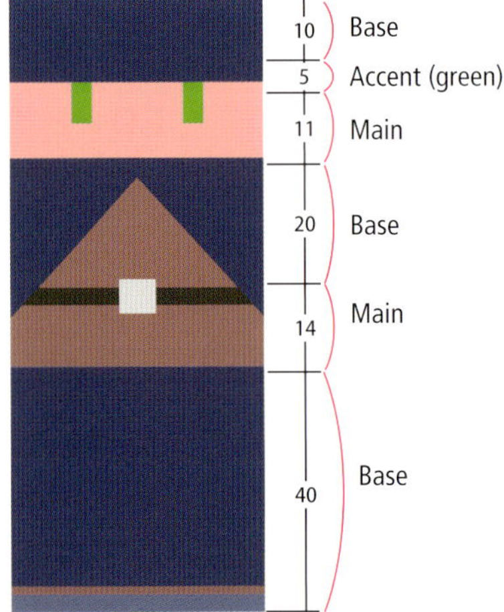

**Abstraction**



( **EXPERT TIP** ) **THICK COATING PROCEDURES**

Caricaturized versions such as chibi-style characters are simple with little visual information, making them easier to judge when used in a color scheme.

Now let's turn this illustration into grayscale (or monochrome). What do you think? Compared to the color version, it looks much plainer because of the loss of color information. What is important here is the brightness of the color; you can clearly see the difference in contrast (lightness, darkness and saturation) when it's made monochromatic.

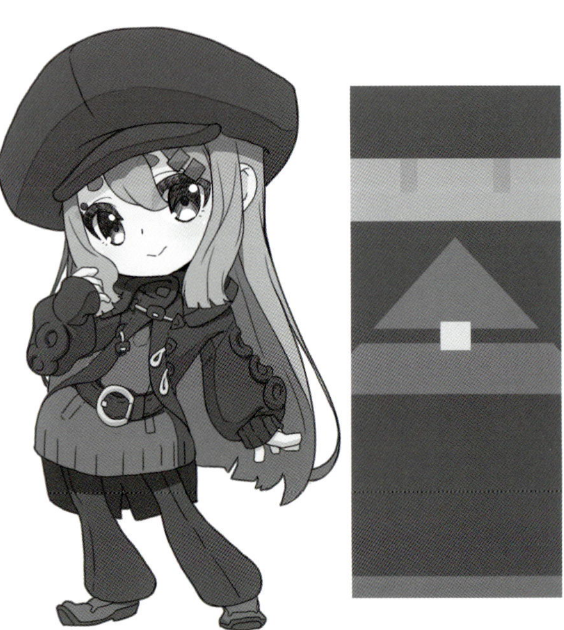

## Color Schemes Guide the Viewer's Eye

Let's use as an example "RX-78-2" from "Mobile Suit Gundam" to explain how color schemes can be used to guide the eye. In anime programs, for production reasons, many of the frames are upper-body shots, and the main focus is on the head and face. In order to draw the viewer's eye to the head, Gundam uses three colors (blue, red and yellow) for each part of the body, with careful consideration given to the coloring. The colors aren't intended to lead the viewer's eye immediately to the face but rather to guide the viewer's eye there by placing the colors in a calculated order on each part of the body. That way, the viewer's eye passes through specific areas and arrives at the face in the order intended by the creator.

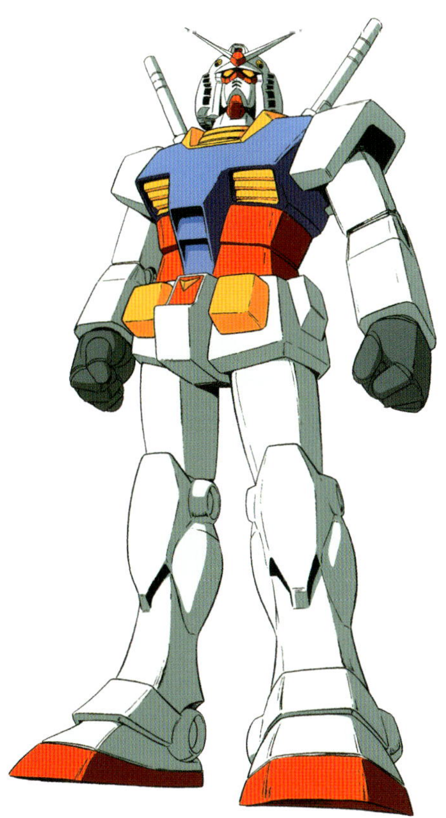

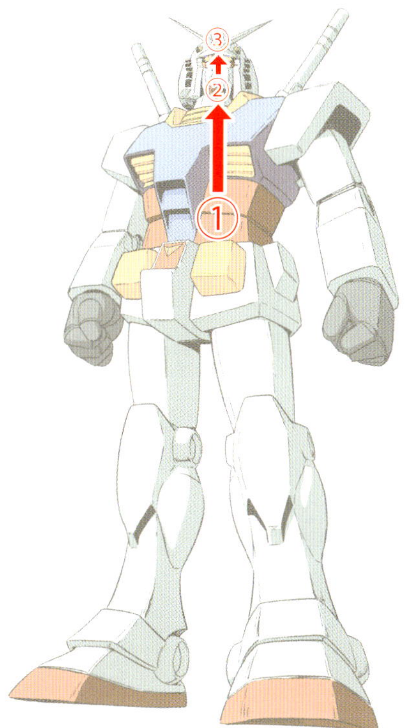

The color scheme is designed to direct the viewer's gaze upward. The original idea was to use only white, but for commercial reasons, more colors were added and the current color scheme was adopted. The blue, red and yellow were chosen because they're colors that are easily recognized by children.

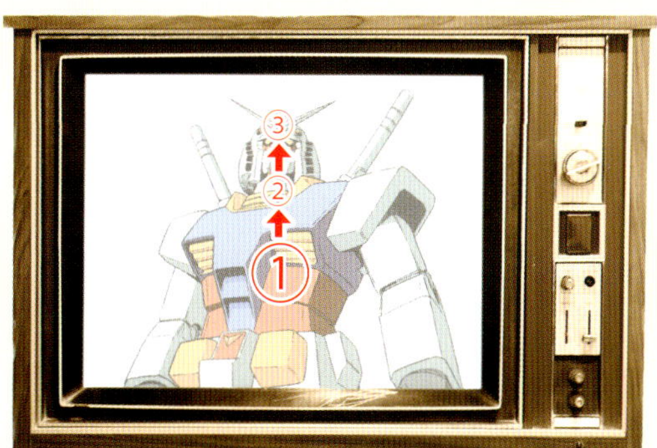

The same color scheme is used in this upper-body shot to direct the viewer's gaze toward the head.

© Sotsu, Sunrise

# Natural-Looking Color Schemes

## Which color scheme is correct?

Doesn't **Ⓐ** seem more natural? **Ⓑ**, on the other hand, seems harsh and imbalanced. This is because **Ⓑ** randomly selects colors without considering saturation and brightness. Here, we'll delve into choosing colors when creating specific color schemes.

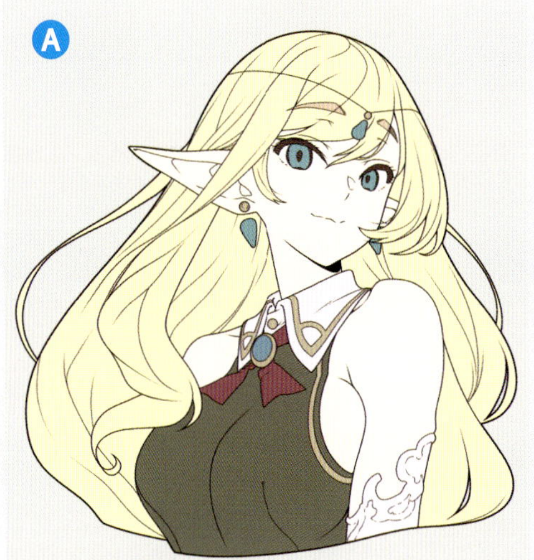

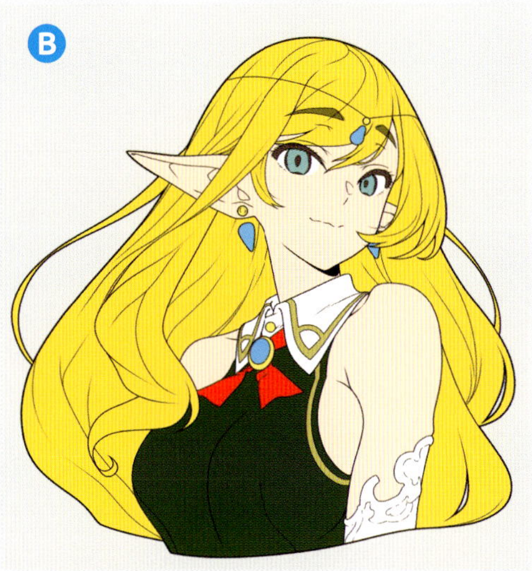

## The Rules of Color Schemes

There are two main points to consider when selecting colors for a color scheme:

- Use color harmony patterns for hue
- Match saturation and brightness

As shown in the Q&A above, even when using the same hue, the choice of saturation and brightness can significantly change the impression. The selection of hues will be explained in "Chapter 2: Color Selection Patterns" (p.48), so here we will mainly discuss the rules of color schemes from the perspective of saturation and brightness.

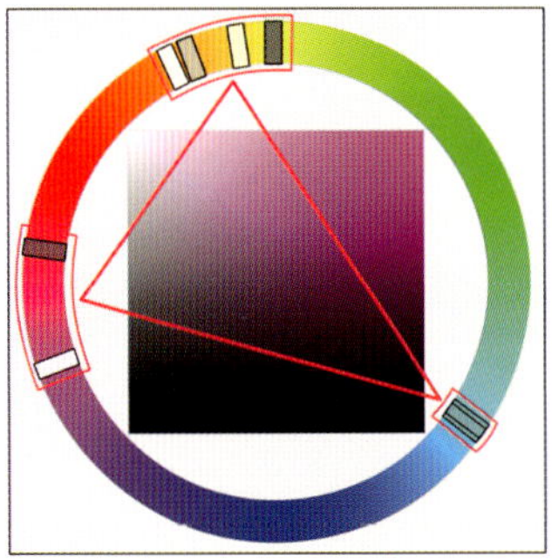

Match hue to patterns

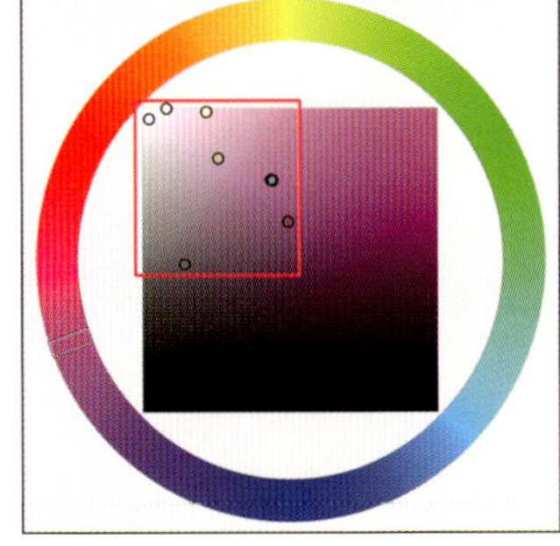

Choose saturation and brightness from similar areas

# Align Hue, Saturation and Brightness

When creating a color scheme, it's important to have a concept in mind and a clear image of the colors you want to use. Avoid selecting too many colors as that can lead to undesired results. Start by deciding on one main color that symbolizes the character, then choose the remaining colors from there. The diagram below shows an actual color scheme. It's based on the split complementary color-harmony pattern (see page 49) and aligns the saturation and brightness areas. The unsuccessful example has inconsistent hues, saturation and brightness. Pay attention to the color harmony patterns and areas when creating color schemes. By following these rules and being mindful of hue, brightness and saturation, you can achieve a cohesive and balanced overall color scheme.

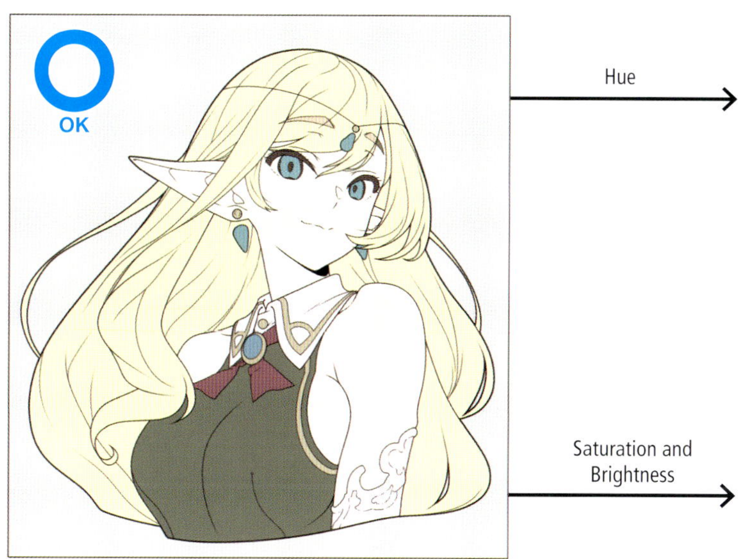


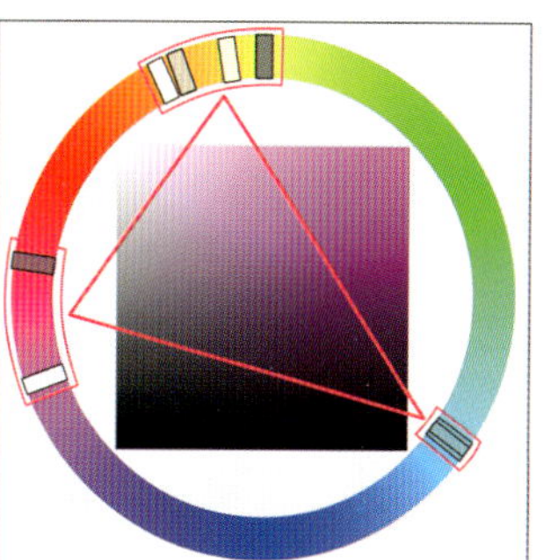

Hue

Colors that form a triangle on the color wheel (the yellow, skin color and green in the example) have a certain harmony when they follow a specific rule.

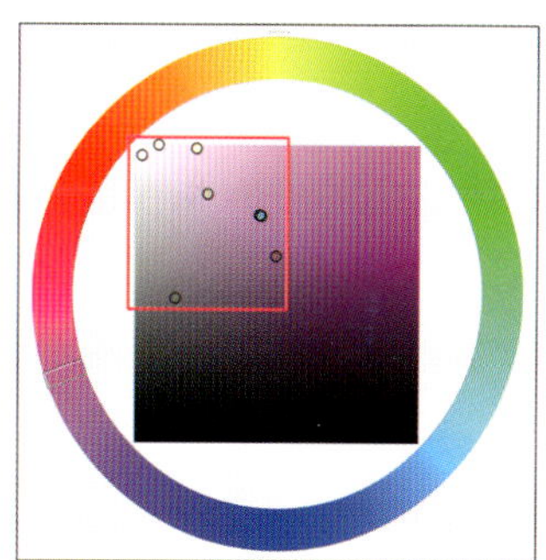

Saturation and Brightness

The chosen colors' saturation and brightness are generally grouped in similar areas. For initial color schemes, focus on selecting from the upper right area of the color circle.

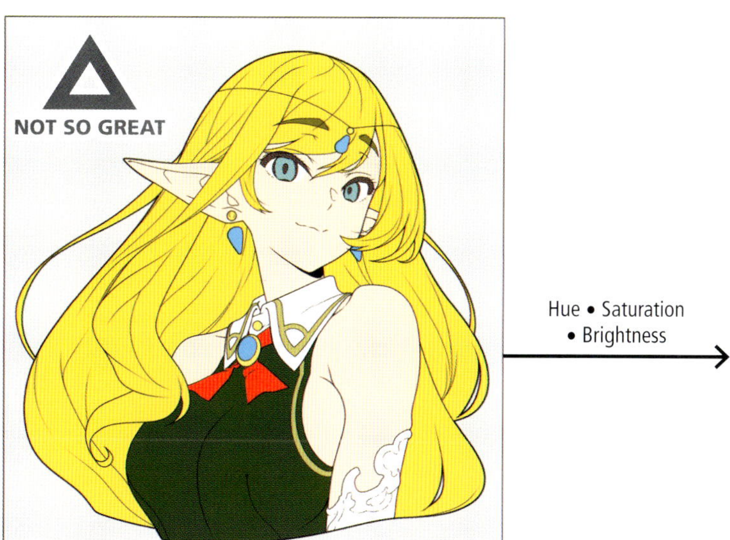


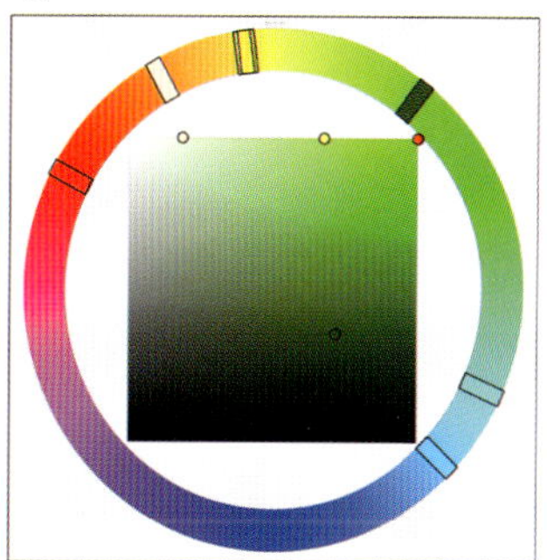

Hue • Saturation • Brightness

The chosen colors are all over the place without any consistent rule, leading to a lack of balance and a sense of discord.

# Achromatic Colors

On page 18, we explained that the ratio for color schemes should be 70:25:5. However, this ratio does not include the achromatic colors: white, black, and gray. Create the ratio within the area excluding achromatic colors. Achromatic-dominant color schemes are explained on page 34.

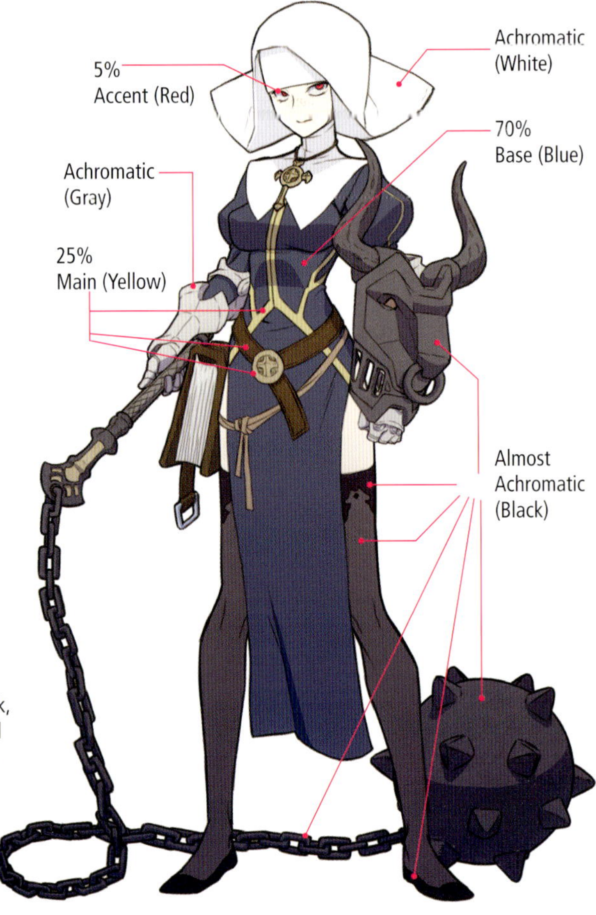


If you want the main color to be white or black, exclude it from the initial distribution and create a 70:25:5 ratio with the remaining colors.

---

**( EXPERT TIP )  WHY ARE ACHROMATIC COLORS NOT COUNTED?**

People perceive color when light reflected off an object reaches their eyes. Achromatic colors like white and black aren't considered colors but rather as modes of lightness. White represents the state of looking at a bright light source like the sun, while black represents complete darkness. Thus, achromatic colors are about brightness rather than color, and therefore, they're not counted or included in color schemes.

While it's theoretically true that mixing the primary colors (cyan, magenta and yellow) creates black, in reality, ink manufacturing and the use of printing machines result in a slight mix of other colors. This means that what we perceive as white or black often contains hints of other colors, supporting the idea of not counting achromatic colors in color schemes.

Similarly, the primary colors of light (red, green and blue) combine to create white, but achieving a perfect white or black requires careful calibration. See the sidebar on page 123 for a bit more on the topic.

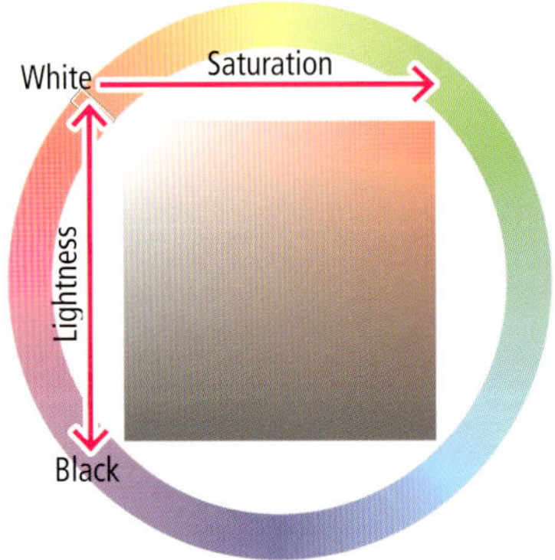


White and black are associated with lightness, not saturation.

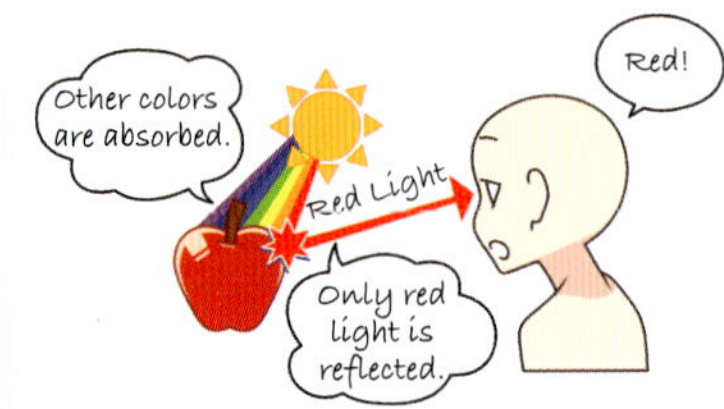

## Colorful Schemes

The illustration below appears very vivid, but upon closer inspection, you'll see that only warm colors (yellow to red) and cool colors (blue-green to purple) are used. The highest-saturation colors used are yellow, orange and red, while the blue cool colors have lower saturation. By increasing the number of low-saturation cool colors and using high-saturation warm colors for accents, you can create an illustration that looks vibrant.

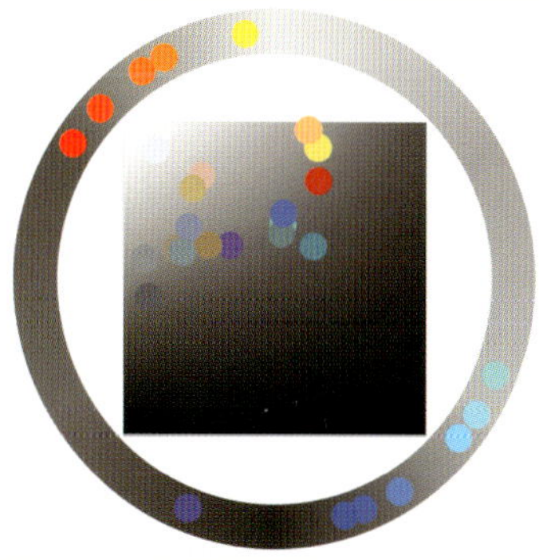

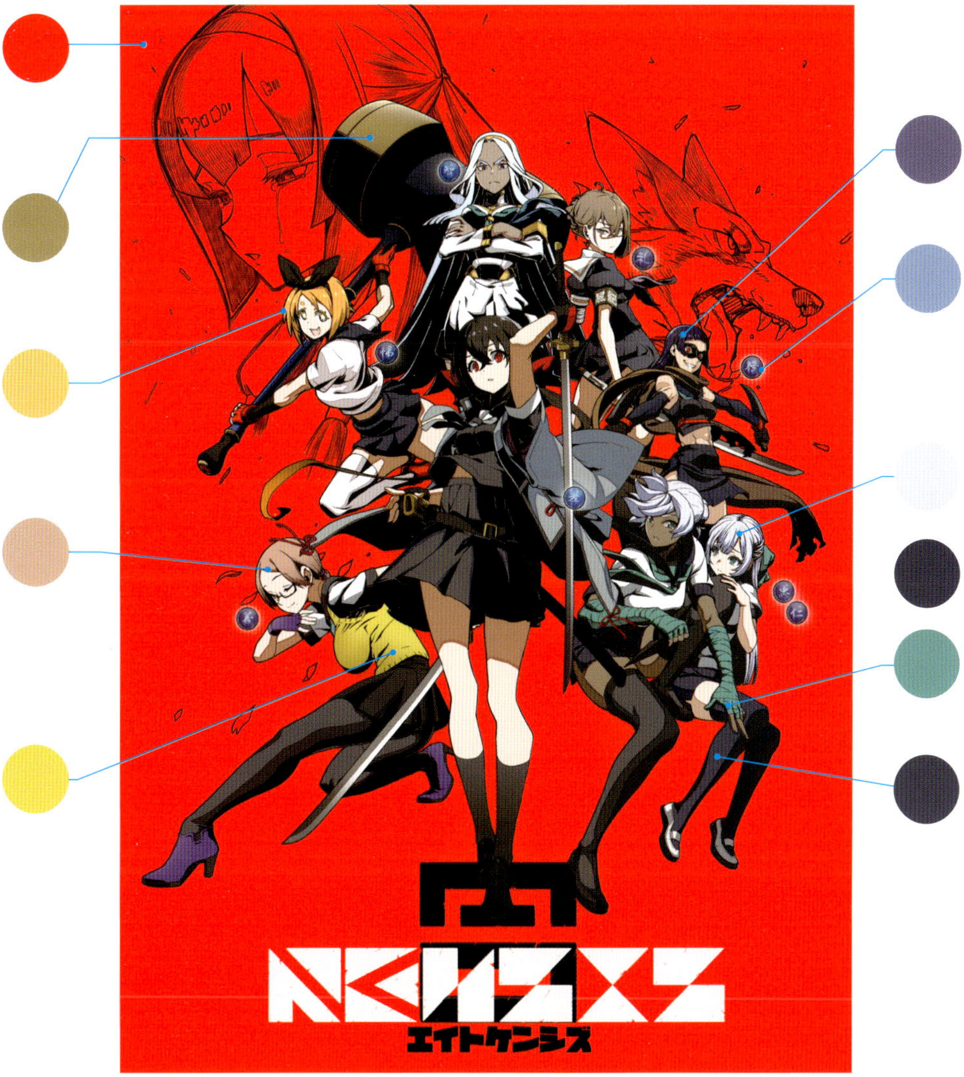

# Recommended Areas for Color Schemes

Let's consider what colors to choose by using the color wheel as an example. First, consider red. When the color wheel is converted to grayscale, area ① appears almost the same as black. Area ② corresponds to the achromatic area explained on page 24. Area ③ is too saturated, making it difficult to create shadows. Especially in area ①, the colors look similar to black, making it difficult to guess the original color. People perceive colors based on brightness (lightness) rather than saturation. To create a harmonious color scheme, avoid colors in areas with extremely high or low brightness.

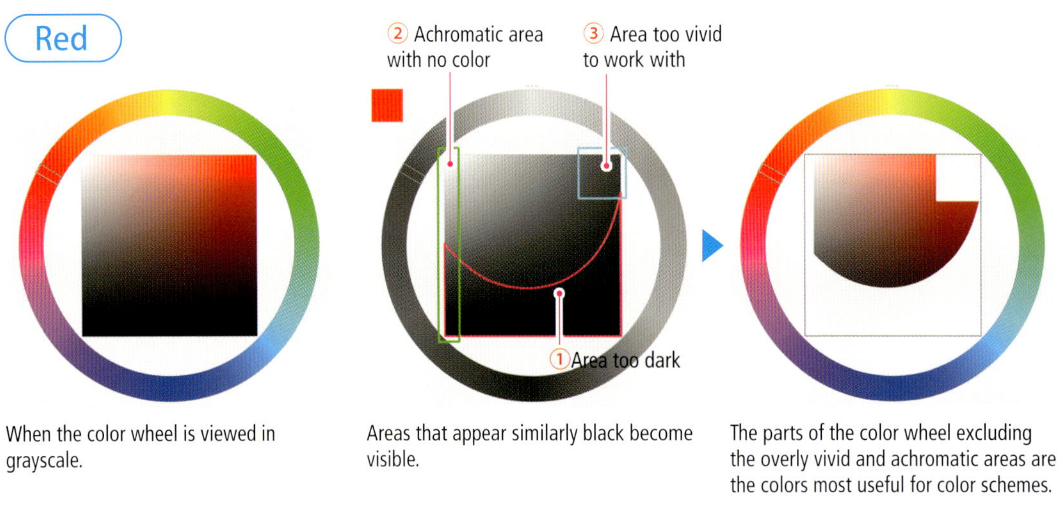



When the color wheel is viewed in grayscale.

Areas that appear similarly black become visible.

The parts of the color wheel excluding the overly vivid and achromatic areas are the colors most useful for color schemes.

We used red as an example, but the areas that are easiest to work with vary by color. Let's look at other colors using RGB and CMYK as references (excluding black as it's achromatic). This comparison shows that blue has the narrowest usable area, while yellow has the widest.

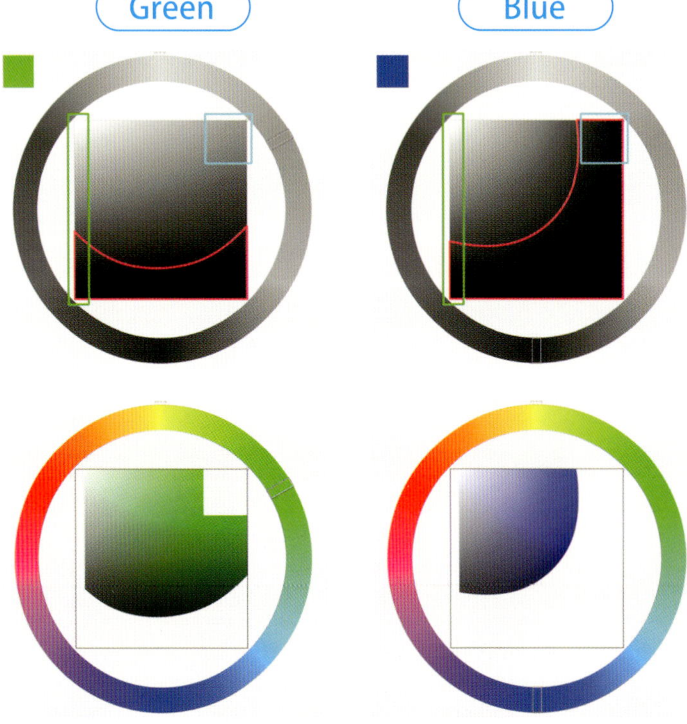

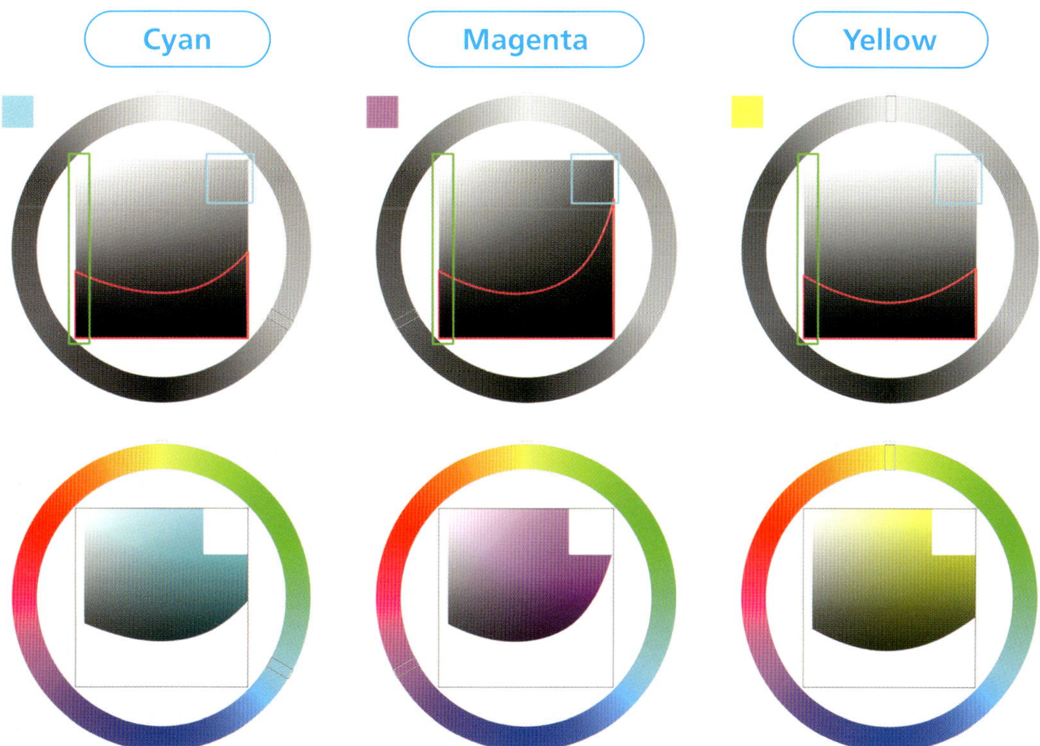



## Adding Shadows

Let's add shadows to the two examples. The result's quite telling. The example on the right, where the color scheme was considered, has a calm finish. In contrast, the mismatched colors in the less successful example on the left compete for attention, making it less balanced and visually appealing. This demonstrates how the initial choice of colors impacts the final illustration.

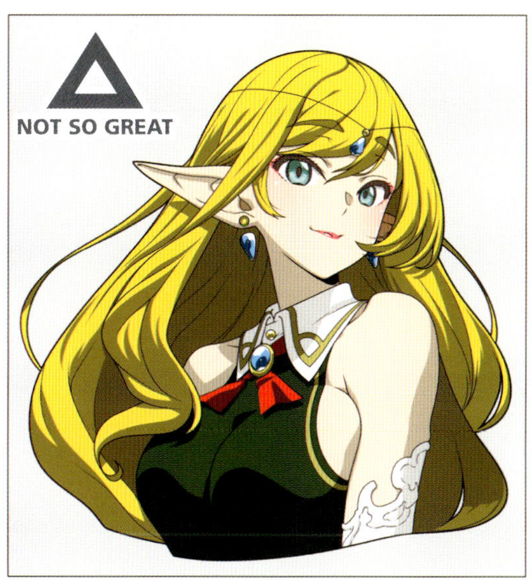



The ribbon is particularly noticeable because red and green are complementary colors, causing the highly saturated red to stand out.

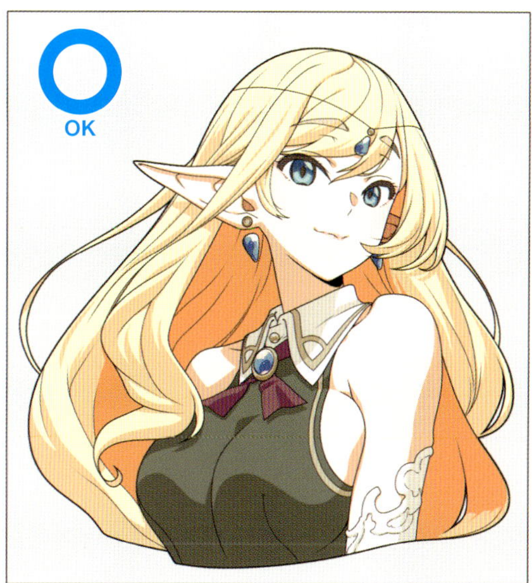

# How to Create a Cohesive Illustration

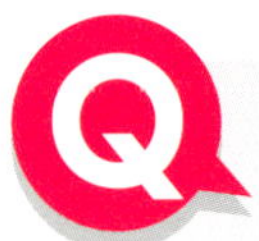

### Which looks more cohesive?

**B** appears more unified and cohesive because the colors are consistent. While **A** is unique, it uses too many colors, making it difficult to determine the character's defining or theme color. Here, we'll look at how to select appropriate colors to emphasize a character's individuality.

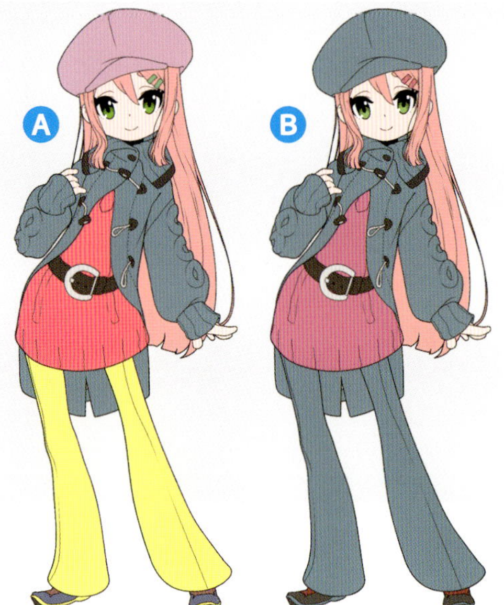

## Avoid Using Too Many Colors

When creating a color scheme, beginners should choose one base color and avoid using too many other choices. Characters benefit from having a distinctive "image color," which strengthens and defines their impression. In the example on the right, blue is used extensively in the jacket, pants and hat, establishing it as the image color.

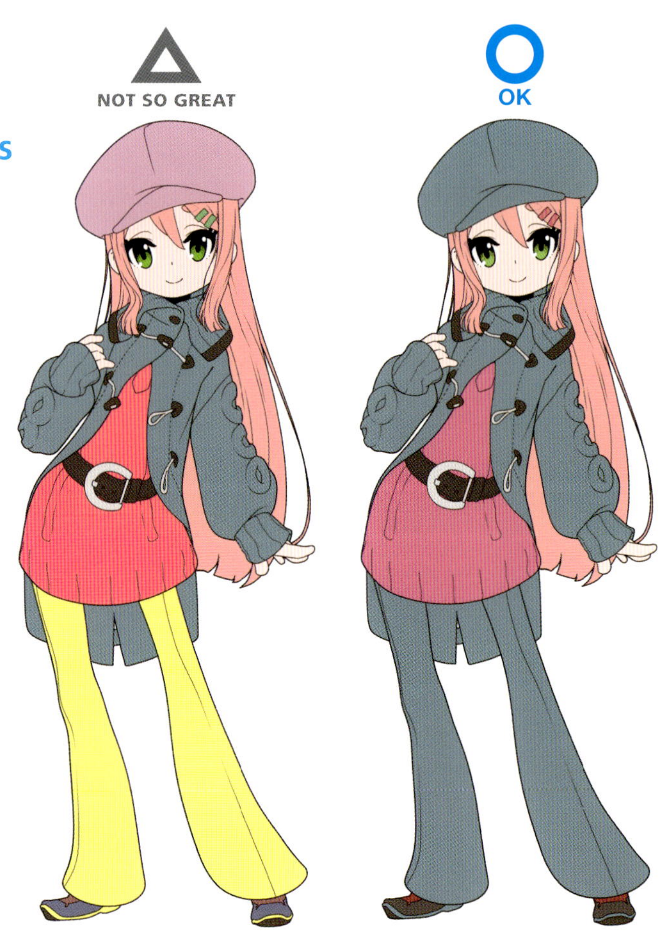

# Start with Gray

When coloring, begin by turning everything gray and then decide on colors one by one. Start by filling 70% with the base color, then allocate 25%, and finally add the accent color, which should be 5%. This method helps to create a balanced look.

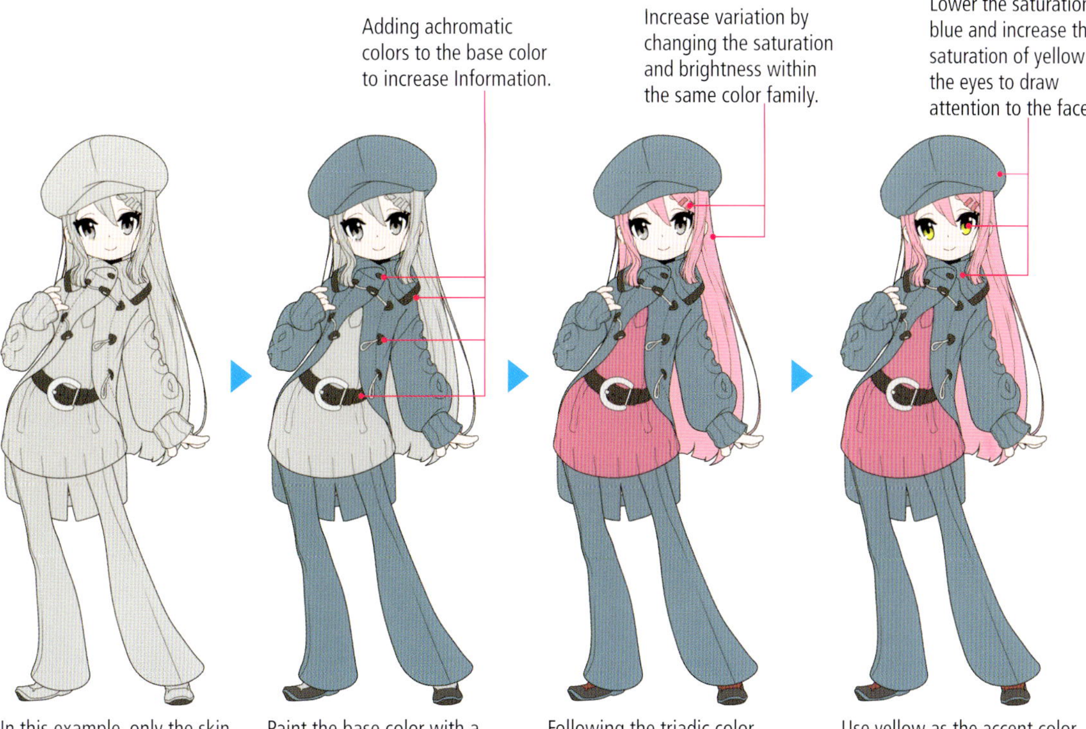



In this example, only the skin color is left, but it's O.K. to make everything monochromatic initially. Start with as little color information as possible.

Paint the base color with a 70% distribution. In this case, a triadic color scheme is used (see page 58).

Following the triadic color scheme, use pink as the main color and paint it at a 25% distribution.

Use yellow as the accent color, painting it at 5% distribution. Since it's an accent, increasing its saturation will make it stand out more. Additionally, since yellow is the complementary color of blue, placing yellow between the blue of the hat and jacket enhances its prominence.



In the example, three colors were chosen based on the triadic color scheme. However, three colors may not be enough for all the areas you want to color. If that's the case, divide each color into several shades within the red family, yellow family and blue family before starting to color.

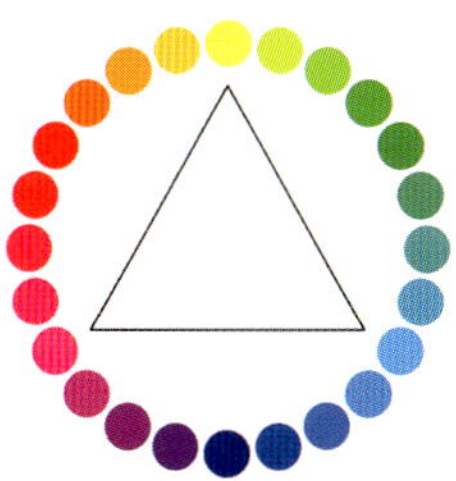

**This is the most basic color scheme. Since the colors are mutually complementary, they don't clash. Other color patterns are explained on page 48.**

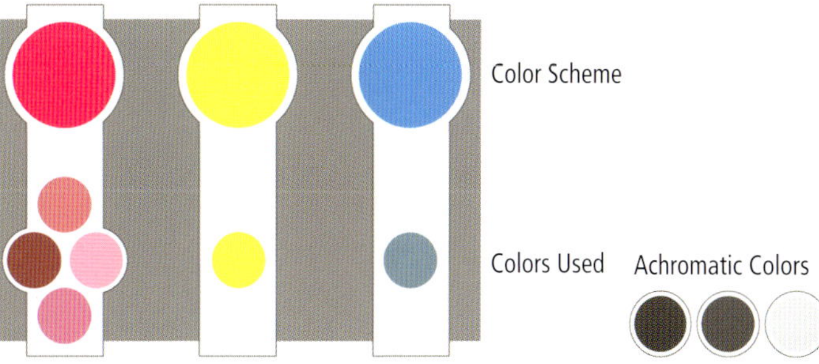

# How to Choose Colors from the Image Color

Now let's consider how to create a color scheme after determining the image color. Unlike the previous example, this illustration is designed to make the red jacket the most prominent feature. In this case, to make the red stand out more, the saturation and brightness of other colors need to be lower than that of the red, Especially since the hair is green, which is complementary to red on the color wheel, it should be adjusted by either increasing the brightness to make it lighter or lowering the saturation to create a pastel tone.

The hair, which you want to stand out next after the image color, should have a high brightness but not necessarily a high saturation.

Using Split Complementary (see page 49) Referencing the split complementary scheme, use pink tones as the main color.

Highlighting the Jacket Since the base color is red, the jacket color should have the highest saturation to make it stand out the most. This way, red is easily recognized as the image color.

Based on the base color, lower the brightness. To create contrast with ④, increase the saturation slightly.

Based on the base color, lower the brightness.

④ and ⑤ are in the same color family as the base but have low saturation and brightness, making them blend in without standing out.

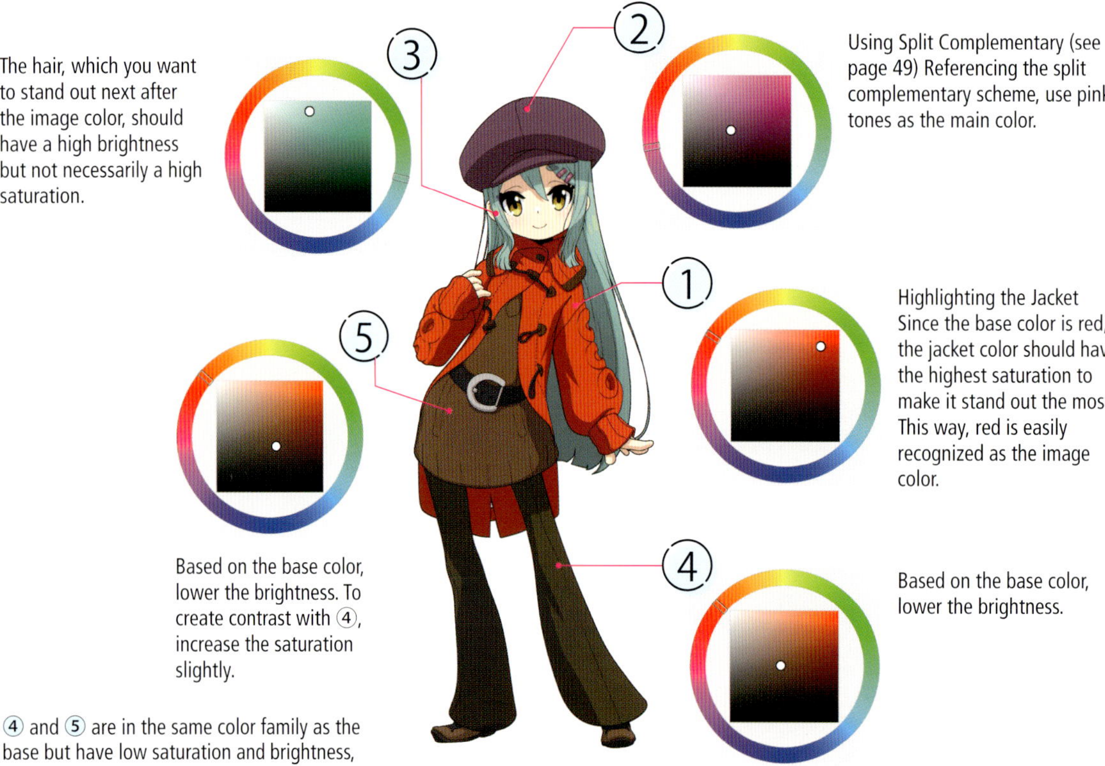

---



## EXPERT TIP — MAKING COLORS STAND OUT

Colors with high saturation tend to stand out. If you want the eyes to be striking, choose a vivid color as the accent for the eyes. If you want the clothing to be more noticeable, make the jacket color vibrant. Use high-saturation colors in areas you want to emphasize according to the character's image.

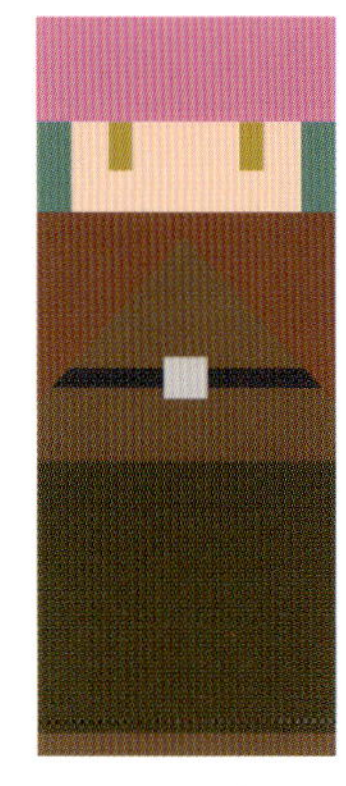

Directs attention to the hat

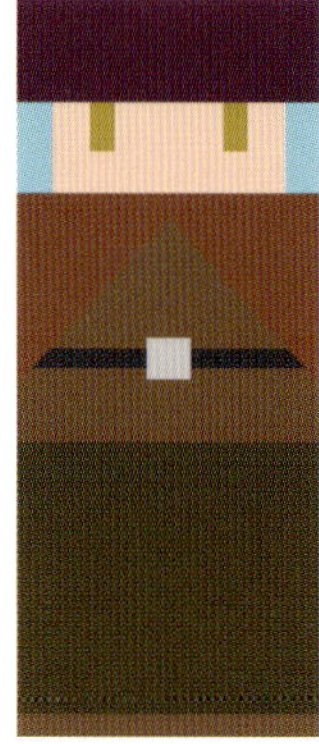

Directs attention to the hair

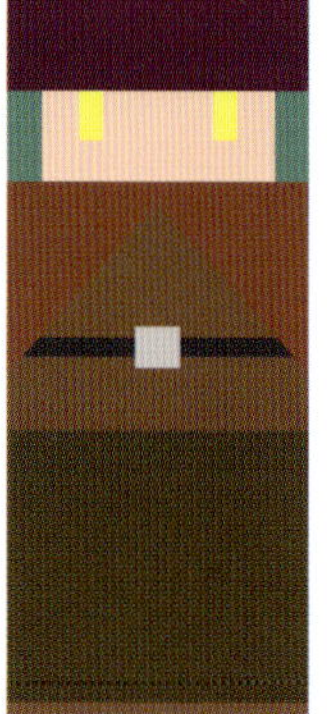

Directs attention to the eyes

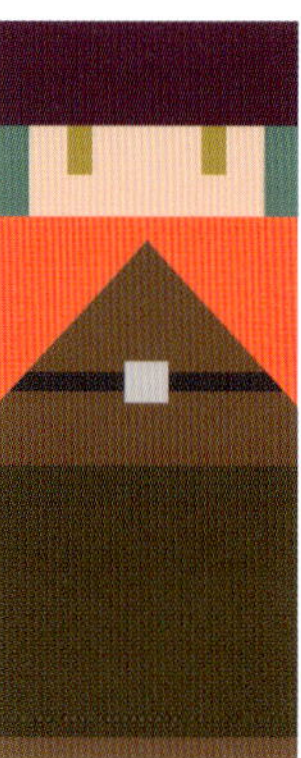

Directs attention to the jacket

# When You Want to Add More Colors

When you want to add more colors to a completed illustration, how should you go about it? In the following illustration, a triadic color scheme is used. To add more colors, you can shift the initial triadic color scheme's triangle slightly on the color wheel to select a range of harmonizing colors.

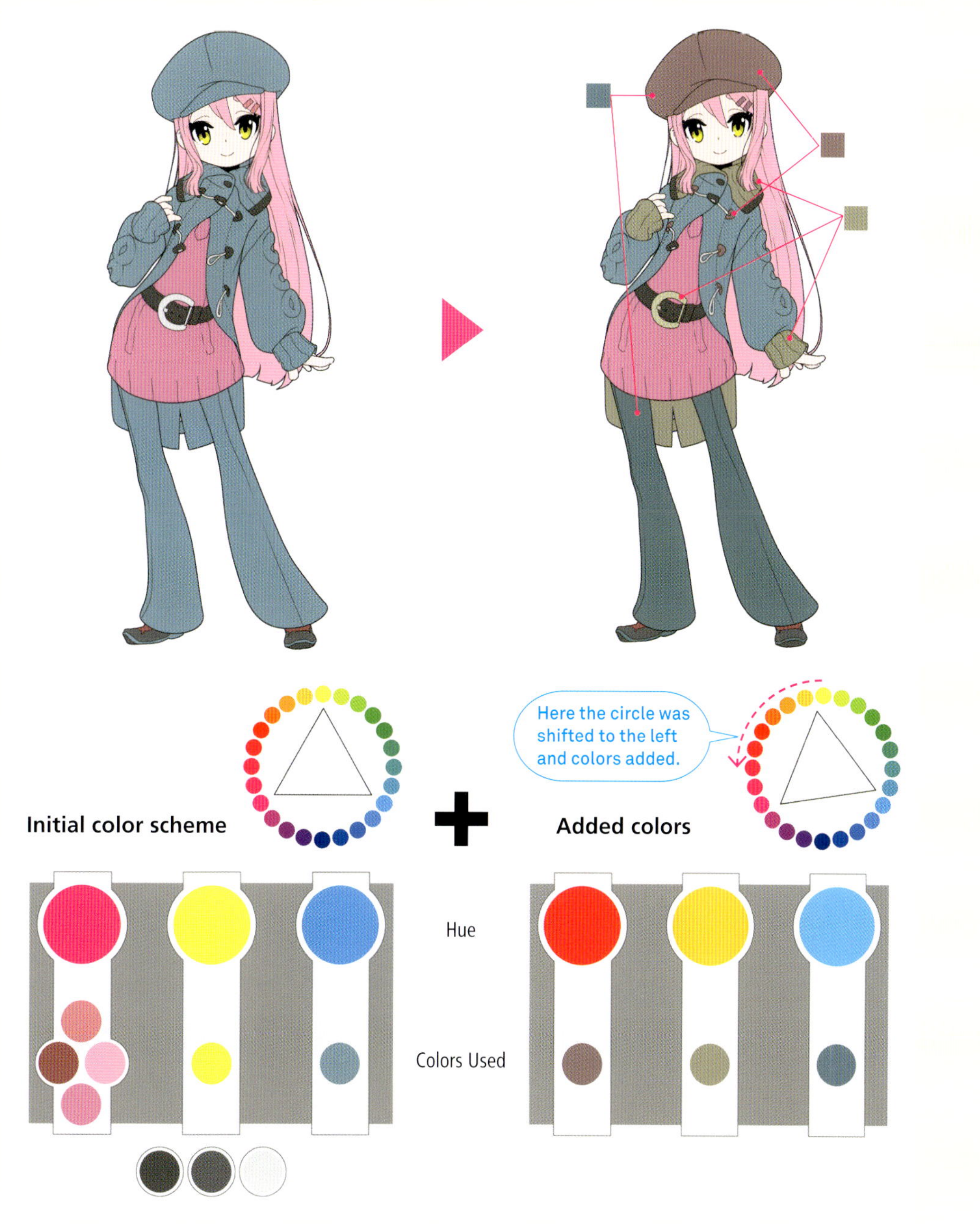

# Saturation Changing the Impression

## Which one is more memorable?

Between **A** and **B**, which one has green as the image color? The only difference between the two is the saturation of the color, but doesn't **A** make the green look like the image color? In **B**, the vibrant red catches the eye, making that seem like the image color. Color can change its impression through saturation, so let's take a look at how to choose saturation to create the intended impression.

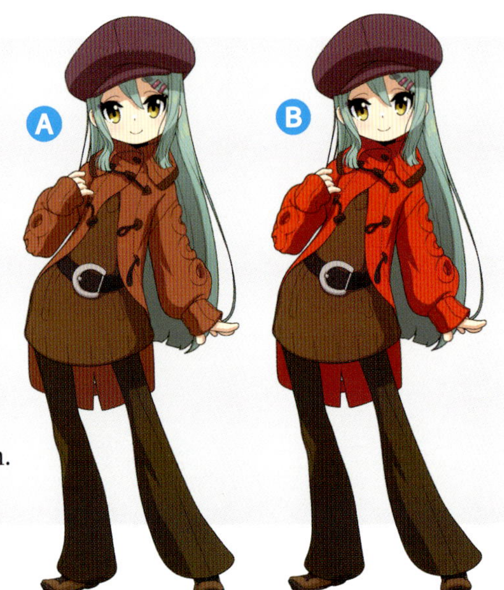

## Emphasize the Image Color

When you add colors, it's easy to be drawn to high-saturation ones. However, if asked to identify this character's defining visual feature, many would likely say the green hair. This is because the green hair has the highest brightness and saturation among the colors used. So if you want green to be the image or defining base color, lower the saturation and brightness of other parts like the jacket and clothes so they don't distract or draw too much attention.

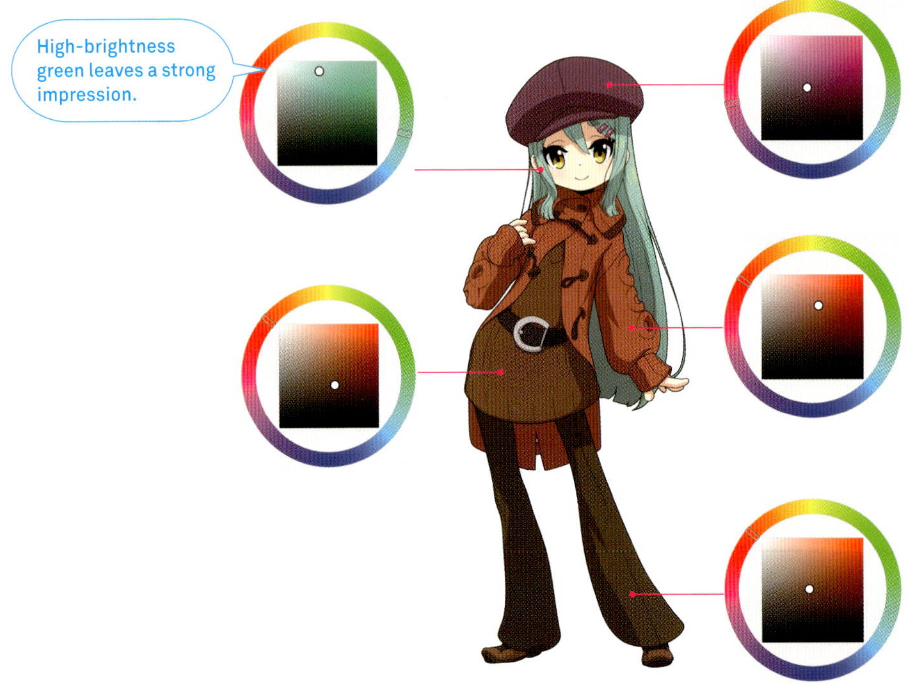

## The Impression Changes with Saturation

Now, let's significantly increase the saturation and brightness of the red jacket. What happens then? The first thing that now catches the eye is the garment. If asked to choose the character's defining visual element, people would now likely say the red jacket. People decide the impression of an image based on the color they notice first. By increasing the saturation of the color you want to emphasize and lowering the saturation and brightness of other colors, you can direct the viewer's attention to the desired color.

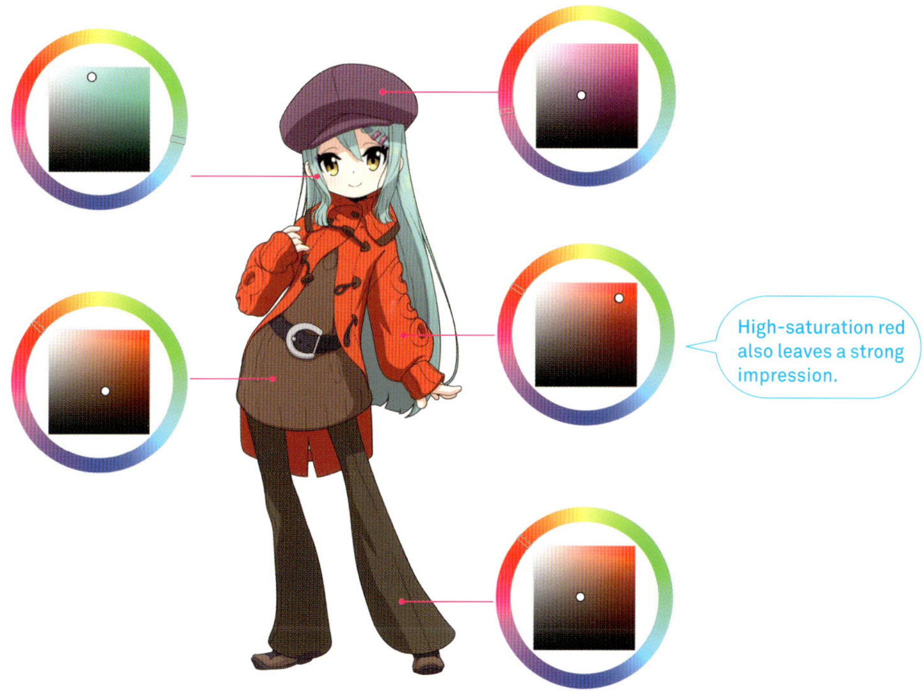



## Simplify Your Thinking

It's difficult to consider these factors when you're not familiar with them. Instead, think of simple shapes as shown in the diagram below. Balancing colors in a complex drawing requires experience, but it's easier to achieve the desired impression in simple drawings like these. When simplified, you can see that the left drawing draws attention to the hair, while the right one draws attention to the vibrant jacket. Even in these cases, consider the "70:25:5" color-scheme rule explained on page 20.

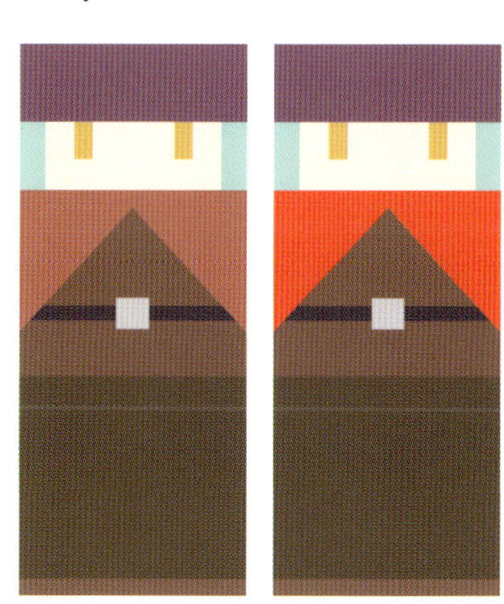

( EXPERT TIP )  **THINK SIMPLY**

**You can also use simplified characters or caricature-style characters as on page 20.**

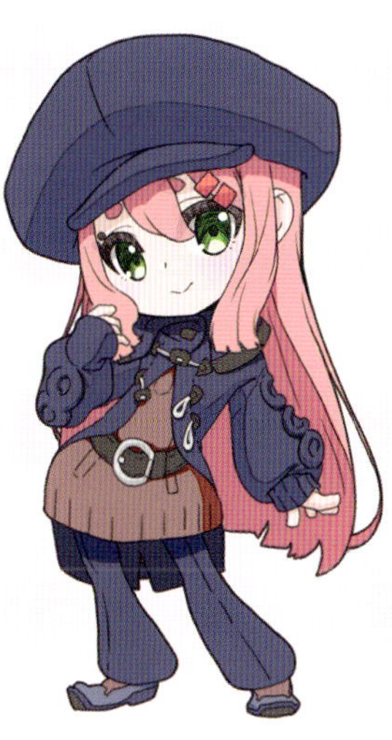

# One Point in Achromatic Colors

Achromatic colors like white and black are not counted as colors. So what should you do if you want to make colors close to black or white as your main image color? When using achromatic colors as the image or defining base color, instead of sticking to three colors, you can create a harmonious look by adding a single point of color or mixing a bit of color into the gray or white. When adding colors, follow the color scheme rules explained on page 48.

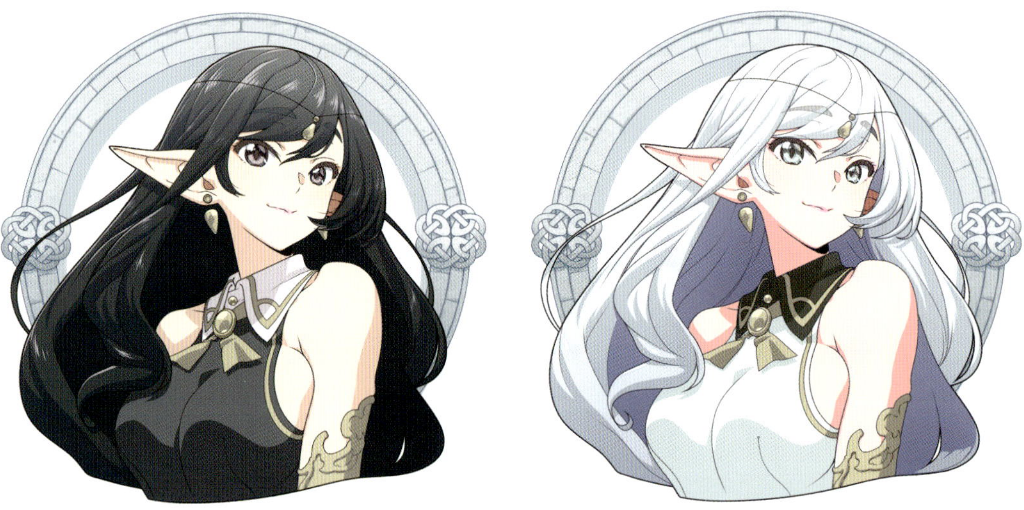

The image colors are achromatic black and white, but a bit of yellow is placed on the chest ribbon as an accent.

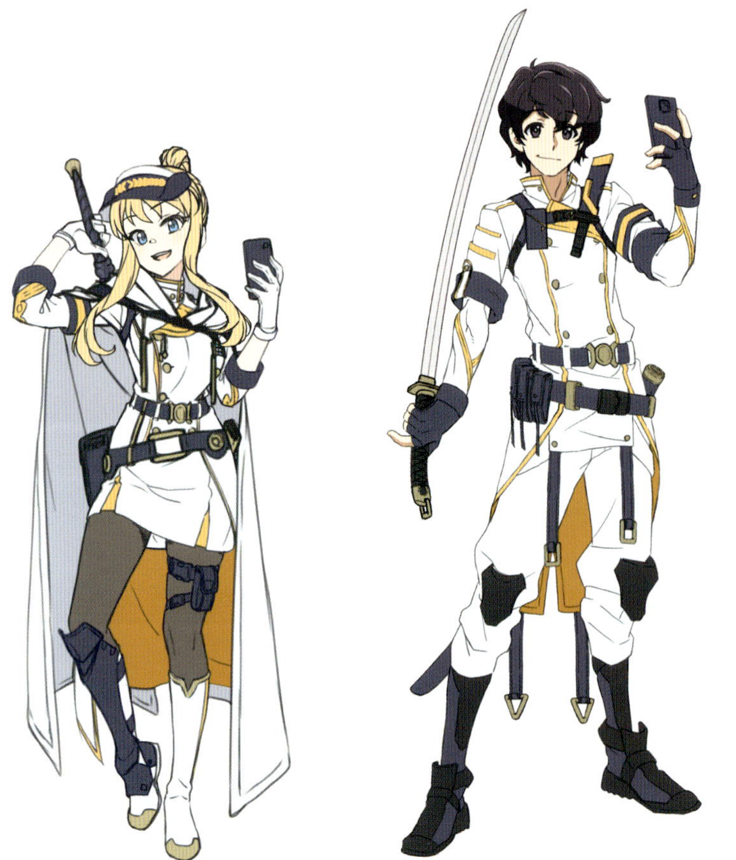

As an accent, a similar yellow is placed on the inside of the cape or the lines of the clothing.

# Painting in Grayscale

A painting method called grisaille or grayscale remains popular in digital art, where shading is done only with gray and then colors are layered on top. This method is effective when coloring fails to create proper shading and results in a flat look. Looking at the illustration below on the left, even though the coloring is finished, it still feels lacking. The reason becomes clear when you look at the illustration on the right where the color in formation has been removed, and you can see the differences in brightness. Due to the lack of contrast, the finished colored picture appears incomplete. So, using the grisaille method, try painting with only the light and dark tones of gray. Using only gray can result in creating effective contrast. On page 128, a coloring method using a gradient map, an advanced application of this technique, is explored, so refer to that as well.

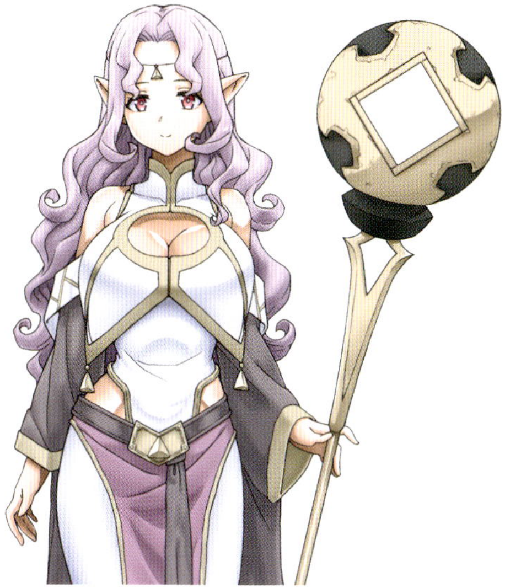

① Do you feel something is off with the completed illustration? That's because you're being misled by the brightness differences in the colors.

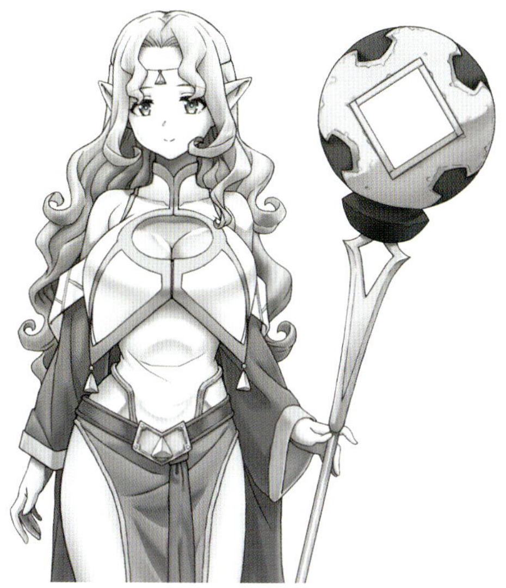

② When converted to grayscale, the colors feel pale over all and don't look the same as the colored version.

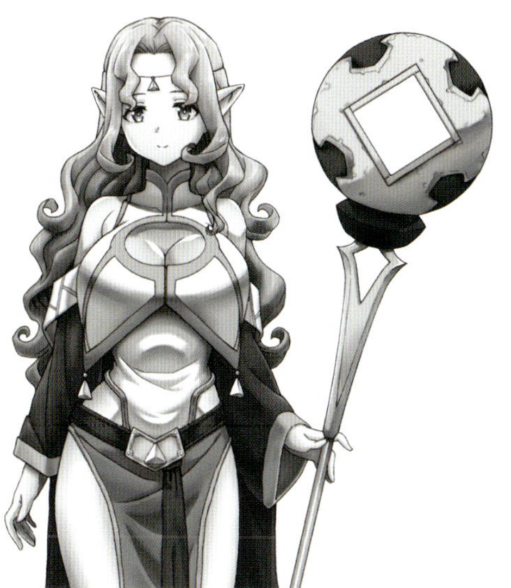

③ First, create strong contrast using only the light and dark tones of grayscale.

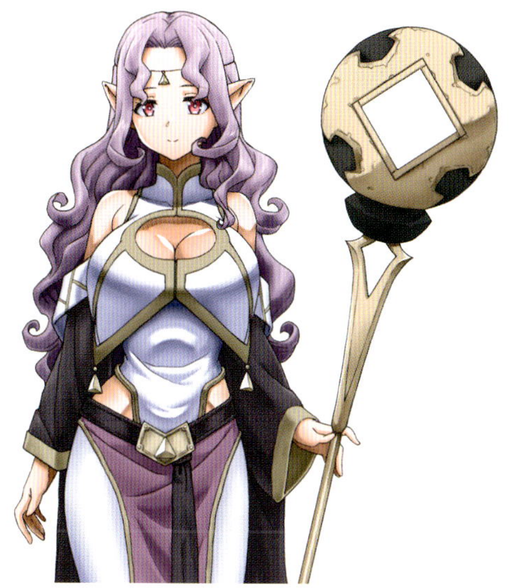

④ Coloring over the gray will result in an illustration with solid contrast.

# Weight Is the Balance of Light and Dark

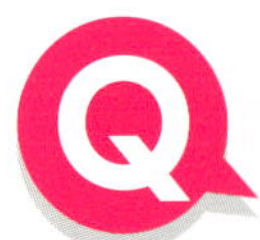

## Which one looks lighter?

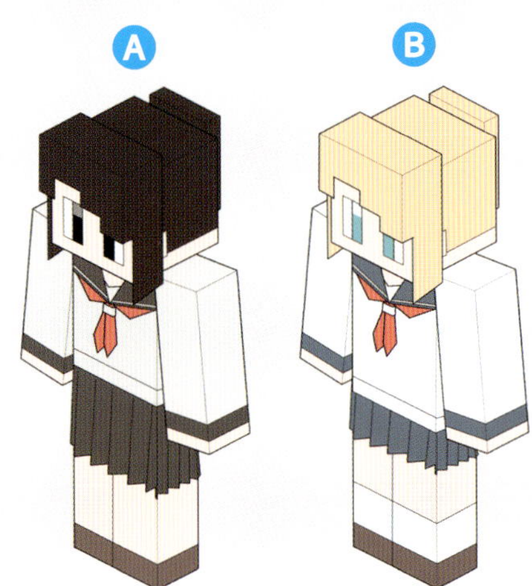

Doesn't **B** look lighter? It uses bright colors over all, with the skirt in blue. Additionally, the white socks give a lighter impression. On the other hand, **A** feels heavier because it's centered on achromatic colors. By adjusting the balance of saturation and brightness, you can control the character's impression.

## Expressing Weight with Light and Dark

The first one from the left has a balanced distribution of light and dark, the second one uses more light colors, and the third one uses more dark colors. What's important here is how to allocate light and dark and in what order to place them. By being aware of this, you can appropriately capture the character's image when creating a color scheme. When there are more light areas, the character will have a lighter impression, and conversely, more dark areas give a heavier impression. Be mindful of placing colors while considering the balance of light and dark that matches the character's personality and atmosphere.

**EXPERT TIP** **ARRANGING LIGHT**

Separating the placement of light and dark either vertically or alternately can make it easier to achieve a cohesive final illustration.

**Light = Dark**

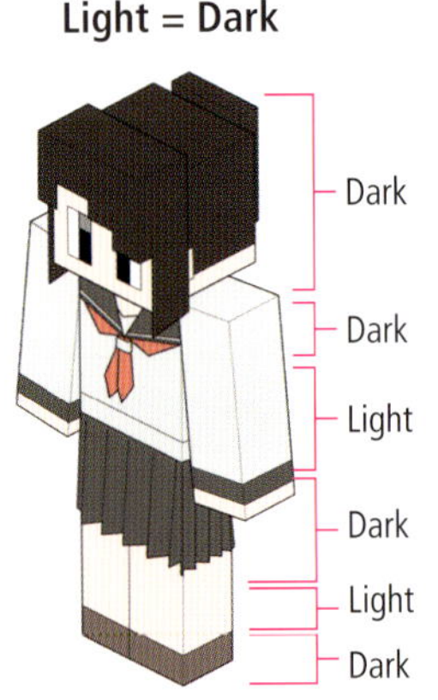

A good balance of light and dark

**Light > Dark**

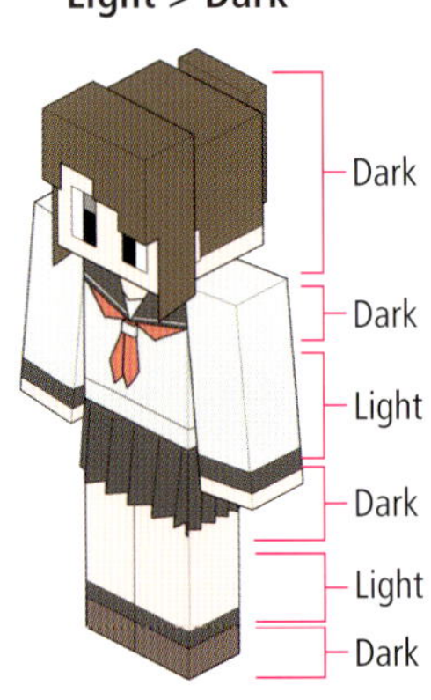

A balance with more light achieved by the skirt length or hair color

**Light < Dark**

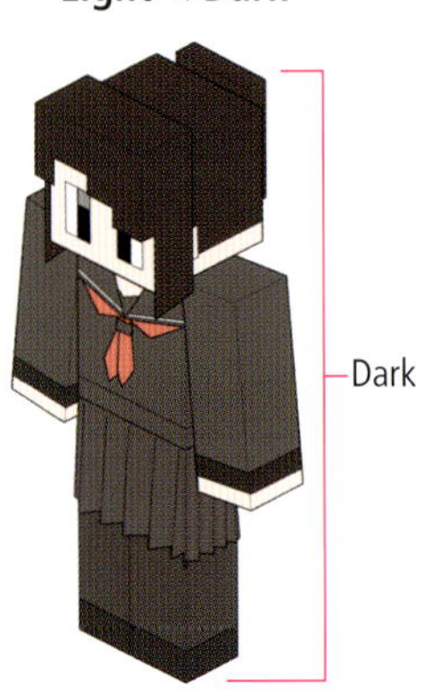

A balance with more dark by making the overall picture darker

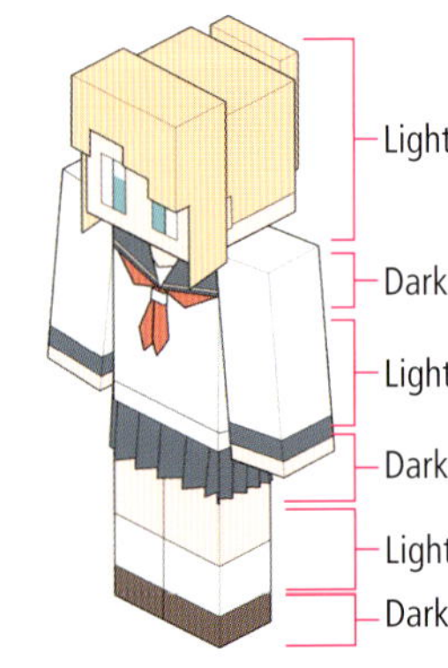

Conversely, a balance with an overall lighter impression

# When the Combination Looks Too Dark

Even when using the recommended areas for color schemes (see page 26), the overall atmosphere can sometimes appear too dark, as shown in the example below on the left. You want the color to look as intended when layering the base and shadow colors, but if the base color is dark, the final result will be even darker. This is especially true for blue and purple, which tend to appear dark and dense. Therefore, it's better to lower the overall brightness and saturation when using these colors.

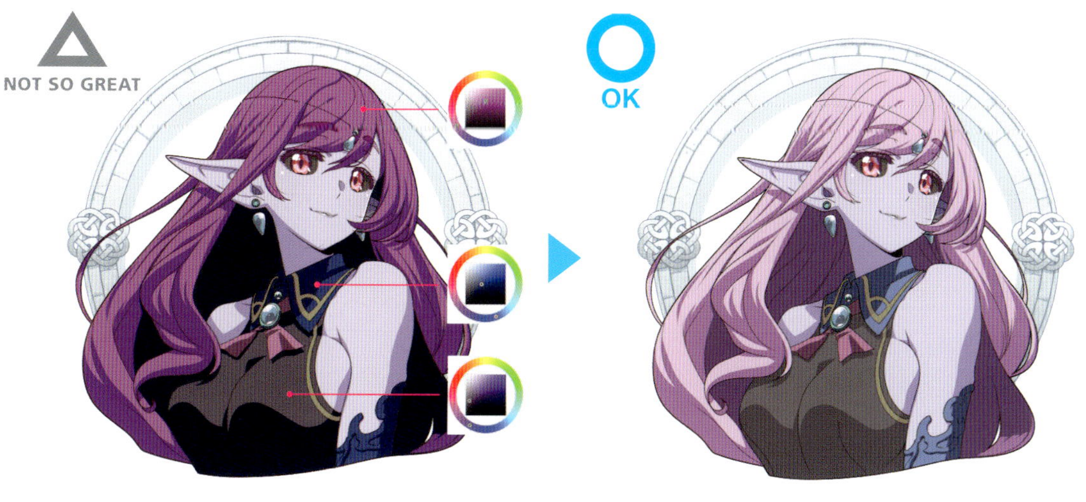


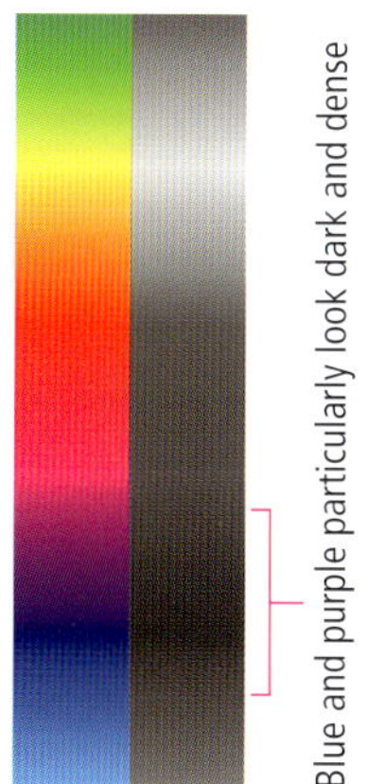


Even if blue and purple are not highly saturated, they still give a dark, dense impression. This is due to the inherent darkness and density of these colors.

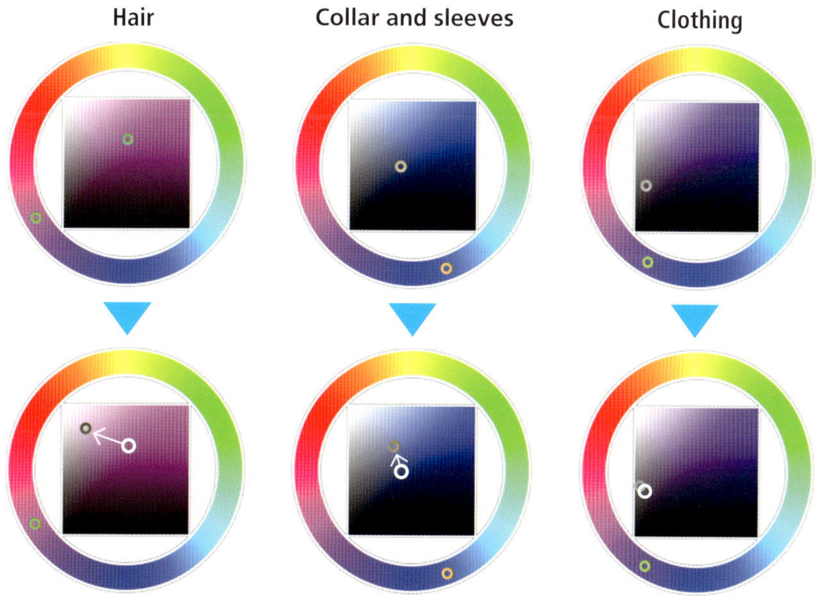


It becomes easier to adjust if you think about the desired darkness of the final color as the combination of the base color and the shadow color.

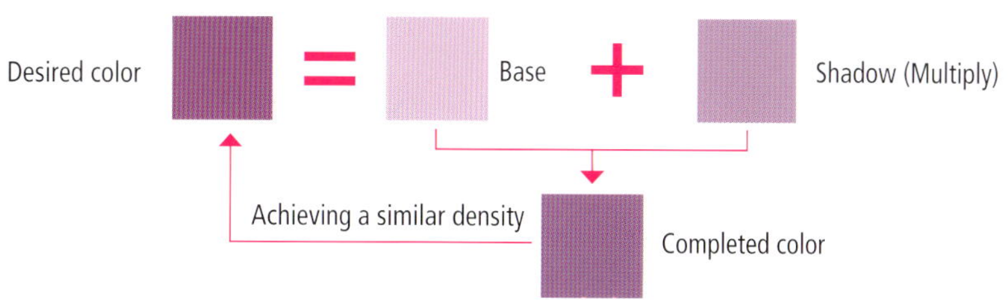

# Beware of Poorly Applied Schemes

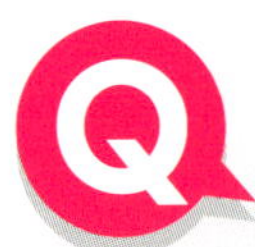


## Which one is easier to look at?

Doesn't **B** appear to have more effectively rendered hair? **A** has too strong a black base, making the shadow color less visible and reducing the sense of three-dimensionality. Let's look more deeply into the key points of using white and black, as well as some color combination cautions.

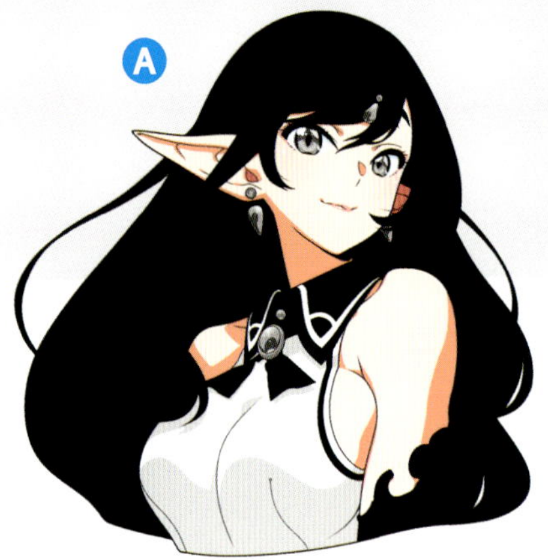


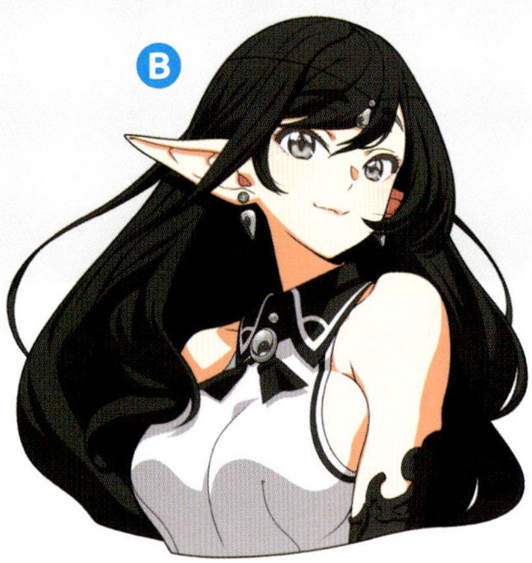


## Frequently Used Areas of Saturation and Brightness

On page 26, we looked at the areas of the color wheel that can be used for base colors. Now let's consider those areas used for highlights and shadows. As shown in the diagram below, try to select colors mainly from the upper left. This is because colors become stronger in brightness and luminosity toward the lower right, and using them indiscriminately can lead to choosing overly dominant colors, making the finishing process difficult. Beginners should focus on using upper-left selections to reduce the likelihood of making mistakes in the coloring.

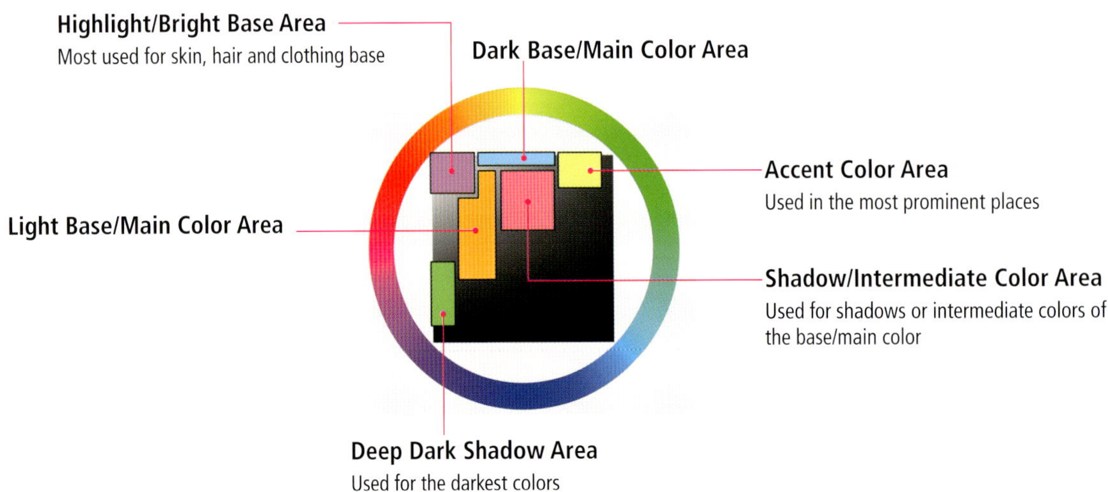

# Avoid Using Full Black and Full White

When creating color schemes, avoid using pure white (full white) and pure black (full black). White and black are considered modes of brightness rather than actual colors, so avoid using pure black or pure white in color schemes except in special cases. If you want to create a drawing that taps into or attempts to create such an atmosphere, choosing a color that's nearly white (or black) but with a slight tint will help achieve a more harmonious and balanced result.

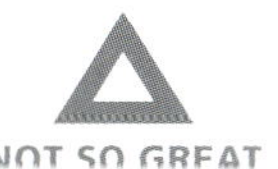


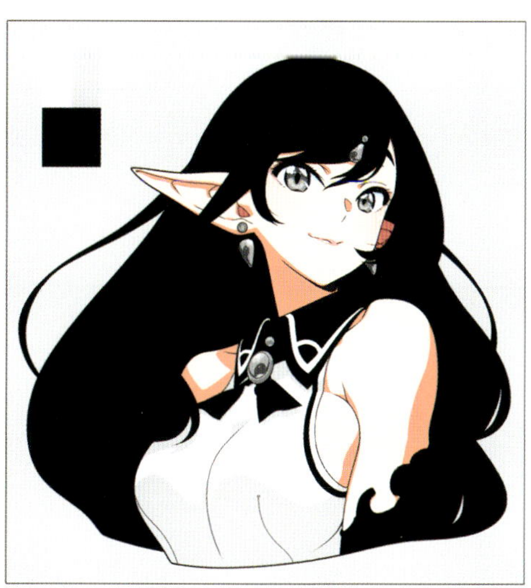

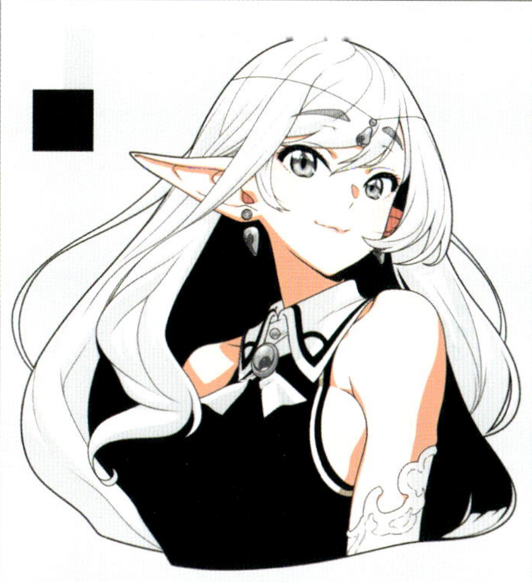

Pure and pure black have the strongest impact in terms of brightness, so they should be avoided and used only as accents. This approach will give your illustration a more balanced look.

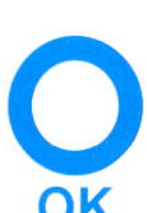


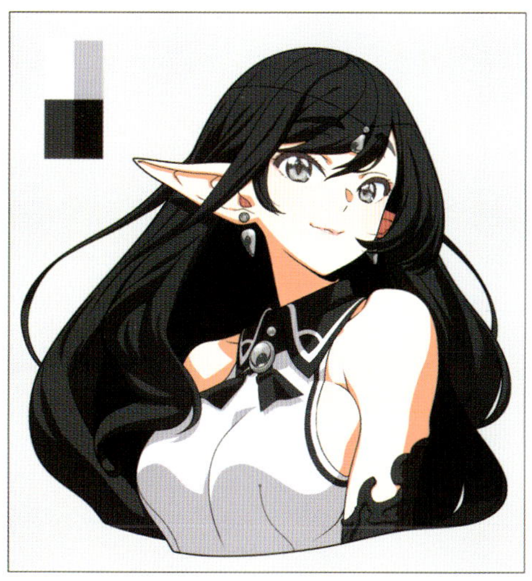

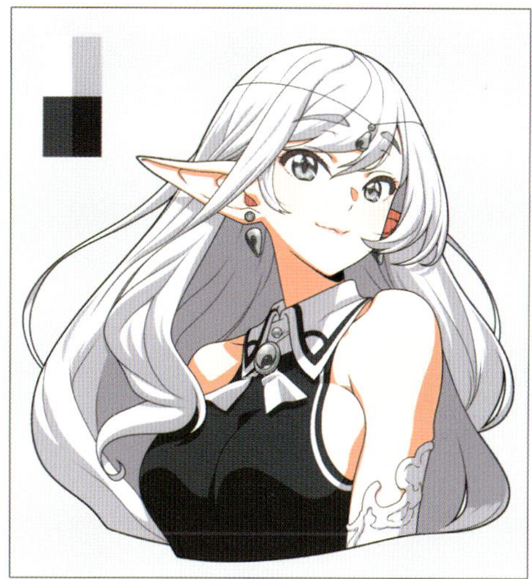

For the base color of black, use a dark gray, and for shadows, use a heavily darkened red. For the base color of white, use a nearly white blue, and for shadows, use a grayish purple. This way, you can express white or black without using pure white or pure black.

# Halation: What Is It?

Sometimes, in informally examining an illustration, you can use the phrase "hurts the eyes" for colors that are imbalanced or extremely applied. This refers to the phenomenon known as halation. It most commonly occurs by combining two colors with similar brightnesses and high saturations. However, even under the same conditions, some combinations are less likely to cause halation. Below are some patterns that are prone to halation and those that are not. It's important to understand these combinations well so as not to create halation effects in your drawings.

**Examples of Halation Patterns**

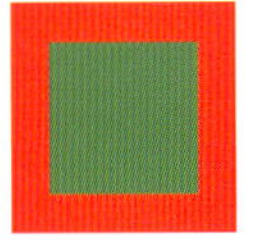 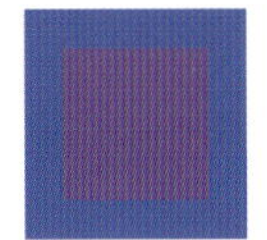 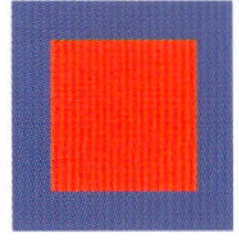

Complementary color combinations are prone to halation.

**Highly Visible Halation**

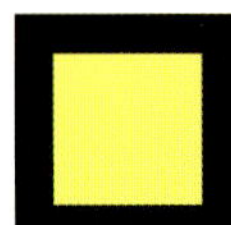 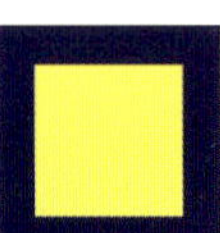 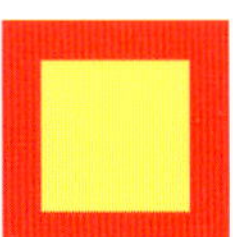 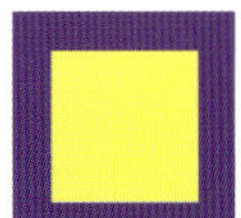

Purple and yellow, although complementary colors, don't cause halation.

( **EXPERT TIP** )  **SPECIAL PATTERNS**

Colors like white and red, or black and red, can potentially cause halation, but when used skillfully, they can be effective inclusions. In this illustration, halation is avoided by balancing black with the red background. However, the balance in placement greatly depends on experience and skill, so it's a good idea to experiment and seek feedback.

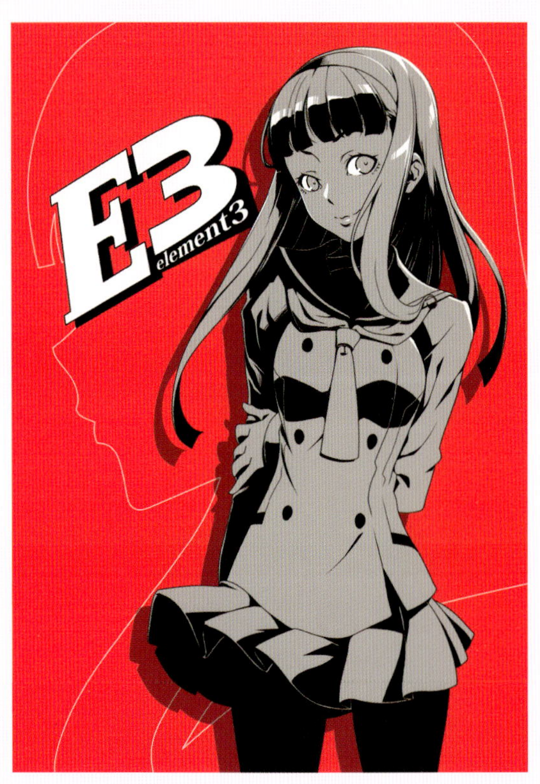

# How to Deal with Halation

To resolve halation, the solution is very simple: insert an achromatic color between the two conflicting colors. Look at the diagram below. At the top, since the colors are separated, there's no visual discord. However, when placed next to each other, halation occurs. By inserting an achromatic color, the previous halation effect is alleviated. Thus, avoiding placing colors prone to halation next to each other can resolve the issue to some extent.

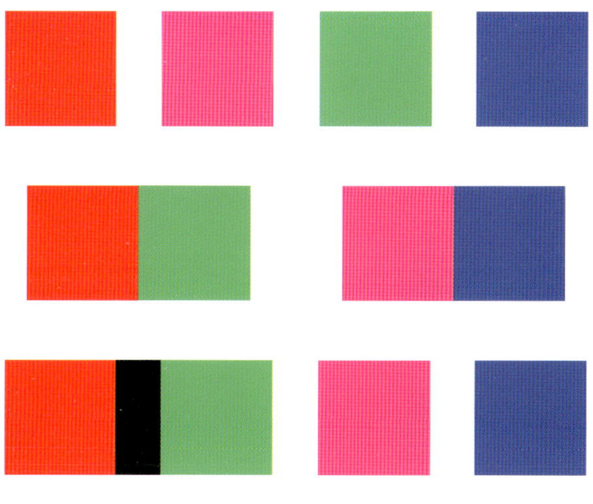

There are two pairs of similar colors: red and purple, green and blue. This arrangement doesn't cause a clash.

Now, let's place them together. The color boundaries appear glaring and discordant, don't they?

To resolve this, inserting an achromatic color between the two colors alleviates the visual conflict.

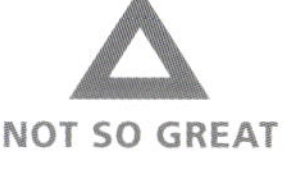

**NOT SO GREAT**

When painting the character green, halation occurs, so let's try the solution.

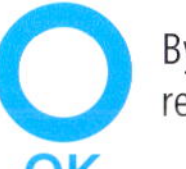

**OK**

By inserting white in between, the glare is reduced, resulting in a calmer result.

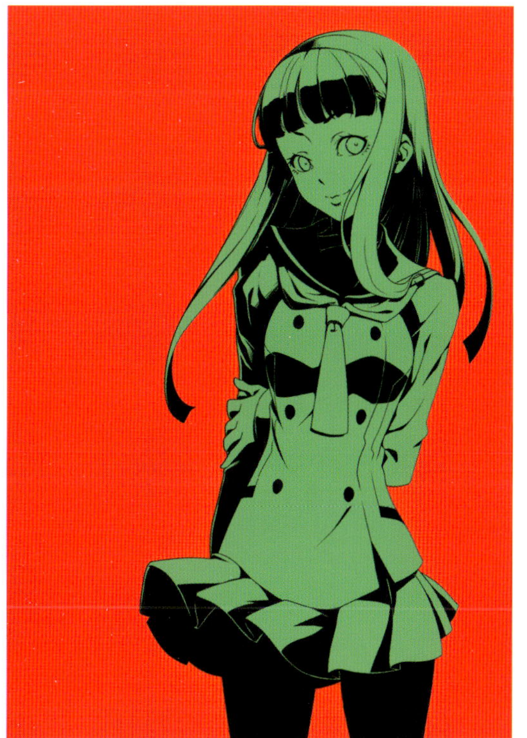

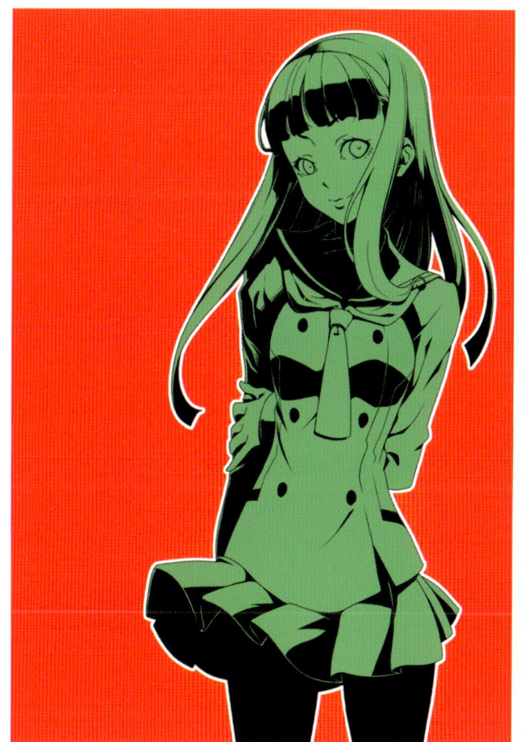

# Colors That Don't Cause Halation

What color does the clothing in this picture appear to be? At first glance, it might look green. However, it's actually yellow. This illustration uses three colors: yellow, blue and red, with red used for the ribbon. If the clothing were green, it would be complementary to the red and could cause halation, so a dark yellow was used as green. As explained on page 40, adjacent colors can cause halation and contribute a visually jarring effect to the finished illustration. To avoid this, you can use another color that looks similar in such situations.

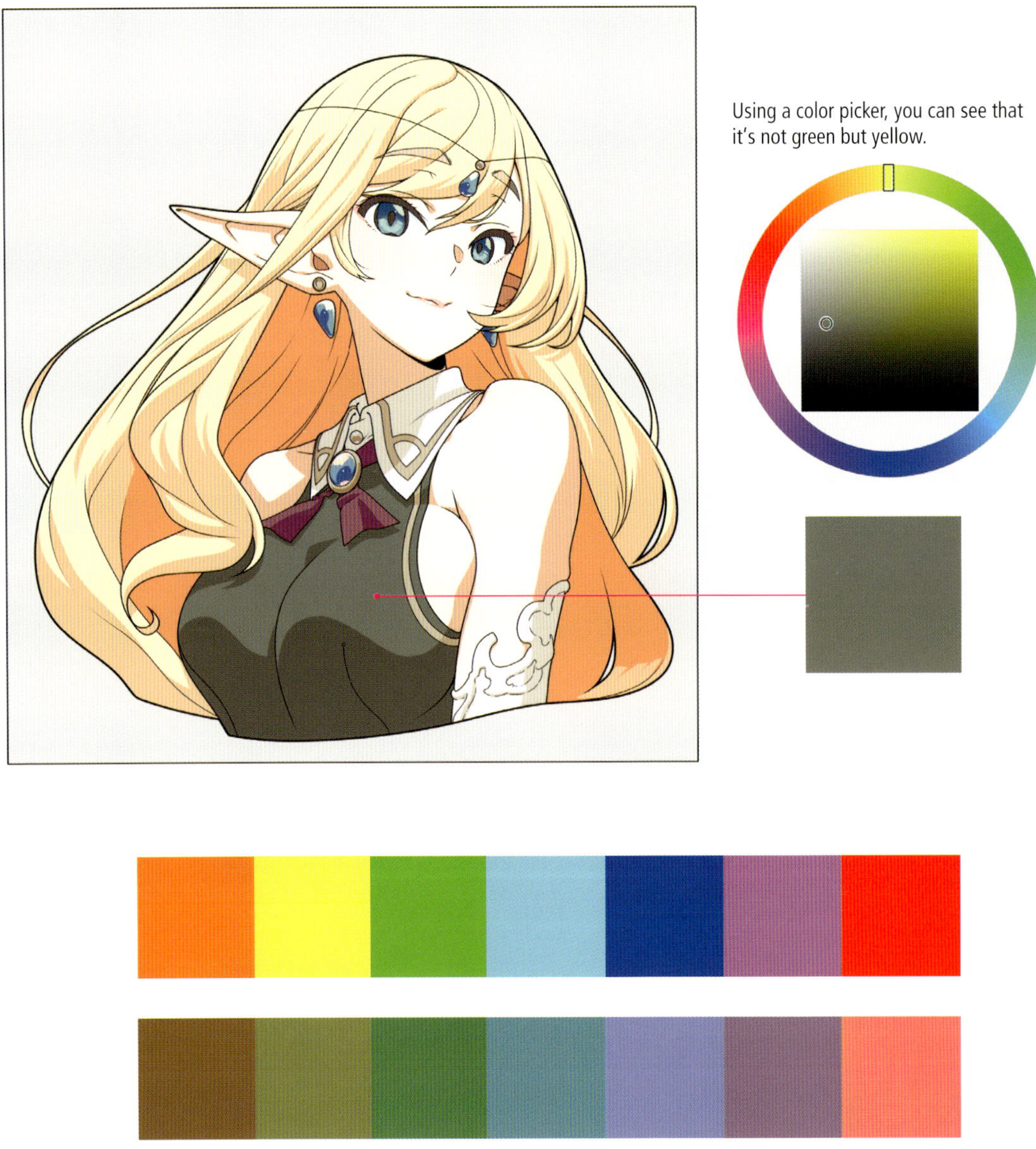



Even if the hues are the same, changing the brightness and saturation can make them appear as different colors. Especially with yellow, low brightness can make it look green, and with red, low saturation can make it look orange.

# Consider Warm and Cool Colors

Understanding this method allows for even more interesting possibilities. In the diagram below, the upper body is based on cool colors, while the lower body uses warm colors. However, by using red only for the eyes as an accent, increased attention is drawn to them. This is just one method, but being able to distinguish between warm and cool colors and use them accordingly allows you to guide the viewer's gaze with color.

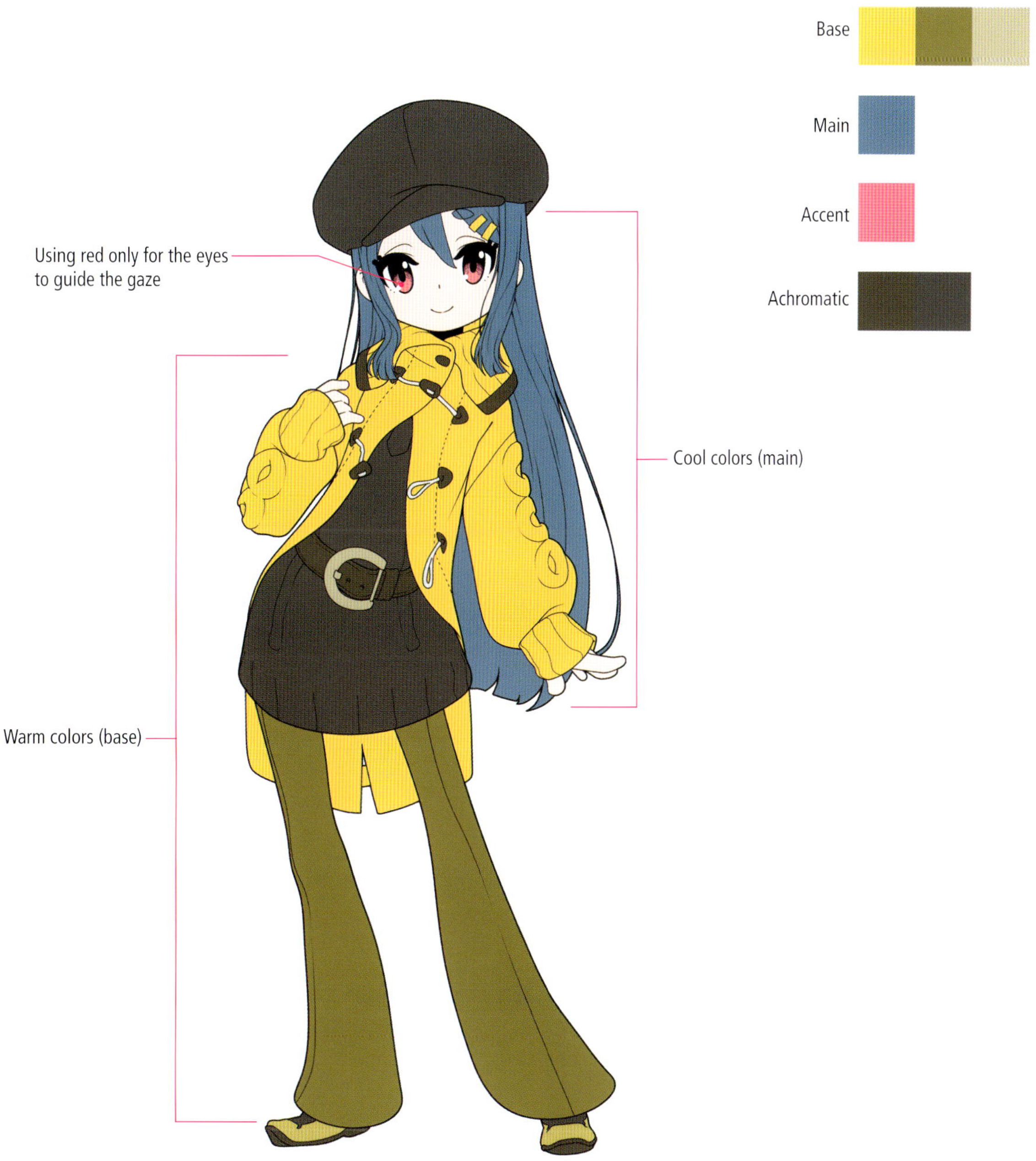

# Considering the Difference in Brightness and Darkness

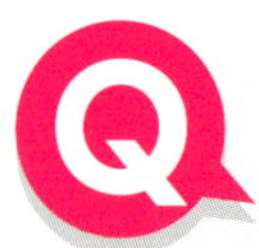

## Which color scheme matches the skin better?

While both may not be incorrect, doesn't **A** seem to be more suitable? **A** leaves a lasting impression with its translucent white skin, while **B** appears dull as the dark skin blends with the clothing color. Additionally, **A** draws the eye due to the contrast difference, whereas **B**'s small difference makes the colors appear similar and less memorable. Let's look more closely at color schemes and highlighting their contrast differences.

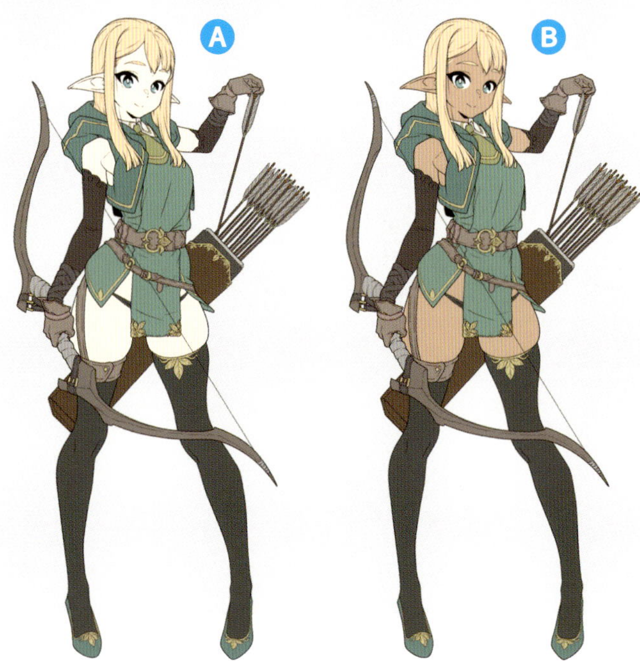

## Skin Tone

How can you make character with varying skin tones, like in the two examples, more striking? For darker-toned characters, one method is to use achromatic white for the clothing. This creates a significant brightness difference between the skin color and the clothing, like the result achieved in **A**.

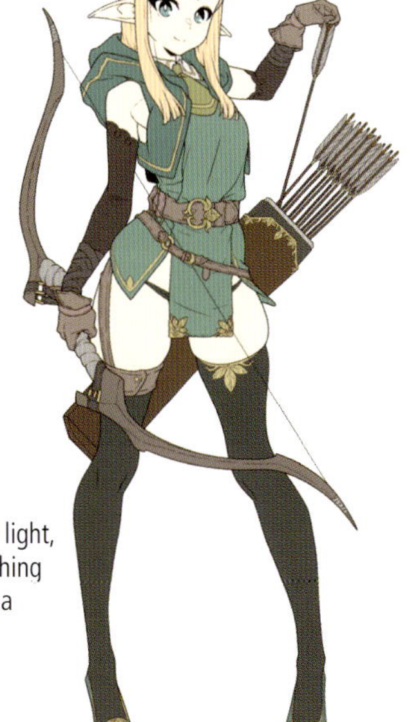

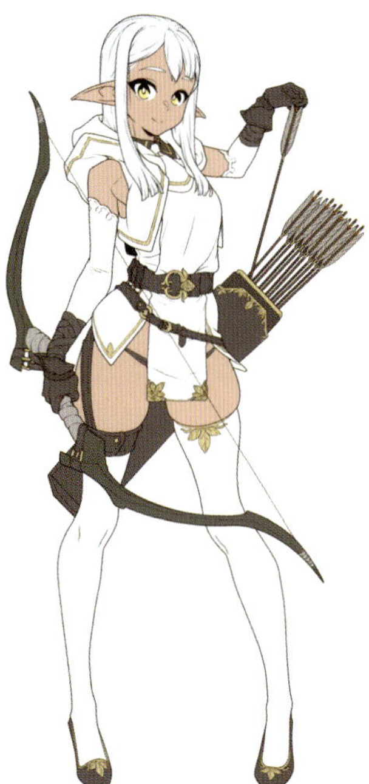

If the skin is dark, make the clothing light, and if the skin is light, make the clothing dark to enhance the contrast. This is a classic technique commonly used to make illustrations more impactful.

# Standing Out from the Background

Now let's consider the balance of light and dark between the background and the character. Four examples are given below, but the basic principle is the same. First, look at the top two. It's easier to understand if you check them with the color infor- mation removed. If the brightness of the background and the character is similar, the character will blend in; but by clearly separating the brightness of the character and the background, the character stands out all the more.

**When the character's color scheme is bright**

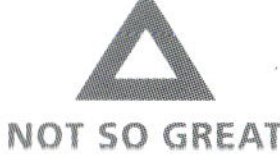
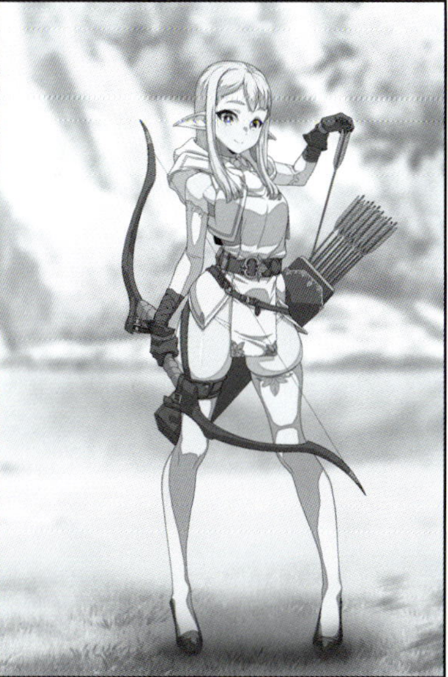

When both the character's color scheme and the background are bright, the character blends in.

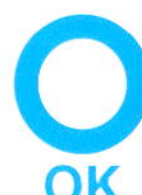
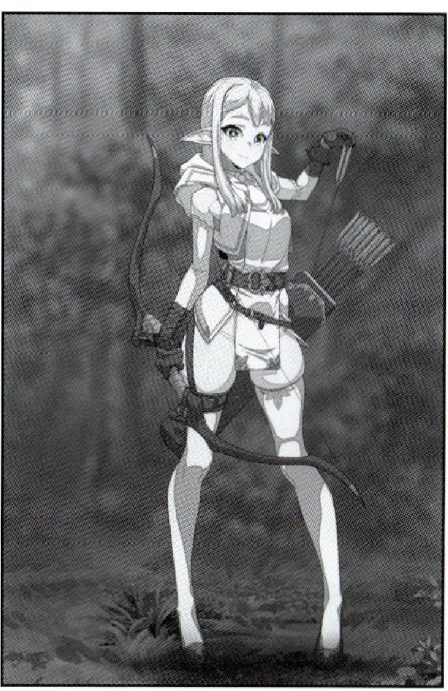

By making the background color darker, opposite to the character's color scheme, the character stands out more.

**When the character's color scheme is dark**

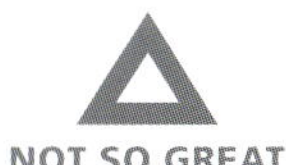
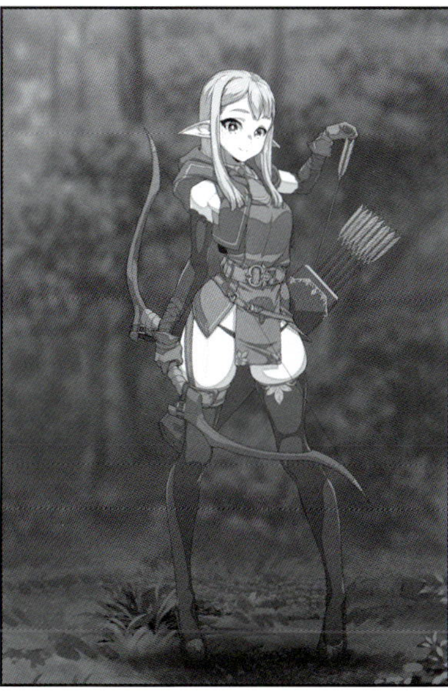

Conversely, when the character's color scheme is dark, a dark background makes the character blend in.

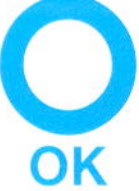
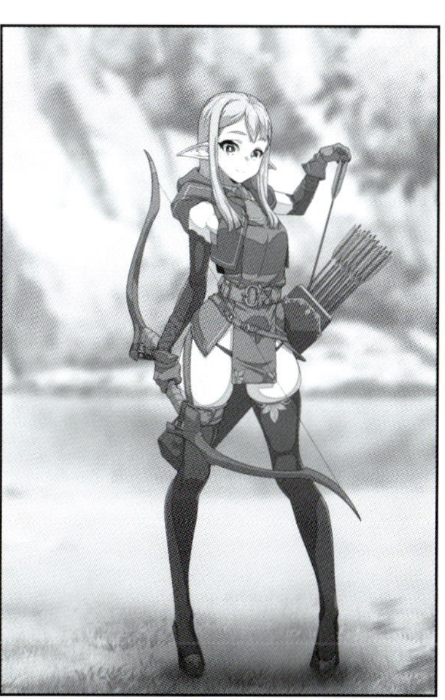

By brightening the background, the character stands out.

## Character and Background

The illustrations below feature the same character and background with the same composition, but doesn't the one on the left seem more convincing? The left illustration lowers the saturation of the background relative to the character, making the character stand out. On the other hand, the right illustration has high saturation for both the character and the background, giving a slightly lighter impression. When both the character and background have high saturation, the character doesn't stand out, and the overall impression of the finished illustration is shifted. A similar technique involves using light and dark differences to make the character stand out. This is explored in greater depth on page 106.

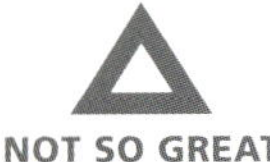



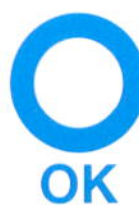



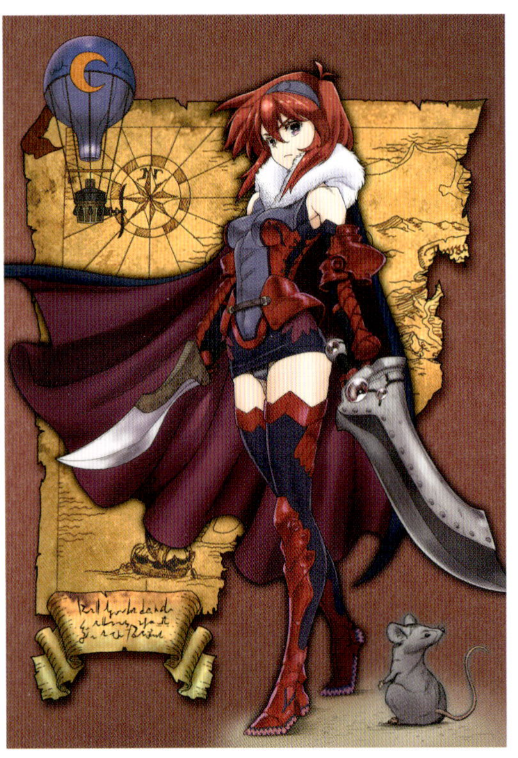

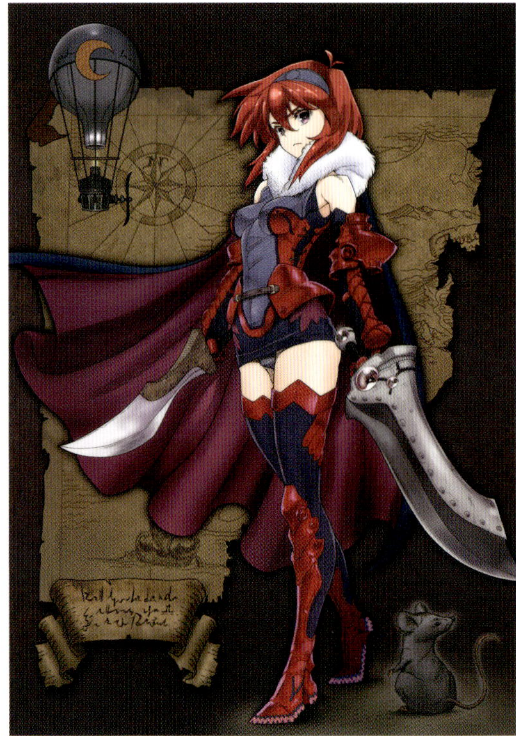

# Consider Brightness and Saturation Separately

At first glance, these two illustrations don't look very different, but upon closer inspection, there are slight differences in the shadow colors. The left illustration uses high-saturation shadow colors, while the right uses low-brightness shadow colors. Even with the same base color, the left illustration pops more, while the right appears relatively calm and more subdued. By choosing different shadow colors, you can change the atmosphere of an illustration even with the same base color. Decide on the brightness and saturation based on how you want your finished illustration to look.

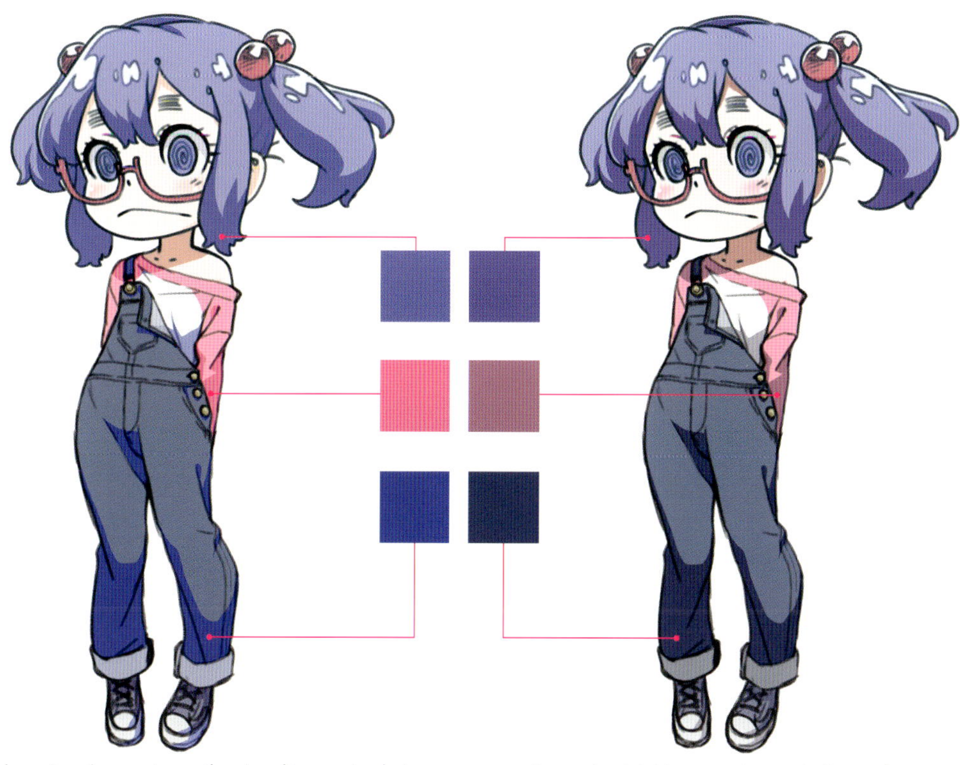

Increasing saturation creates a vibrant and impression but requires caution as colors may conflict more easily.

Decreasing brightness creates a calm impression, but the result may appear slightly dull.

Now let's consider just the skin color. Using the same base color, shadows with increased saturation are applied to **A**, and shadows with decreased brightness are applied to **B**. The sphere in **A** appears vibrant, while **B** has a calmer impression, doesn't it? Even with the same skin color, changing the saturation and brightness of the shadow color can significantly alter the impression. To make it vibrant, increase the saturation, and for a calmer look or result, lower the brightness.

For reference, animation and watercolors, typically use high-saturation colors, while thick painting uses low-brightness colors, matching the appropriate mood. The selection of shadow colors for skin is examined more closely on page 70.

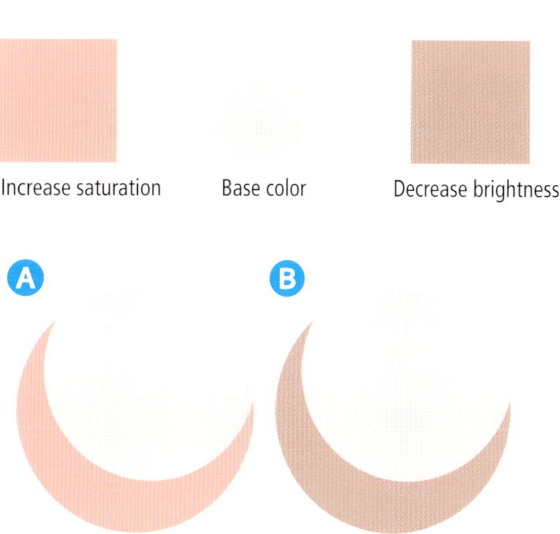

# Ready to Use! Color Patterns & Rules

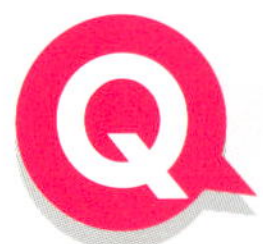

## Which one looks more cohesive?

When compared, **A** appears more cohesive. **B** lacks uniformity in its color schemes across the various parts, making it look somewhat disjointed. Let's look at the rules and principles that guide selecting the main colors you use.

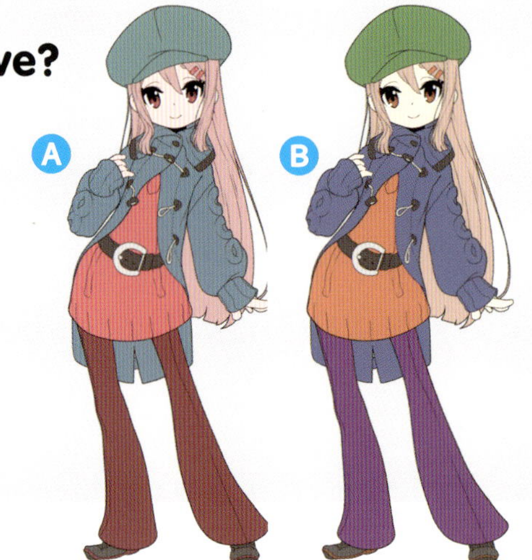


## Color Scheme Patterns

Choosing colors based on spontaneous ideas or on-the-spot inspiration can lead to poor cohesion and balance. There are various color scheme patterns, and following them can reduce the chances of making mistakes. There are many different patterns, but here we introduce some that are easy to use.

### Dominant Color

A color scheme that changes brightness and saturation within one hue is called a dominant color scheme. By choosing colors from one hue, it creates a monochromatic or analogous color scheme, making it easier to convey the character's defining or base image color. However, using the same hue can lead to a generic effect and might lack immediate visual impact compared to other color schemes. You of course don't have to choose from just one hue; analogous colors can also be used to create a cohesive scheme.

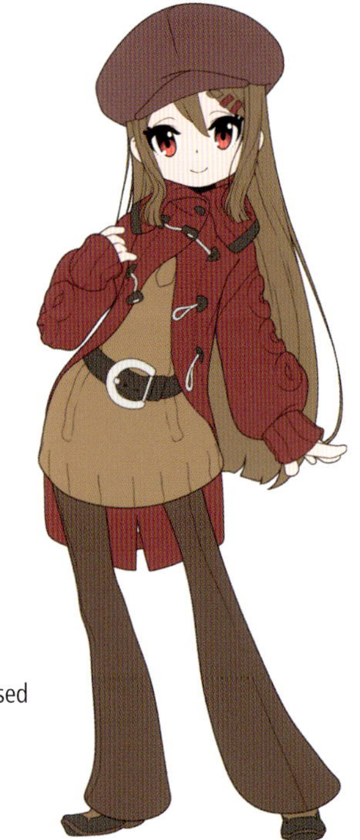

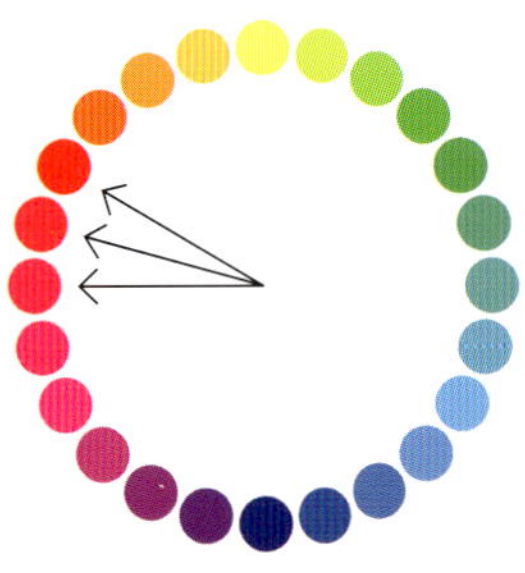

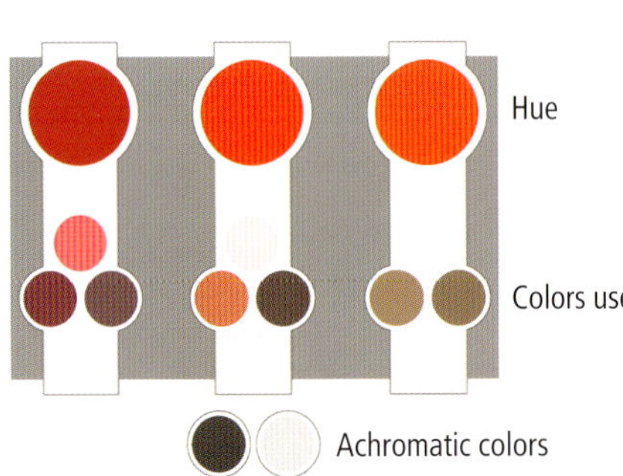

A two-color scheme using opposing complementary hues creates a tight overall impression, creating eye-catching effects at first glance. You can select any two colors, as long as they're complementary on the color wheel. Compared to three-color schemes, adding more colors to a two-color scheme can easily result in a dull impression, so choose carefully.

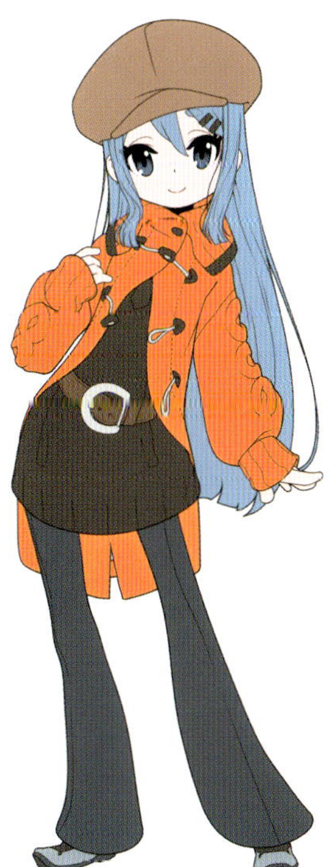

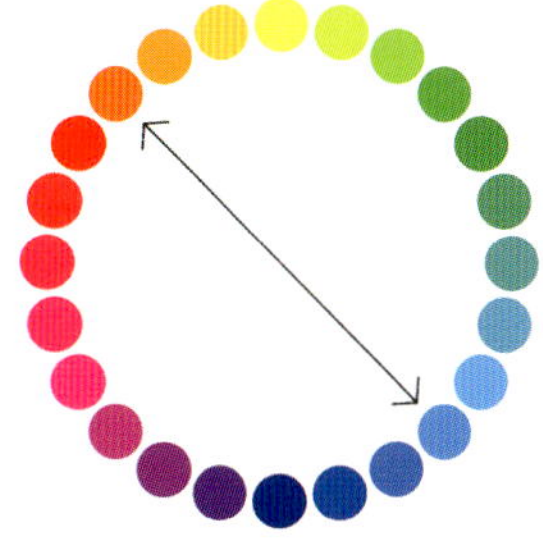
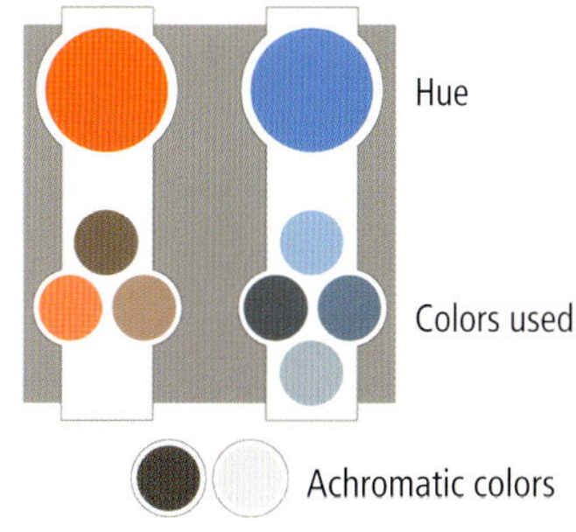


**Split Complementary**

A color scheme where you choose one color first and then use the two colors adjacent to its complementary color is called a split complementary color scheme. While it's similar to a two-color scheme in using complementary colors, the slight shift from the complementary color makes it a safer choice. This scheme has fewer chances of failure, but the color selection can be monotonous and lack individuality, so careful consideration of the chosen colors and their placement is necessary. Additionally, as the number of colors increases, the placement becomes more challenging. For example, in this illustration, placing a green hat next to green hair can make the face area, which is meant to be a focal point, less noticeable. Therefore, attention to color placement is essential.

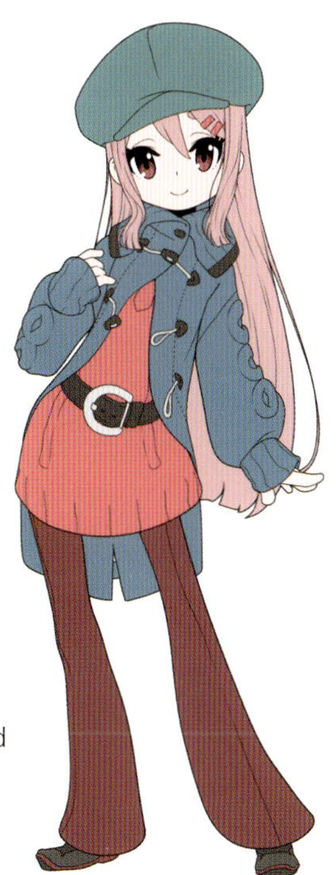

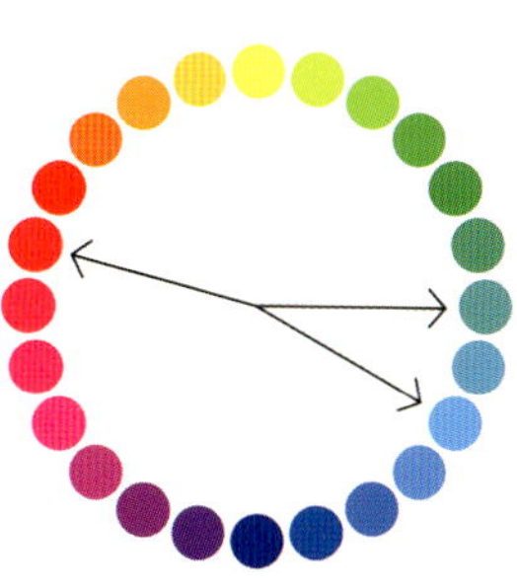
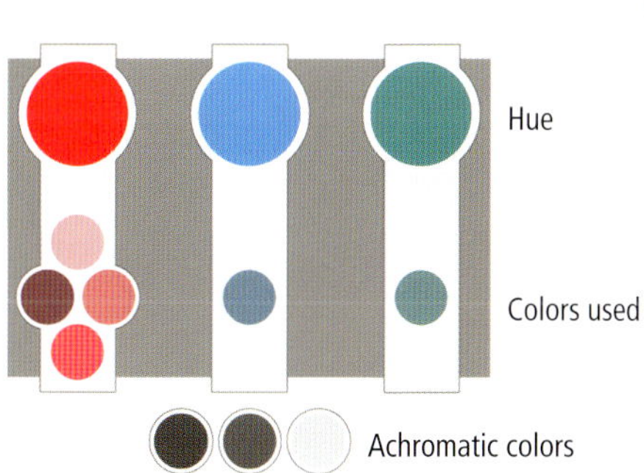

A color scheme that takes three colors forming an equilateral triangle on the color wheel is called a triad color scheme. While the split complementary scheme forms an isosceles triangle, the triad scheme forms an equilateral triangle. This creates a highly balanced color scheme, and although none of the three colors are complementary, they're unrelated colors, resulting in a clear and distinct illustration. Depending on the choice of colors, the hues can become strong and pronounced, so pay attention to the overall balance.

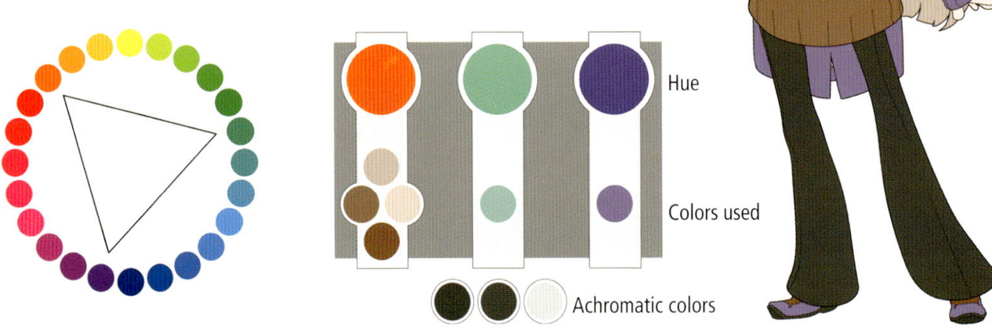


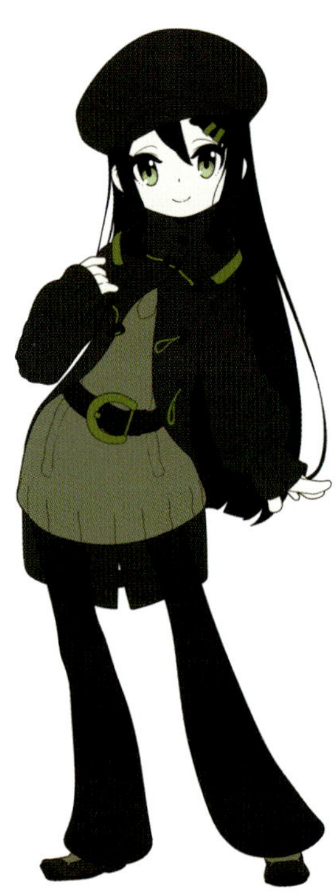

## Monotone

A color scheme composed of a single color close to achromatic colors yields a monotone effect. In the illustration below, colors like dark green and light green are used. Be careful not to choose completely achromatic colors. Since monotone schemes are mostly achromatic, they help the image stand out. It's typically a color scheme method suitable for advanced users with skills in both color scheme and placement.

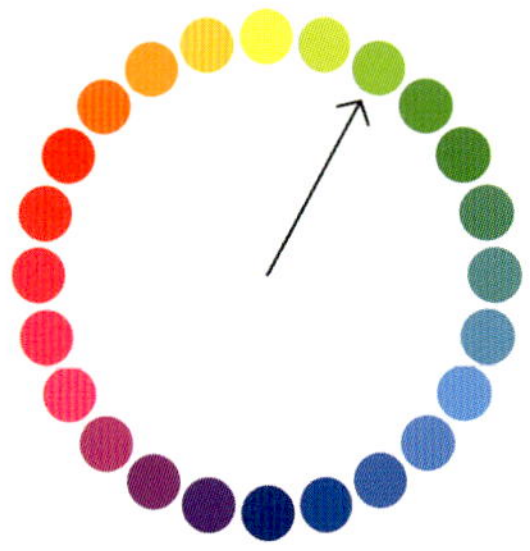

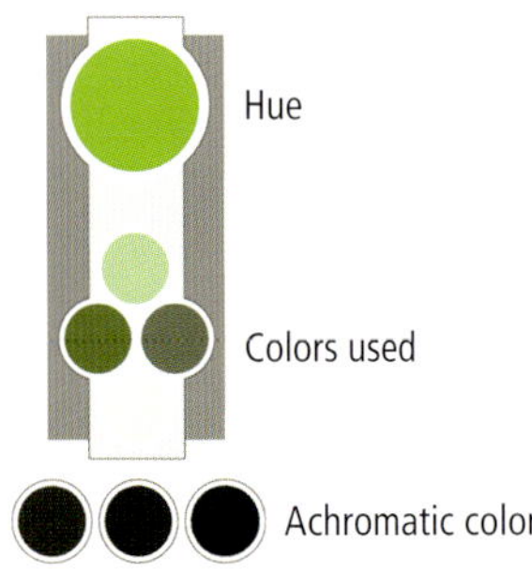

# Using Pastel Colors

Choosing highly saturated colors can create strong contrasts and brightness differences, resulting in an imbalanced color scheme. Therefore, initially aim to use pastel colors with high brightness to avoid these potential problems.

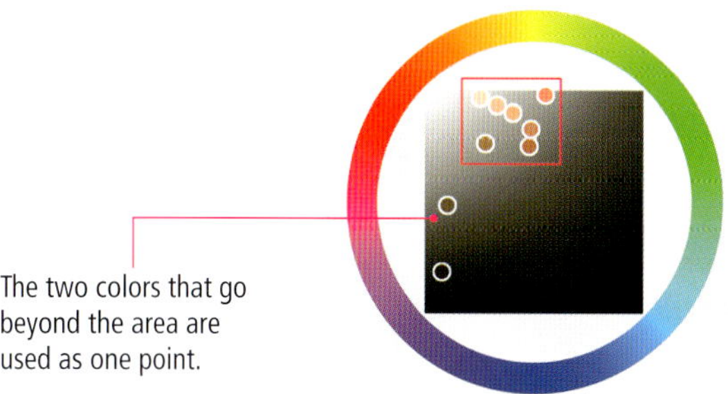

The two colors that go beyond the area are used as one point.

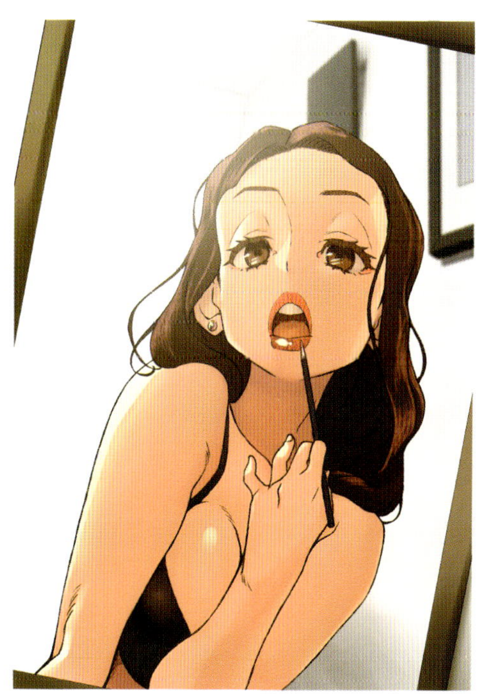

If you use the eyedropper tool to pick colors from the illustration on the right, most of them fall within the area enclosed by the red box. This area has just the right saturation, allowing you to choose colors that don't create overly strong contrasts in terms of shadows and finishing touches.



## CHOOSING SKIN TONES WITH PASTEL COLORS

The right diagram shows an example of combinations when choosing skin tones based on pastel colors. The colors there are chosen from within or close to the pastel color area marked by red in the diagram below. In the less successful example on the left, colors are chosen from outside the area or have mismatched hues, brightnesses and saturations, resulting in a sense of discord. By choosing highlights, base colors, and shadows from pastel colors, you can create a cohesive impression with minimal adjustments required.

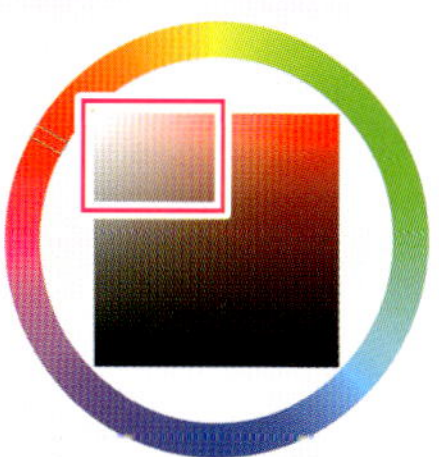

Choose colors from the pastel color area near the upper left of the color circle.

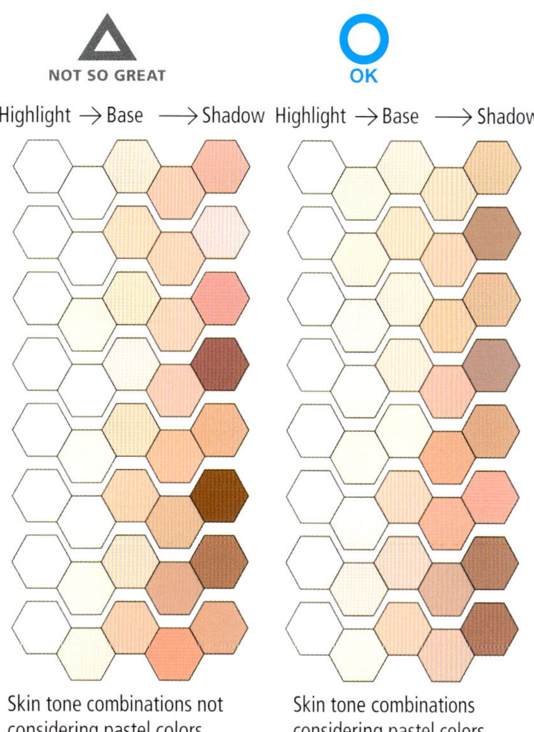


Skin tone combinations not considering pastel colors

Skin tone combinations considering pastel colors

# Vivid Color Schemes

The most vivid colors are highly saturated. Using these high-saturation schemes can make it difficult to achieve a harmonious look. A few tips make it easier to manage the use of vivid colors effectively. First off, align the brightness of the colors. In the example below, the main colors are selected and converted to grayscale. You can see that their brightness levels are almost the same. By aligning the brightness to some extent, you can introduce several additional colors while maintaining a cohesive color scheme.

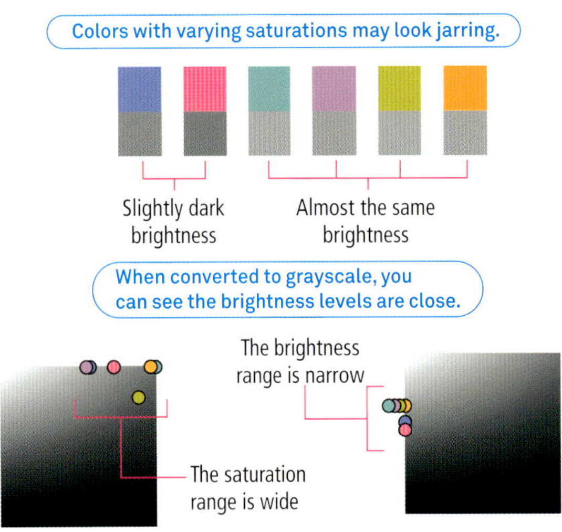


However, simply aligning the brightness might make the scheme monotonous. By adding complementary colors to small areas, you can enhance the vividness. Balancing with brightness rather than hue or saturation helps the colors harmonize better.

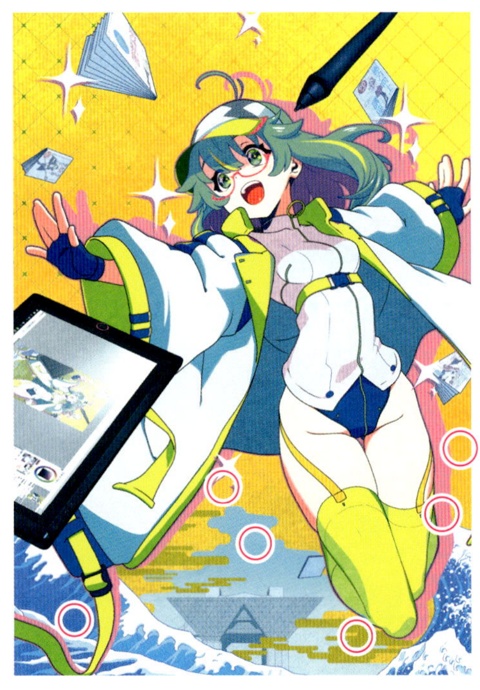

The blue, being the complementary color, is used in a smaller area than the yellow to create a balanced look.

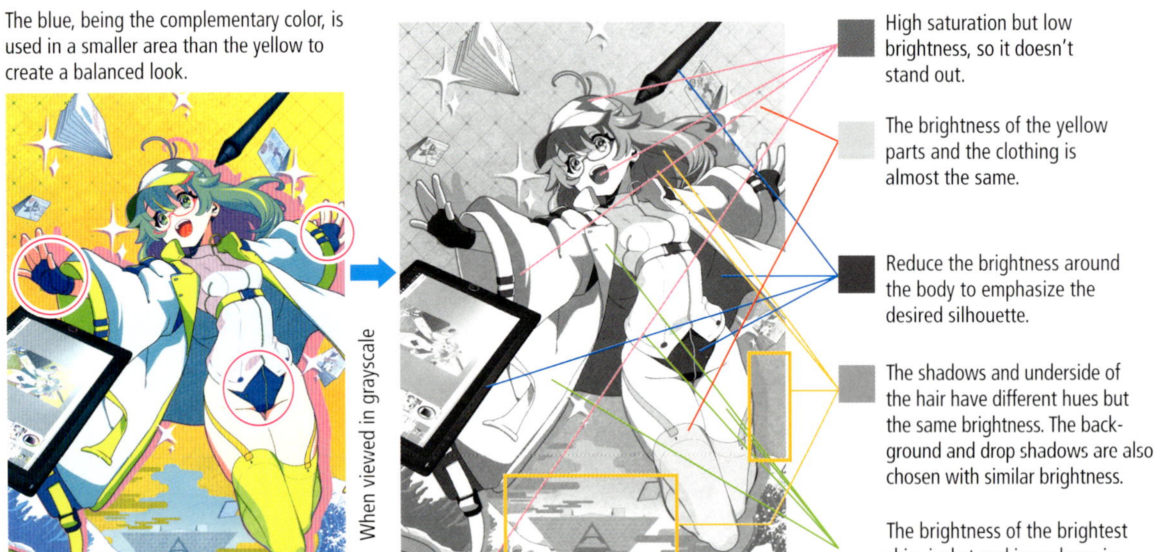

# Color Preferences by Age

There are patterns in associated colors and palettes depending on the age or generation, although naturally there are individual differences that your illustrations and characters will reflect. Let's take a closer look at the tendencies and patterns of color preferences by age group.

## Infancy

Infants are said to prefer bright, primary colors. Therefore, toys and everyday items for infants are often made in pastel tones. However, colors with more subdued saturations are also a common choice.

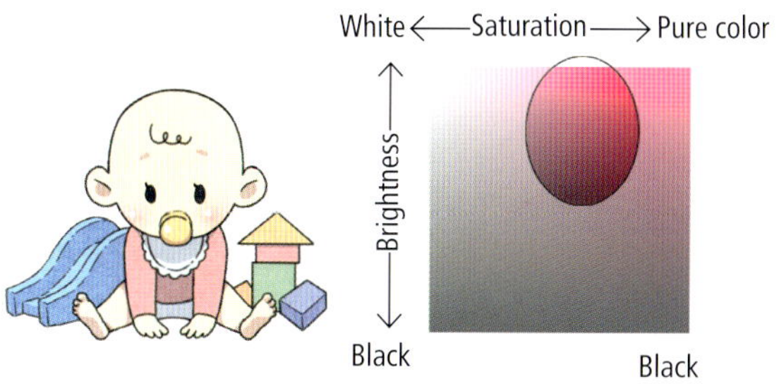


## Early Childhood

From age five, children tend to prefer or gravitate to colors closer to the vivid "pure" colors. The more complex palettes reflect a more sophisticated understanding of the world around them.

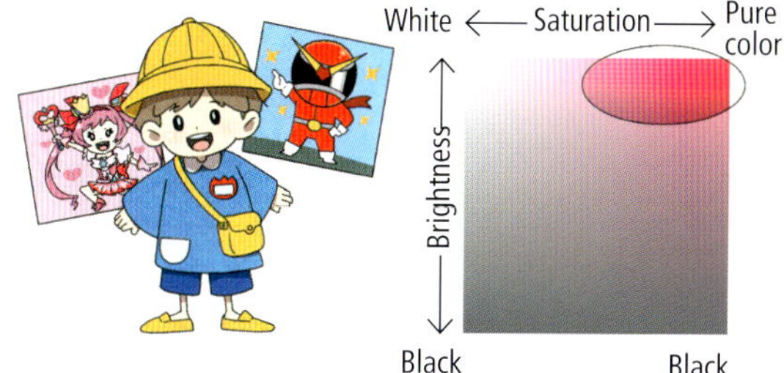


## Adolescence

In adolescence, the interest expands to a wide range of tones. This diversity is related to the wide variety of clothing and the diverse tastes and preferences in this demographic.

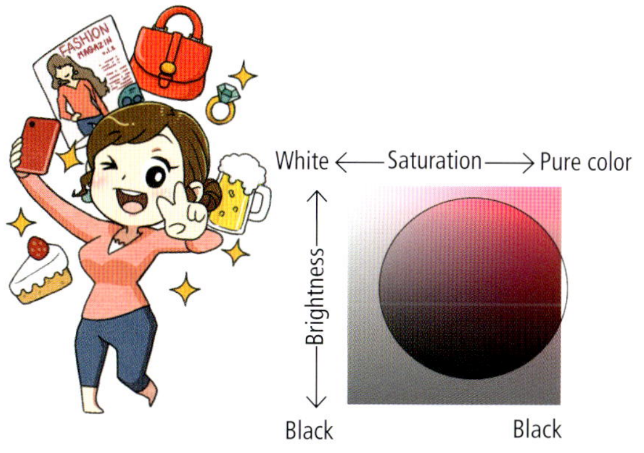


## Middle and Older Age

In middle age, preferences narrow significantly to darker, more subdued tones. This is largely due to these tones being perceived as calm and dignified. Conversely, an extreme shift toward vivid colors in an attempt to appear younger, such as flashy tiger stripes, can be an overt flouting of subdued tones.

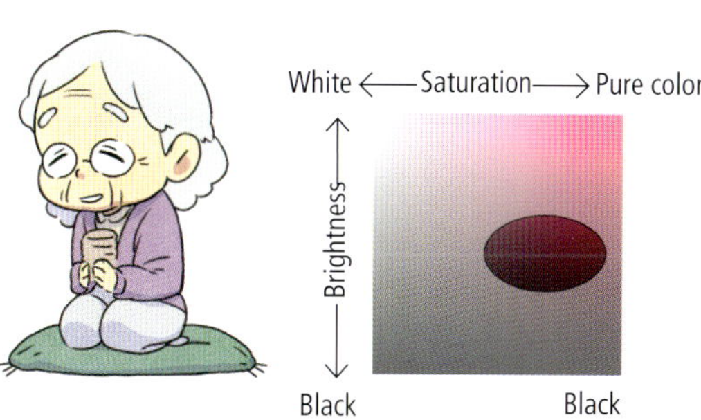

# Color Schemes and Finishing the Cover Illustration

Let's look at the color scheme and the process at work to finish the cover character.

## Color Scheme

### COLOR ROUGH

First, decide on the color scheme. During the creation of the color rough, the basic color scheme is determined. Here, an analogous color scheme pattern, which uses similar colors, is adopted. The base color is in the red range, the main color is in the orange range and the accent color falls in the yellow-green range. This time, because there are many accessories, we first thought about the color scheme without the accessories.

### ANALOGOUS

An analogous color scheme is composed of three colors that are next to each other on the color wheel. This scheme allows for a wider range of colors than the dominant color scheme (see page 48), providing more options. Using similar colors makes it easier to achieve harmony and reduces the risk of clashes.

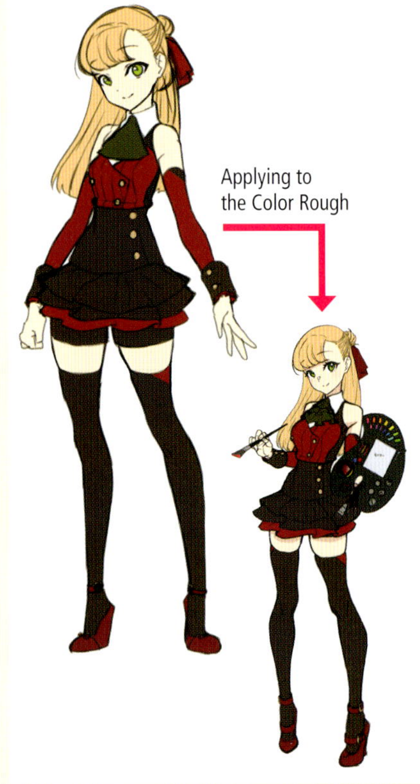


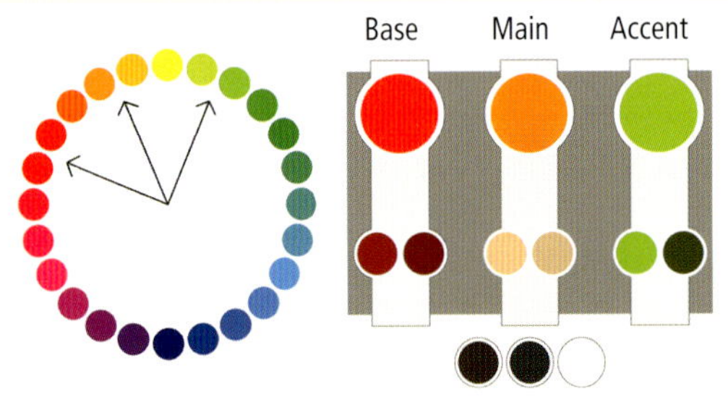


### GRAYSCALE CONVERSION

Convert to grayscale to check the balance. The focus is on the face, so the hair (the main color) near the face is kept bright, while the clothes and accessories (the base and accent colors) are kept dark to create contrast and draw attention to the face. The colors of the palette held by the character are also adjusted to have a similar brightness to the clothes to avoid any sense of discord.

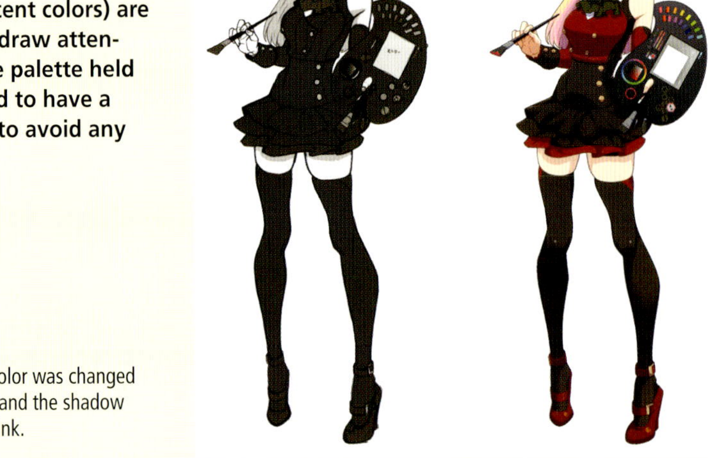

The hair color was changed to yellow and the shadow color to pink.

The character coloring is not complete until it has been processed and the colors adjusted. The methods for color adjustment and processing are explained in Chapter 6 and beyond. Here, we'll explore how the cover illustration is processed.

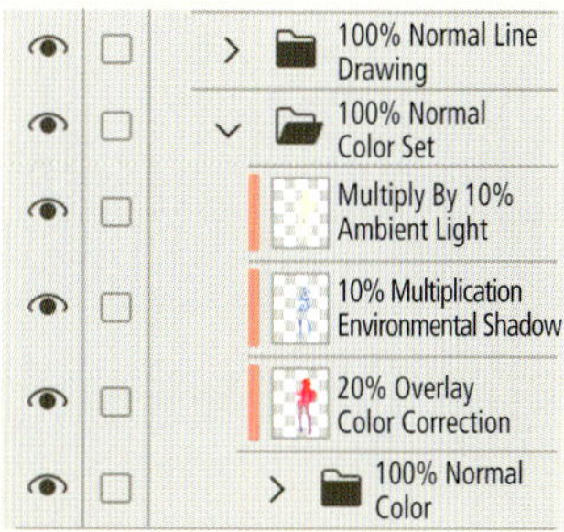


Three layers are created above the character coloring, each with its own color.

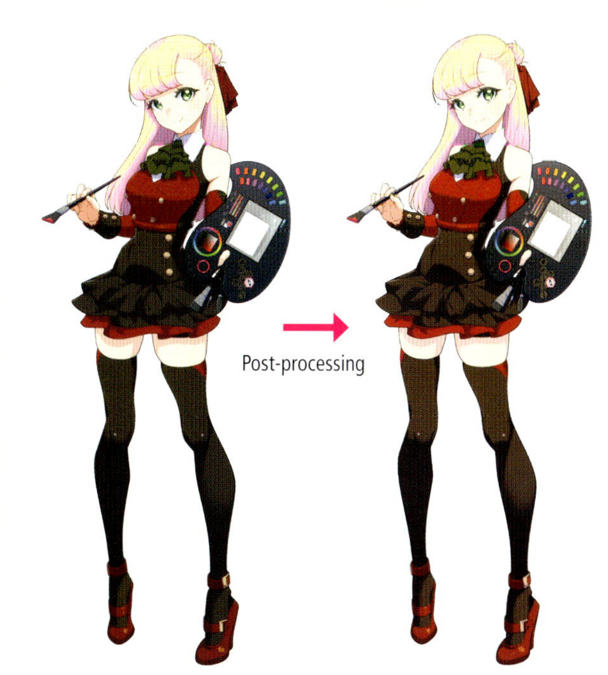

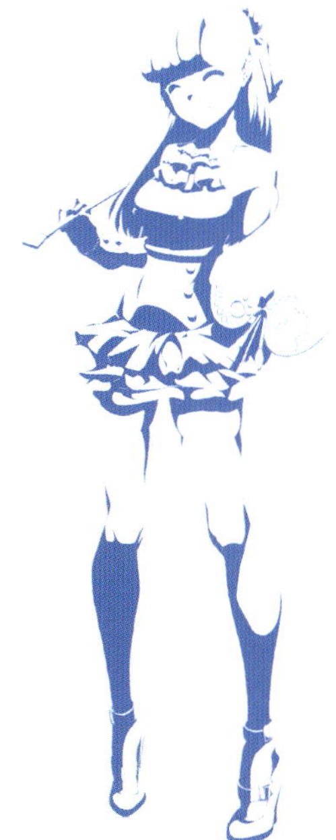

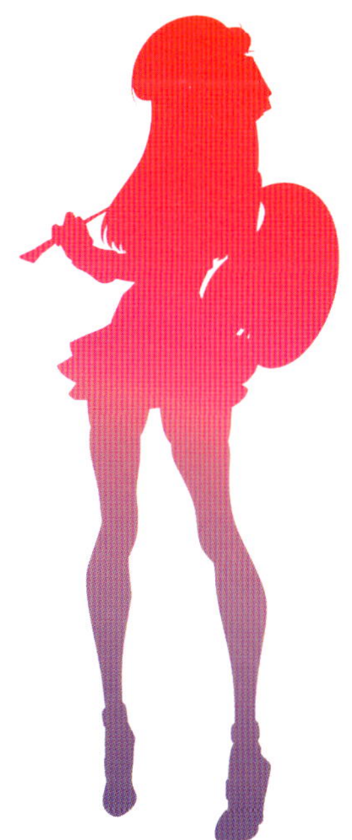

**Ambient Light**
Apply ambient light from daytime (see page124) to the entire character. (Multiply, layer opacity 10%)

**Ambient Shadow**
Apply ambient shadow from daytime only to the shadow areas. (Multiply, layer opacity 10%)

**Color Adjustment**
To enhance the red base color and add a reddish tint to the skin, a red to pink gradient is overlaid on the entire character. (Overlay, layer opacity 10%)

# Control Your Viewer's Gaze with Color

## Which one draws the viewer's gaze to the eyes?

Both direct attention to the face, but **A** likely draws more attention to the eyes. **A** uses an accent color on the eyes, demonstrating how color usage can control focal points. This section explains color schemes designed to guide the gaze.

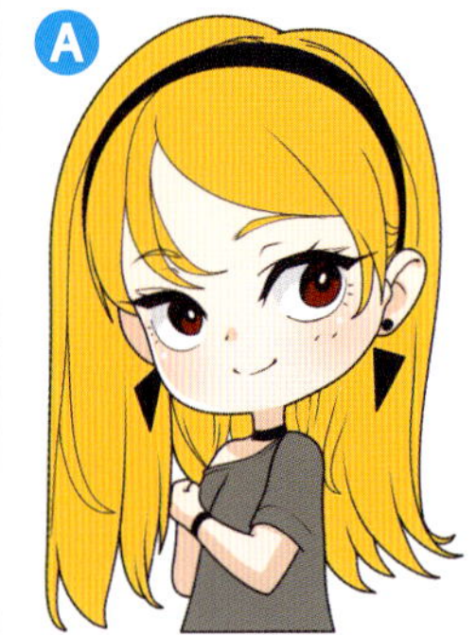

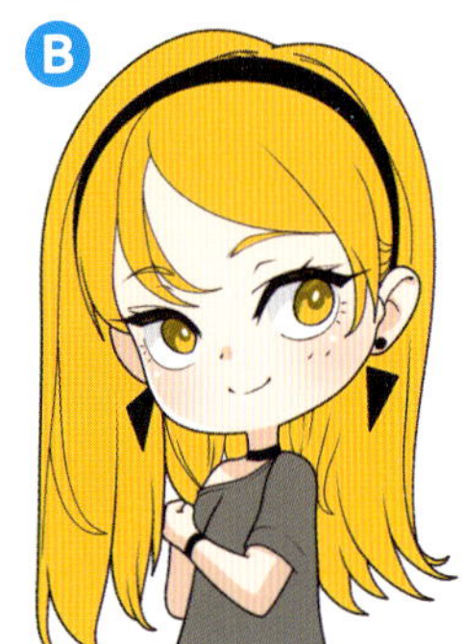

## Techniques for Guiding Gaze

Look at the illustration on the right. This is Alphonse Mucha's "Gismonda" (1894). Note how techniques for guiding the gaze through the use of color have been employed. The area around the face is meticulously colored, with detailed line work, while the face itself, set off in green, is less detailed. This contrast in information density ensures that the gaze is first drawn to the face.

Darker colors are also concentrated at the top of the painting, while the lower part features lighter pastel colors, directing the overall gaze upward. These techniques for guiding a viewer's gaze with color have existed since ancient times and remain fundamentally unchanged today even with digital platforms.

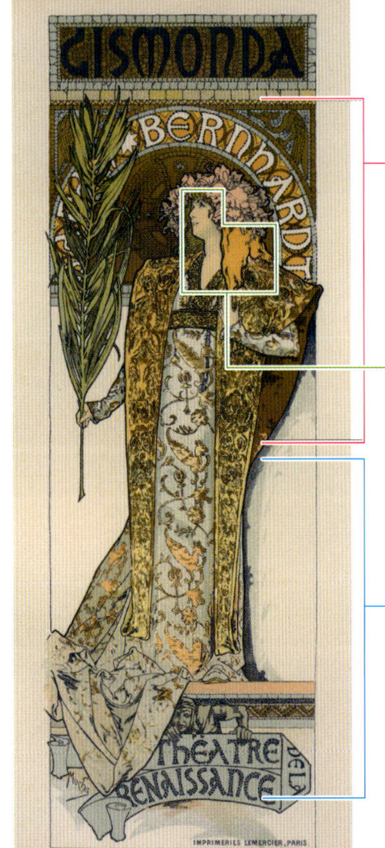

**High-Information Density**

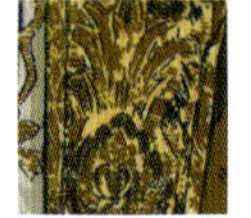
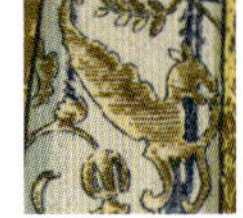

In areas with high-information density, the less dense areas like the face and hair attract the gaze.

**Low-Information Density**

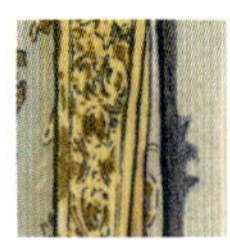
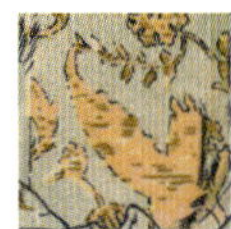

# Using Color to Guide the Gaze

The illustration on the right is painted with guiding the viewer's gaze in mind, creating two gaze pathways. The first is the red line, and the second is the yellow line.

The red line decreases in colorized areas as it moves downward, guiding the gaze from the hat → chest → abdomen → waist. The yellow line places star-shaped marks at various points, directing the gaze from the head down to the feet.

By using such color schemes to guide the gaze from top to bottom, the viewer's attention is directed throughout the entirety of the illustration.

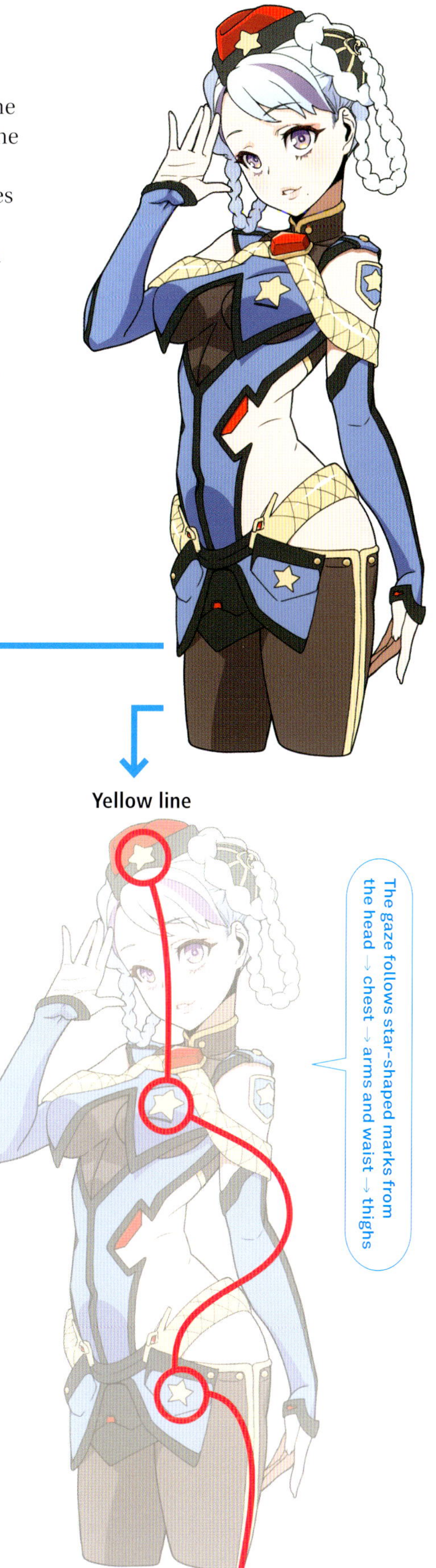

**Red line**



**Yellow line**

# Guiding Gaze with Differences in Brightness, Hue and Saturation

In the previous section, you learned how to guide gaze using the density and arrangement of colors in illustrations. Here, we'll delve into what specific color schemes are effective. By controlling brightness contrast, hue contrast and saturation contrast, you can highlight certain colors. A significant difference enhances contrast, which is crucial for guiding gaze.

Take a look at the three examples. None of them have extreme saturation differences, but they all use contrast to guide the gaze. Many people think of changing brightness to adjust contrast, but contrast can also be strengthened through differences in hue and saturation.

## Brightness Contrast

When the hair is bright, and the eyes are dark, the gaze is drawn to the eyes. A small dark area on a large bright surface also attracts attention. This is similar to how a single black dot on a white sheet of paper draws the eye.

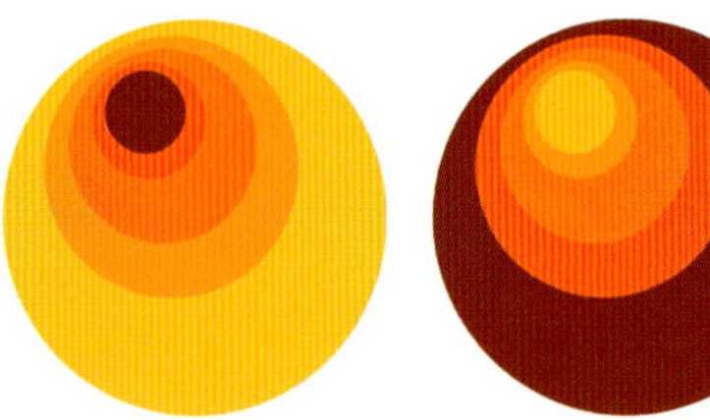

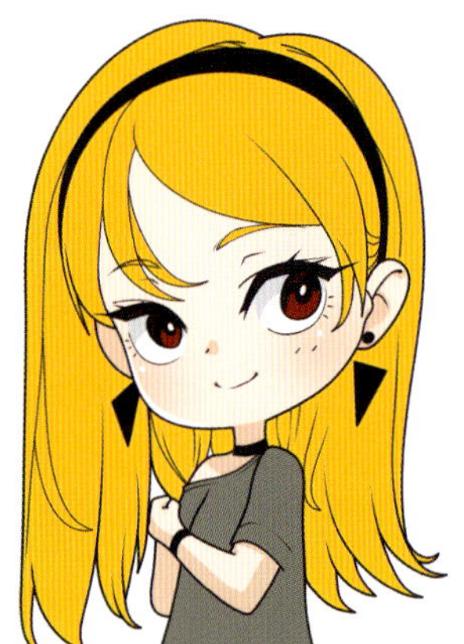

## Hue Contrast

Using complementary colors directs the gaze to smaller areas. Green hair with red eyes forms a complementary color relationship, guiding the gaze to the eyes.

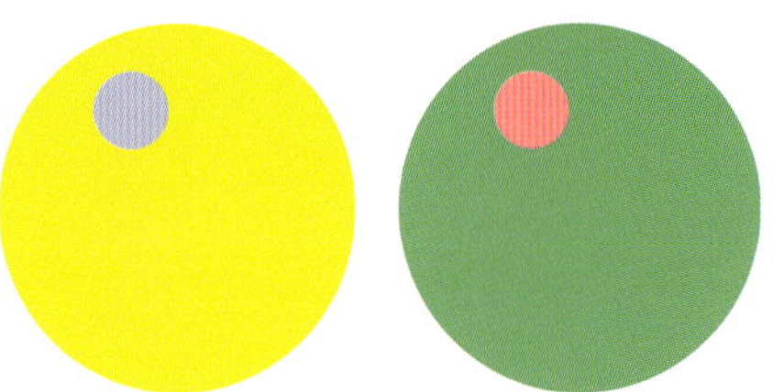

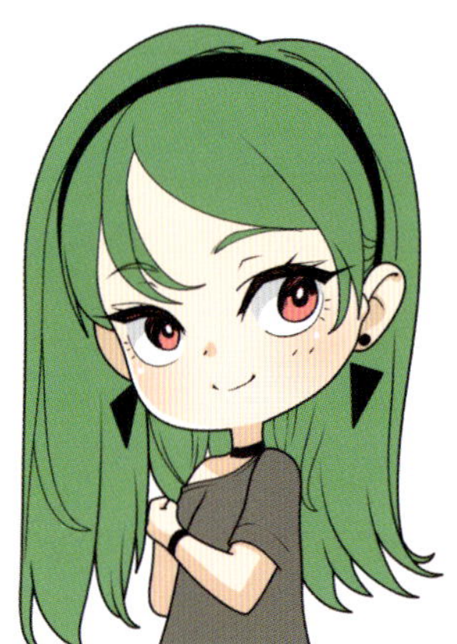

## Saturation Contrast

Using the same hue but significantly changing the saturation can also guide the gaze to the eyes. Placing vivid blue eyes against low-saturation light blue (white) hair directs attention to the high-saturation eyes.

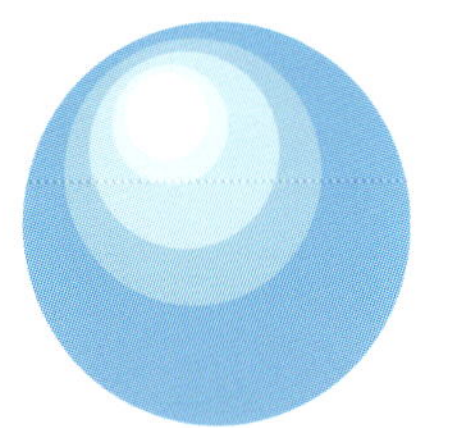

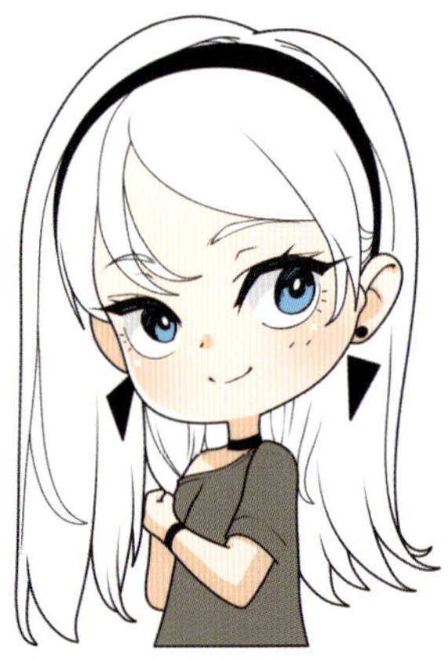

# Consider the Ease of Communication

Designs for advertisements or flyers consider essential elements like visibility, legibility and identifiability to communicate their visual messages effectively to viewers. This principle applies not only to advertising but also to all design fields, including illustrations and videos.

## VISIBILITY

A clear example is road signs. They use contrasting colors to ensure they're noticeable even at driving speeds. Warning colors like yellow and black, though not complementary, are adjacent and thus highly noticeable.

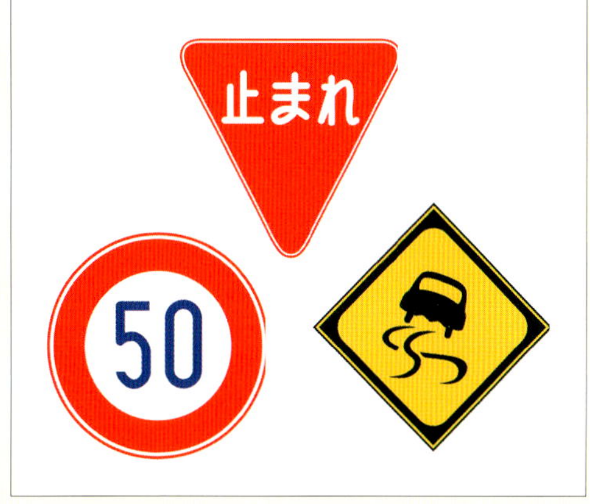


## LEGIBILITY

Not just words need to be legible, but icons and images need to as well. Examples include Exit signs and wheelchair-accessible areas. These designs are intended to be immediately recognizable for their purpose at a glance.

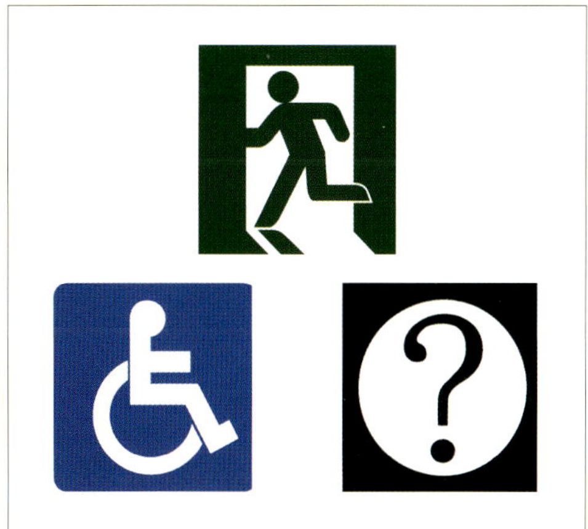

## IDENTIFIABILITY

Identifiability means designs that are easily distinguishable at a glance. Examples include gender signs on restrooms and hot and cold water faucets. Complex designs like subway maps are also made with high identifiability to distinguish various routes easily.

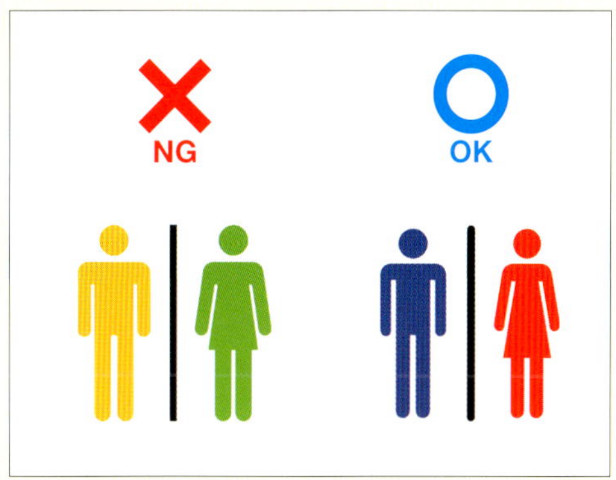

# Guiding Gaze in Vivid Illustrations

Even in vivid illustrations using a range of colors, guiding the gaze using color is still possible. Let's use the illustration from page 52 as an example to explain some of the key points.

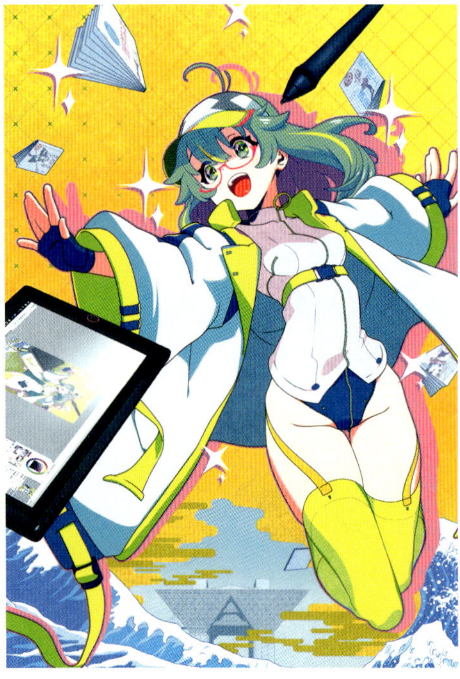

 **SILHOUETTE STANDOUTS**

**By using dark colors on the lining of the clothes, the character's body lines are made more distinctive and stand out, presenting a more definied silhouette.**

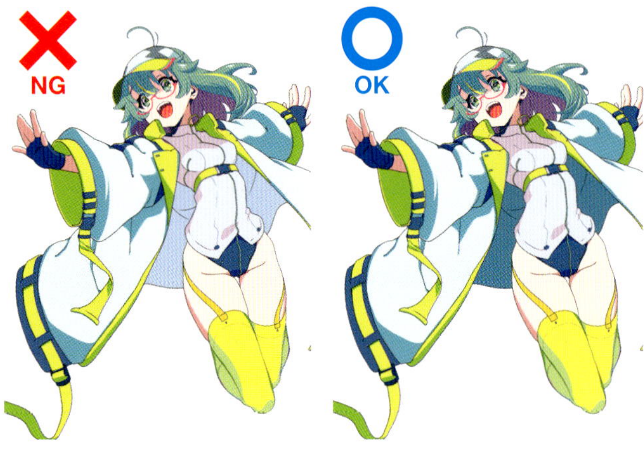


If the lining color is made the same brightness, the body lines and clothes appear as one solid mass.

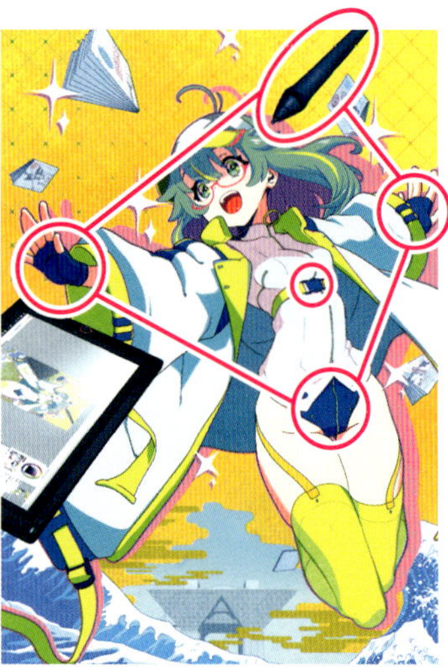

By connecting the dark blue areas, they surround the face, making it easier for the viewer's gaze to be drawn to the upper body.

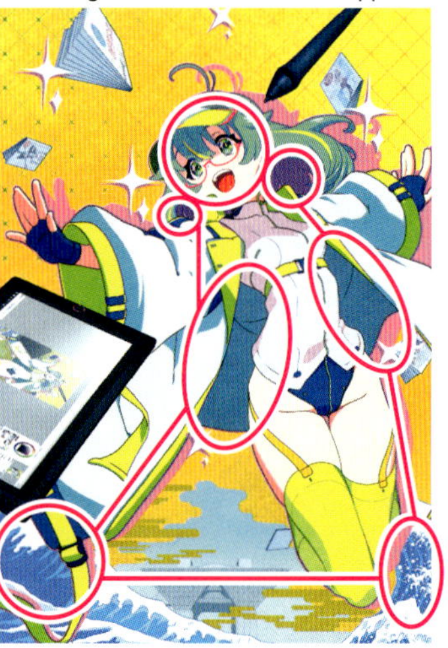

Connecting the blue areas forms a triangle, directing the viewer's gaze toward the face.

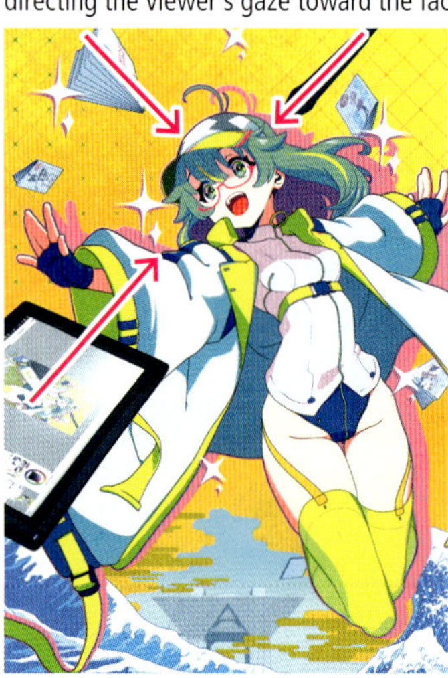

Arranging items like the pen tablet and books to point toward the face effectively directs the viewer's gaze.

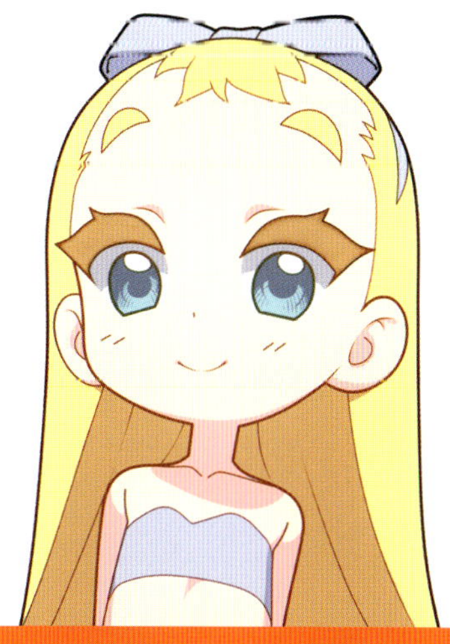

# LIGHT AND SHADOW

Light, shadow and color: how do they create a three-dimensional effect? How do you choose shadow colors? These and many more questions are explored in this chapter!

# A Triangular Relationship: Light, Shadow and Color

### Which light appears warmer?

Even though the shadow colors are different, doesn't **A** give a warmer impression? This is because using complementary colors in the shadows intensifies the color impression, making it look warmer. Here, we will explain the relationship between light and shadow and also discuss shadow colors.

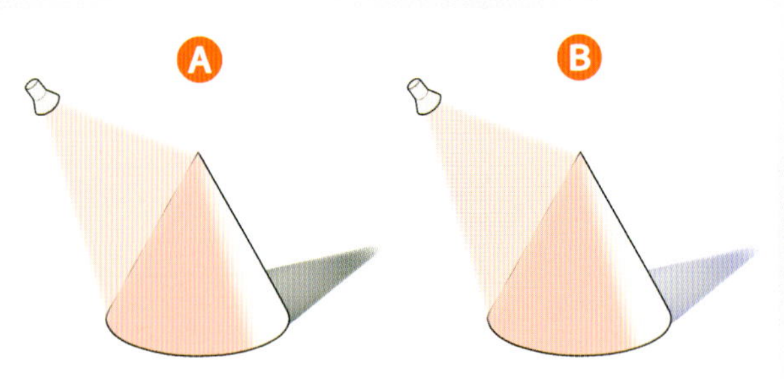


## Relationship Between Light Source Color and Shadow Color

Please refer to the diagram below. Warm-colored light (orange) and cool-colored light (blue) are projected onto a round cone. When warm-colored light is applied, cool-colored shadows are generated, whereas when cool-colored light is applied, warm-colored shadows are generated. Thus, depending on the color of the illuminating light, shadows are determined

to be either warm or cool. Understanding these properties allows you to more convincingly depict shadows and more accurately and precisely represent the time of day (daytime, twilight or night) to establish the setting of your scene and to increase the visual information the illustration conveys.

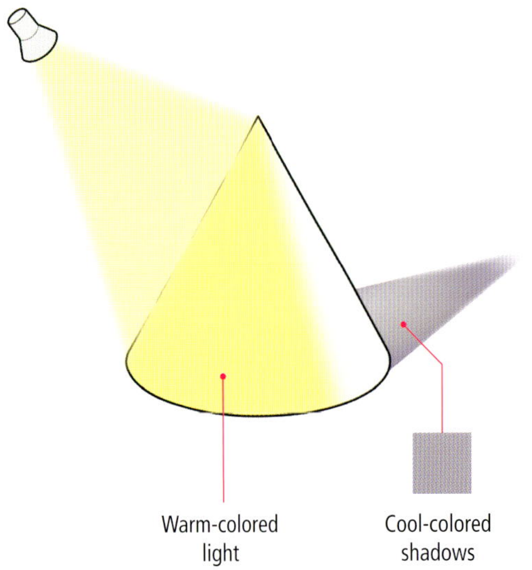


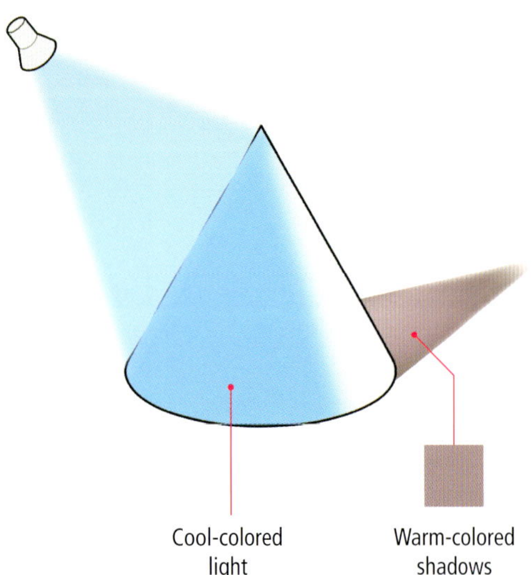

Why does this happen? When it's daytime, the background is filled with the blue sky, and yellow sunlight proliferates. Since the predominant colors in the space are blue and the yellow of sunlight, shadows take on the strong complementary color, blue. In the evening, as the sun sets and the sky gradually darkens, the side where the sun sets turns orange, while the opposite side becomes tinged with purple. In this scenario, with orange sunlight emanating, shadows appear purple. The principle is similar for nighttime. In the dark blue world illuminated by the moon's pale yellow light, shadows take on a navy blue tint.

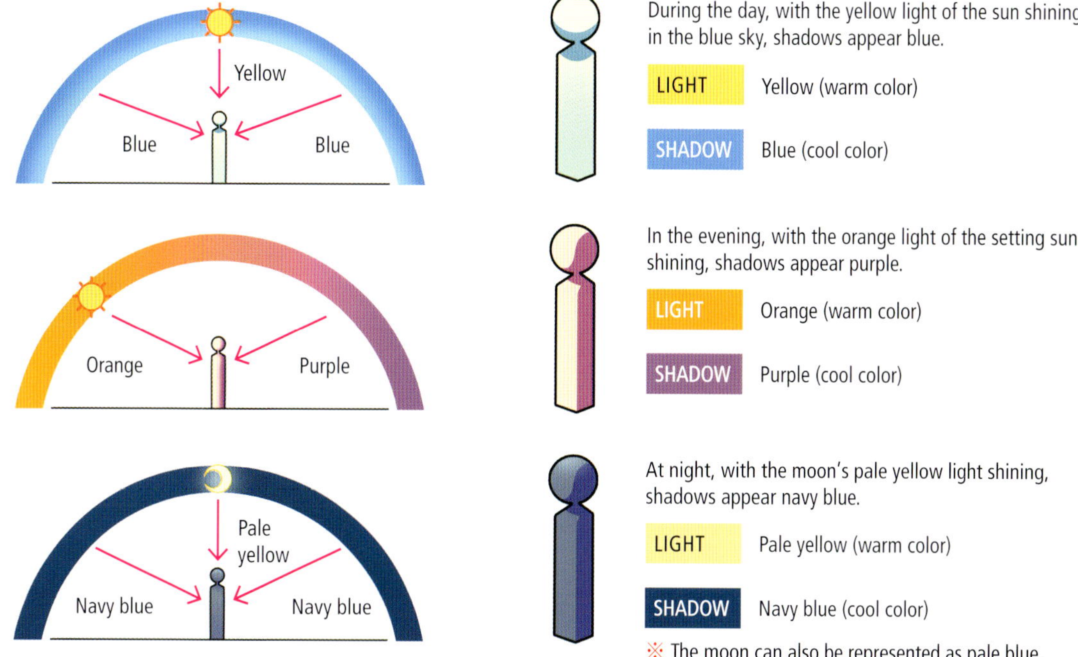



## Choosing Shadow Colors by Considering the Relationship Between Light and Shadow

By applying these concepts, you can create a balance between light and shadow by using two colors that are complementary. The left diagram below shows cool-colored shadows against warm-colored light. Normally, light and shadow exhibit this type of relationship; but as depicted in the diagram on the right, making shadows the complementary color of the light enhances the contrast between warm-colored light and dark complementary shadows, thus emphasizing the color of the light source. This technique is also used in painting and graphic design to enhance the work's impact on the viewer.

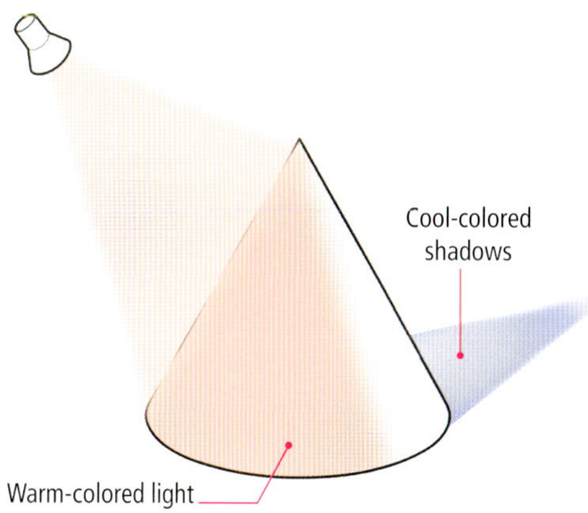



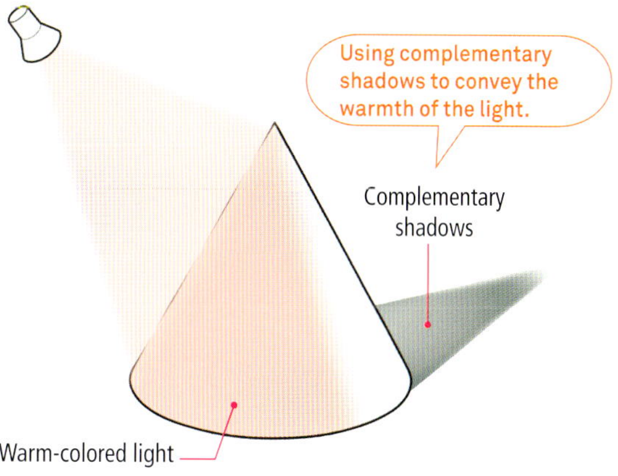

# Creating 3D Effects with Lighting

## Which one looks three-dimensional?

Doesn't **B** appear more three-dimensional? This is even though both have minimal shadows, but **B** has highlights added. Thus, even with minimal shadows, you can express three-dimensionality by adding highlights. Let's take a closer look at the concept and learn how to produce these essential effects.

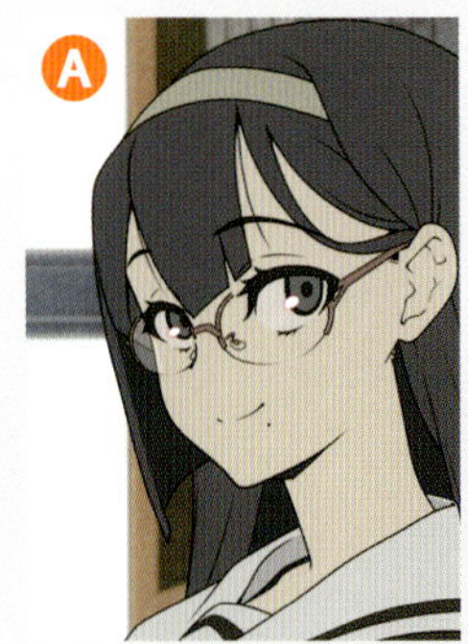

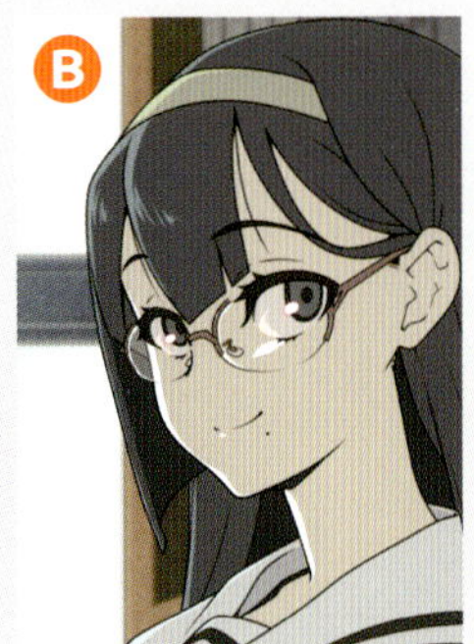

## Creating Three-dimensionality with Highlights

It's a common approach to paint the base color and then add shadows to create a sense of three-dimensionality. Thus, it's often thought that three-dimensionality is created with shadows. However, you can also create three-dimensionality with highlights. A technique similar to oil painting, where light is added on top of shadows, is also a common approach.

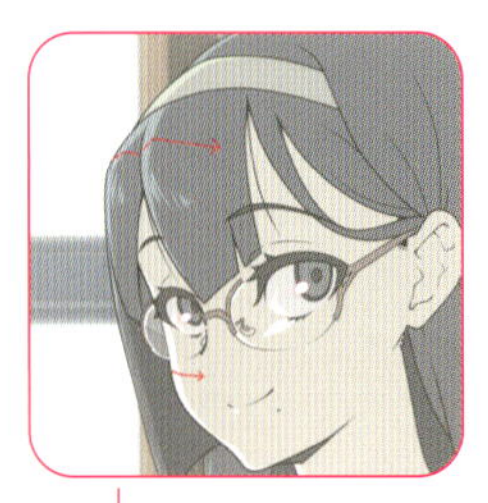

By adding highlights as if tracing the line drawing, the surfaces are emphasized, creating a sense of three-dimensionality.

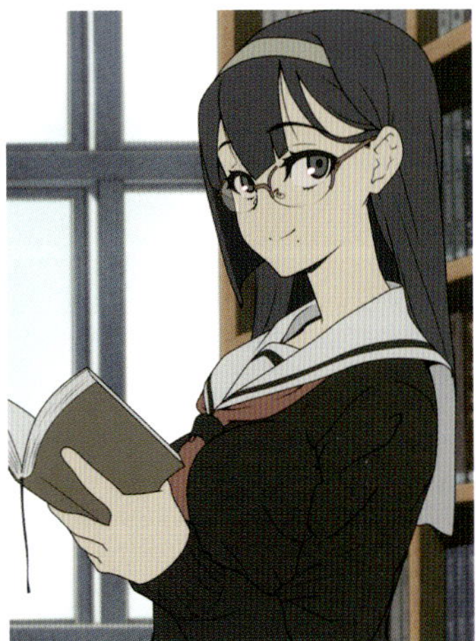

**Base Color Only**
This is after the base color has been added. Depending on the illustration, it may be acceptable, but it still appears flat in terms of its dimensionality.

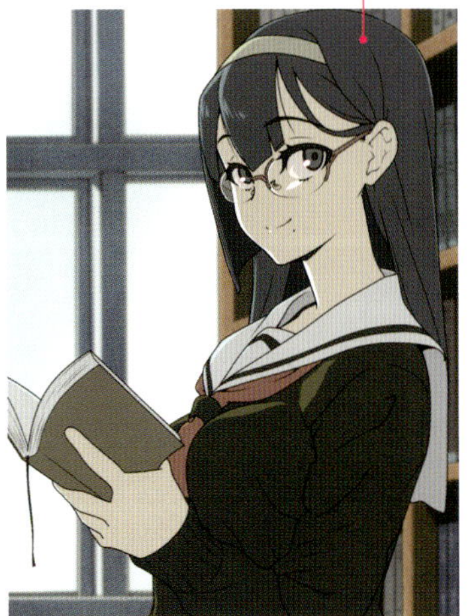

**Highlights**
Highlights have been added to the illustration to create a greater sense of three-dimensionality.

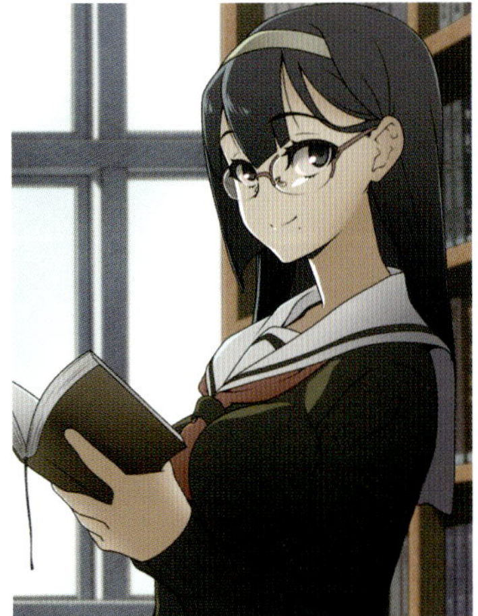

**Highlights + Gradient**
Without adding distinct ones, shadows are expressed with gradients, and highlights are introduced. This alone is sufficient to suggest three-dimensionality.

Let's now take a look at the relationship between shadows and highlights using simple shapes like a sphere and a cube. Whether adding shadows or light, you can express three-dimensionality by creating a contrast between light and dark.

When it comes to three-dimensionality, the tendency is to add shadows, but that alone isn't necessarily the only way to express or suggest three-dimensionality. Try coloring or painting your illustration while consciously adding light and its effects.

## Sphere

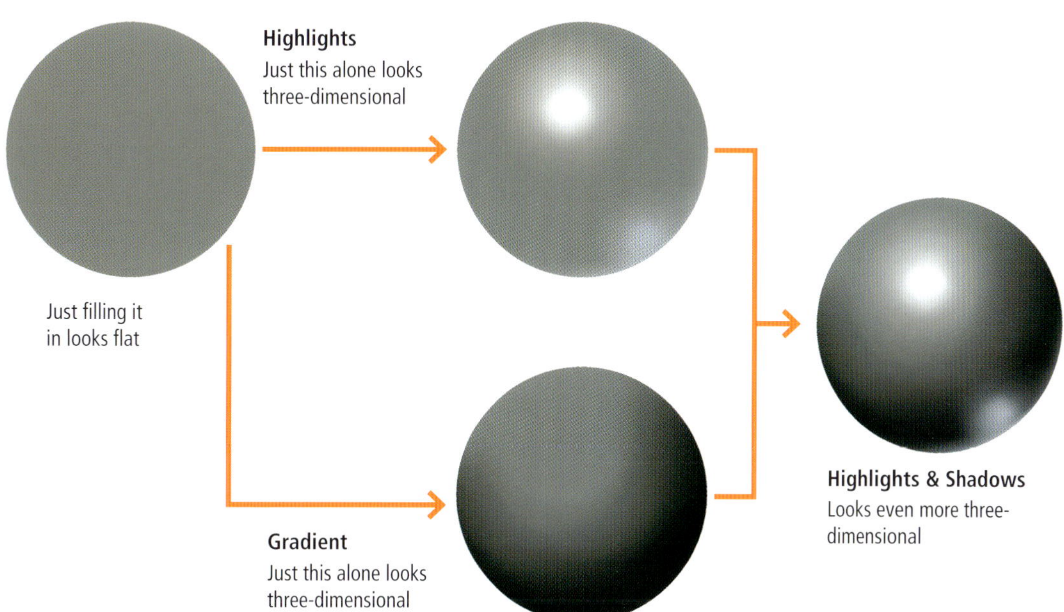



## Cube

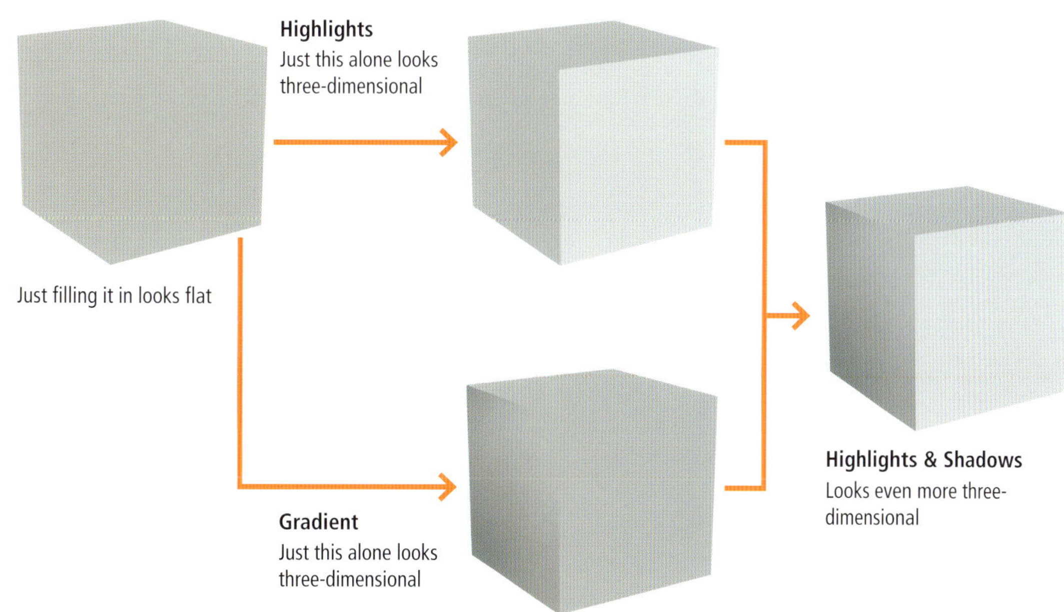

# Reflected Light

Light has the property of reflecting off surfaces in all directions, illuminating objects from various angles. Additionally, reflected light contains the color of the object it reflects off and is weaker than the original light. As shown in the diagram below, light reflected off blue and red walls carries the color of the walls and is slightly weaker compared to direct light from the source. However, since illustrations are stylized, being overly conscious of too much reflected light can make it look unnatural. It's good to start by being aware of simple light sources and nearby reflections.

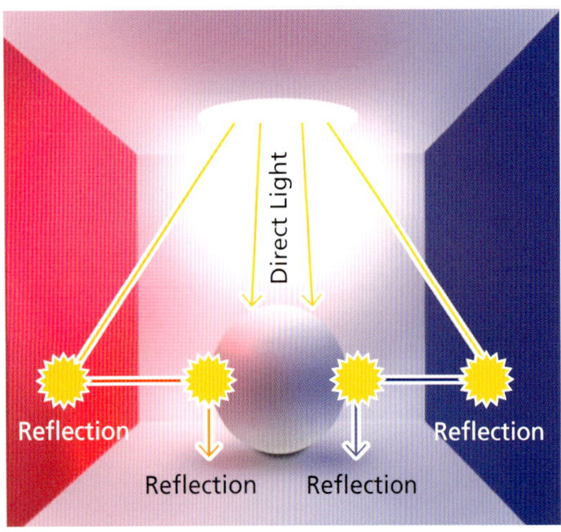


Light from the source reflects off the wall, coloring the ceiling, floor and the far wall in red and blue. Additionally, light hitting the walls reflects onto the sphere, further reflecting onto the floor, resulting in shadows tinted with red and blue.

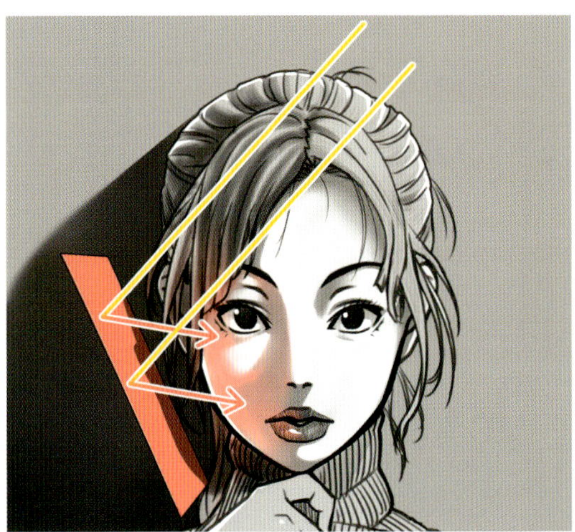

To avoid overly vivid effects, remember that reflected light is not as bright as colored light sources

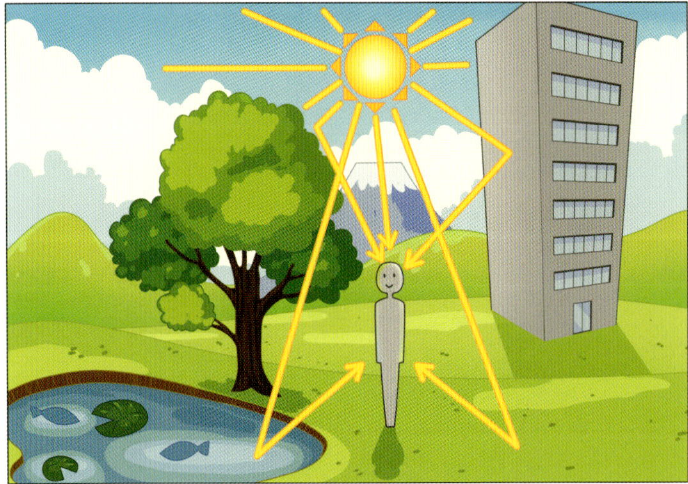

Especially outdoors, sunlight reflects off various objects, casting reflected light onto the subject.

# Cylindrical Shadows

Light is fundamentally waves; it's made up of a range of varying wavelengths. Therefore, the shadows created by light also have gradients. For some, it's easier to understand the changes in light and shadow by intentionally visualizing them as angular solids. Similarly, when considering the human body, if you simplify it into cylindrical shapes, you can grasp the rough positions of shadows. However, if you exaggerate or alter the proportions, especially with human bodies, it can look odd. So, keep it to a rough understanding of the positional relationship.

To more easily understand light's effect on and movement across surfaces, let's think about it in polygonal form.

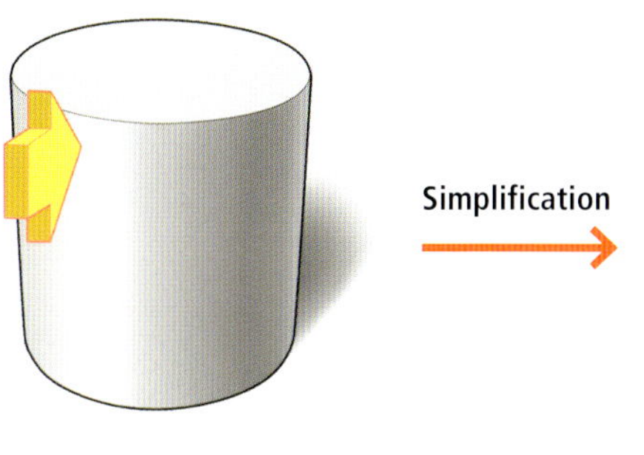

**Simplification**

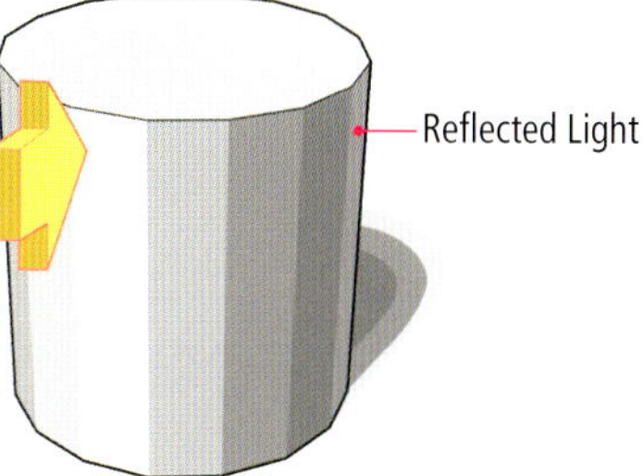



The farthest place from the light source will be the darkest. It becomes easier to understand if you consider it gradually brightening from there.

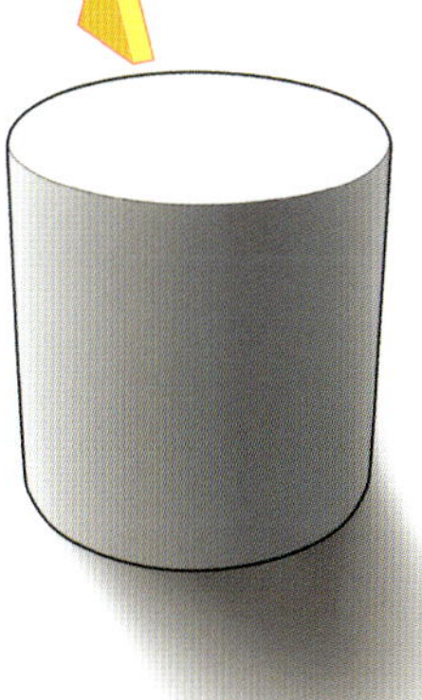

**Simplification**

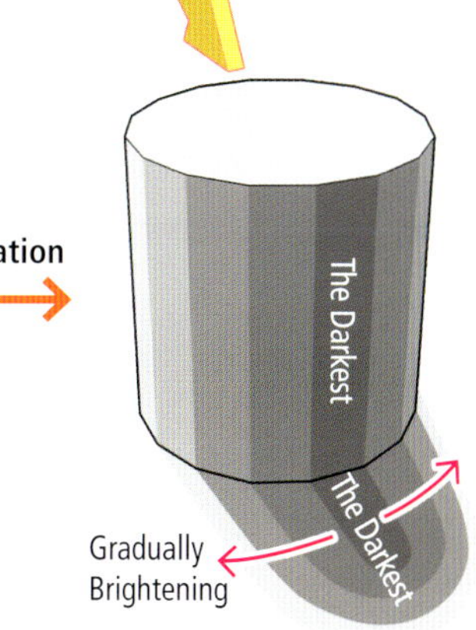



Even body parts like arms and legs can be simplified into cylindrical shapes. When unsure how to add shadows, try simplifying things first.

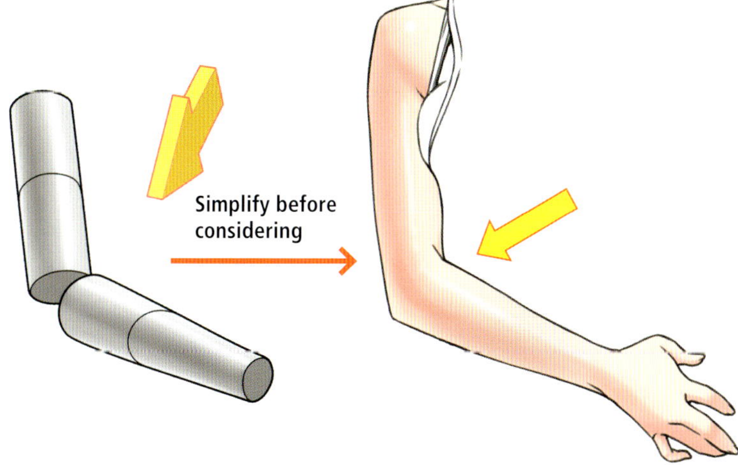

# How Shadows Are Created by Different Light Sources

The diagram below illustrates how shadows fall on a face, with the yellow arrows indicating the direction and source of the light. These shadow patterns represent common scenarios, but they can be simpler or partially omitted depending on your style and goal. It's important not only to understand the position of the light source but also to grasp the basics of facial sketching and three-dimensionality. Using this as a reference and experimenting with variations will help you improve your skills.

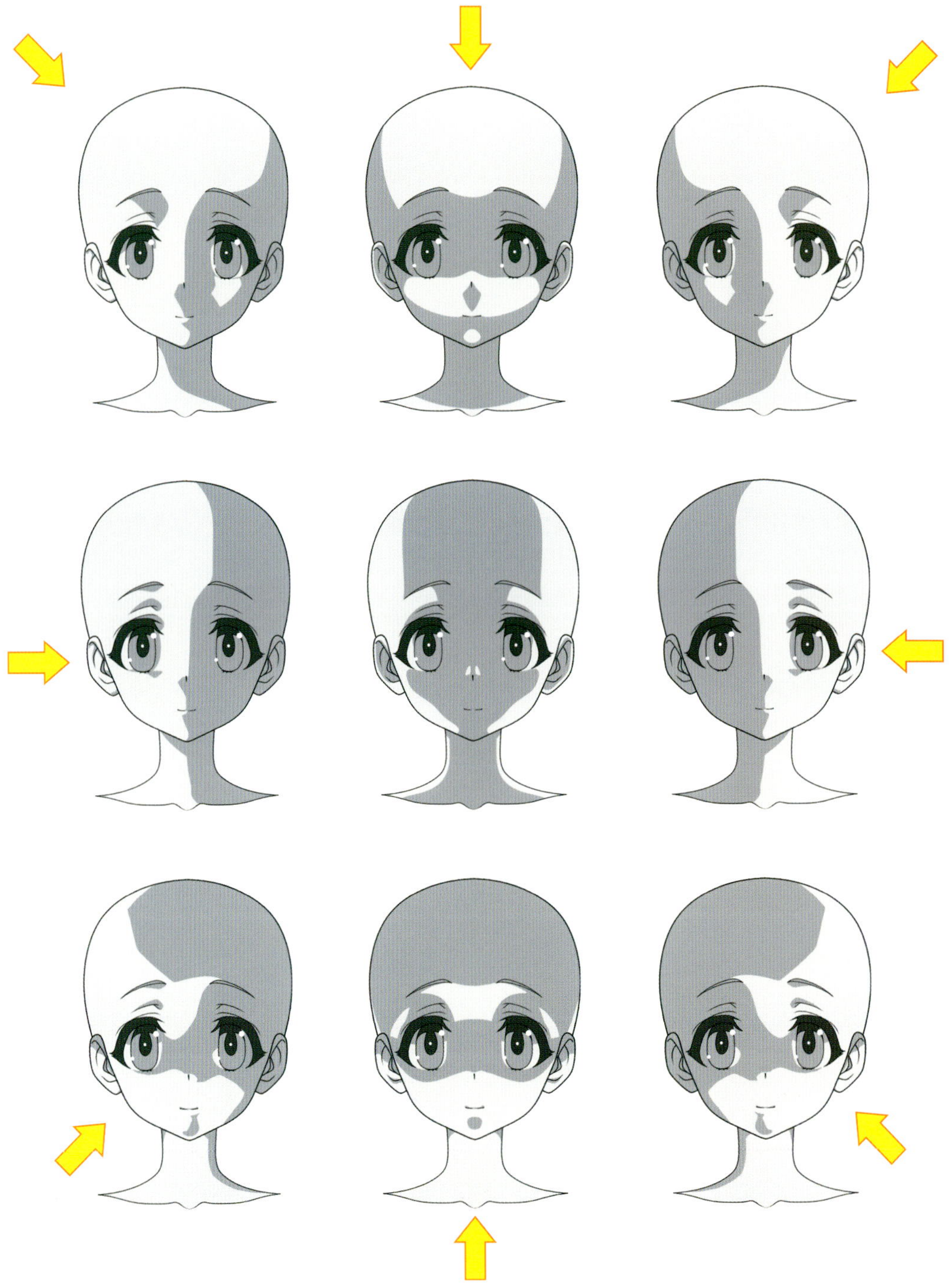

# How Shadows Form from Multiple Light Sources

In reality, light comes from various directions, so the concept of a single light source is somewhat unrealistic. While illustrations use a single light source for simplicity, adding multiple light sources can enhance and heighten the sense of realism. However, having too many light sources can create a sense of discord. Therefore, it's best to start by mastering shadows with a single light source before experimenting with multiple sources. Additionally, if all light sources have the same brightness, the result can be monotonous, so vary the intensity to create a more interesting and detailed image.

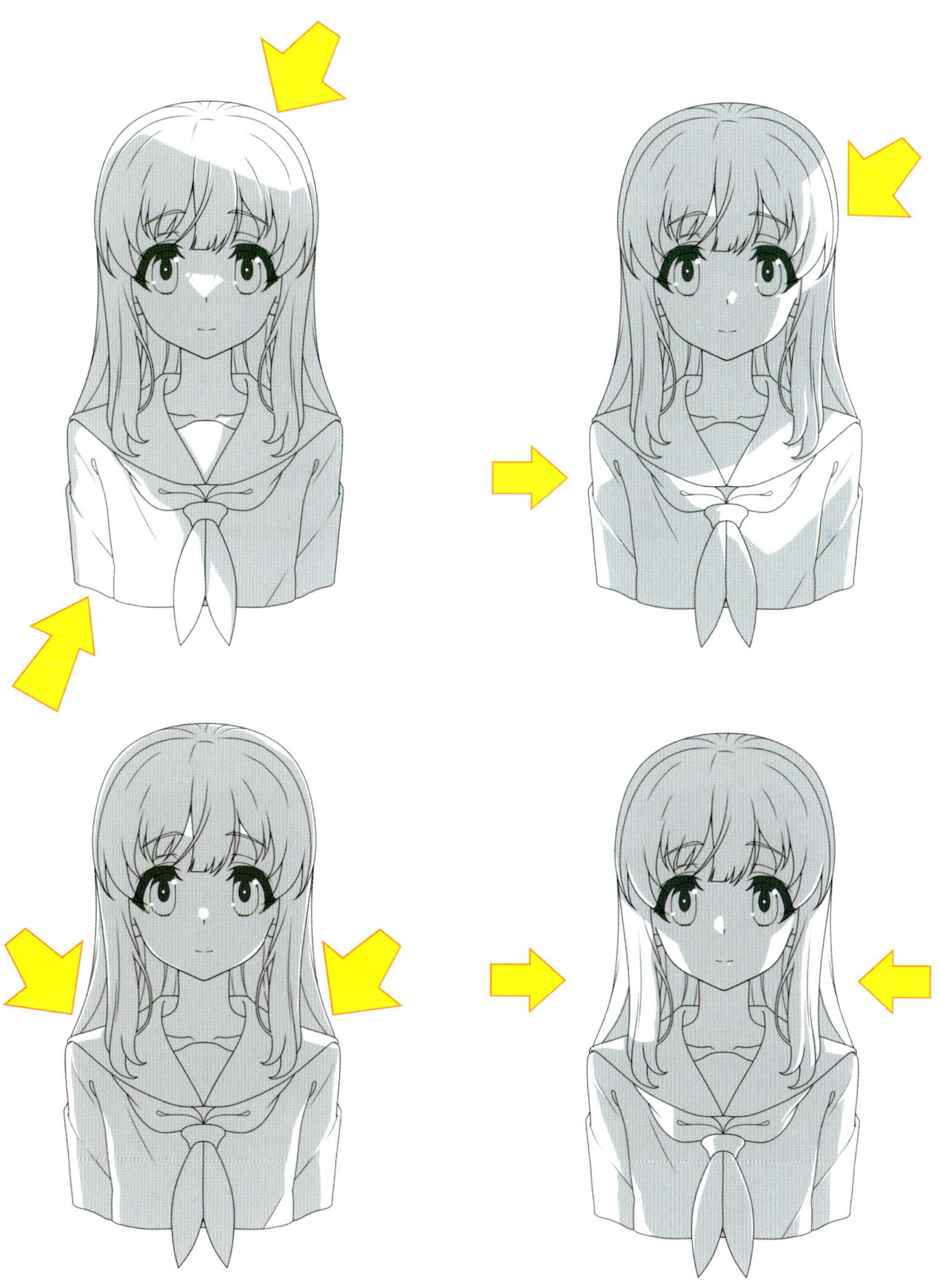

# Shadow Effects

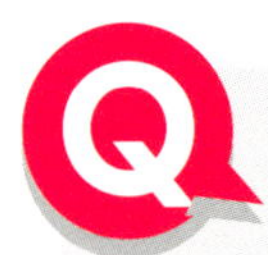

## Which looks brighter?

The base colors of the hair and skin are the same for both, but the shadow colors are different. Doesn't **A** look brighter? That's because the same color can appear different depending on the adjacent colors, creating an optical illusion. So how exactly do you choose colors to achieve this effect?

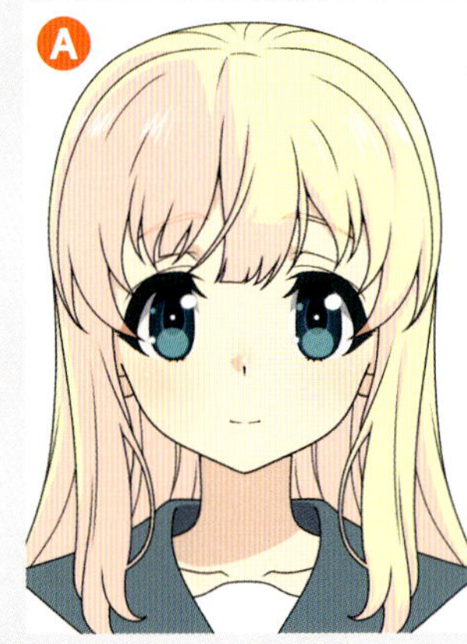

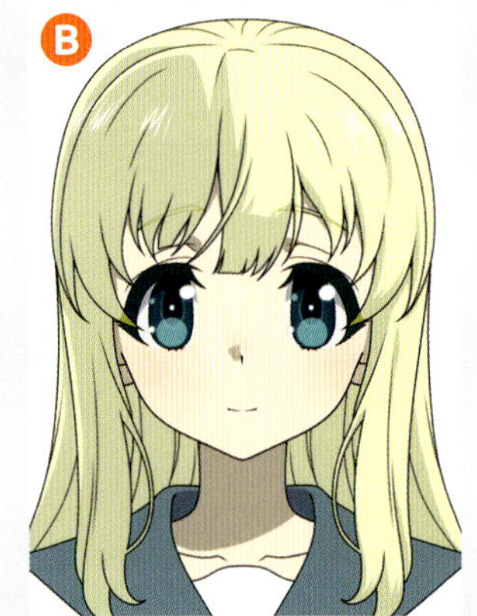

## Illusions Caused by Color Combinations

In the diagrams below, the base color is the same, but the shadow colors are different. On the left, the shadow color has a lower brightness, making the base color look dull. On the right, the shadow color has higher brightness and saturation, making the base color look brighter. This is due to the influence of the adja-cent shadow colors, creating an optical illusion. If you cover the shadowed half of the two sets of circles below and compare, the base colors should look the same. Since the appearance changes depending on the shadow color used, we need to take a closer look at how to choose shadow colors to avoid this phenomenon.

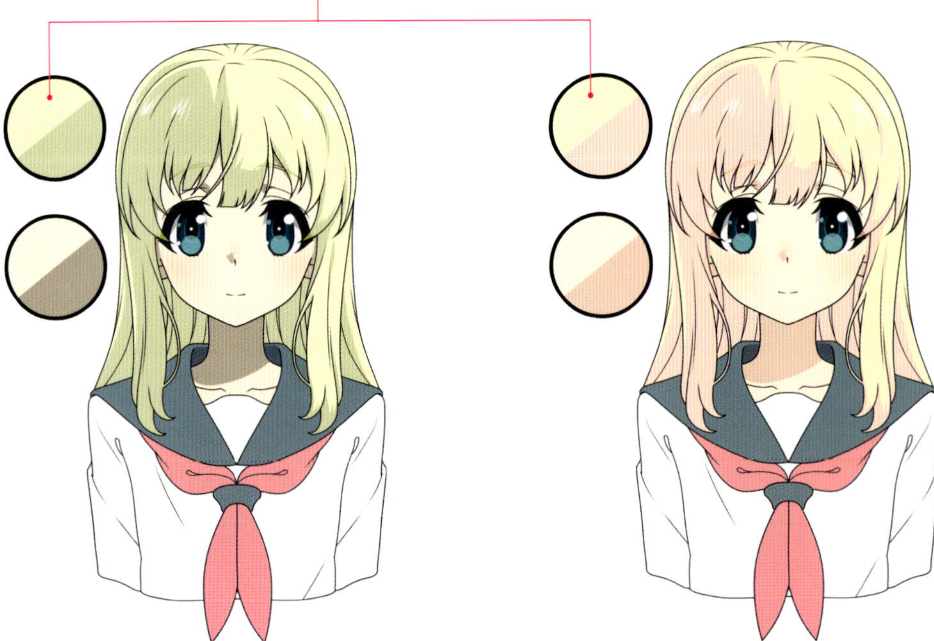

# Choosing Colors to Avoid Illusions

Skin tones serve as a good way of examining how to choose shadow colors that are less likely to cause dullness or murkiness due to optical illusions. First, use a color wheel to familiarize yourself with the areas for the base skin color, highlight color and shadow color in terms of brightness and saturation. Select colors from the areas indicated in the diagram to the right. Choose a base color with high brightness and low saturation to avoid making the shadow color too dark or overly saturated. The diagram below shows how to choose colors with actual pen movements.

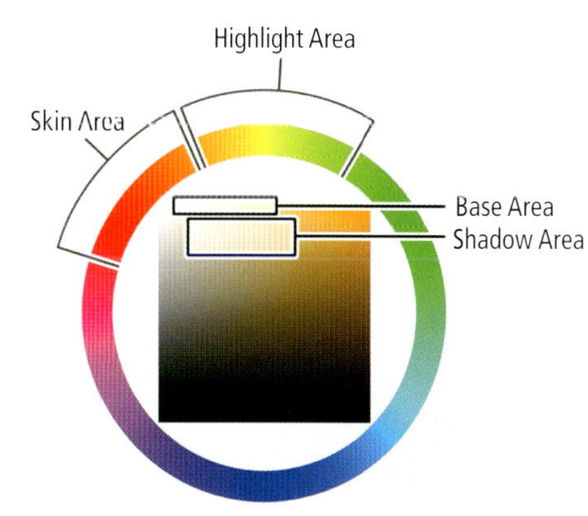


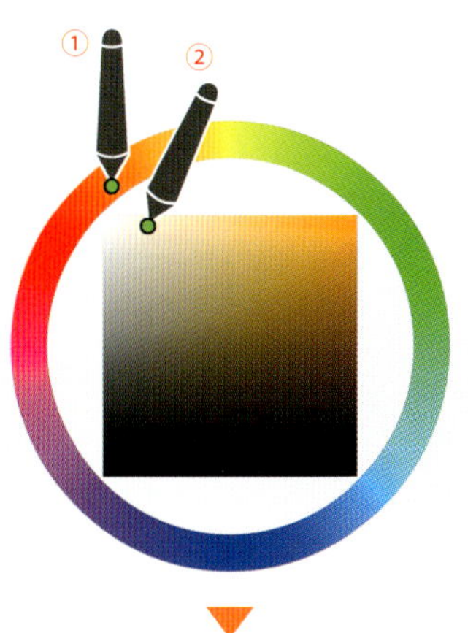

**Base Color**

Choose a skin color from the hue area of the skin and confirm it from the base area.

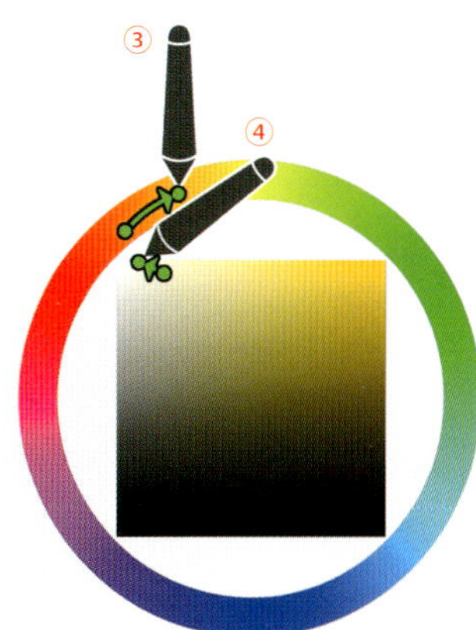

**Highlight**

Shift clockwise from the base hue, increasing brightness and saturation toward white.

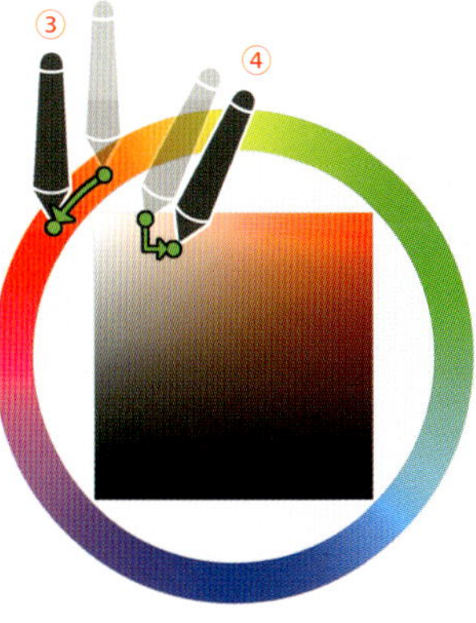

**First Shadow Color**

Shift counterclockwise from the base hue, slightly lowering brightness and increasing saturation.

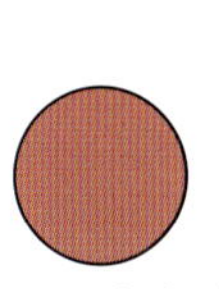
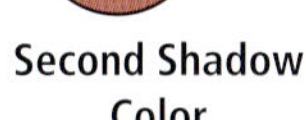

**Second Shadow Color**

From the hue of the first shadow color, shift counterclockwise, lowering the brightness more and increasing the saturation compared to the first shadow.

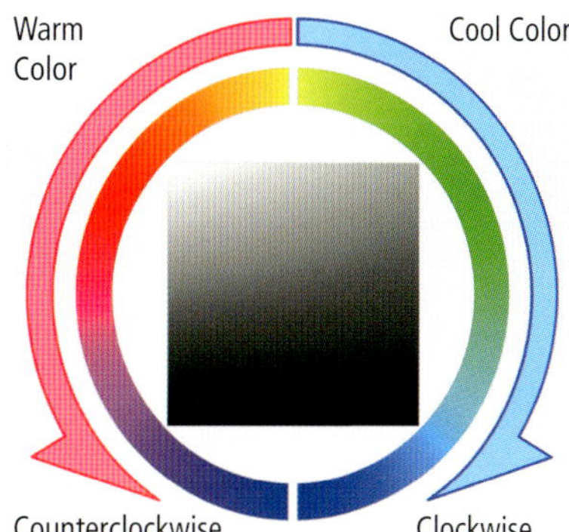


For selecting shadows for areas other than skin, if the base color is a warm color, shift the hue counterclockwise. If the base color is a cool color, shift the hue clockwise to prevent illusions.

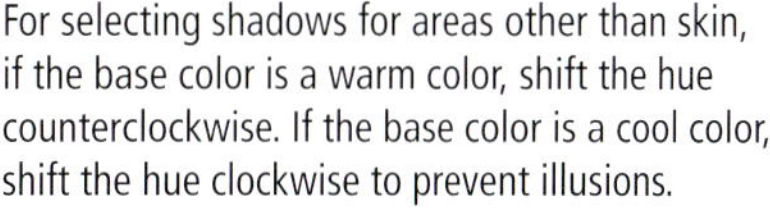

|  | Warm Color | | Cool Color | |
| --- | --- | --- | --- | --- |
|  | Bright | Dark | Bright | Dark |
| Color Wheel | Clockwise | Counter-clockwise | Counter-clockwise | Clockwise |
| Color Picker | Top Left | Bottom Right | Top Left | Bottom Right |

# How to Choose Shadow Colors

Lowering the brightness to create shadows can result in dull-looking colors, as seen in example ❶ due to an optical illusion. Building on the details discussed on page 71, choose a shadow color by lowering the brightness and increasing the saturation, as shown below in ❷.

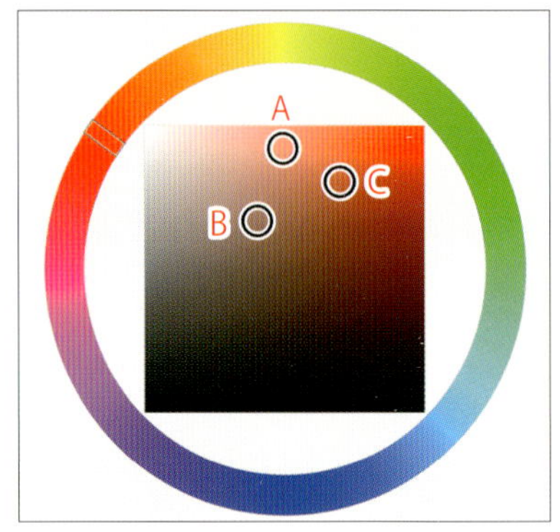

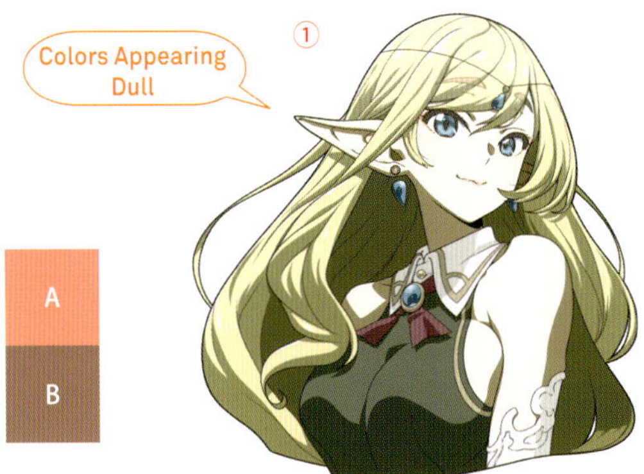



Shadows created by only lowering brightness.

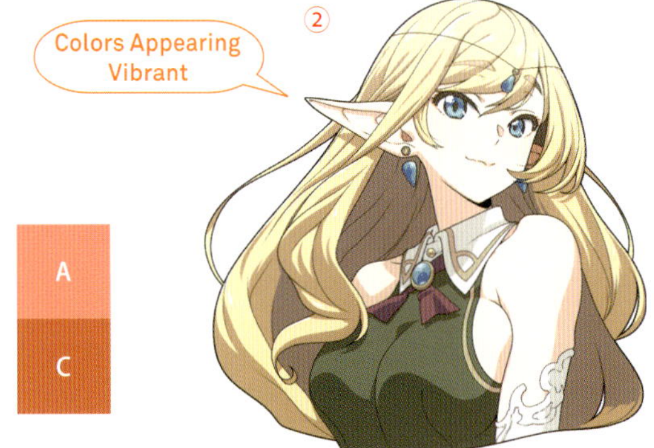



Shadows created by increasing saturation after lowering the brightness.

**EXPERT TIP** — **REDDENING THE SKIN**

When finishing the skin coloring, you can red or pink to the cheeks. It makes the skin appear healthier and emphasizes the roundness and three-dimensionality of the cheeks. Be careful not to use a pink that's too intense, as it can look unnatural.

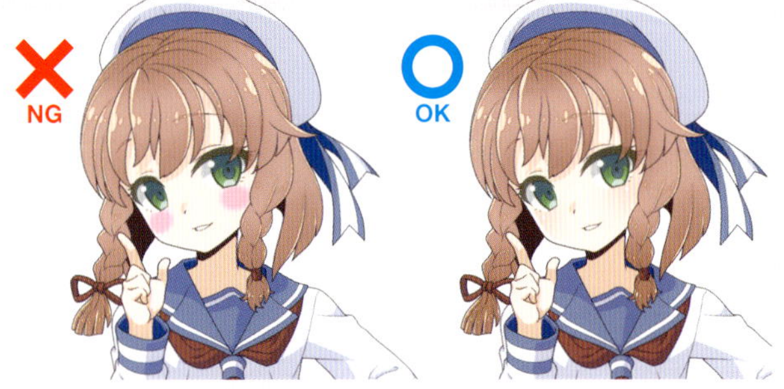



**How to add redness**

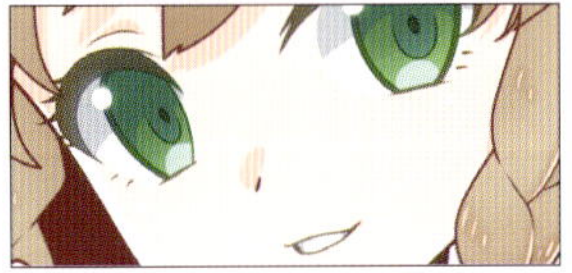

In this state, the highlights are hard to see.

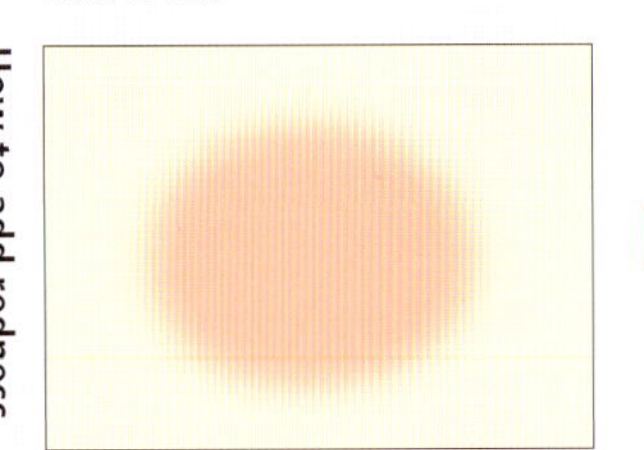

Use the airbrush tool in multiply mode to add a small amount of redness.

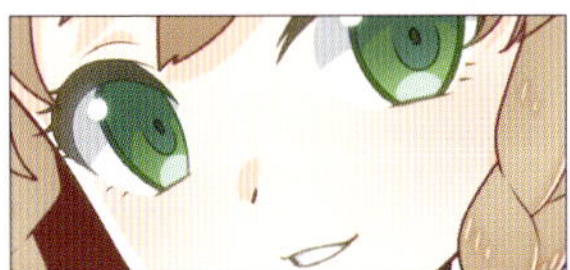

For the redness, add it lightly and subtly, and blend the edges well.

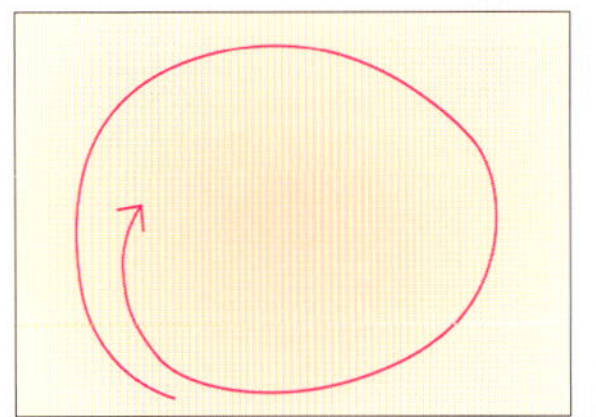

Blend it with the skin tone using a blur tool in a circular motion.

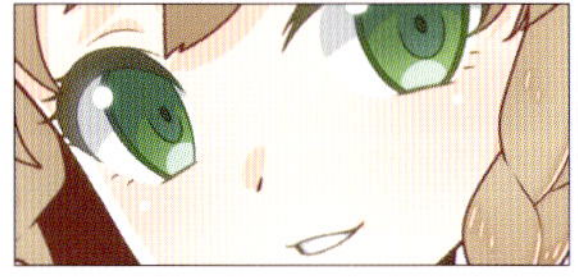

When combined, the highlights will stand out clearly.

Add highlights to finish.

When choosing shadow colors, you need to decide on the color while imagining the finished image. Colors can become dull due to optical illusions, but if you want to create that atmosphere intentionally, you can deliberately integrate those colors into your illustration. The diagram below compares shadows with the same base color but with different attributes:

shadows with reduced brightness, shadows with increased saturation and shadows with a reddish hue.

As you can see, the choice of shadow color changes the overall atmosphere. Decide how you want the final image to look and choose the shadow color accordingly.

## Shadows for a Subdued Look

It's often thought that shadows should be dark, but when a bright color (base color) and a dark color (shadow color) of the same hue are adjacent, the colors look subdued, making it effective for a calm atmosphere.

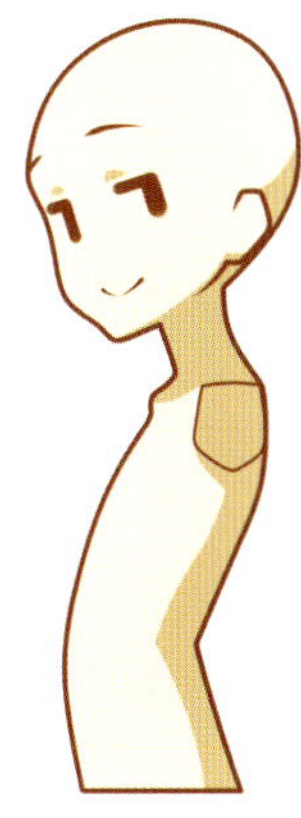

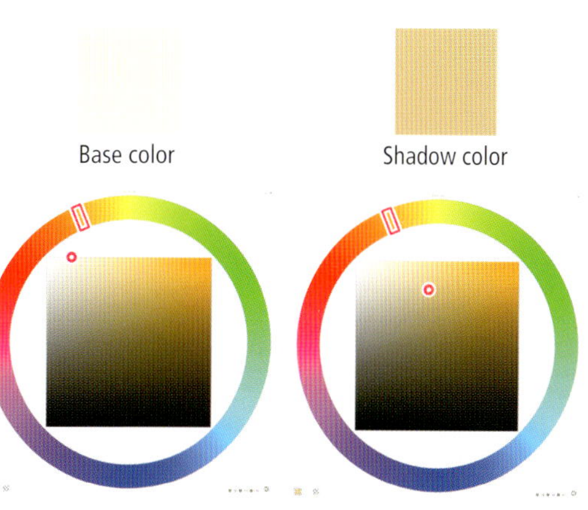


## Shadows for a Unified Look

Even if you use a high-saturation color for the shadow, it can still be used as a shadow color. However, with the same hue, the overall image can look yellowish, making it effective for creating a unified look or for matching tones.

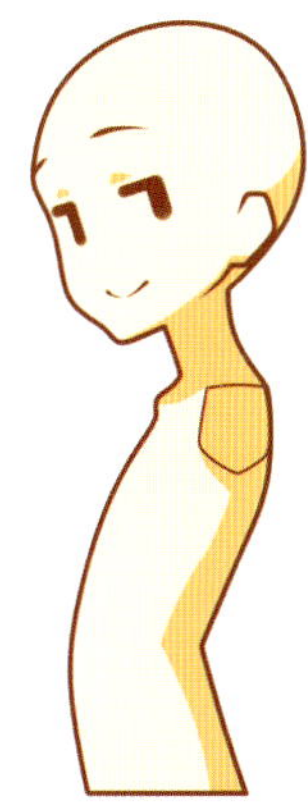

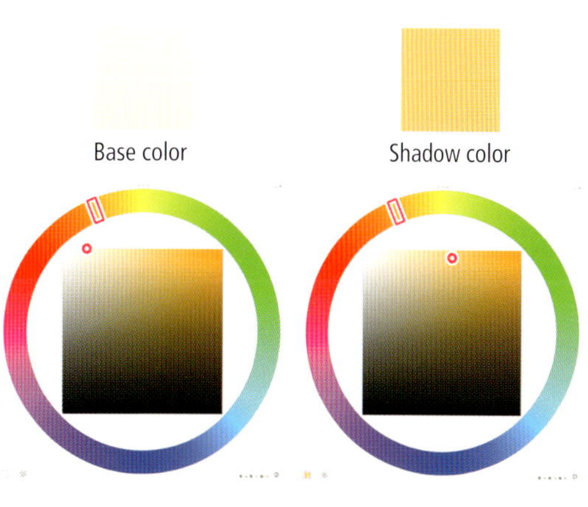


## Shadows for Healthy-Looking Skin

If you want the skin to look bright and healthy, you can choose a color that shifts slightly toward the red side of the hue and increase the saturation to make it look more realistic and healthful.

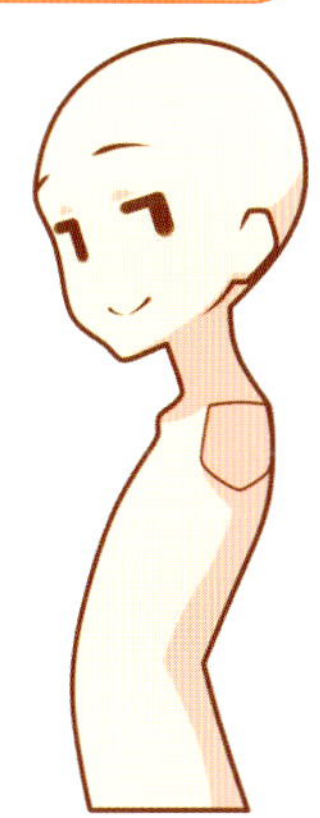

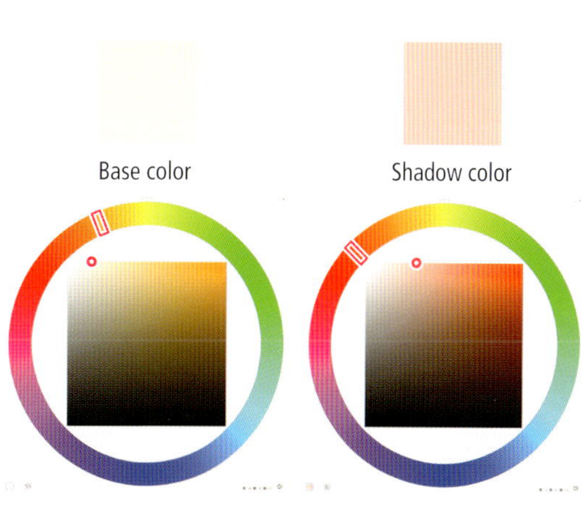

# Universal Shadow Color

Now let's look at a technique and concept called universal shadow color. This method differs from the previous approach, being mindful of color illusions, as it involves using the multiply layer mode to apply shadow color. The universal shadow color is easy to blend with any base color and is a relatively fail-safe way of introducing shading.

| Warm-colored shadows | Pastel-colored shadows | Slightly cool-colored shadows |
|---|---|---|

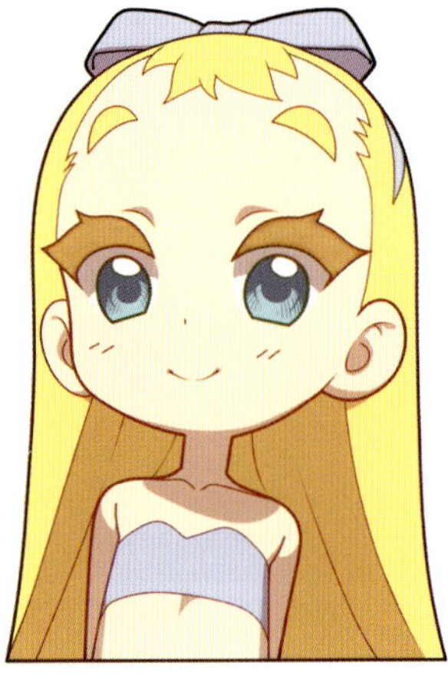

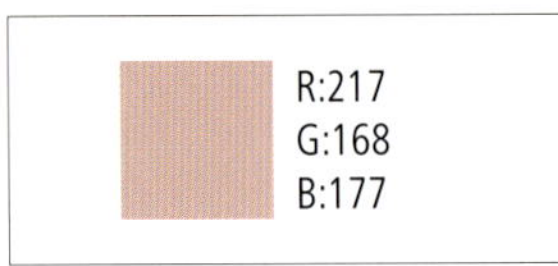
R:217
G:168
B:177

These shadows create a warm color palette. However, they don't pair well with cool colors.

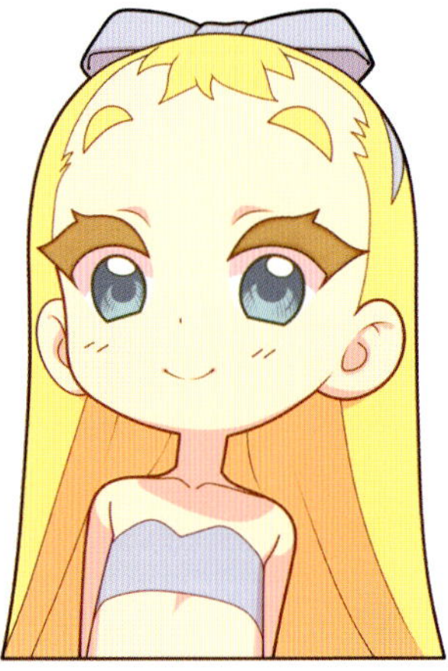

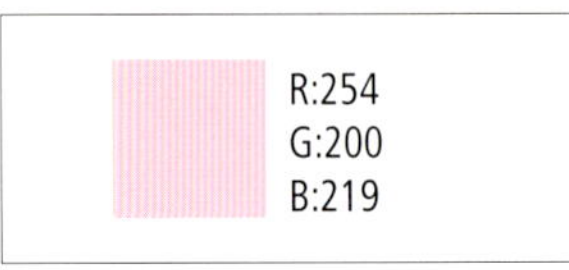
R:254
G:200
B:219

These shadows work well with both warm and cool colors but can clash with some colors due to their high saturation.

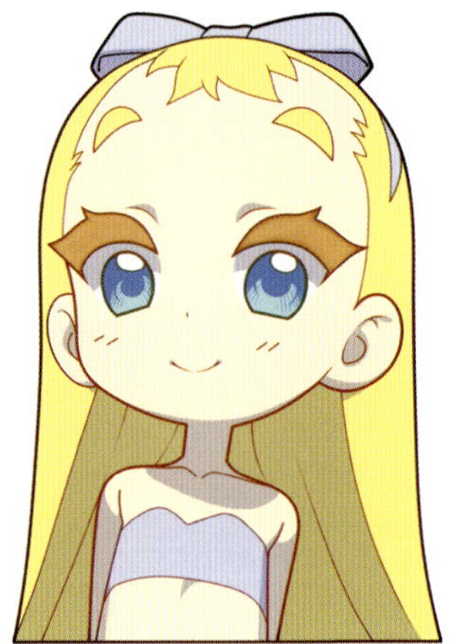

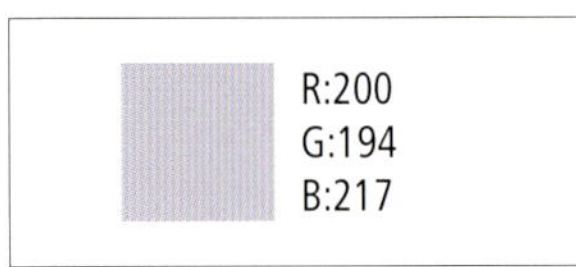
R:200
G:194
B:217

These shadows create a clean and calm impression but do not pair well with warm colors, particularly with skin tones.

**EXPERT TIP) CHOOSING THE UNIVERSAL SHADOW COLOR**

**When finishing skin coloring, you might add red or pink to the cheeks. This can make the skin appear healthier and emphasize the roundness and three-dimensionality of the cheeks. Be careful not to use a pink that is too intense, as it can look unnatural.**

RGB values are provided, but the colors don't need to be precisely match or reflect them. You can choose colors that are simply close to these values.

When actually applying these shadow colors, don't use only one color. Instead, use different colors depending on each part. No matter how "universal" the shadow color is, using it too liberally can create color illusions, making the colors look dull.

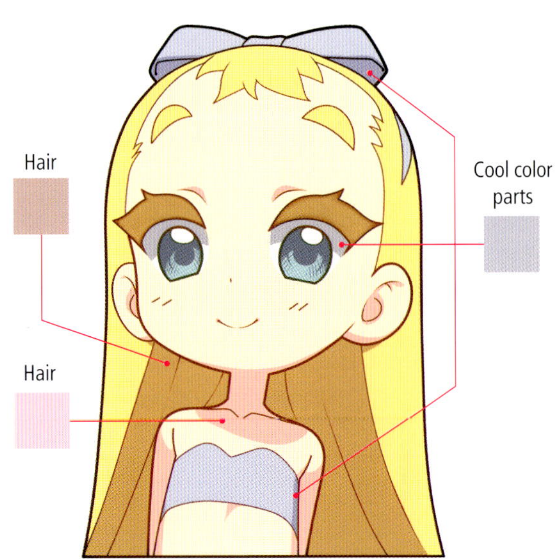

# Why Are Cool and Warm Shadows Considered Universal?

We perceive color through the reflection of light. The universal shadow color is related to the light source, sunlight, that causes this reflection.

Look at the photo below. If you use an eyedropper tool to pick colors, you'll notice that areas near where sunlight reflects off an object become warm colors, incorporating the colors of the ground or the object. Conversely, areas farther from the point of reflection tend to be cool colors, close to the color of the sky, which is blue. The universal shadow color is considered universal because it selects colors that are close to these sunlight colors (and the wavelengths we're able to perceive with our eyes).

However, in certain laboratories or indoor/underground spaces, there might be no light sources or objects to reflect light. In these settings, the universal shadow color might not blend well, so adjust it according to the illustration. In photography, light sources are taken into consideration to ensure correct color representation during shooting.

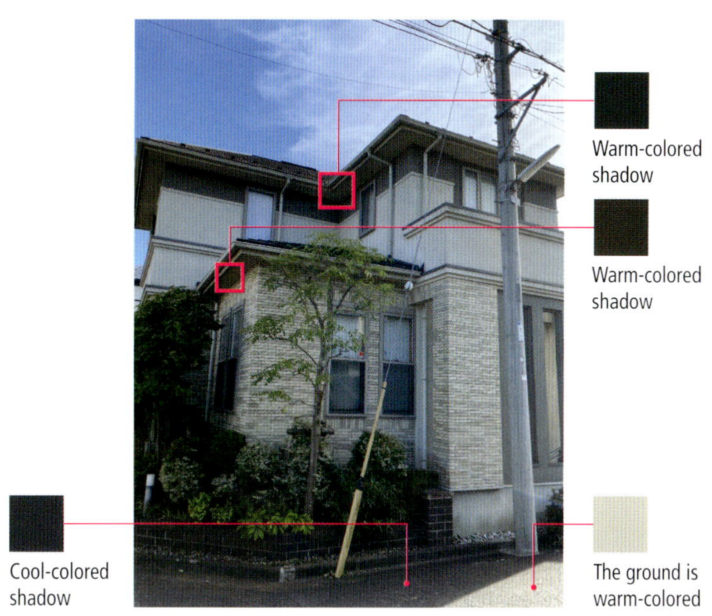


Because the shadows of objects are influenced by the environment's color, colors like the universal shadow color blend well.

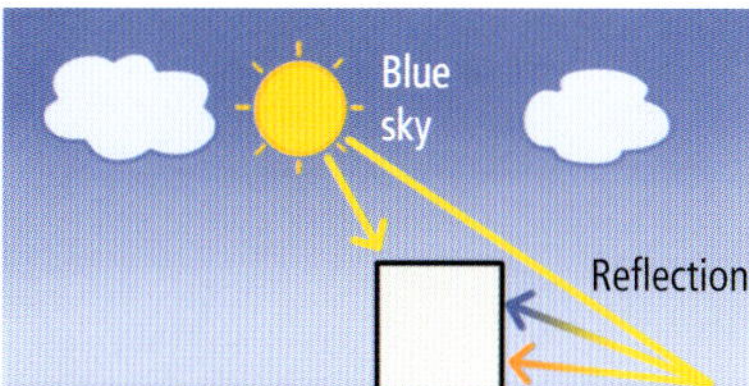


Reflected light changes the shadow color based on distance. This is why universal shadows are red and blue.

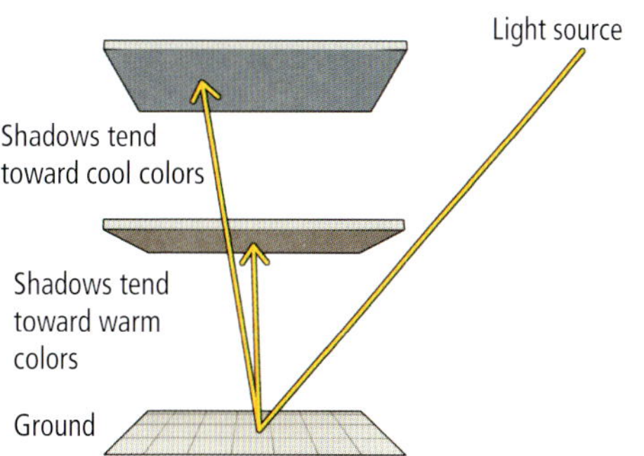

## Expressing Texture with Color

Look at the diagram below. The top three illustrations use low saturation and weak shadow contrast, giving them an overall soft texture. In contrast, the bottom three illustrations use high saturation and strong shadow contrast, making them appear heavy, hard and more defined. By adjusting the color tones and brightness, you can significantly change the impression your illustrations create.

|  | High | Low |
|---|---|---|
| Saturation | Hard | Soft |
| Brightness | Soft | Hard |

Higher saturation makes objects look harder, while higher brightness makes them look softer.

**SOFT-LOOKING EXAMPLES**

**HARD-LOOKING EXAMPLE**

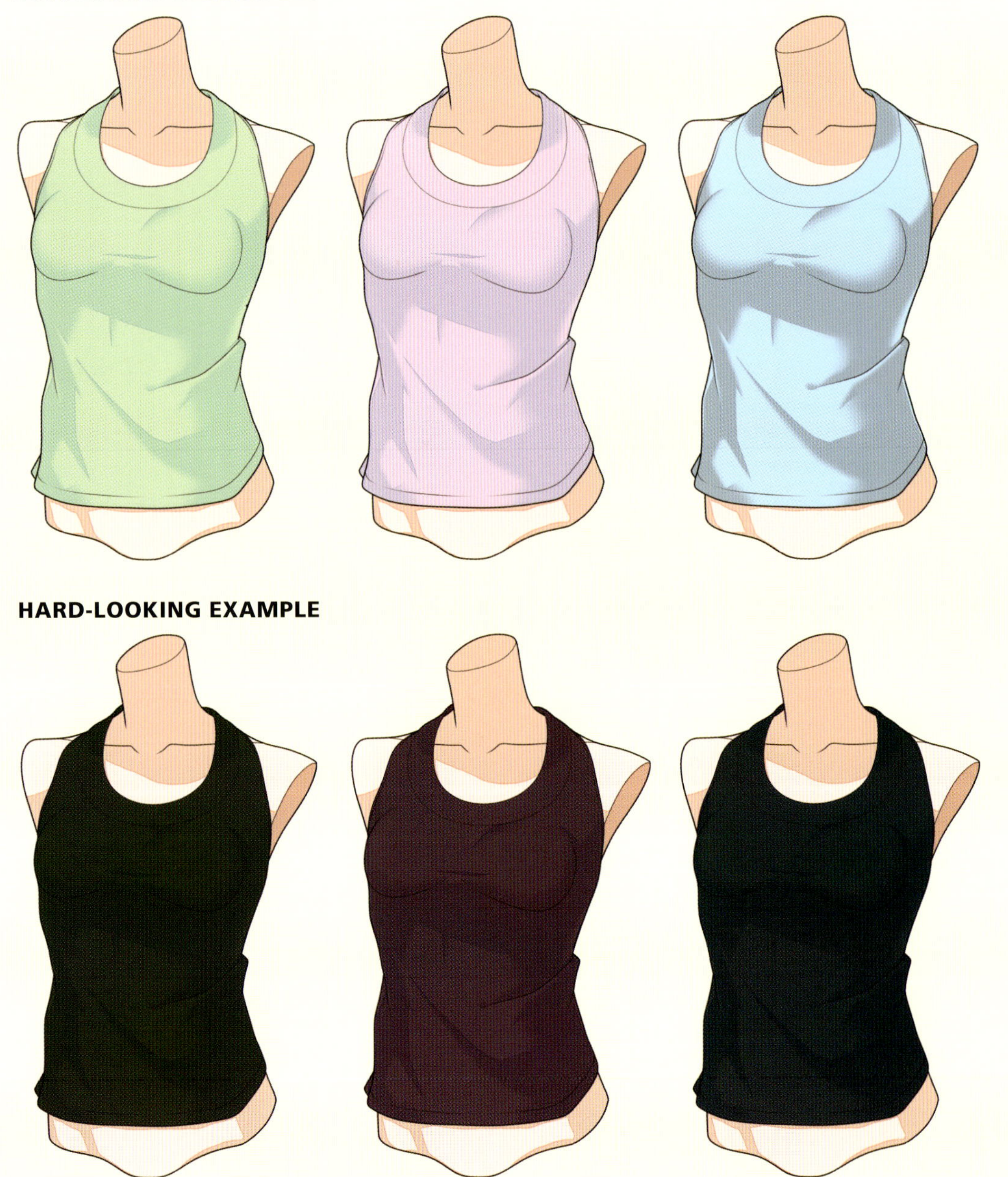

Changing saturation affects and influences the overall impression.
You can also express texture by changing the shadow color. Considering
how much light the object reflects, you can place or locate shadows to
achieve a deeper expression.

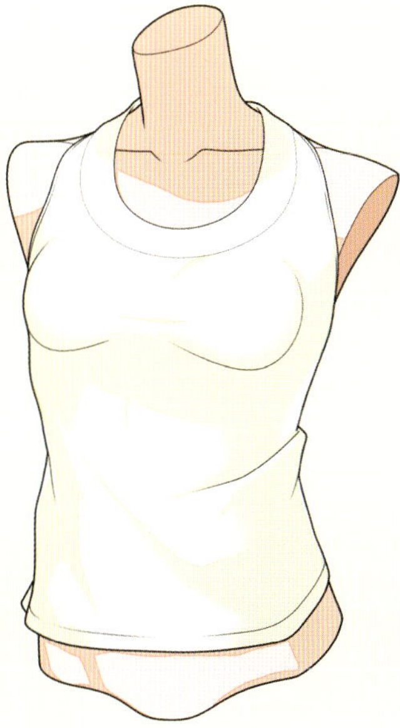

### Thick Material

Thick materials tend to absorb light,
so intentionally dulling the colors
expresses weight.

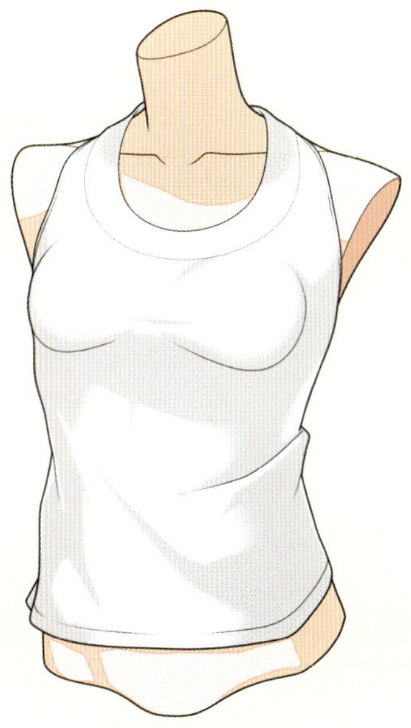

### Silk

Place shadows with slightly lowered
brightness on a neutral color base to
show silk's highly reflective surfaces.

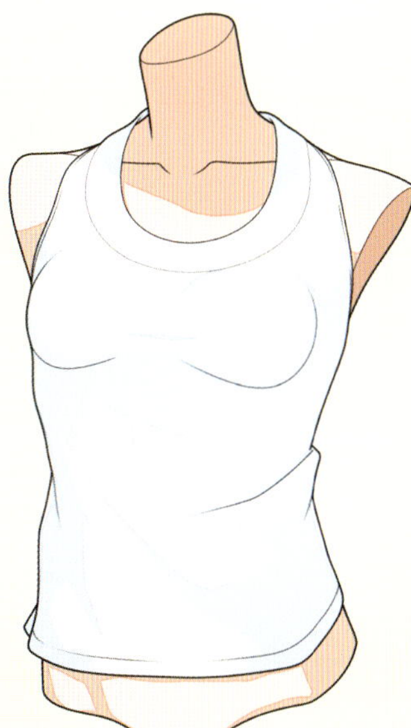

### Whiteness of a New Shirt

New fabrics are more highly reflective,
so placing cold-colored shadows with
high contrast on neutral colors enhances
the effect.

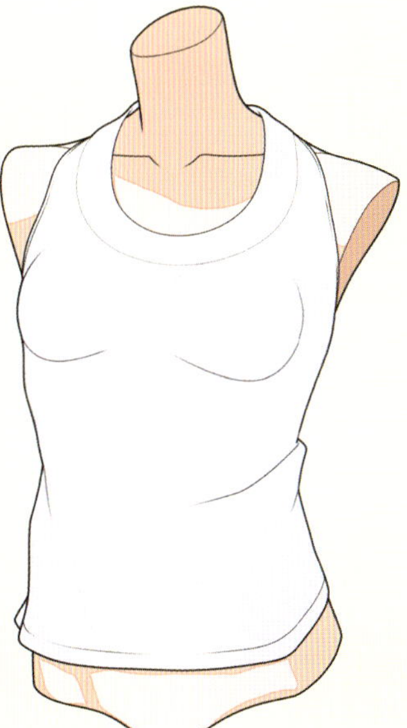

### Softness of a Worn-In Shirt

Compared to new garments, washing
reduces a fabric's reflectivity, so use
slightly warmer shadow colors to capture
the effect.

# Changing the Color of the Light Source

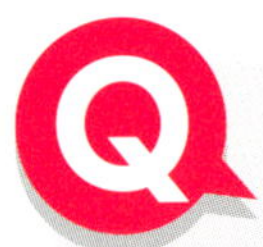

## Which highlight looks more natural?

In image **B**, the highlight on the person matches the green light of the staff. However, in image **A** the highlight color doesn't match the staff's light. Although both images have a similar atmosphere, **B**, with the matching light color, looks more natural. Let's take a closer look at how to choose colors that match the light source.

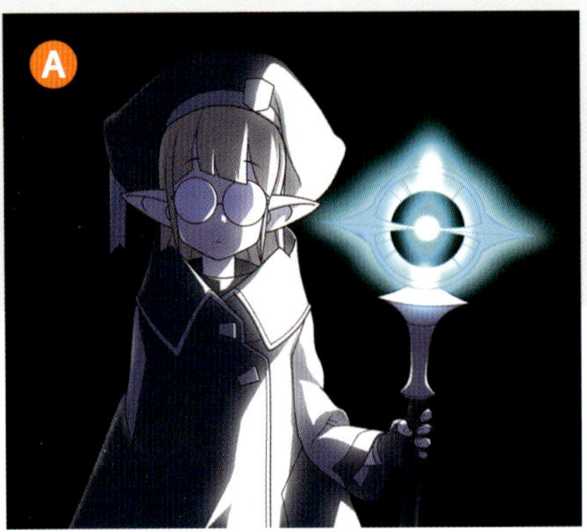

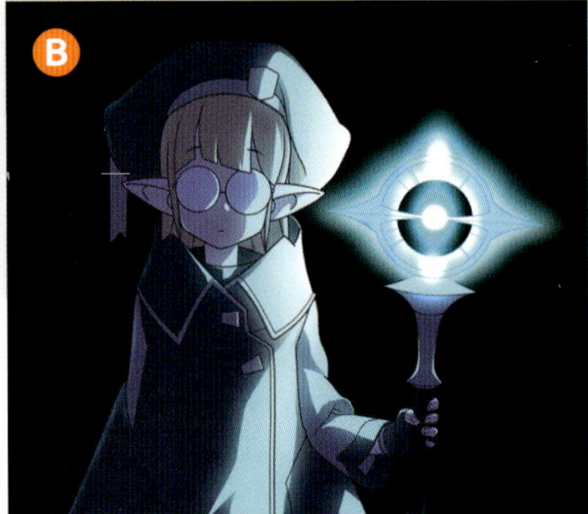

## Be Aware of the Light Source Color

In the diagram on the right, the character's staff emits yellow light, so the highlight is also yellow. Not only should the highlight be yellow, but the colors of the clothes and skin should also blend well with the light source color to effectively capture the illumination's glow. It's important to understand that as the light source color changes, so does the color of the light hitting the character.

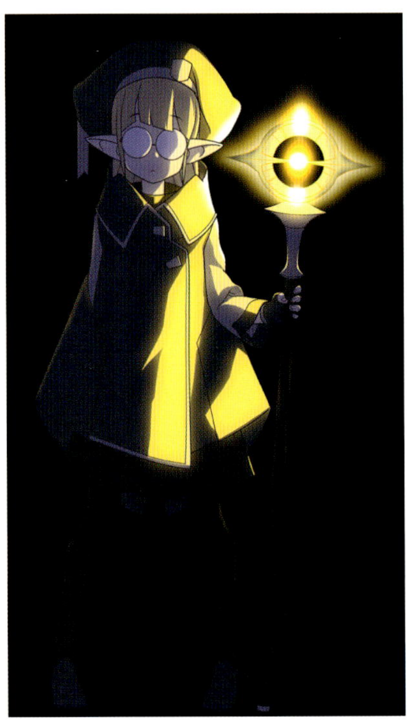

## Distance from the Light Source

Here, the staff is a bit distant from the light source. The highlights change depending on their distance from the light source, so it's important to understand the relationship between relative distance and the light source.

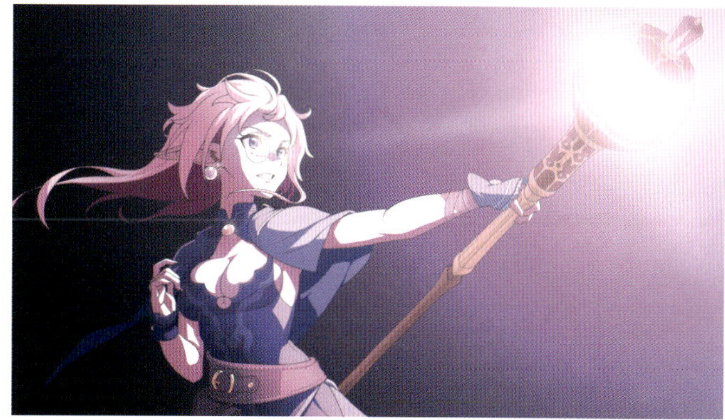

In the diagram on the right, the distance of the light source is varied for a simple sphere. At the top, the light source is the farthest away, so the surface of the sphere has only a slight amount of light on it. As it gets closer, the amount of light illuminating the sphere increases, and the highlight becomes a stronger white light.

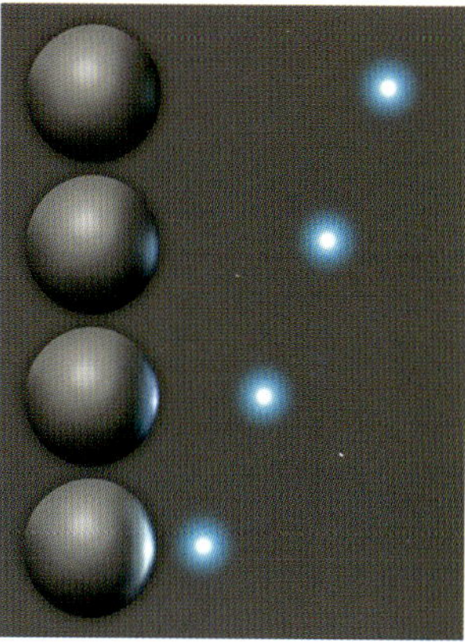

Let's see this in an actual illustration.
When the character and the staff are close, a stronger light is emitted, so the light on the face and body is mostly white. When the character and the staff are farther apart, the light source color is more prominent, so the highlight is mainly yellow. Thus, as the distance from the light source changes, the color of the illuminating light also changes.

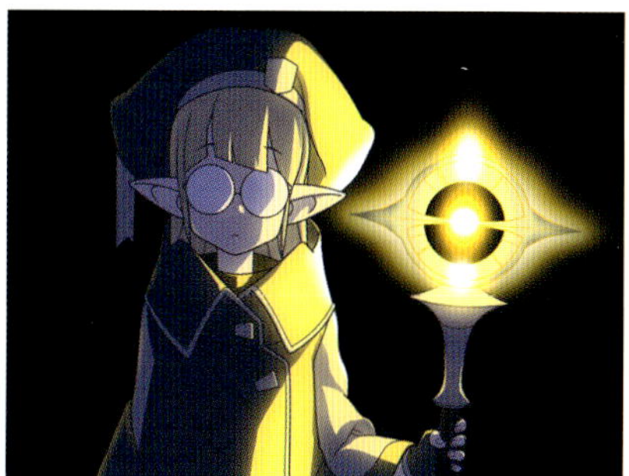

The light source is close.

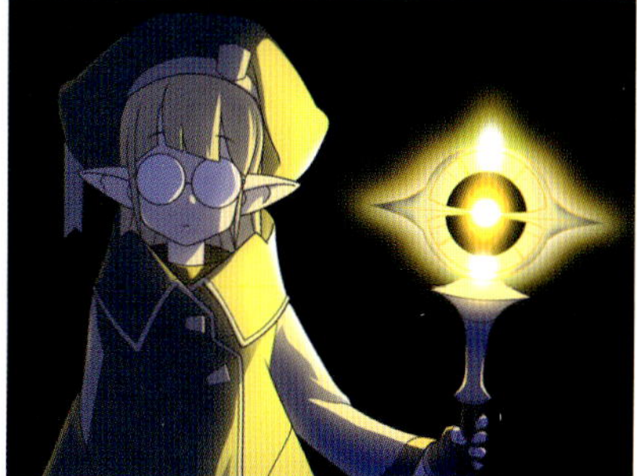

The light source is farther off.



**YOU'RE GLOWING!**

When you want to create or suggest a glow, a common method is to blur the color, but this alone can make it look weak or distant. Simply placing a white circle doesn't necessarily suggest a glow either. However, by combining these methods, you can create the proper effect.

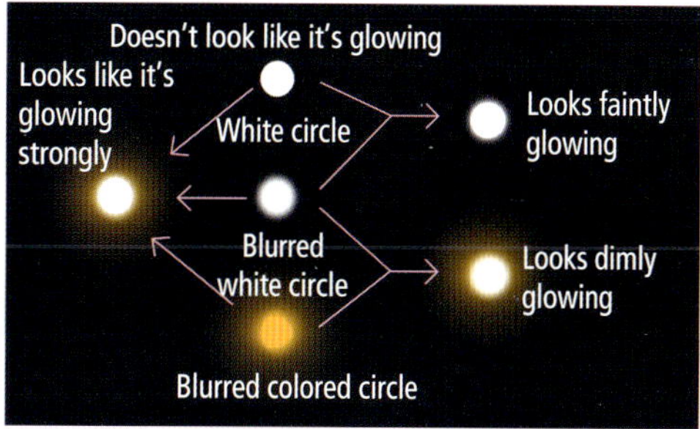

# Changing the Image with Light Source Color

Now let's become familiar with adjusting the overall atmosphere of a work by examining the light source color. In the example below, cyan and magenta are used as the light source colors to create a science- fiction atmosphere. These two colors were chosen because they're often used on gaming devices. Additionally, artificial lights like those used in electronic circuits or neon signs often create these hues, making the mechanical impression stronger when these colors are used as the light source.

**Near-Futuristic Look**

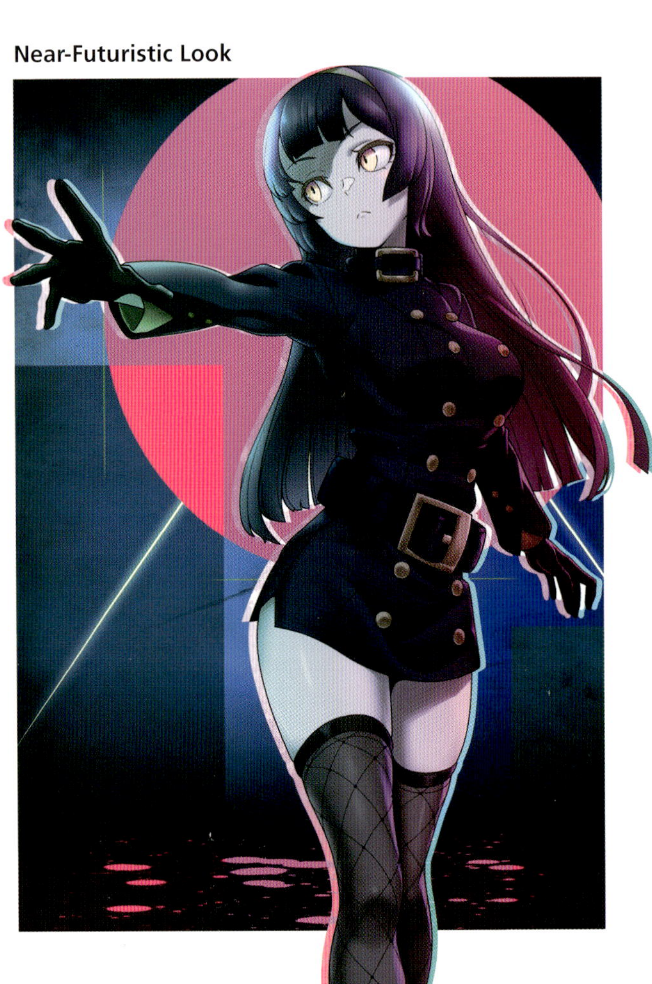

The technique of influencing the overall style through the light source color is commonly used in photography and film shooting.

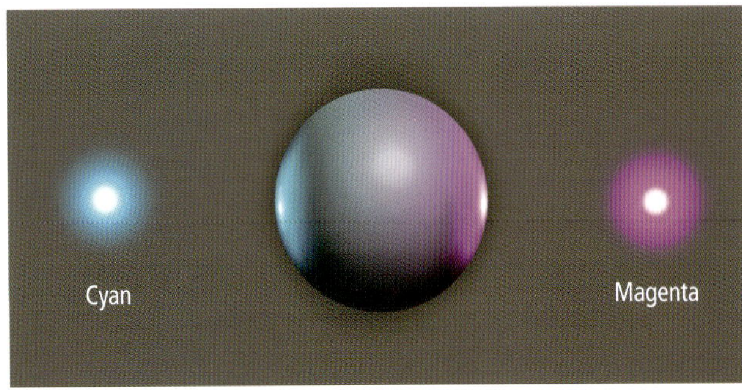

The example below uses a technique called orange and teal to adjust the light source. This method has been used in the film industry since the 1990s to create or enhance a nostalgic impression or mood. Recently, it's also become popular in illustrations and photographs, often using cyan tones (green in this case) and orange. The effect of these complementary colors emphasizes the skin tone while enhancing the background atmosphere with green.

**Nostalgic Look**

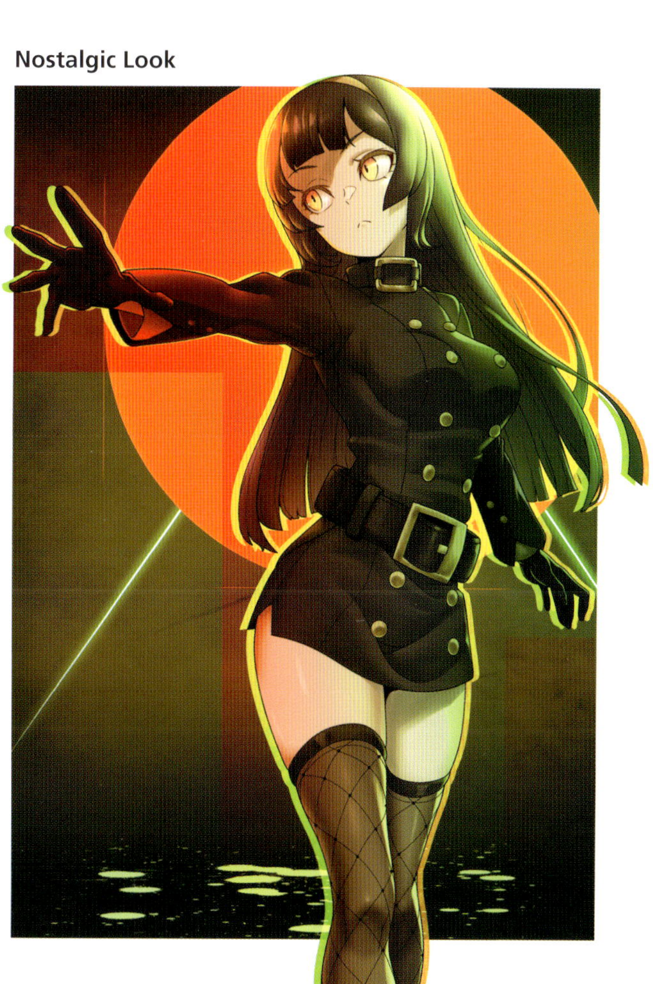

By being mindful of the light color, you can unify the overall atmosphere of an illustration or guide it in the intended direction.

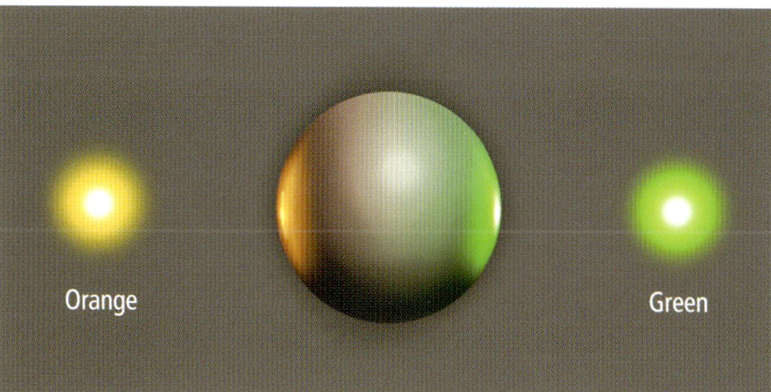

# Shadow Tips

## Which has more transparent skin?

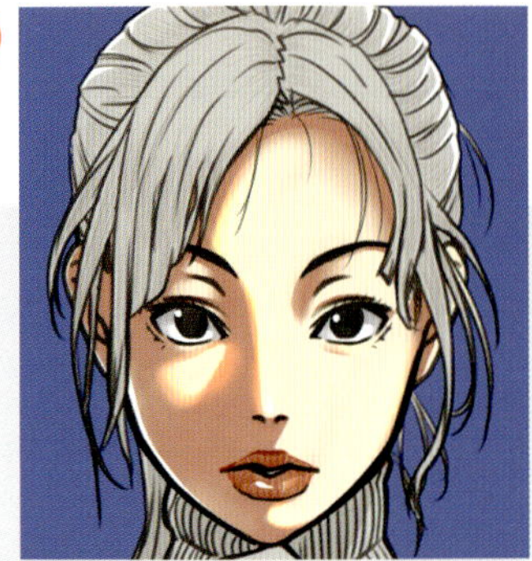

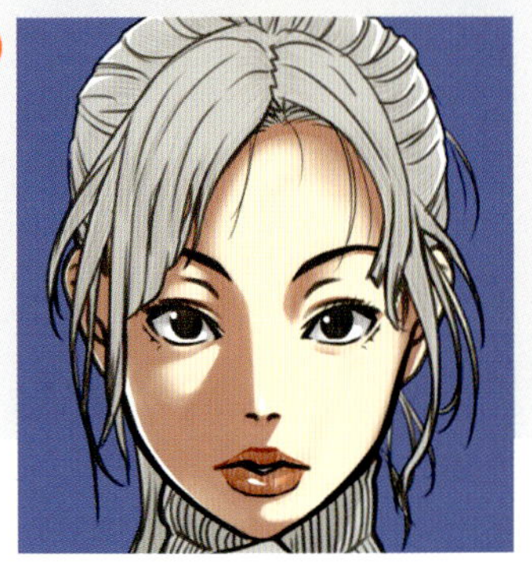

In **A**, there's a slight color at the edges of the shadows around the eyes and nose, whereas **B** lacks this. Doesn't the presence of bright colors at the shadow edges make the skin appear more transparent? Adding this kind of detail and effect can give the skin a more transparent look. Let's look more closely at this technique and how to add enhancing details and shadows.

## Skin Edges

In some illustrations, the shadow edges are painted with high saturation and with dark colors. In the example, a thin line of color with a higher saturation than the base color is added to the edges of shadows on the arms and chest. This technique is called subsurface scattering.

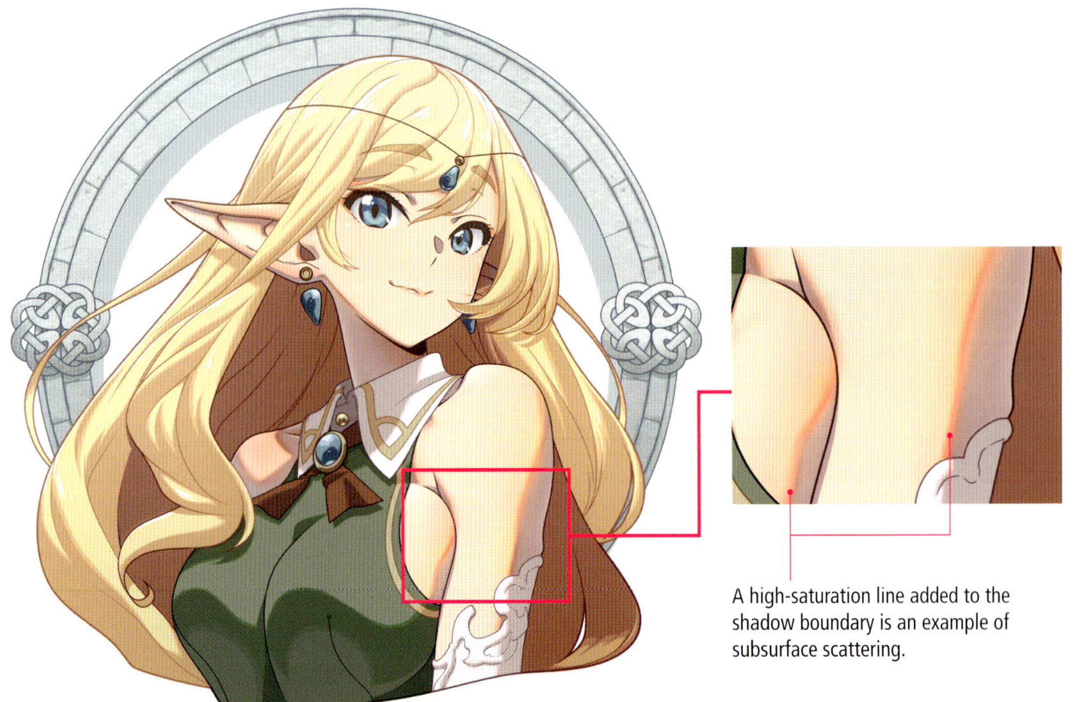

A high-saturation line added to the shadow boundary is an example of subsurface scattering.

# Subsurface Scattering

Subsurface scattering refers to the phenomenon where light illuminating the skin penetrates the surface, reflects off the body and mixes with the skin's surface color to reveal a reddish tint. In the twenty-first century, this effect and expression has been increasingly used in illustrations, enhancing the amount of visual information and detail it contains and making the skin look healthier.

### Enhanced in Illustrations

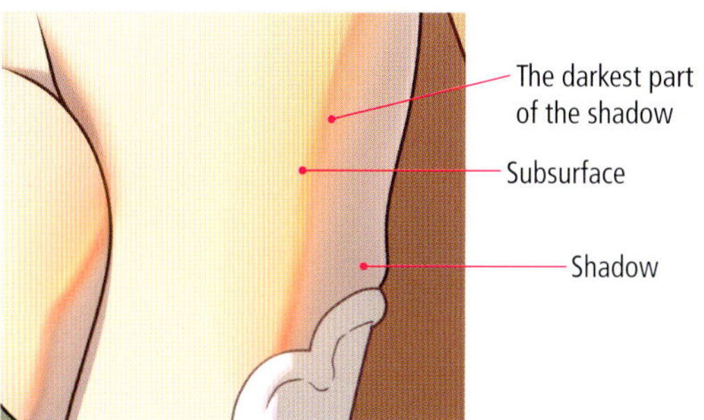


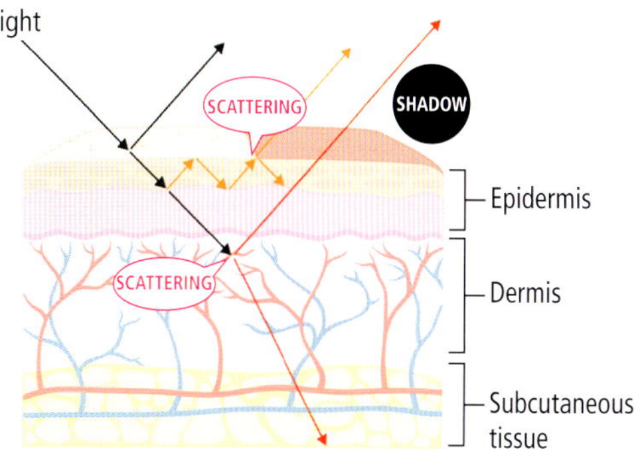


Let's compare illustrations with and without subsurface scattering.

### With Subsurface Scattering

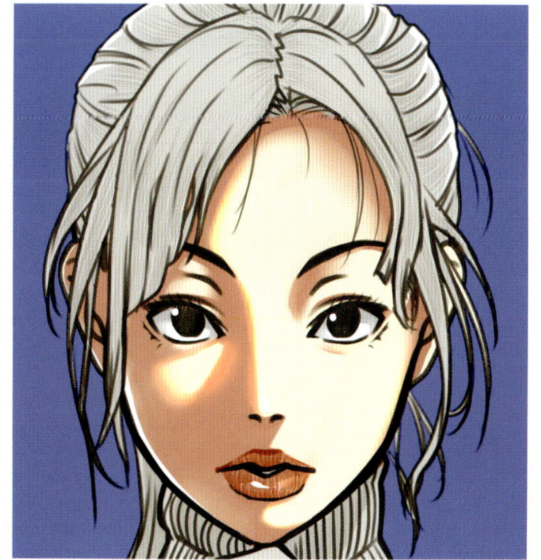

Increases the soft texture and makes the skin look more vibrant.

### Without Subsurface Scattering

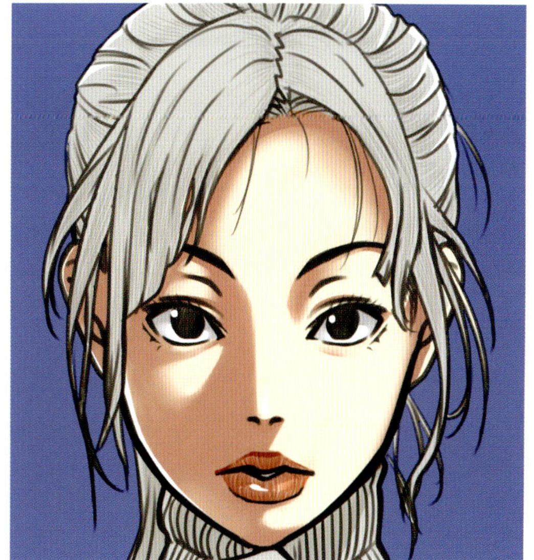

Not wrong, but looks simpler compared to the one with subsurface scattering.

Here are some common mistakes beginners make when shading. In the example on the left, the shadows are added along the character's line art. However, the actual body has contours and complex shapes, so the shadows shouldn't follow the lines of the body in this way. To correctly suggest and capture such shadowing, observe the effects carefully using three-dimensional models, figures and photos or even make note of the effects on your own body to properly place and locate the shadows.

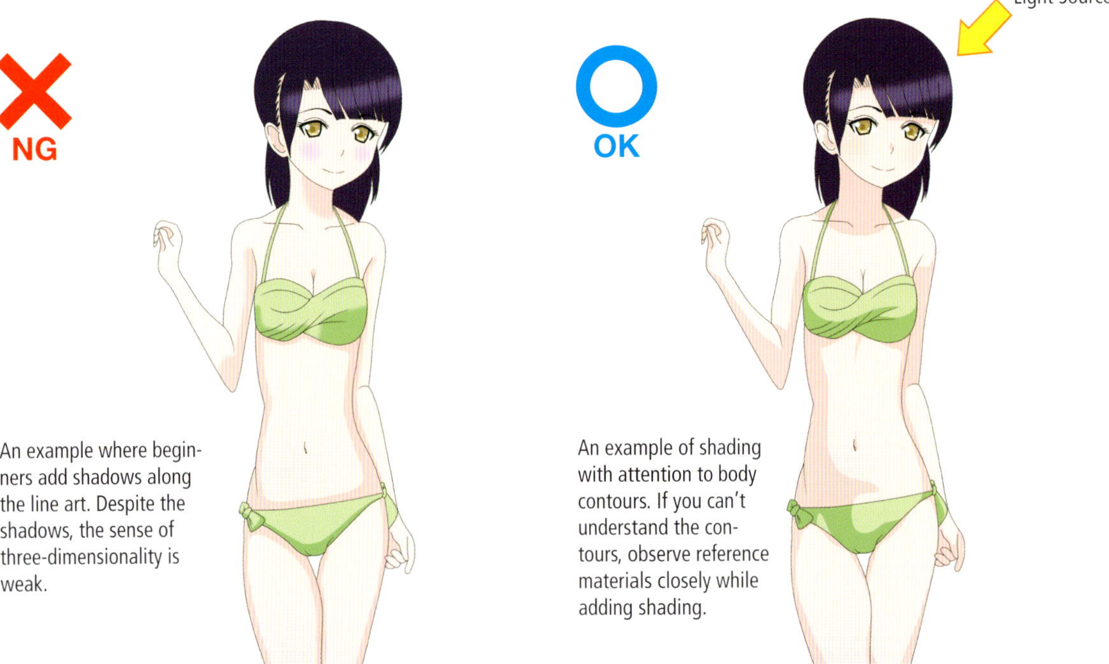


An example where beginners add shadows along the line art. Despite the shadows, the sense of three-dimensionality is weak.

An example of shading with attention to body contours. If you can't understand the contours, observe reference materials closely while adding shading.

---

**EXPERT TIP**   **SHADOWS AND SHADES**

Shading effects can be broadly classified into two categories: shadows and shades. Shadows are the areas where an object casts a shadow, while shades are the dark areas where light doesn't reach when an object is illuminated. These two types of light-based effects are not mutually exclusive. It's important to consider whether the effect you're adding is a shadow or a shade as you apply the color, which will add a greater sense of realism to your illustration.

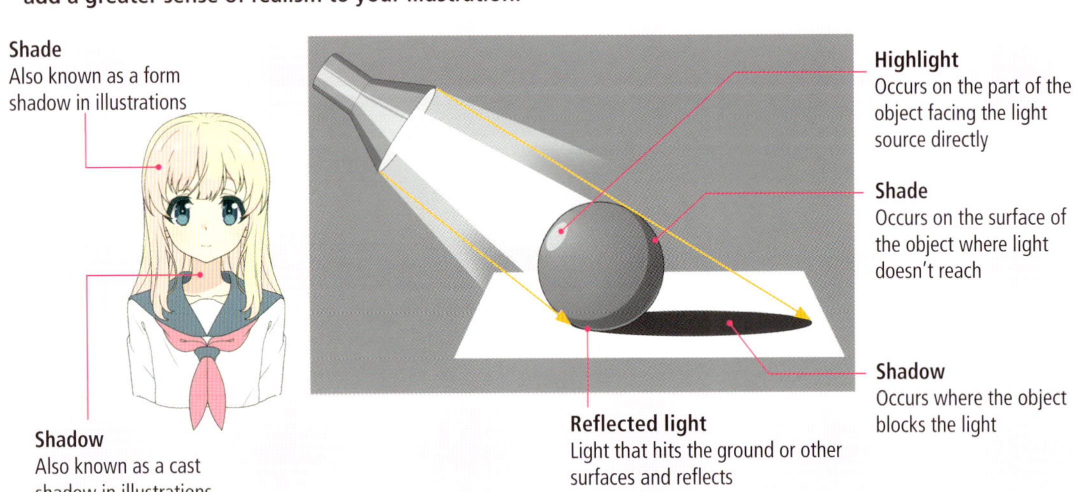

# Erasing with Transparent Color

When shading, you might find the need to erase excess areas. Using the default eraser tool can often make the erased parts stand out because the touch of the eraser differs from that of the brush used to paint. Therefore, try erasing using transparent color. As you can see in the diagram below, drawing tools like CLIP STUDIO PAINT offer a transparent color option. By setting the drawing color of the brush to transparent, you can create an eraser tool with the same texture as the brush. This allows for cleaner corrections that blend seamlessly.

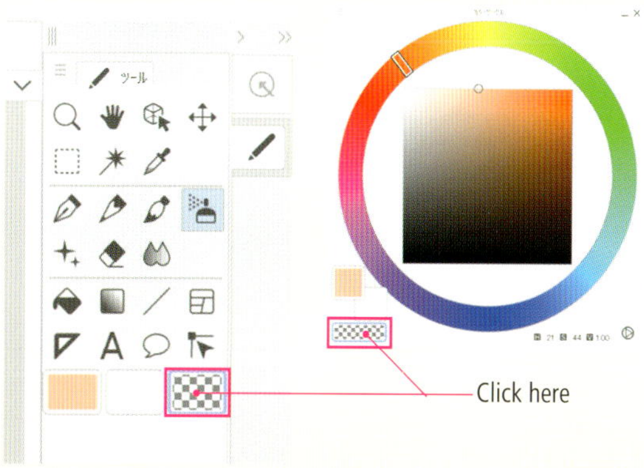


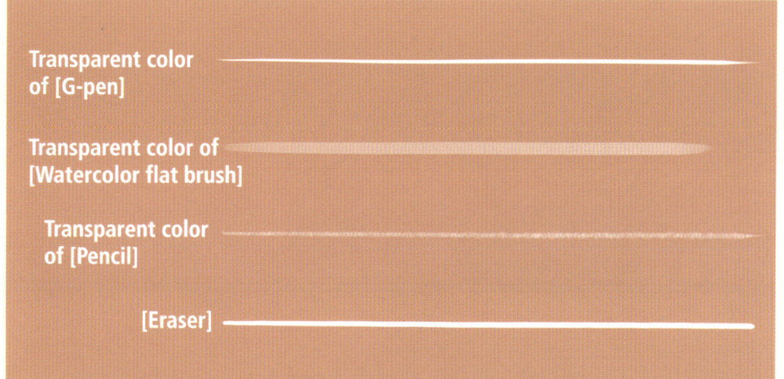


When you want to preserve the touch of the pen while erasing, use transparent color.

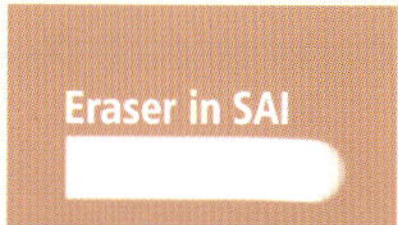


In SAI, the erasing can be less precise.

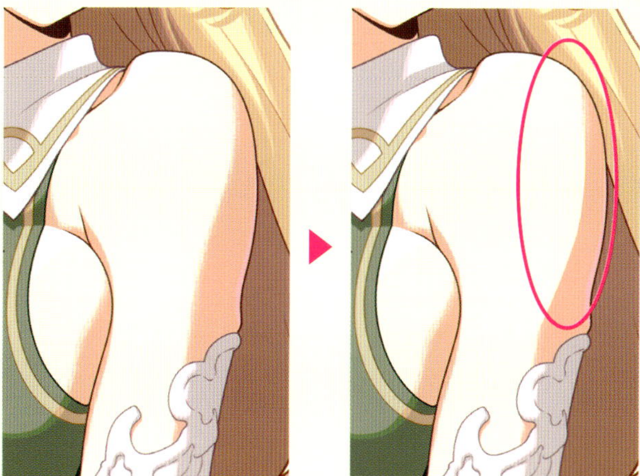

If you use the default [eraser] on shading done with a brush that has an analogue feel, the brush's touch is lost.

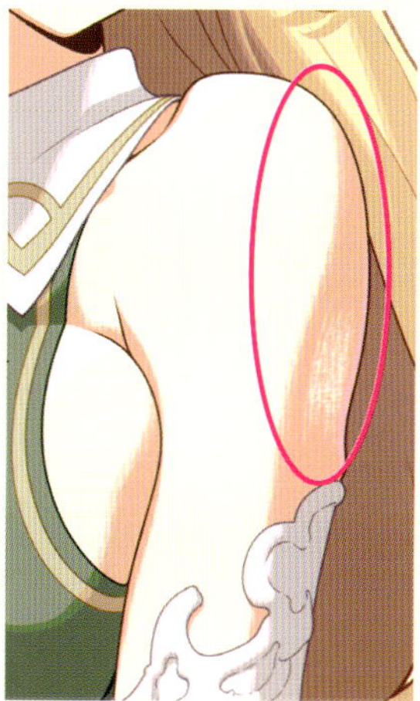

By erasing with the brush's transparent color, you can make corrections while preserving the brush's touch.

# Adding Light Blue to Shadow Colors

After finishing painting the shadow color, sometimes the result doesn't look quite right. In such cases, adding light blue to the shadow color can help you achieve a more cohesive look. The diagram below shows the subject illuminated by yellow light, a warm color. By adding light blue, a cool color, to the shadow color, you create a complementary relationship between the light and shadow. This enhances the finished illustration by tightening the overall effect. The illustration on the bottom right shows the addition of complementary colors to all parts of the shadow color. Although it takes more effort, this approach creates a brighter impression compared to just adding light blue.

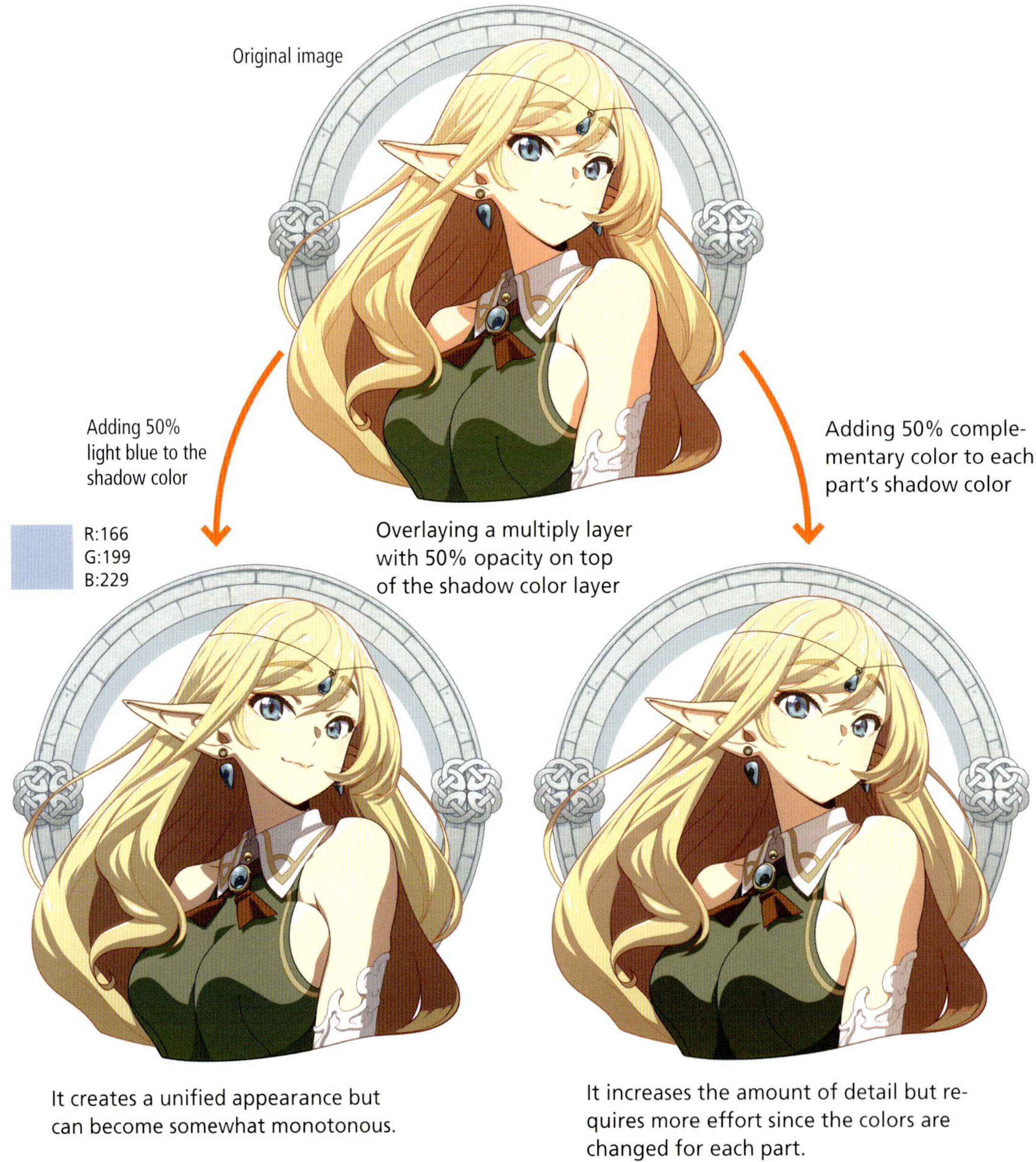



It creates a unified appearance but can become somewhat monotonous.

It increases the amount of detail but requires more effort since the colors are changed for each part.

There's no right or wrong way, so use the colors according to your preference and the atmosphere you want to achieve.

# Shading Techniques

There are two basic options: you can add light to dark shadows or apply dark shadows to light colors. The latter approach is derived from techniques associated with watercolor painting, which involves starting with light colors and then adding darker colors and shadows. While techniques like anime-style shading and watercolor painting can work with either approach, when applying thick layers of paint, it's easier to start with dark colors and then add lighter ones. Feel free to experiment and find which method works best for you.

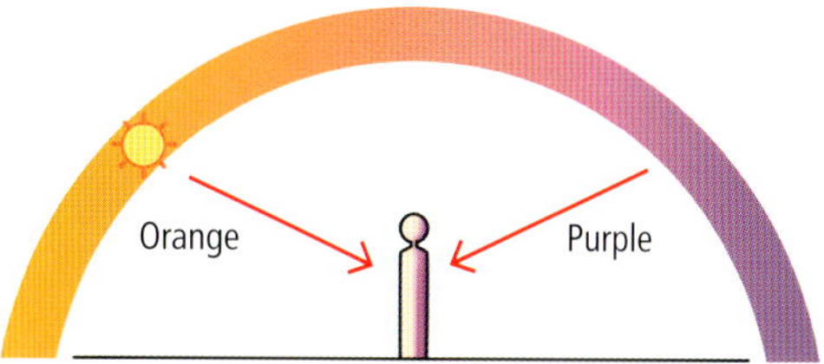


## Shading Technique

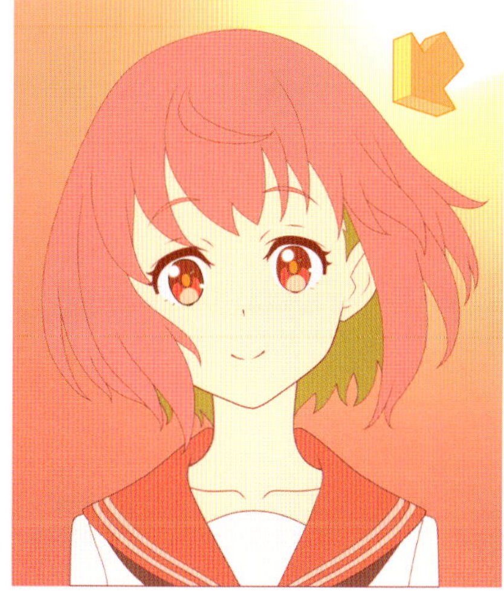

Shade after finishing the base coloring.

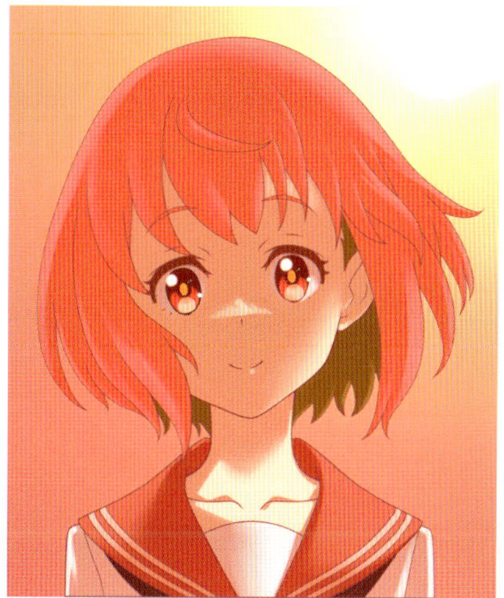

R:227
G:141
B:148
Set the layer blending mode to [Multiply] and apply the shadows.

## Lighting Technique

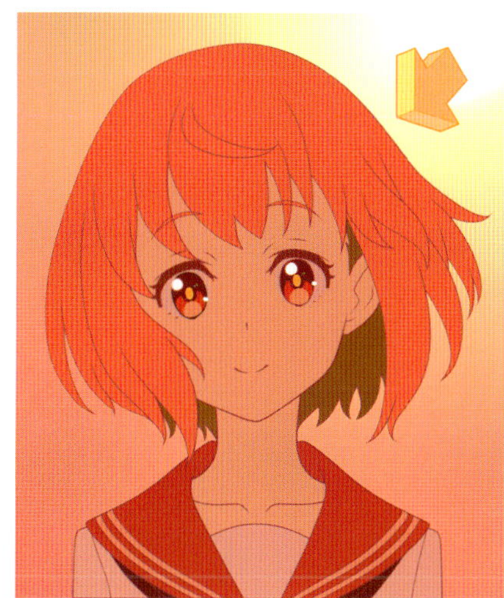

R:227
G:141
B:148
After finishing the base coloring, cover the entire illustration with a purple hue. Set the blending mode to [Multiply] and add the shadows across the illustration.

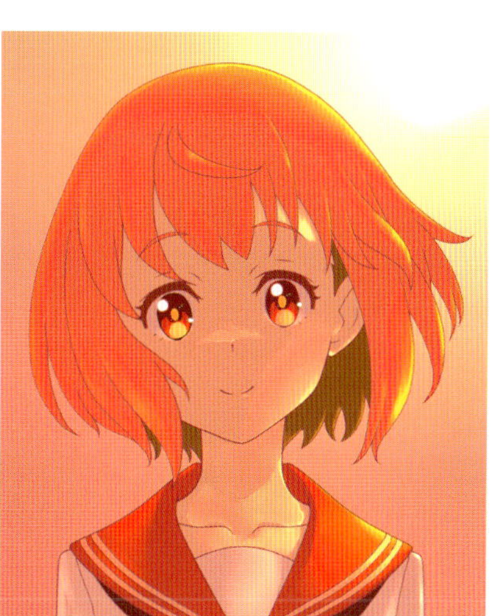

R:255
G:243
B:139
Set the blending mode to [Hard Mix] and use the [Watercolor Brush] to add the light. This method allows for a quick finish.

# Highlights in Natural Light

When adding white highlights to areas painted with dark or low-brightness colors, the high contrast can be a bit too much. For example, when using navy blue as in the top two illustrations, using a diluted version of the inherent color instead of white for the highlights can create a more natural finish. However, when using naturally lighter colors as in the bottom two illustrations, white highlights blend in nicely and don't present a problem.

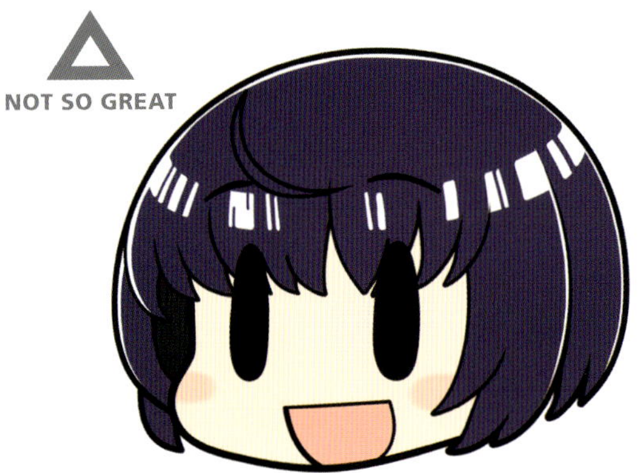



Adding white highlights to dark or dense colors results in high contrast, which feels off.

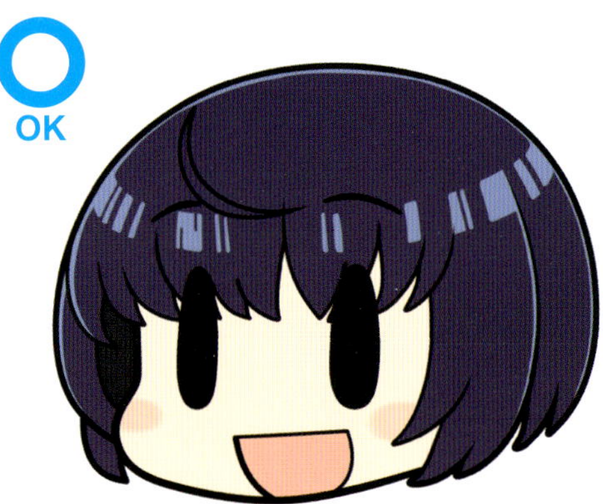



For dark or dense colors, using a color with increased brightness from the base color blends better.

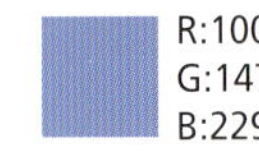

R:100
G:147
B:229

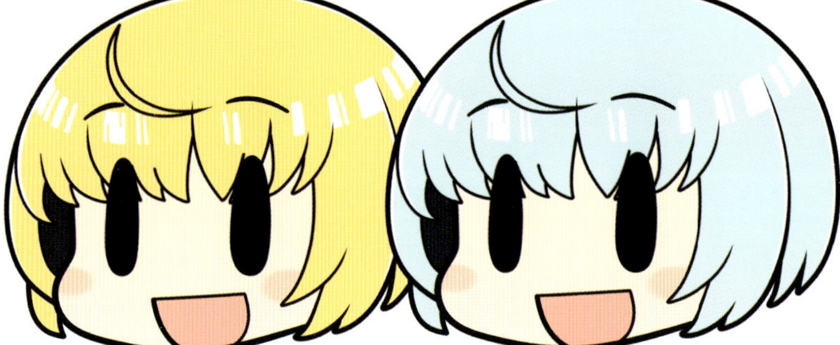

For light or pale colors, white highlights don't feel out of place.

Using multiple colors for highlights is an increasingly popular trend in manga and anime. Known as gaming highlights, by using various colors for highlights, the visual information increases, making the result more eye-catching. Additionally, in recent years, the color palettes used in illustrations has often leaned toward pastel and low-saturation colors, with many techniques intentionally using high-saturation colors for eyes and highlights to enhance the overall impression.

Set the blending mode to [Add (Glow)] and the opacity to 50%

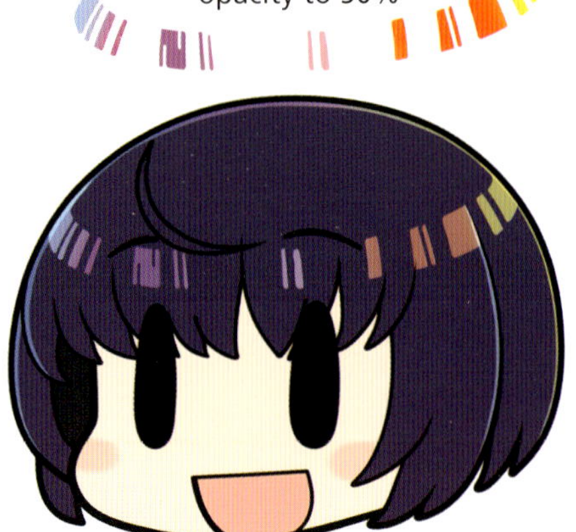

Using rainbow colors for highlights makes them colorful.

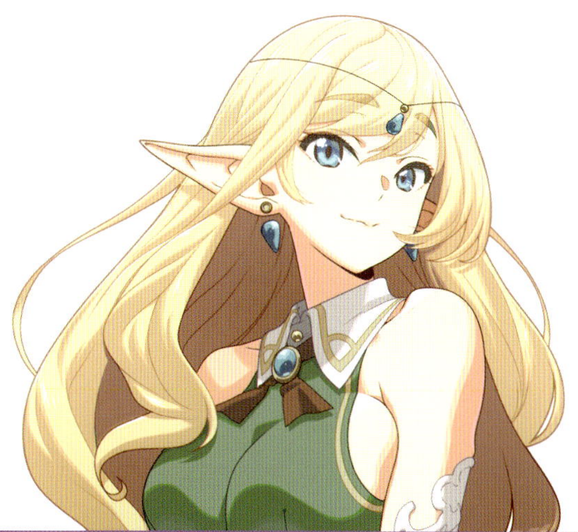

# TIPS AND TECHNIQUES

So you've adjusted the lighting and achieved the perfect effect. Now it's time for the finishing touches. This section explains various refining techniques and shows you what to do when you're stuck in the home stretch.

# Creating a Sense of Unity

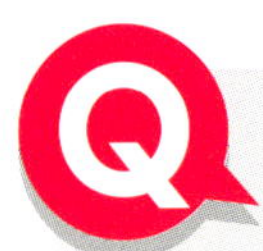

## Which illustration has a better sense of color uniformity?

Which illustration has a better sense of color uniformity? Both seem visually cohesive, but doesn't **B** appear to have better uniformity? **A** is the completed coloring, while **B** has the overall colors adjusted on top of **A**. Although **A** is more vibrant, upon closer inspection, its color saturation lacks uniformity. On the other hand, the adjusted **B** looks neatly unified, an example of how final tweaks and adjustments can create uniformity.

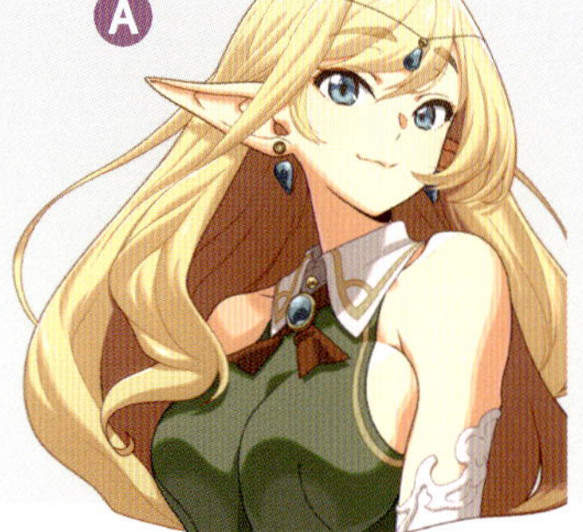

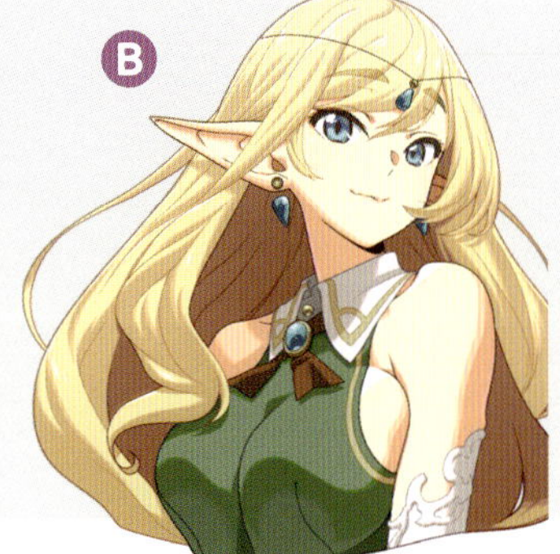

## Creating Uniformity with Overlay

Some illustrations use many colors or complementary colors to enhance their impression, but this can sometimes result in clashing hues, making the final image look out of balance or too stark. If this is the case, using an overlay to adjust the color tone can soften the clashing tones and hues and create a sense of unity.

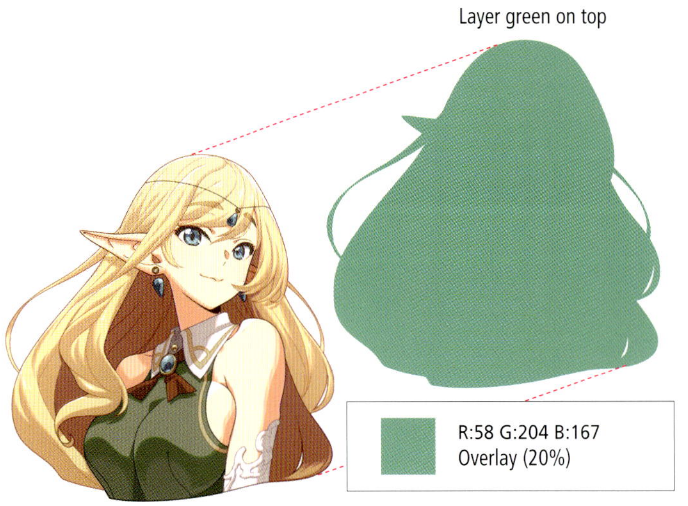


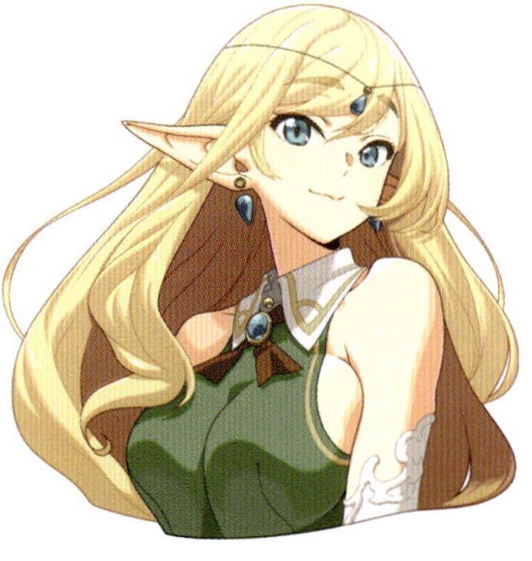

① Create a layer on top of the finished illustration, fill it with the desired color for unification and set the layer's blending mode to [Overlay].

② Set the layer blending mode to [Overlay] and adjust the opacity to about 20%. Adding green throughout will unify the colors.

※ Adjust opacity or use gradients to match the desired atmosphere.

 ENHANCING SKIN COLOR

**If the overlay color is red, it will make the skin appear healthier.
Try different colors to match the final look of your illustration.**

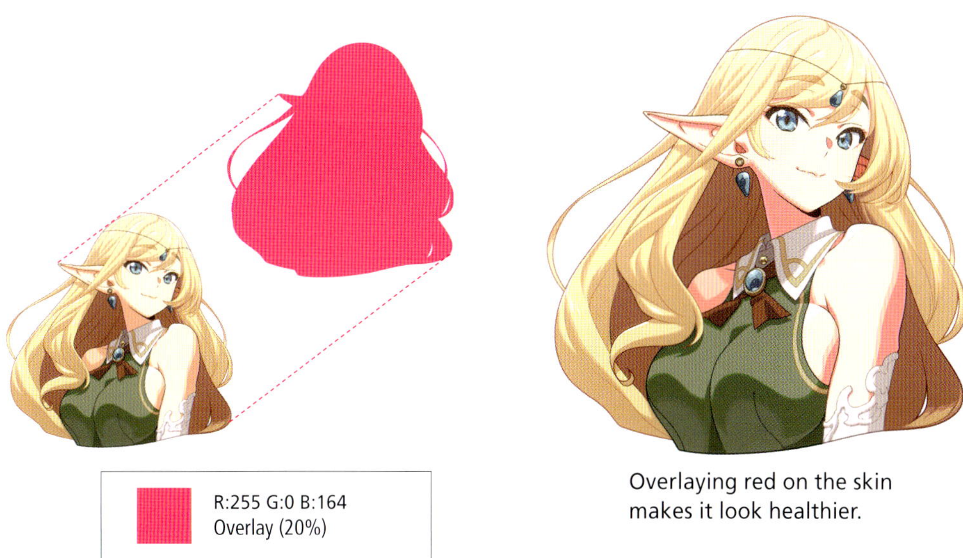

R:255 G:0 B:164
Overlay (20%)

Overlaying red on the skin
makes it look healthier.

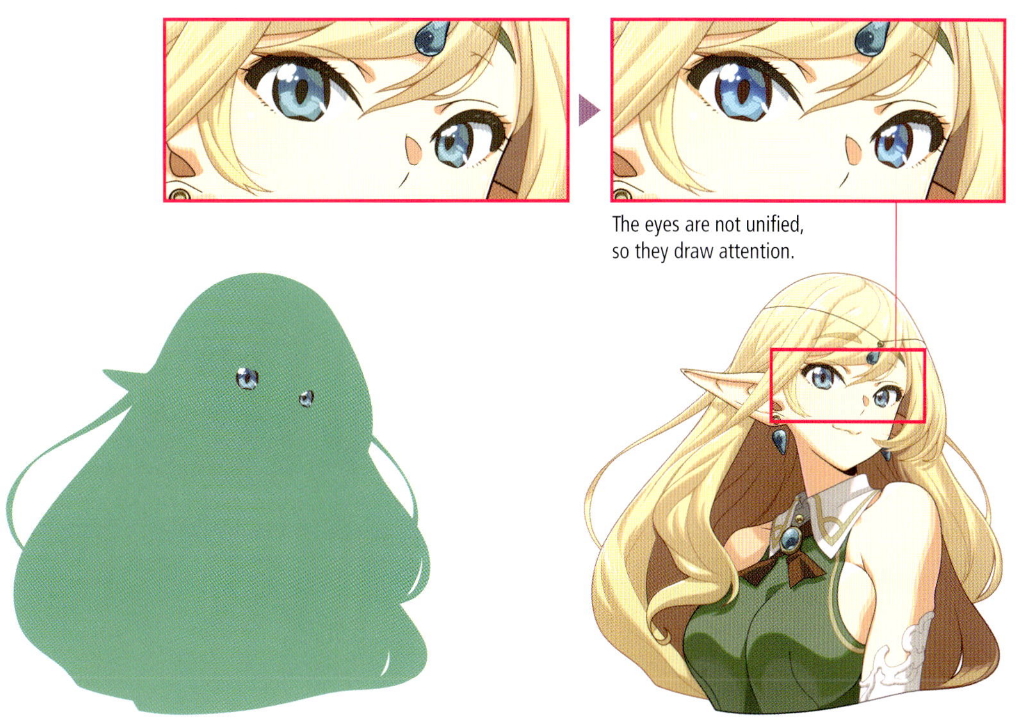

The eyes are not unified,
so they draw attention.

③ If the entire image is unified, it can look flat, so
remove the color from the eyes to draw focus.

④ The completed illustration achieves the
right balance.

# Creating Depth with Overlay

Sometimes a finished illustration still looks flat or the balance seems off. One way to add depth is to repaint or add shadows, but you can also create depth using the effects of advancing and receding colors. First, apply a receding color, such as blue-black, across the entire image. Then, add red to areas that protrude toward the viewer. Finally, add a yellowish color to the brightest areas or the spots you want to emphasize. This method allows you to add depth to a flat-looking illustration without repainting. Now let's adjust the following illustration as an example, so you'll get a better sense of the technique.

① Although the illustration is complete, the placement of shadow colors, brightness and contrast can still make it look flat.

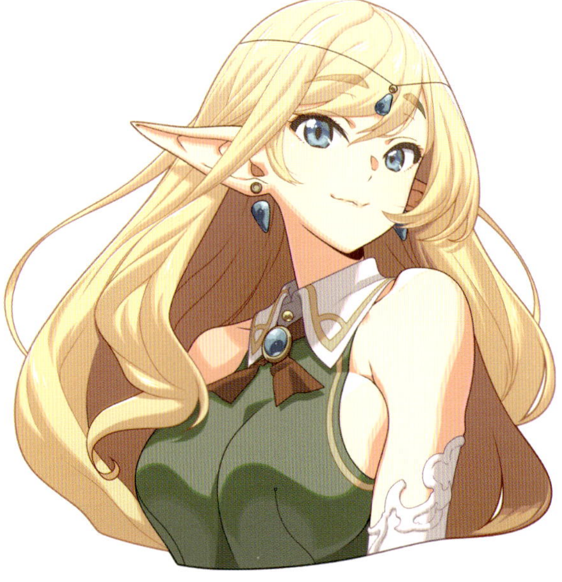

② Duplicate and merge the illustration ①. Place the layer at the top and lock the transparent pixels to protect the transparent areas. To create the dark areas, fill them with blue-black, a receding color.

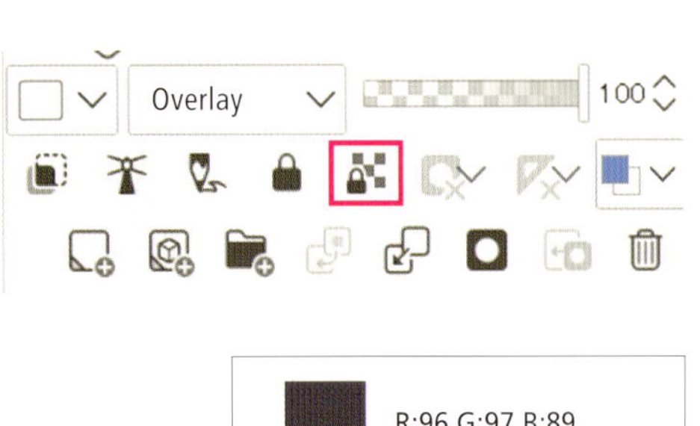

③ Using an airbrush or another soft brush, blend red tones into the areas where light hits, as shown below. If the airbrush blending is insufficient, you can use the blur tool or Gaussian blur.

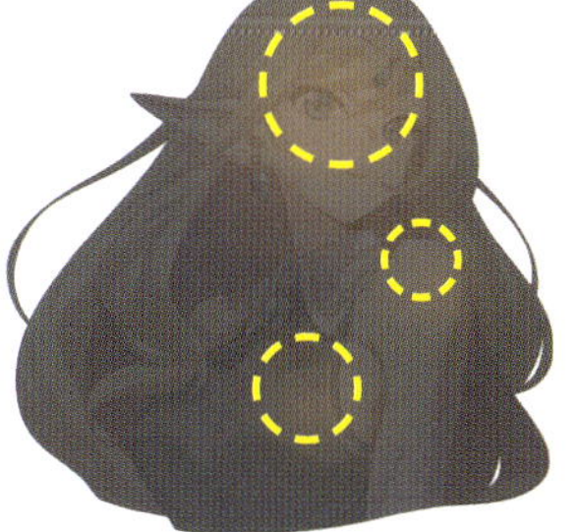

R:128 G:94 B:93

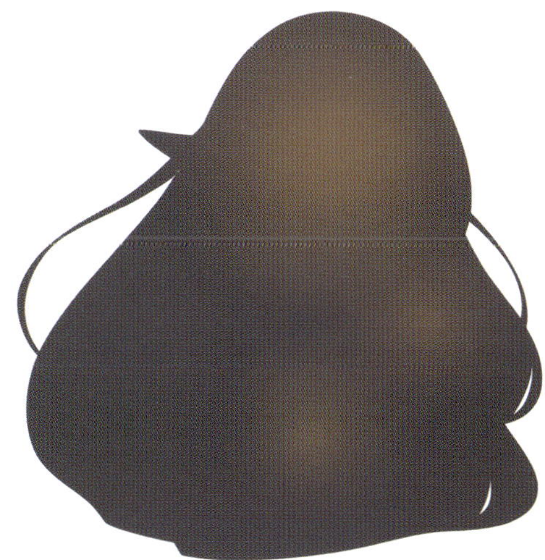

Apply color with an airbrush to areas you want to embellish such as the face, shoulders and chest.

④ For further emphasis, add the brightest highlights in a low-saturation yellow over step ③ and set the layer blending mode to [Overlay]. Adjust the opacity to your liking.

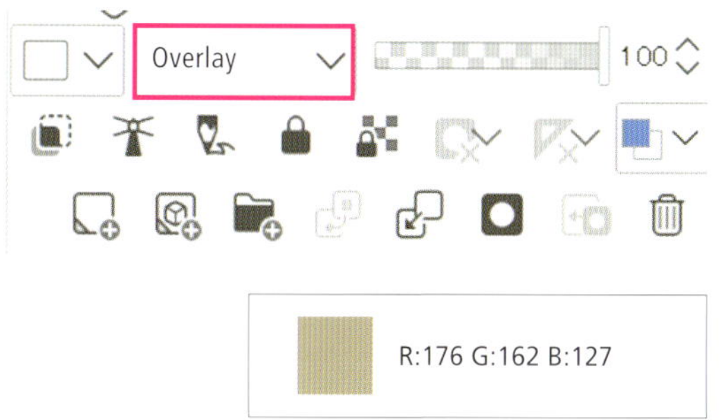


R:176 G:162 B:127

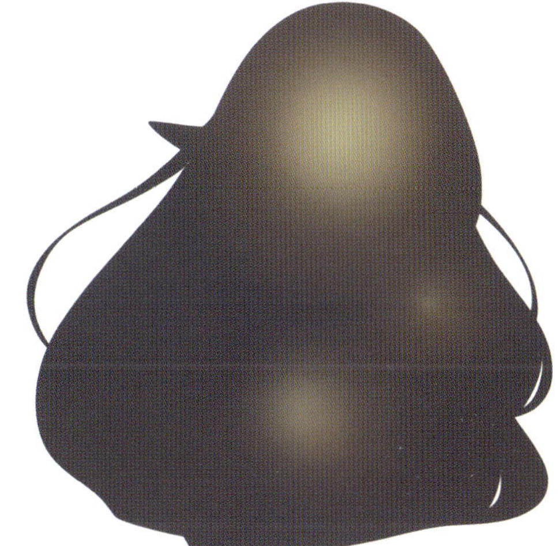

⑤ It's complete! Adding advancing and receding colors has created a greater sense of depth.

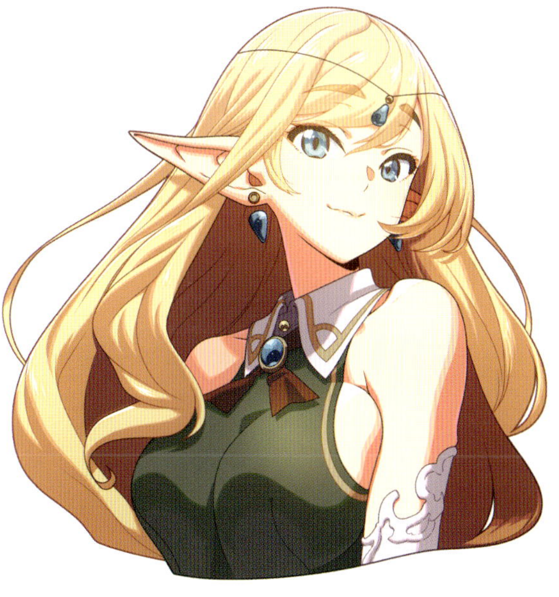

# Adjust Using Tone Curve

If the finished illustration is far from what you expected, you can adjust it to some extent by using tone curves. The first step is to adjust contrast. When the difference between dark and light areas has become small, you can emphasize the difference in brightness or luminance to create an illustration with strong contrast. The second is color adjustment, which can be done for each of the RGB colors (red, green, and blue), so if the saturation of a particular color is too strong or too weak, it can be adjusted to adjust the color tone.

① Duplicate the completed illustration and merge the layers. Right-click on the layer, select "New Color Correction Layer," then "Tone Curve."

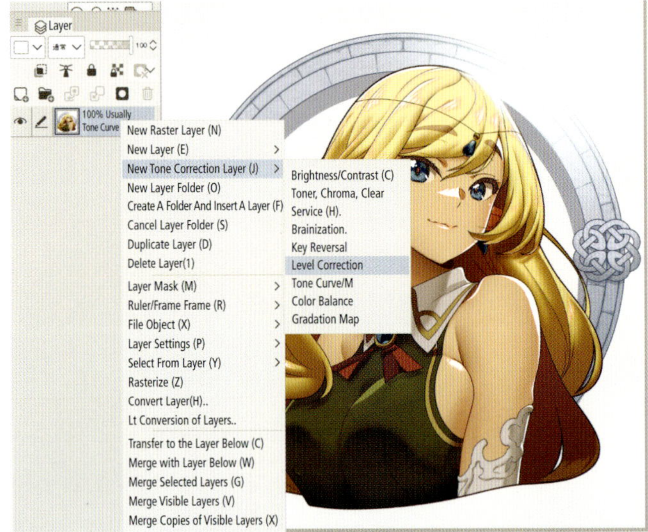


② A dialogue box will appear, and you can adjust the color tone to your liking.

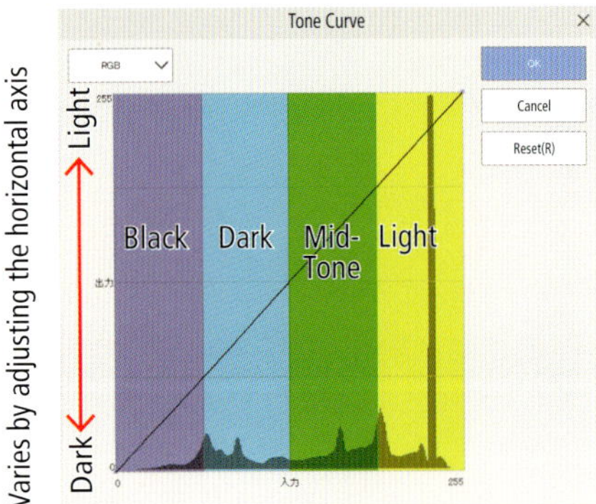


The horizontal axis indicates the lightness or darkness of the original image.

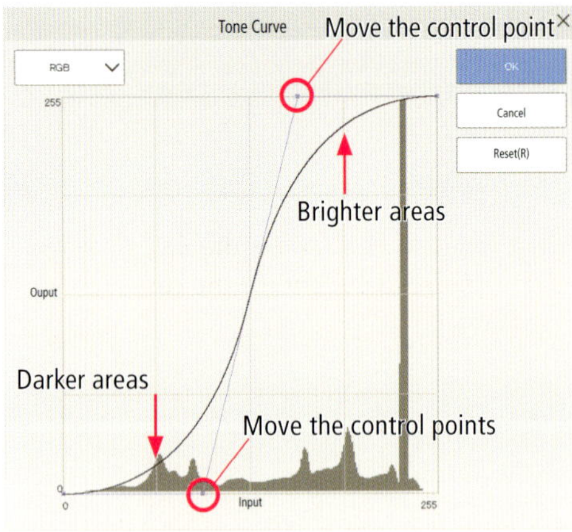


Dragging on the diagonal white line creates a control point, which adjusts the brightness and darkness. To erase a control point, drag it off the screen.

③ Click O.K. to create a color correction layer. Since it is a separate layer, it can be easily restored to the original image by hiding or deleting it when not needed. You can also double-click the tone curve symbol on the layer to redo the adjustment later.

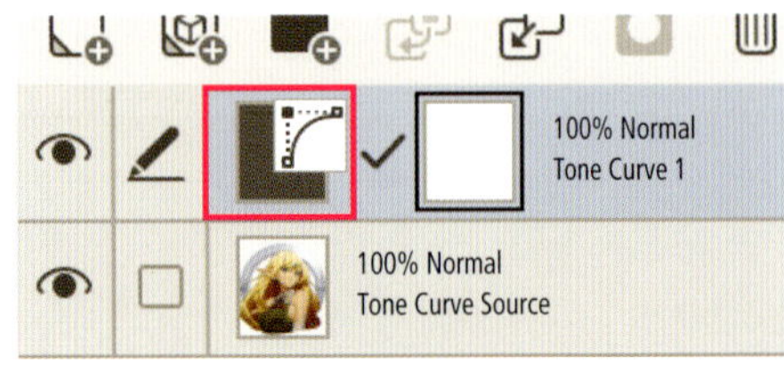

## Example of Tone Curve Adjustment

Here are some examples of tone curve adjustments.

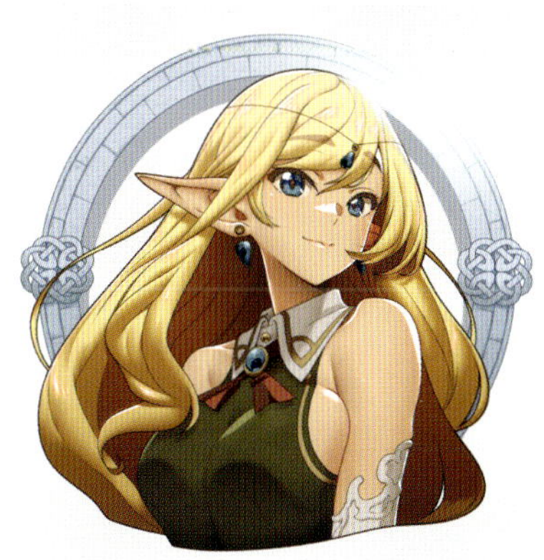

Original Image

**When You Want to Brighten the Entire Image**
Pull up the top part of the curve (light) to make it brighter.

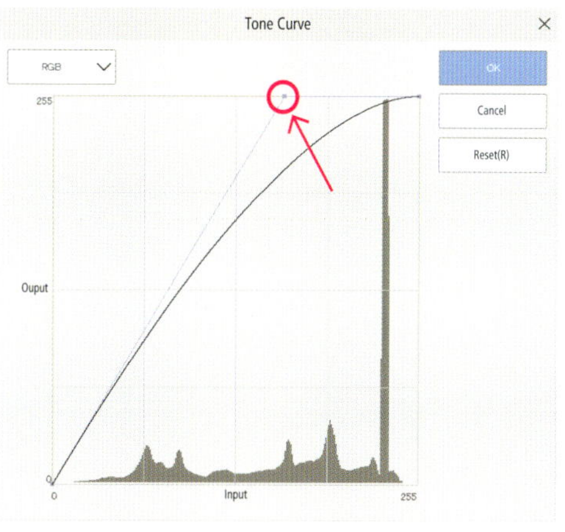


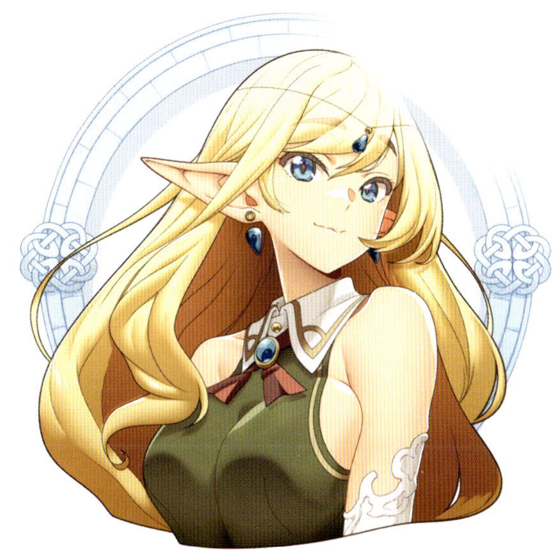

**When You Want to Darken the Entire Image**
Pull down the lower end of the curve (dark) to darken it.

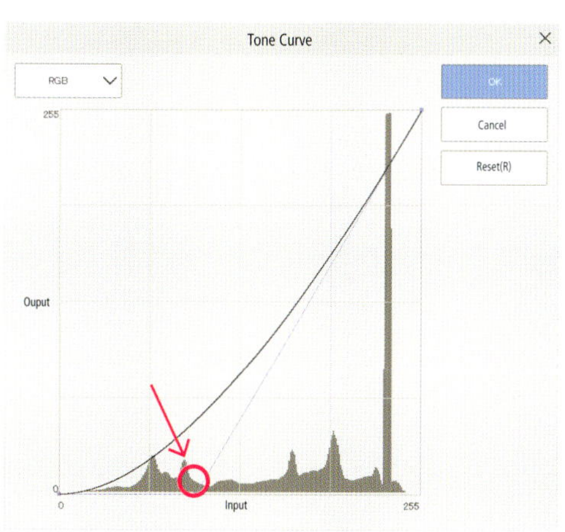


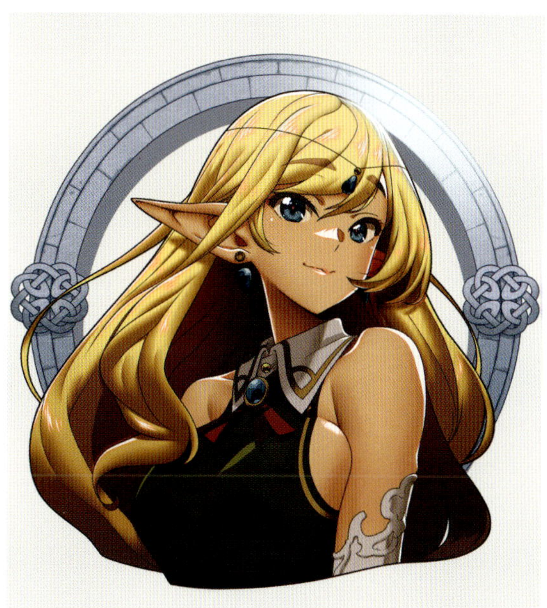

## When you want to increase contrast

Making the curve S-shaped increases the contrast.

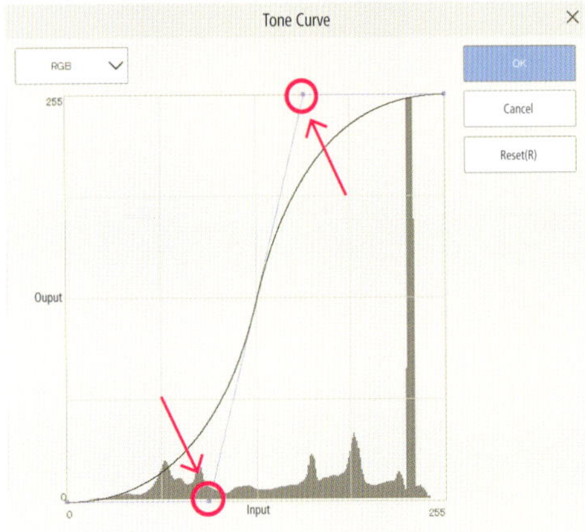
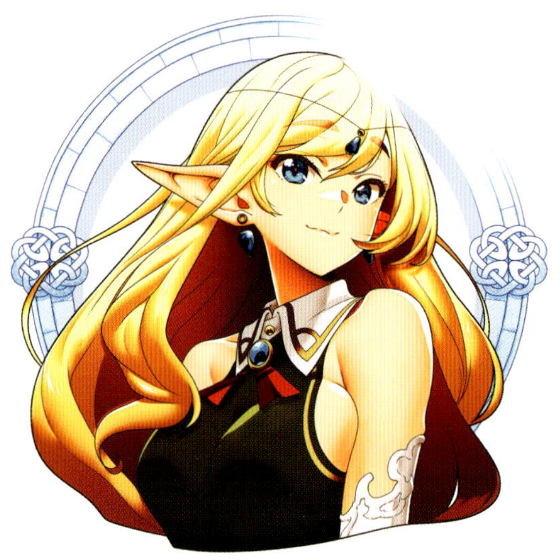

## When you want to decrease contrast

Making the curve inverted S-shaped decreases the contrast.

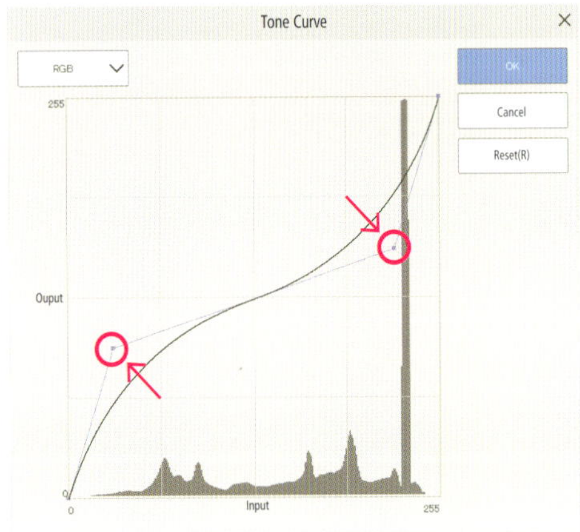
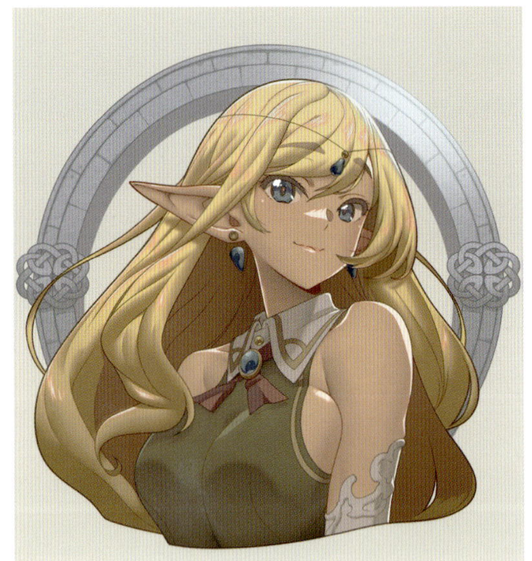

**When you want to adjust each RGB individually**

From the top left dropdown, select [Red], [Blue], or [Green] to make adjustments.

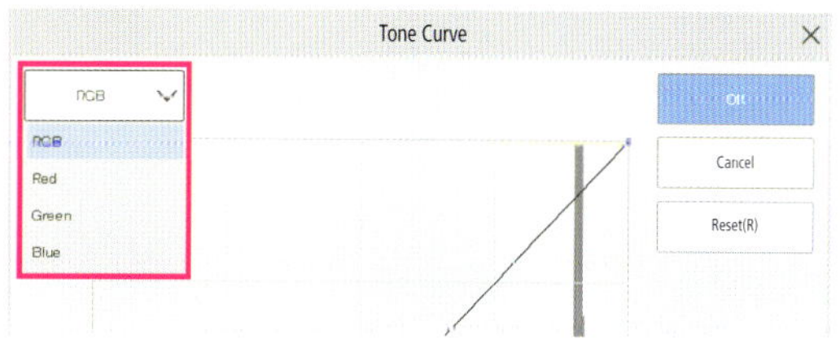

In the case of adjusting the level of blue, moving the control point up makes the image more blue.

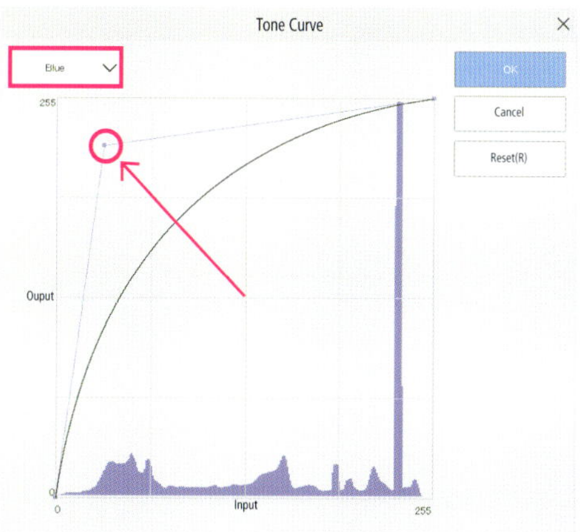

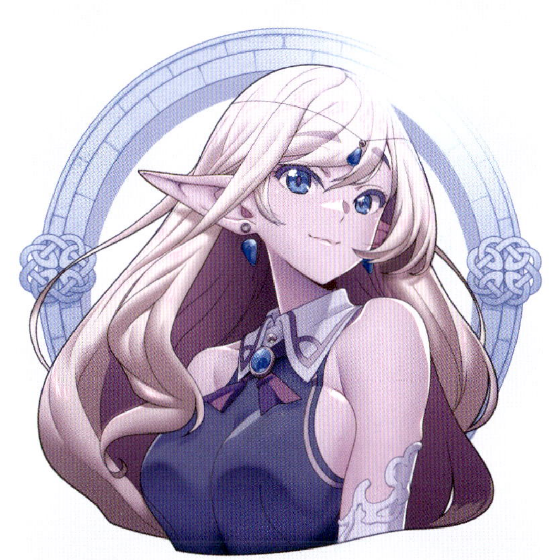

Moving the control point down increases the yellow tint, which is the complementary color of blue.

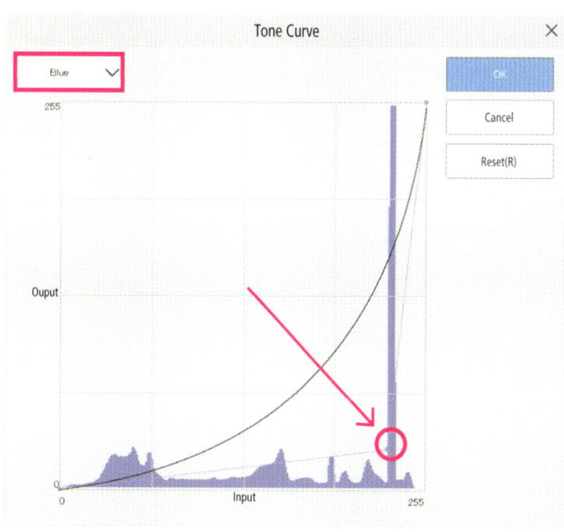

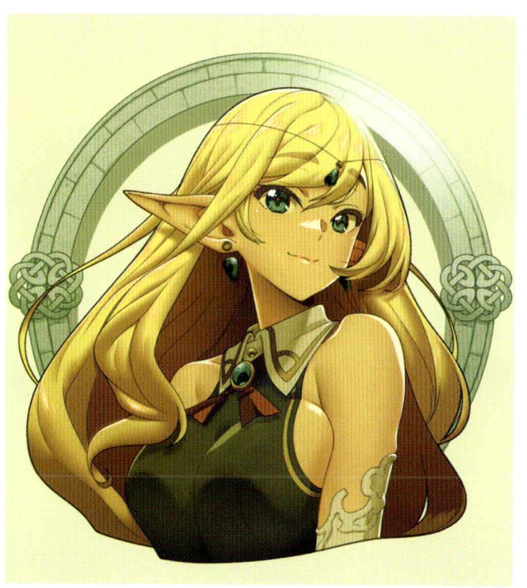

# Effective Finishing Processes

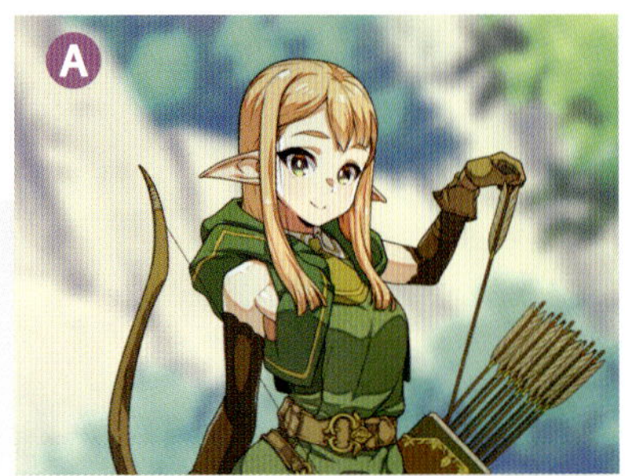

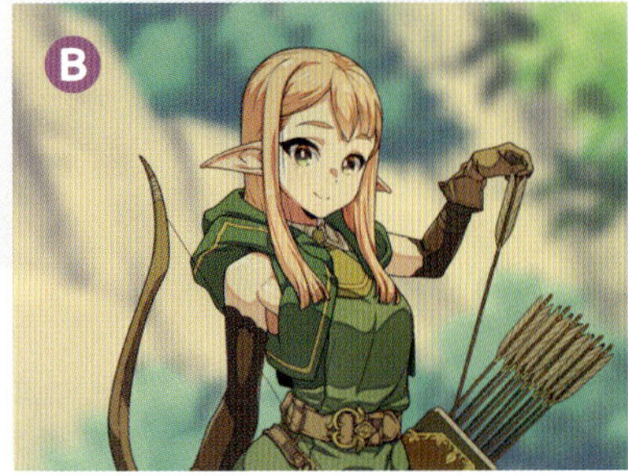

## Which gives a retro impression?

Is it **A** or **B**? Doesn't **B** look more like an old-fashioned retro illustration? **A** is the one that has been painted, and **B** is the one that has been processed to give a retro impression. In this way, you can change the impression by processing the completed illustration.

## "Nostalgic" Overlays

By adding a layer on top of the first layer of the completed illustration, filling it with a specific color and setting the composite mode to overlay, this technique can be used to add specific effects, such as altering the overall color tone of the completed illustration. Adjust the number of layers and opacity according to the situation.

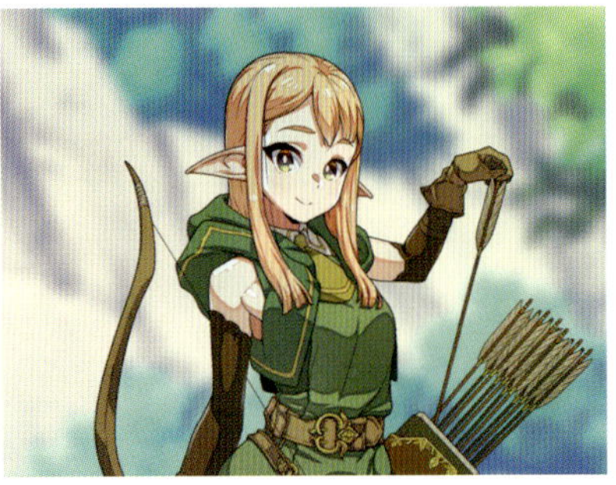

① Duplicate the completed illustration and merge it into a single layer.

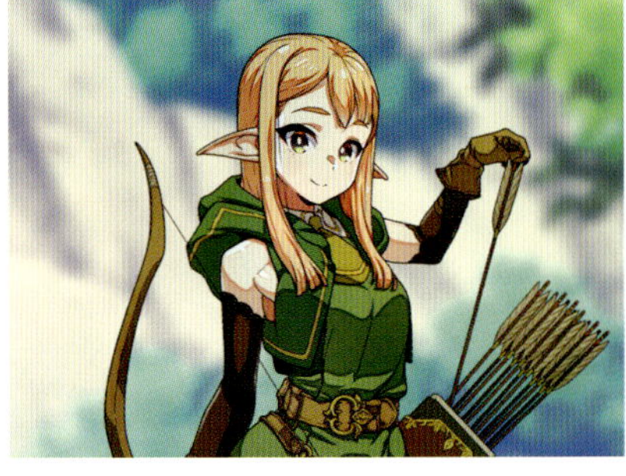

② Set the duplicated layer's Composite Mode to Burn-in Color and set the opacity to 20%.

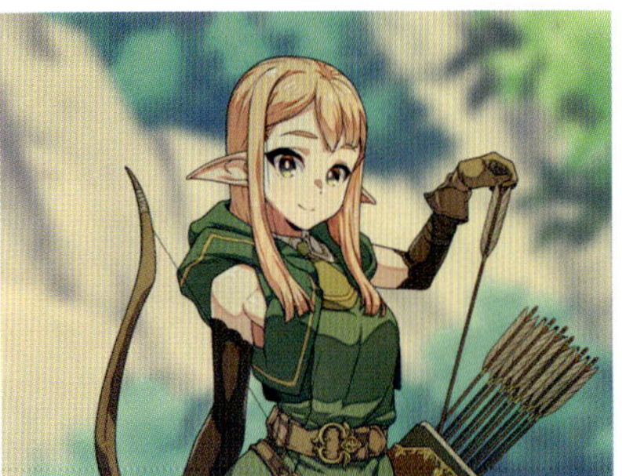

③ Create a new layer on top of (2) and fill it with blue. Set the composite mode to [Exclude] and opacity to 50% to complete.

R:43
G:93
B:204

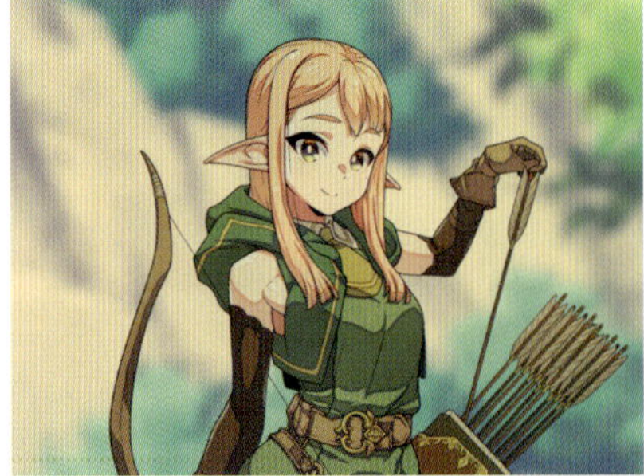

④ Setting the composite mode to [Overlay] in (2) will give a softer impression. Use different modes depending on the atmosphere you want to achieve.

# Backlighting for Emotional Moments

Backlighting refers to when light seems to emanate from or shine through the lines that make up a character's body. This technique can be used in a variety of situations and is effective for reminiscences, such as the nostalgia effect, as well as for scenes where characters are making a first or a dramatic appearance or for moments when you want to make a strong impression, such as emotional scenes. This technique is also used to enhance a character's physical appeal or to add a narrative to the illustration. It's also employed in situations where the light source is behind the subject or when a particular visual mood is the goal, such as an evening or nighttime scene.

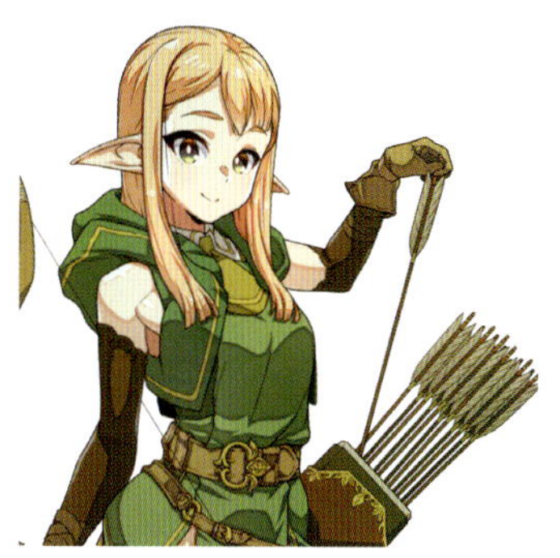

① Duplicate and integrate the completed illustration.

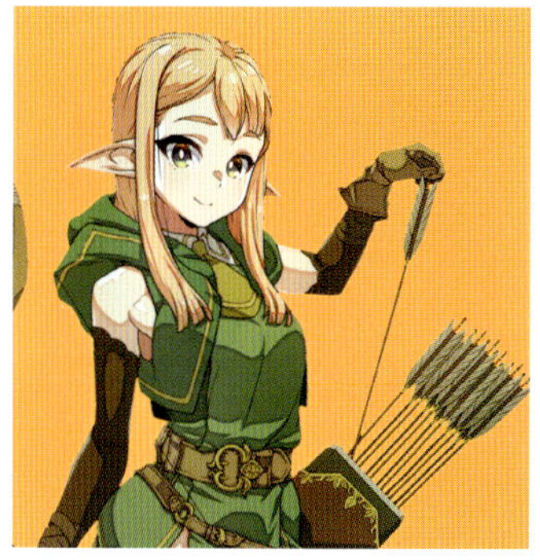

② Create a new layer and place it over the character. Select the outside of the character and fill it with orange. Duplicate and overlap the filled layer on top of the line drawing until a little color is added.

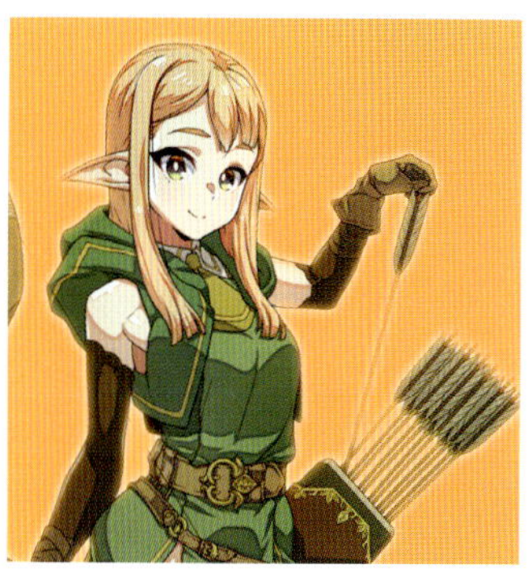

③ Merge the filled layer and the duplicated layer and blur them with Gaussian Blur.

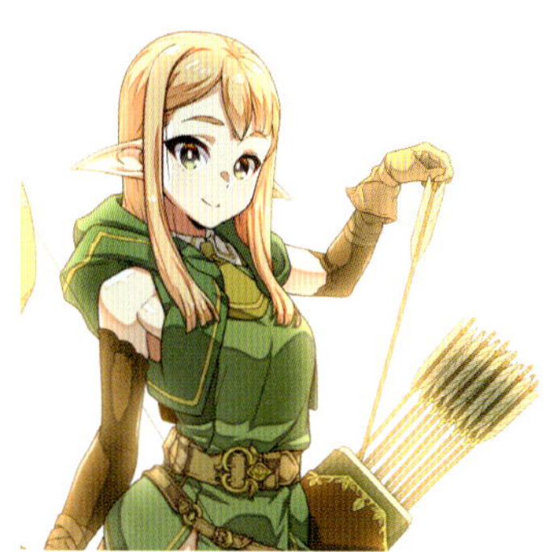

④ Set the composite mode of layer ③ to [Cover (Luminous)]. The same effect can be achieved with [Add (Luminance)].

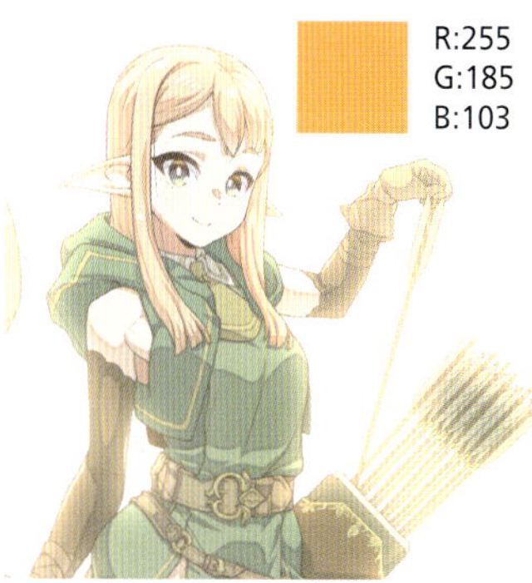

R:255
G:185
B:103

⑤ Create a new layer and place it on top of the character layer. Fill it with white and set the opacity to about 40%.

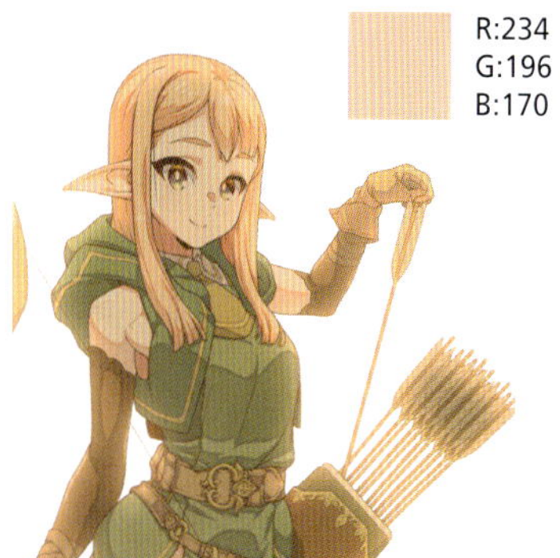

R:234
G:196
B:170

⑥ Create a new layer on top of 5. Clipping on the layer below, fill in orange and set the composite mode to [Multiply] to complete.

# Glow Effect

The glow effect, also known as diffusion, started being used in the 2000s when anime production went digital. It was used to soften the overly hard-edged quality of digital images, giving them a less rigid, more gentle appearance. By duplicating the finished illustration and changing the layer modes, you can make your illustrations appear softer and brighter as a result.

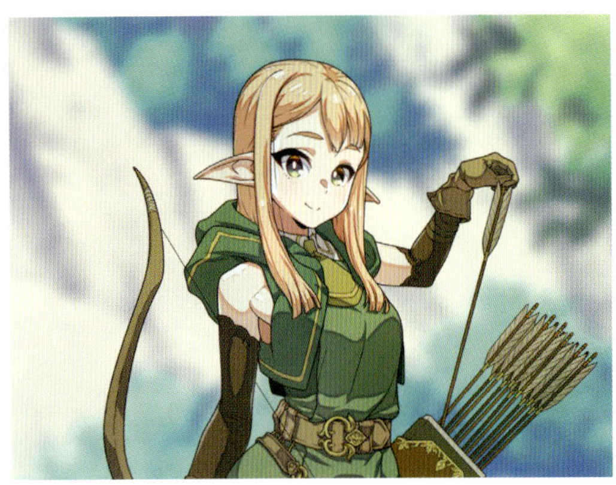

① Duplicate the finished illustration and merge the layers.

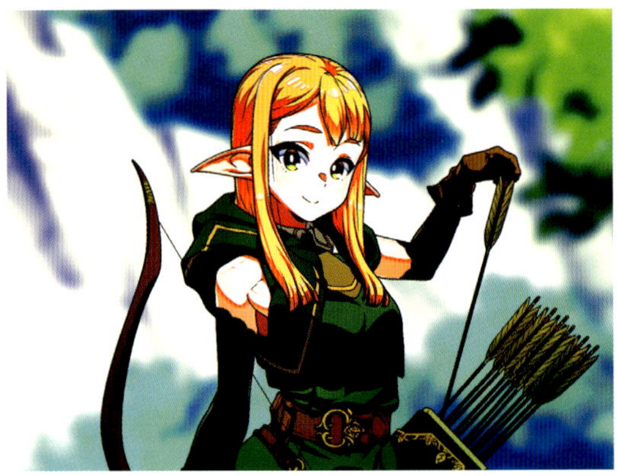

② Adjust the contrast of the duplicated layer by going to [Edit] → [Tone Correction] → [Brightness/Contrast] to increase the contrast.

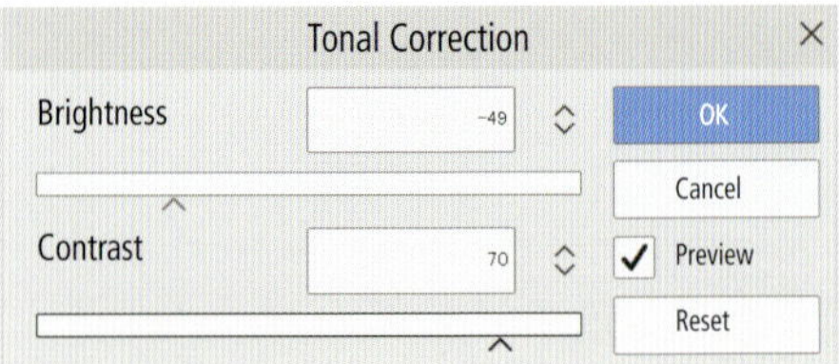


Adjust to make the brightness and saturation differences as clear as possible.

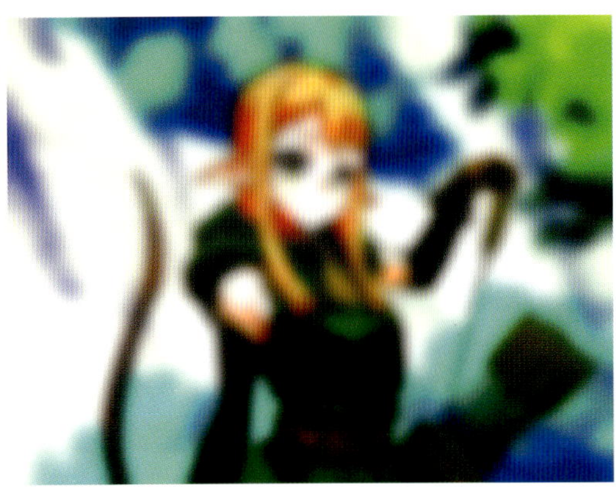

③ Blur layer ② with [Filter] → [Blur] → [Gaussian Blur] set to around 50.

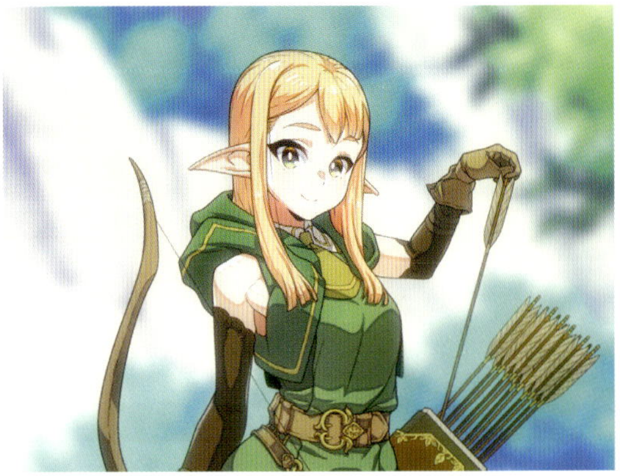

④ Set the blending mode of layer ③ to [Screen] and the opacity to around 40%.

You can switch the order of steps ③ and ④ and adjust the blurring and opacity to your preference.

# Color Aberration

Color aberration occurs when light passing through a lens disperses and causes color shifts in photographs. This technique, also known as RGB shifting, can be applied to illustrations to add information and make the final result more vivid.

① Duplicate the finished illustration three times, create a new layer on top of each, and set the blending mode to [Multiply]. Fill each multiply layer with RGB colors.

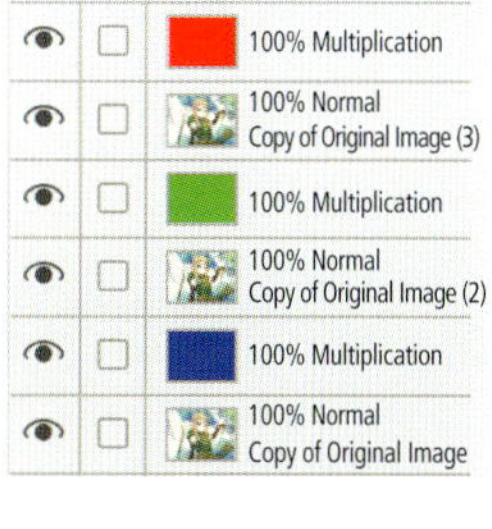

② Merge each multiply layer with the original image, set the top two layers to [Screen] blending mode and leave the bottom layer as normal.

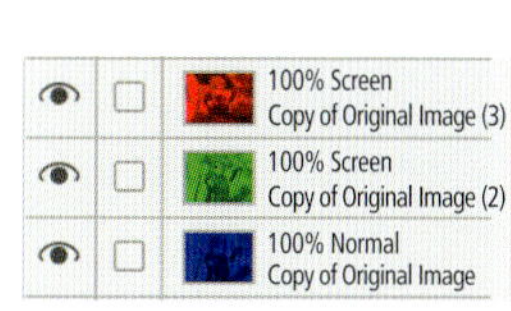

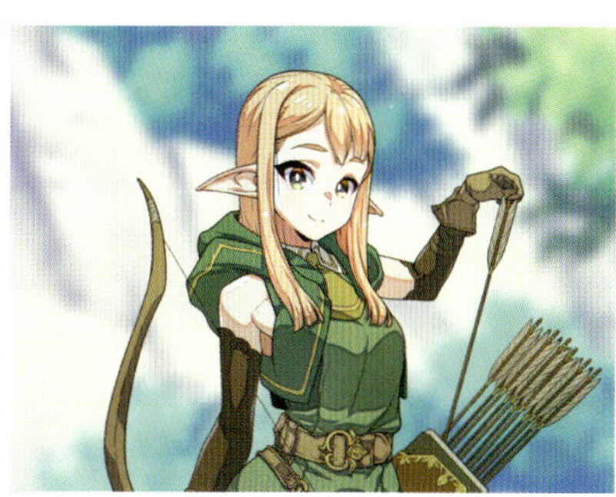

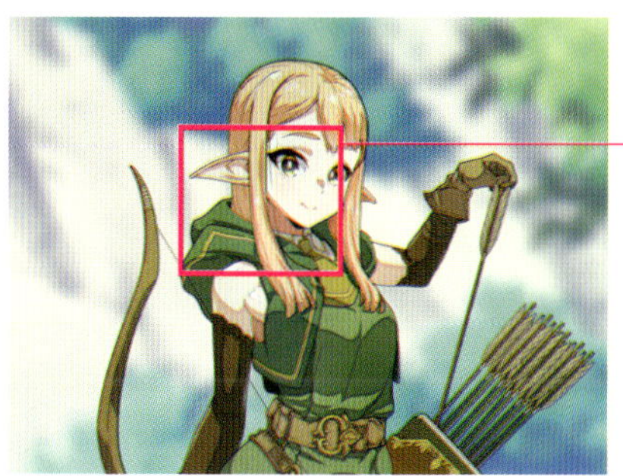

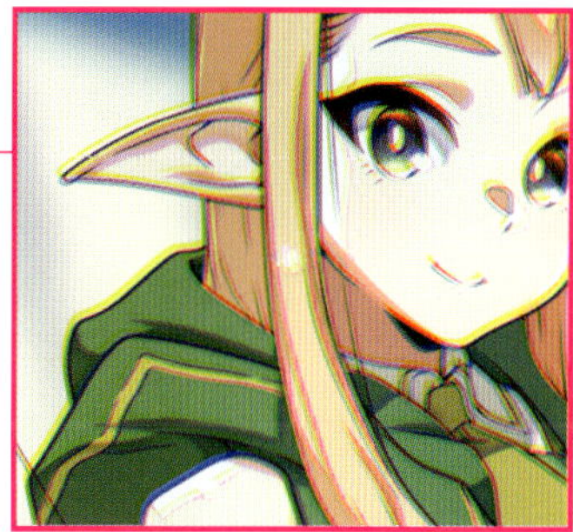

③ Shift the top two layers by a few pixels each to complete the effect. You can freely adjust the amount and direction of the shift.

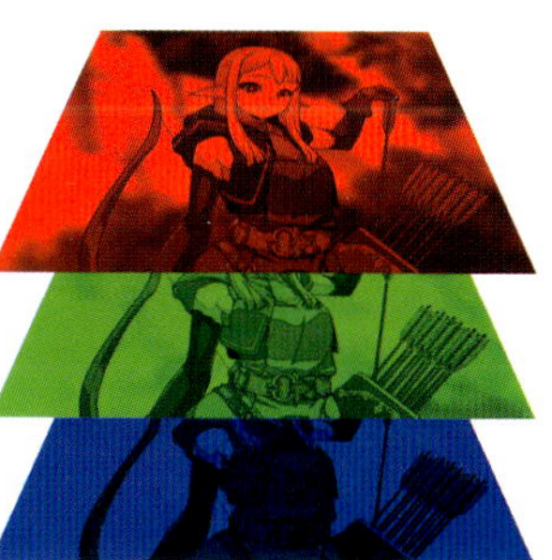




**Another phenomenon related to color aberration is purple fringing, where light reflects strongly around objects illuminated by strong light, causing a slight purple glow.**

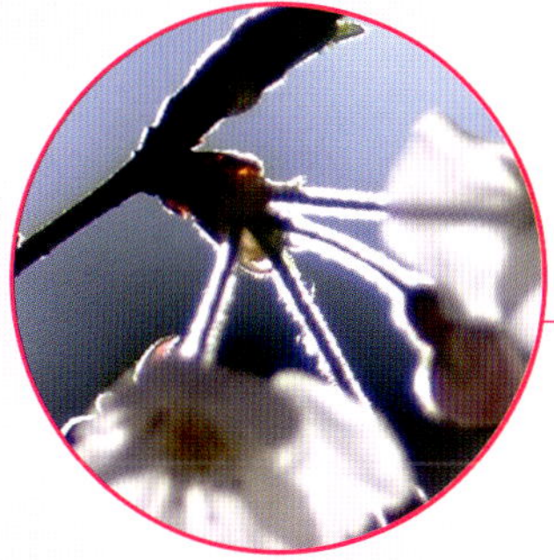

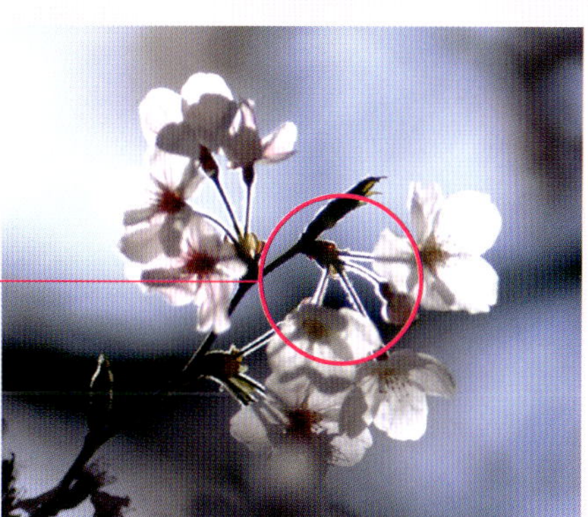

Purple fringing can be seen around the branches.

# Depth of Field

This technique adds a sharper sense of realism to an illustration by dividing the area to be blurred and the area shown clearly. This technique is derived from photography. When taking a picture with a camera, the image blurs as you move away from the area that's in focus. This area in focus is called "depth of field." Let's use the illustration on the right to process an image with depth of field in mind.

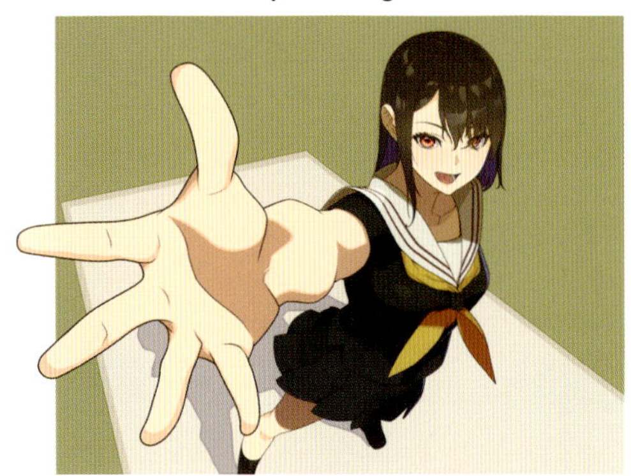



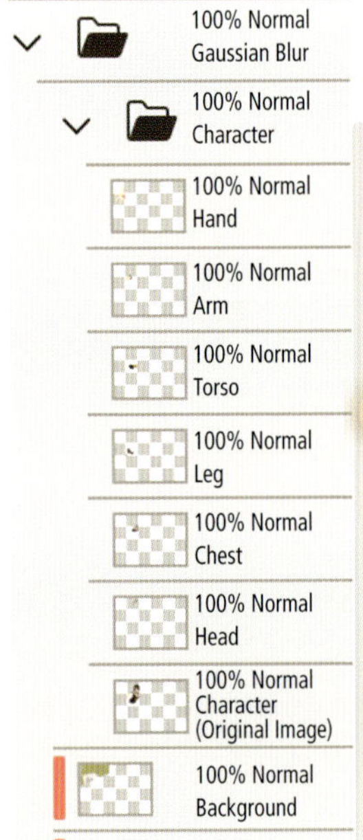



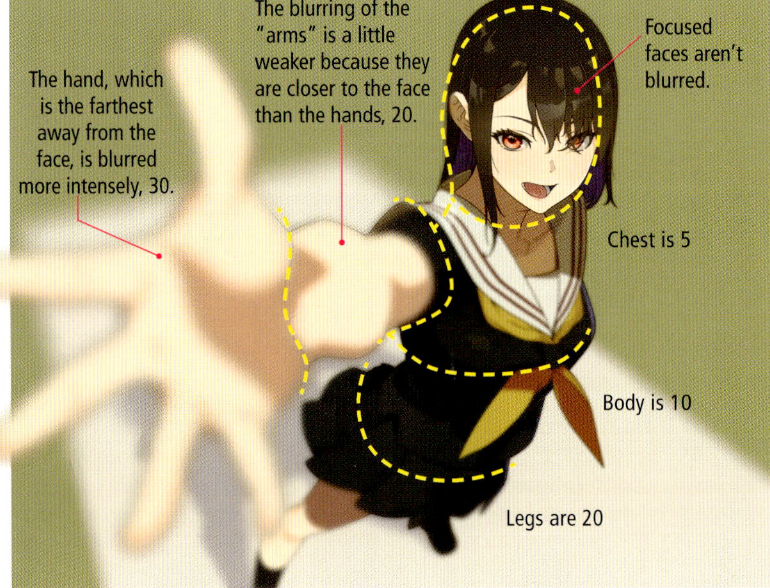



**①** It's fine to use a rough sketch, so separate the parts and put them on separate layers, keeping in mind the distance to the camera.

**②** Assuming that the face is in focus, no blur is applied to the face layer. Since the hand extending into the foreground, far from the face, is out of focus, the hand layer is strongly blurred using [Gaussian Blur]. The arm layer, which is closer to the face than the hand layer, is blurred less. In the same way, the blur value for the body and background is determined by the distance from the in-focus area. *The amount of blur depends on the illustration, so set the value to your liking.

> Depth of field refers to focusing only on the area you want to look at and blurring the rest.

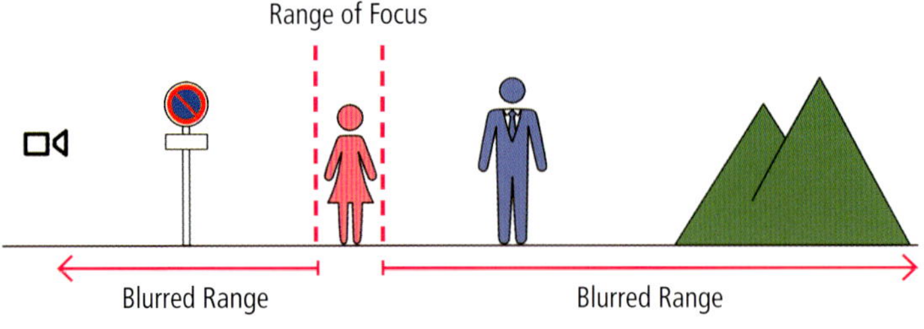



This phenomenon is more likely to occur with a dedicated camera than with a smartphone, so try using one.

# Using Perspective to Add Depth

Air perspective refers to the phenomenon in landscape photography in which the farther away an object is the more it's affected by the layers of air, resulting in a hazy blue or white color. By adding air perspective, a sense of distance and depth can be added. Although this phenomenon doesn't normally occur with people because of their close proximity, it can be used to create a more attractive illustration by increasing the amount of visual information it contains. Now let's process the illustration on the right.



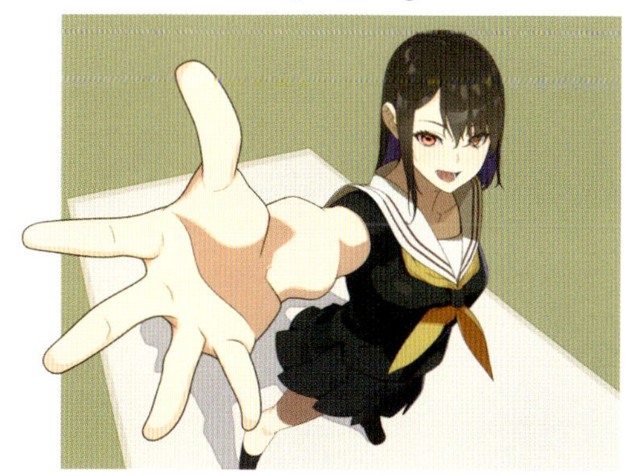

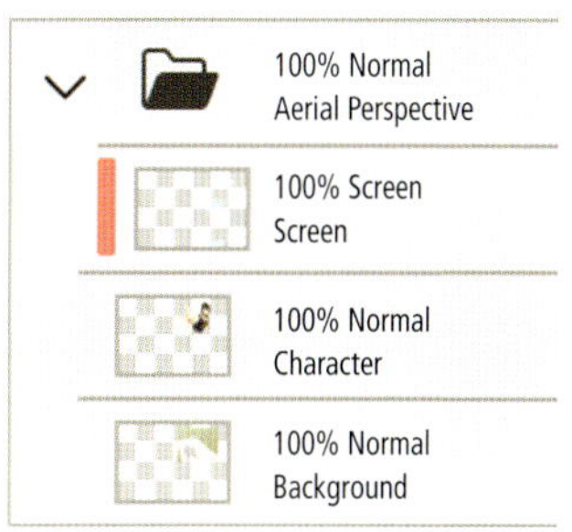



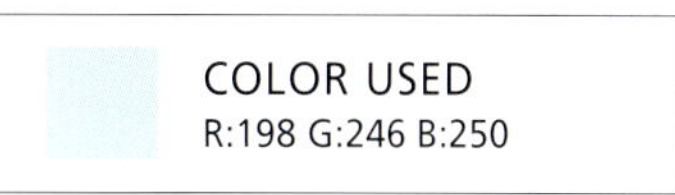



1. Create a new layer on top of the completed illustration and set [Clipping on the layer below].

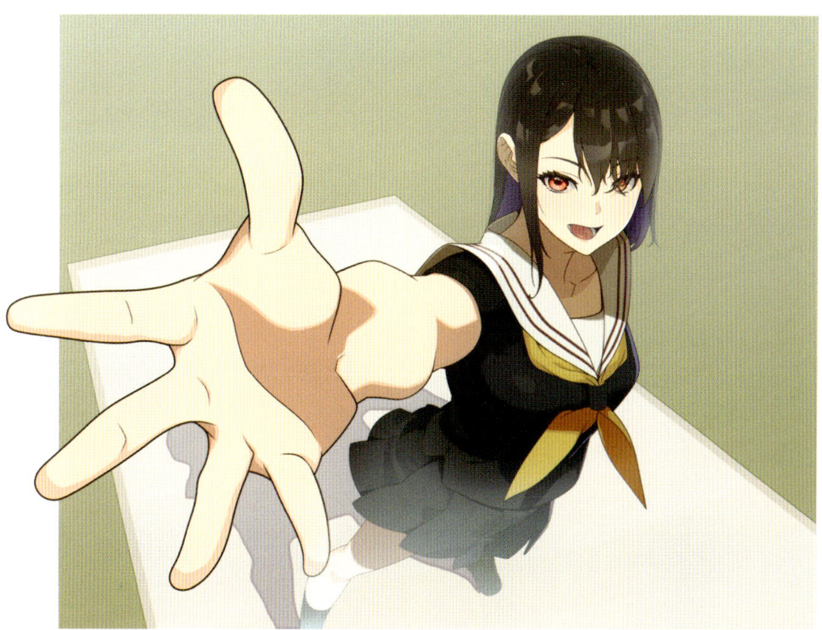

2. To direct attention to the face, put a light blue color on the area behind the face and set the layer's Composite Mode to [Screen] to blend it. The phenomenon doesn't actually occur at this distance, but the light blue color will make the eye focus on the face and hands you want to show.

**Now let's look at actual photographs demonstrating depth of field and aerial perspective.**

**Depth of Field**

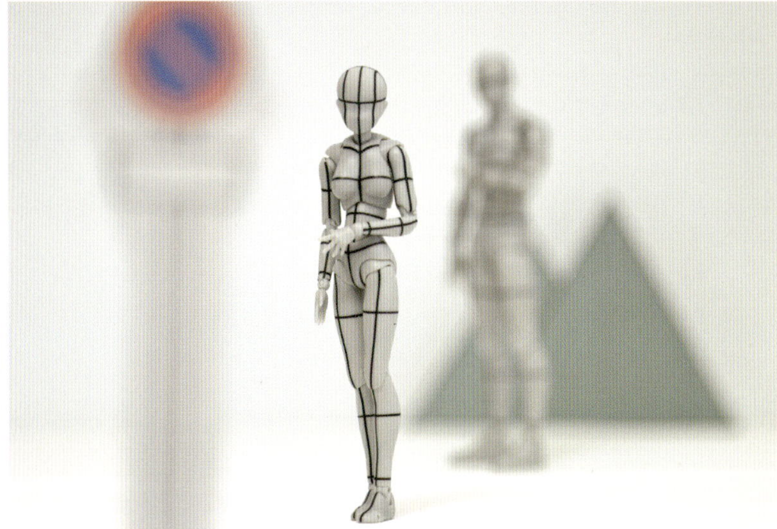

The focus is on the woman, causing the sign in the foreground to blur. Additionally, the man and background behind the woman become increasingly blurred as the distance from the woman increases. (https://tamashii.jp/item/13464/)

**Aerial Perspective**

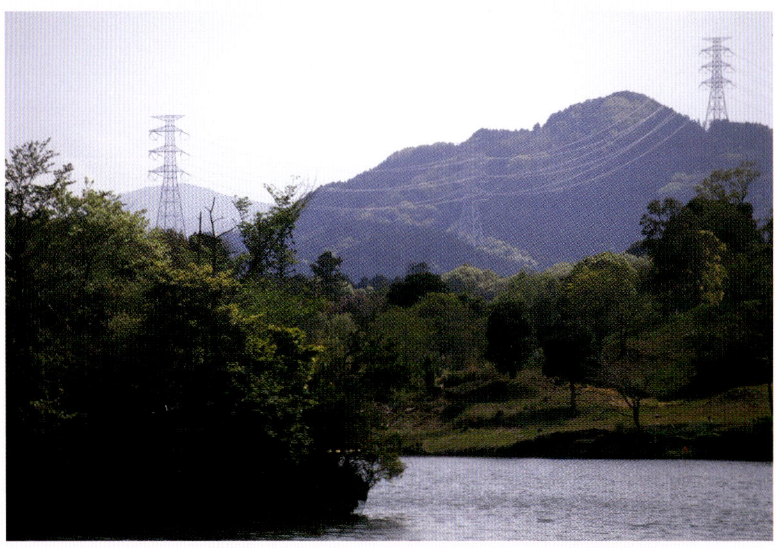

Objects farther away appear hazy due to changes in light wavelength caused by temperature and humidity. In reality, this effect requires a distance of several hundred feet to a few miles, but in illustrations, this technique is used to add depth and a sense of three-dimensionality.

# Guiding the Viewer's Eye with Saturation Differences

This technique involves lowering the saturation of areas you don't want to emphasize, thereby guiding the viewer's eye to the parts you want to highlight. Use an airbrush to apply color to the areas where you want to reduce saturation, then change the layer's blending mode to [Saturation]. Adjust the airbrush strength and layer opacity to tweak the saturation levels as needed. Let's apply this technique to the illustration on the right.

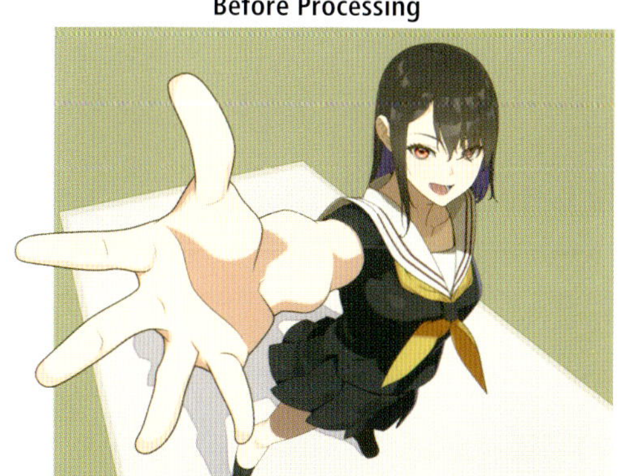


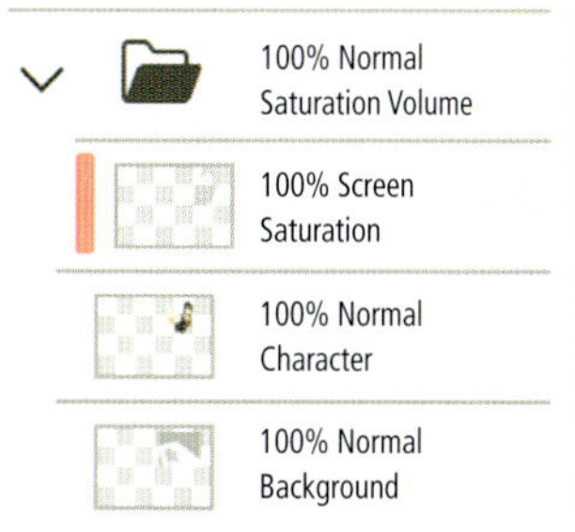


① Create a new layer on top of the finished illustration and clip it to the layer below.

Apply color using a soft brush like an [Airbrush]. You can also use filters like [Gaussian Blur].

Color Used
R:189 G:178 B:189

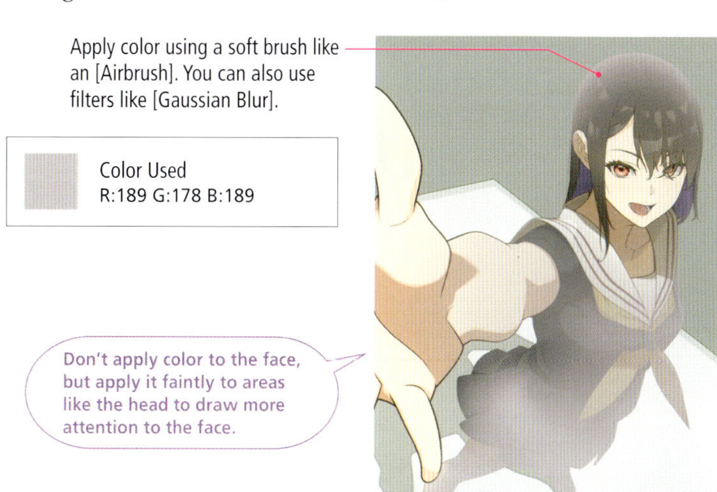


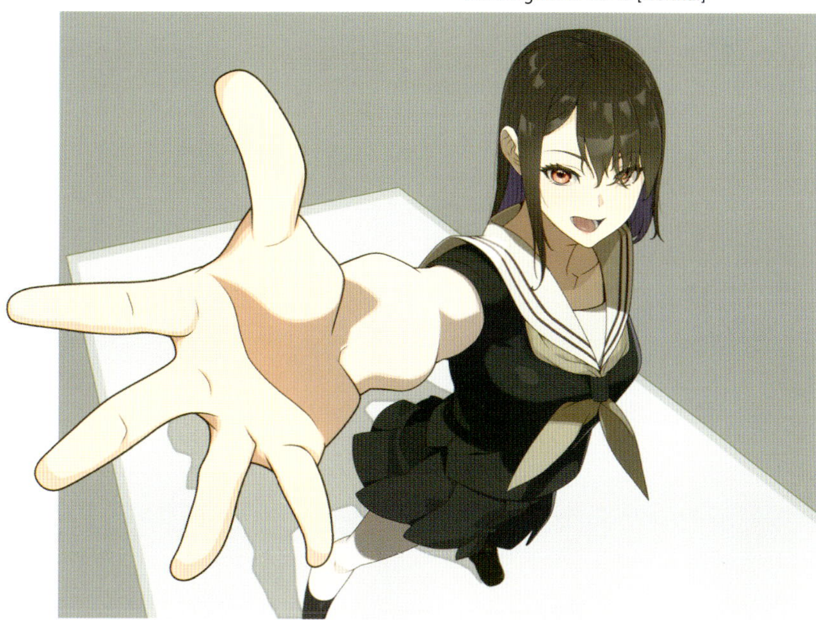

② In this case, we want to guide the viewer's eye from the hand and arm in the foreground to the face. Therefore, apply a low-saturation purple color to the other areas. By setting the layer blending mode to [Saturation], the saturation of the areas where color was applied will decrease, drawing the viewer's attention to the hand and face.

# Techniques for Creating Depth

## CREATING DEPTH WITH LIGHT AND DARK CONTRASTS

This technique is an application of aerial perspective (explained on page 103). In the example on the left, the character is emphasized by making the background hazy and white. In the example on the right, the background is emphasized, so the character is made hazy and white. By using lightness contrast to adjust the parts you want to emphasize and to express the depth to the background, you can clarify which element is the main subject of the illustration.

Increasing the brightness of the background
(from the river and farther back)

Increasing the brightness of the character
and the foreground

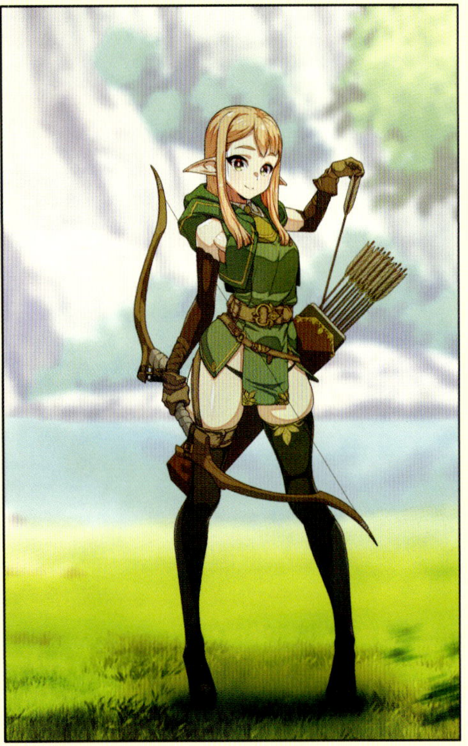

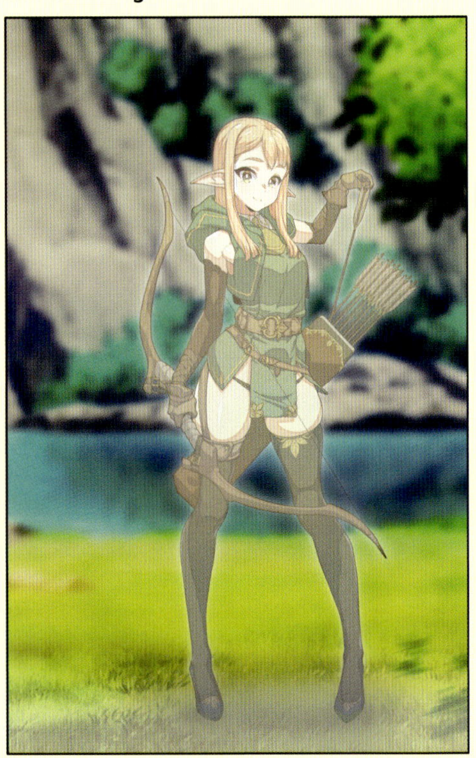

Draws attention to the person

Draws attention to the background

※ The effect is slightly exaggerated for clarity.

This can create the same effect as aerial perspective or depth of field.

## CREATING DEPTH WITH ADVANCING AND RECEDING COLORS

Look at the red and blue designs to the right. Doesn't the red appear to pop out while the blue seems to recede? Now try looking at the book or screen upside down. It will look the same, but red feels closer, and blue feels farther away. By applying a red filter in the foreground and a blue filter in the background, you can create a greater sense of depth in the image.

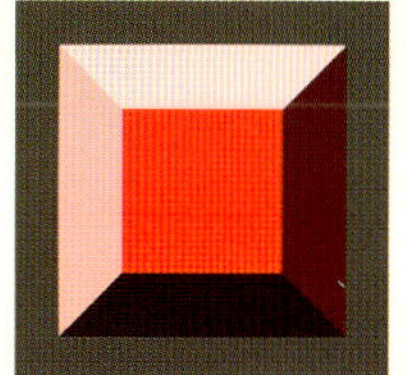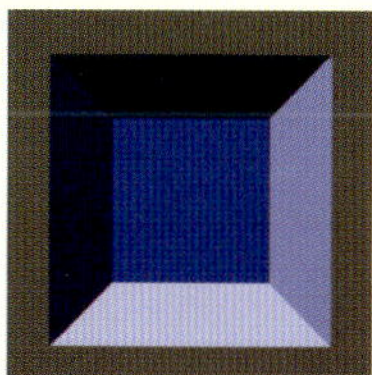

**Without filter**

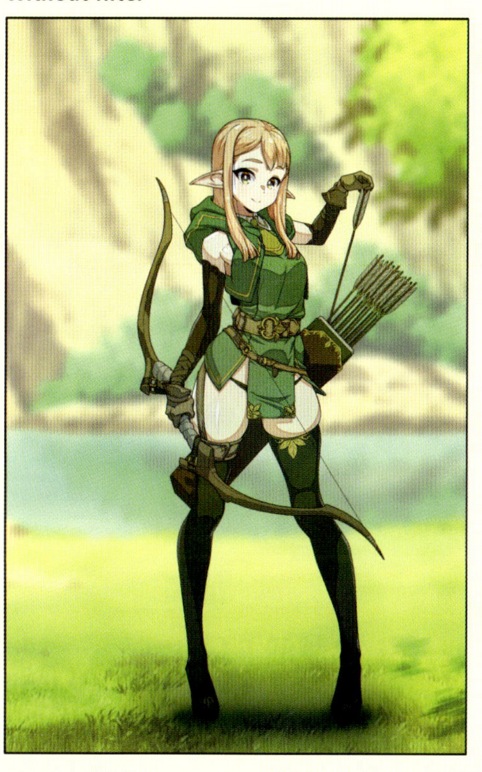

**With filter**

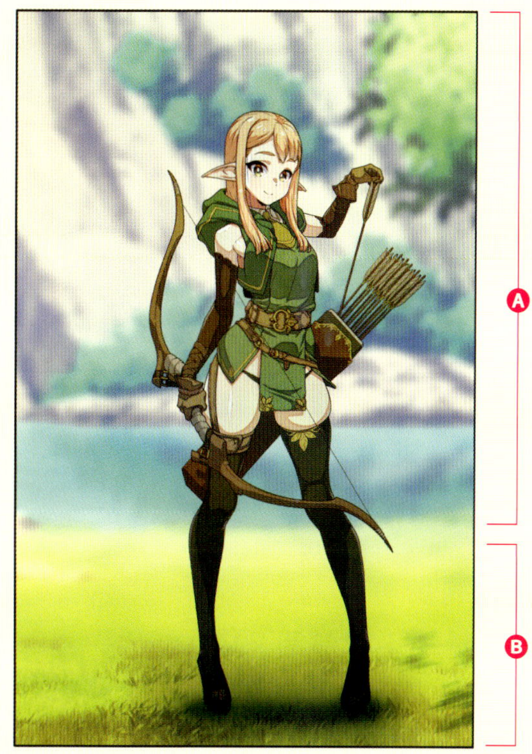

(A) Apply a blue overlay to the upper background.

(B) Apply a red overlay to the character and the lower background.

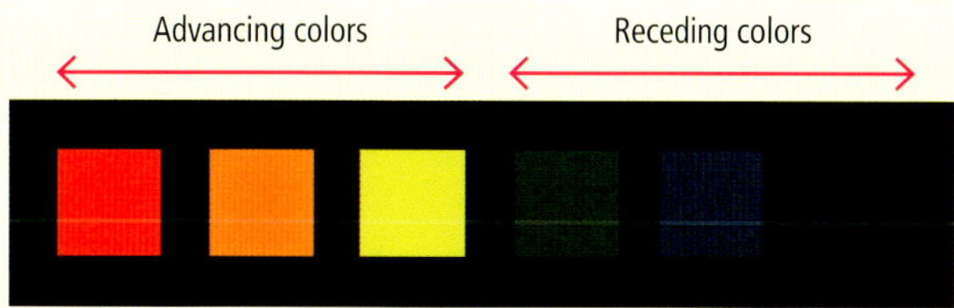


Additionally, warm colors, bright colors, and high-saturation colors are advancing colors, while cool colors, dark colors, and low-saturation colors are receding colors.

# "Pop" Dotting Technique

This technique can give your finished illustration a pop art feel. It's also used to intentionally add texture (weathering) when the finished artwork looks too monotonous. In drawing, the quality of the paper and the texture of the drawing materials affected the artwork, but in today's digital era, such influences have been eliminated, leading to the use of this technique.

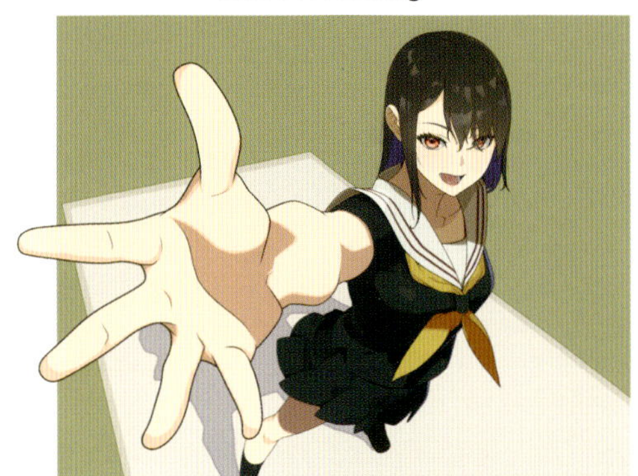
**Before Processing**

① Duplicate the finished illustration and convert it to a tone pattern from [Layer Properties]. For this example, a tone line count of 50 was used, but you can choose the line count based on your preferences.

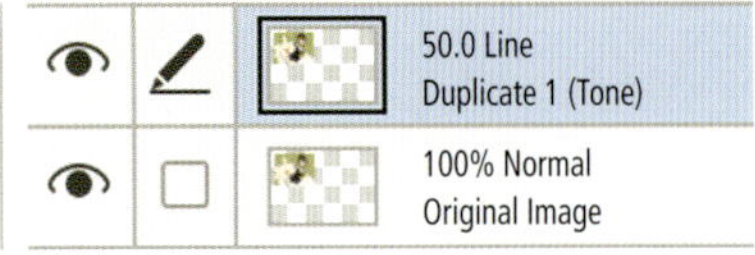

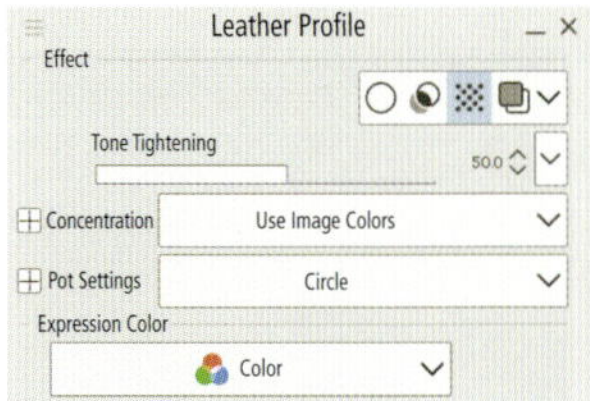


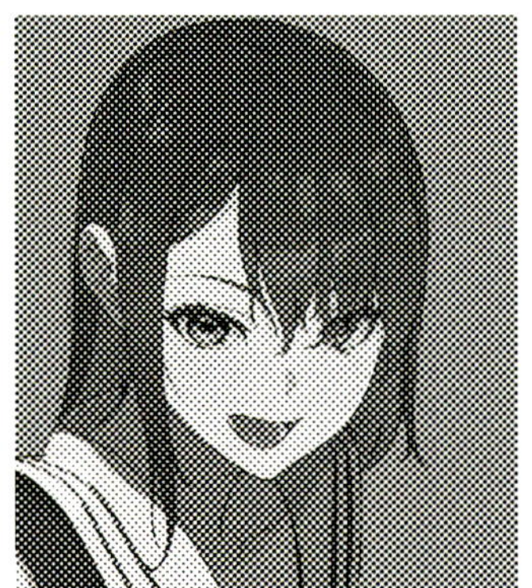

② Duplicate the finished illustration again and clip the layer to the one from step ① using [Clip to Layer Below], then merge the two layers.

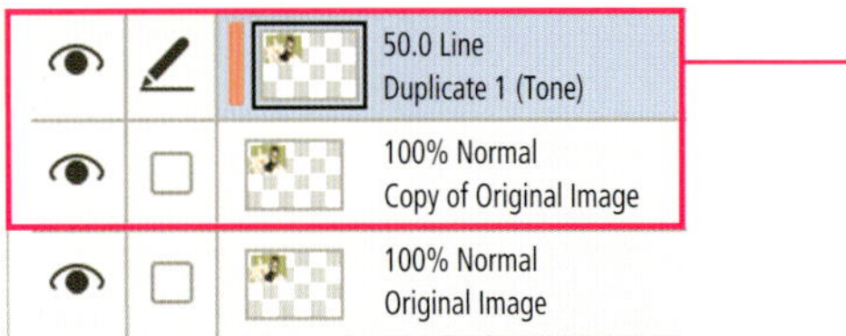


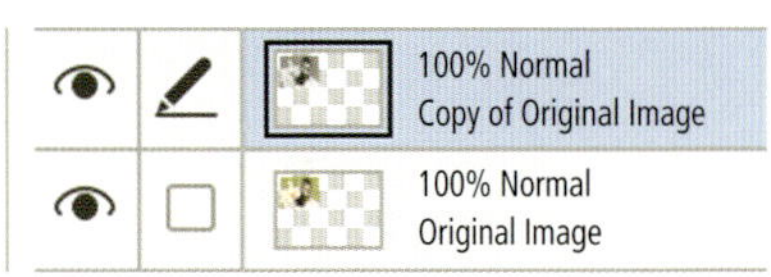


③ Set the blending mode of layer ② to [Add].

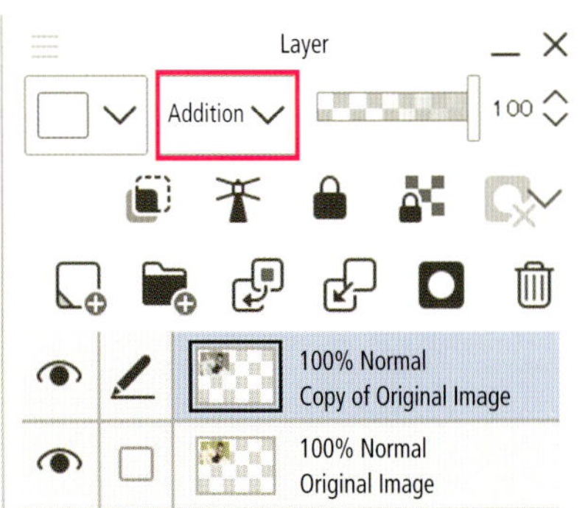


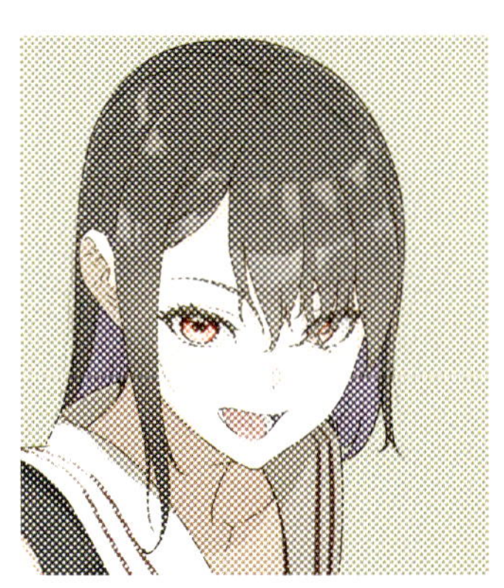

④ Change the opacity to about 15% to complete the process. Feel free to adjust the opacity to your liking.

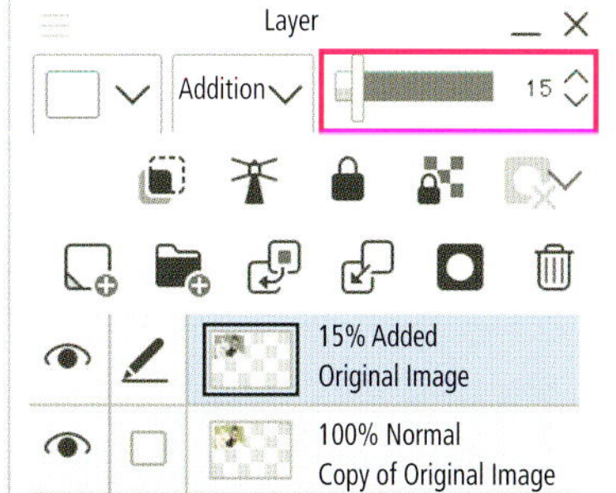



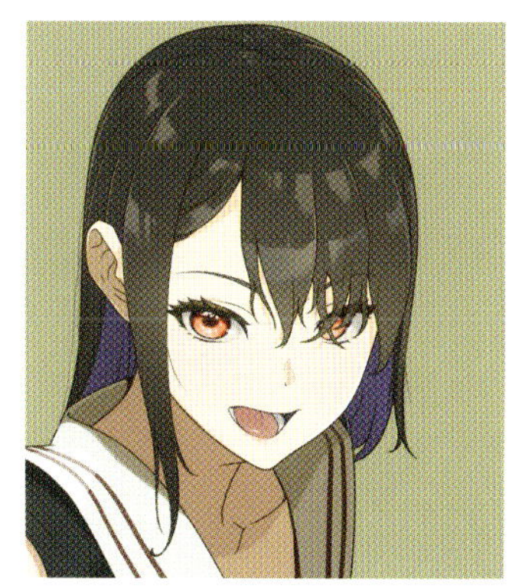

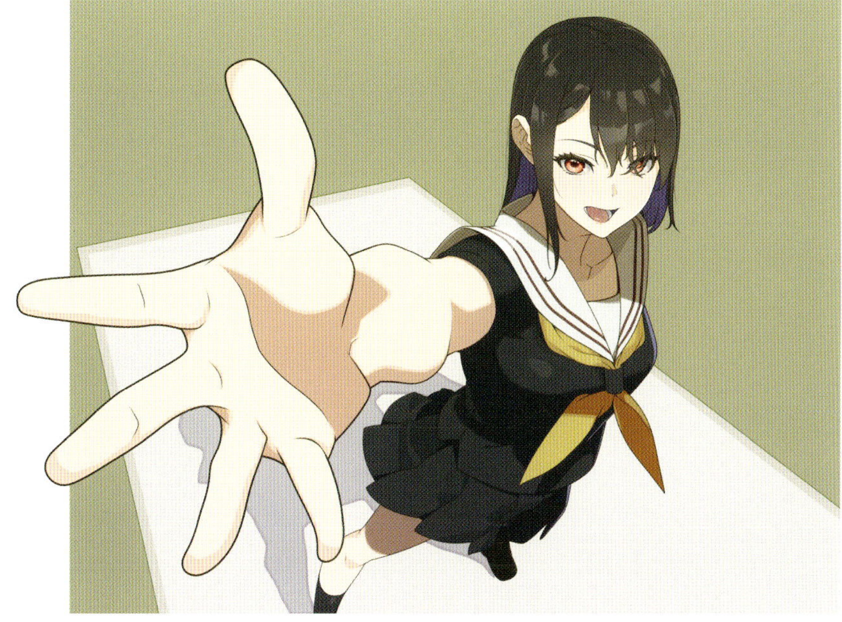

⑤ Complete

---



## ADJUSTING THE DOTS

When processing this way, dot patterns may appear on the face. If you don't want patterns on areas like the skin, adjust the brightness and contrast of the duplicated layer from step ① using [Edit] → [Tone Correction] → [Brightness/Contrast] until the skin becomes more pale, then apply the tone pattern. This will prevent the pattern from being applied to those areas.

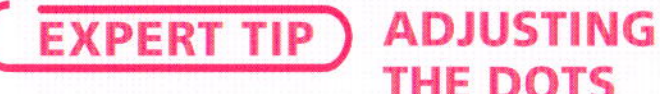

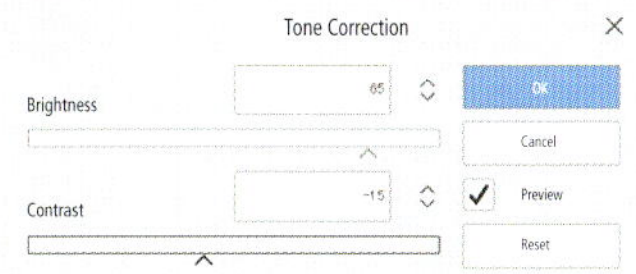


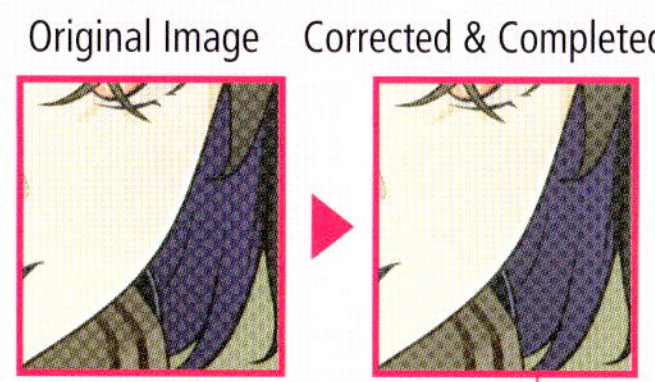
Original Image    Corrected & Completed

**Brightness/Contrast**

**Tone Pattern**

**Complete**

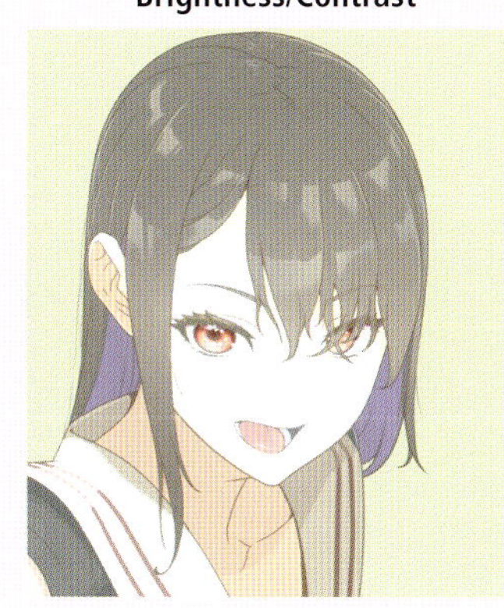

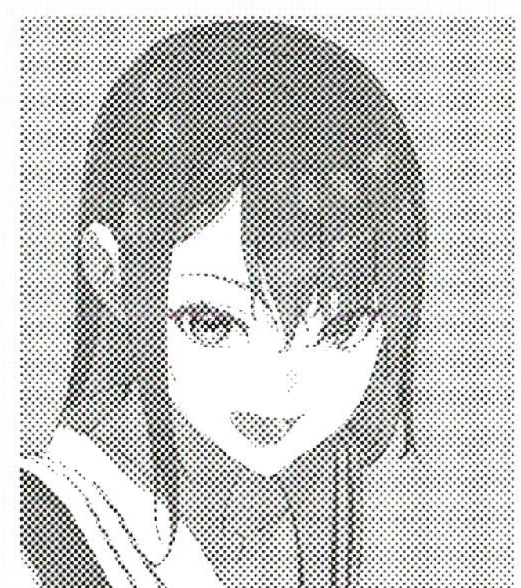

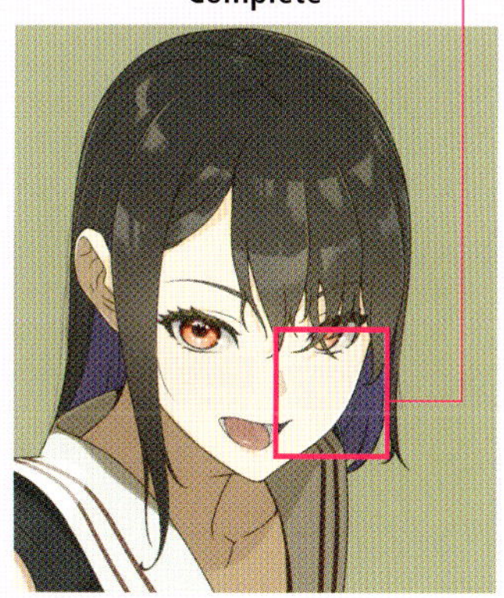

# "Retro" Vignette Effect

The vignette effect darkens the corners of an illustration. This effect is based on the phenomenon that occurs in camera lenses. Depending on the lens, the amount of light it can capture varies, or the amount of light captured is intentionally controlled. As a result, the corners of photos can sometimes appear darker based on the shooting settings, adding a retro impression. Vignetting is most effective when paired with strong blurring effects, so combining this with depth of field considerations (see page 102) can create a more compelling and cohesive illustration.

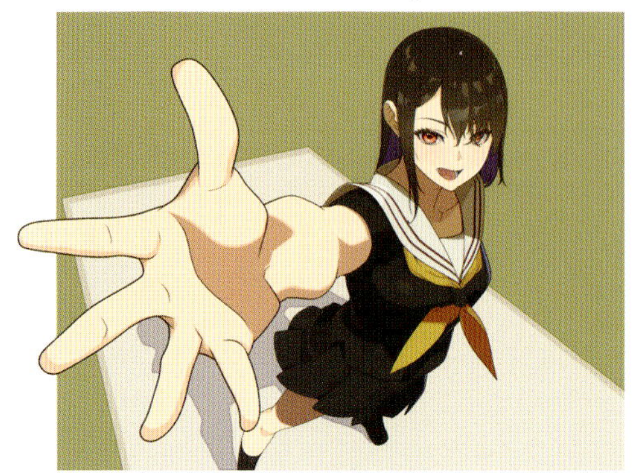

**Before Processing**

① Create a new layer on top of the finished illustration, and use the [Gradient Tool] set to [Radial] to darken the corners. In this example, the blending mode is set to [Overlay] with 100% opacity, but you can also achieve this effect with [Soft Light], [Multiply] or [Subtract], so feel free to experiment.

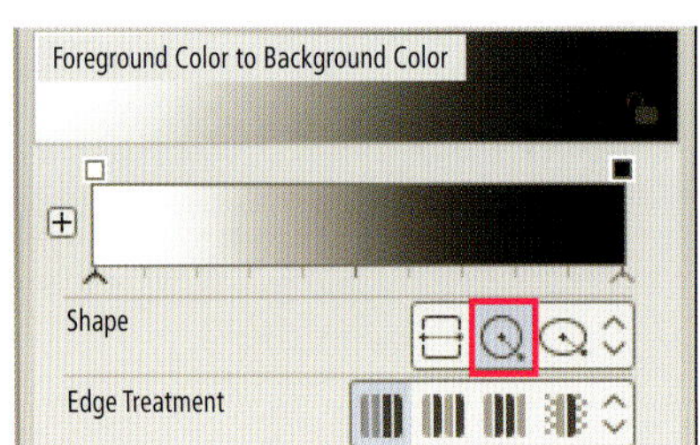

② To blend the effect with the illustration, duplicate the line art layer, apply [Gaussian Blur] with a value of 2.5 and set the layer opacity to around 50%, placing it on top of the original line art.

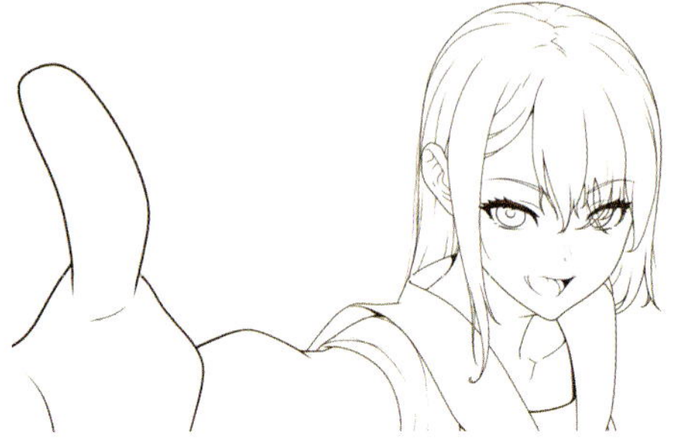

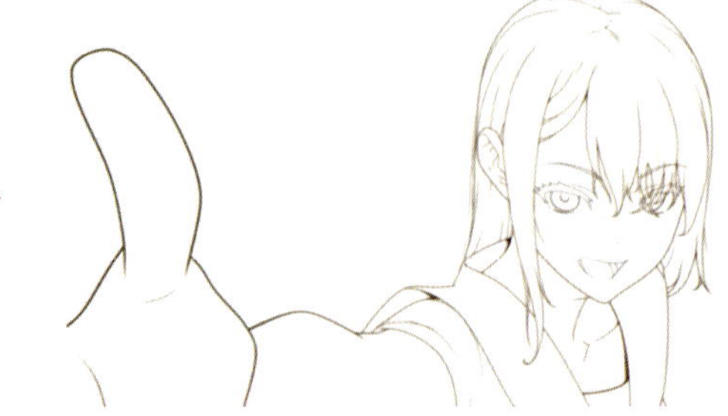

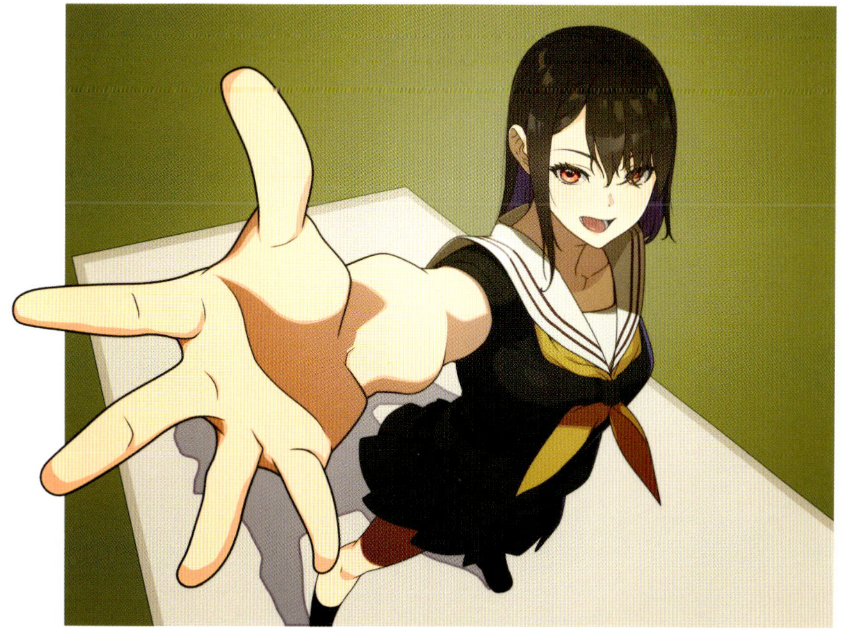

(3) Complete.
The dark corners and blurred lines enhance the retro feel of the illustration.

## Variations

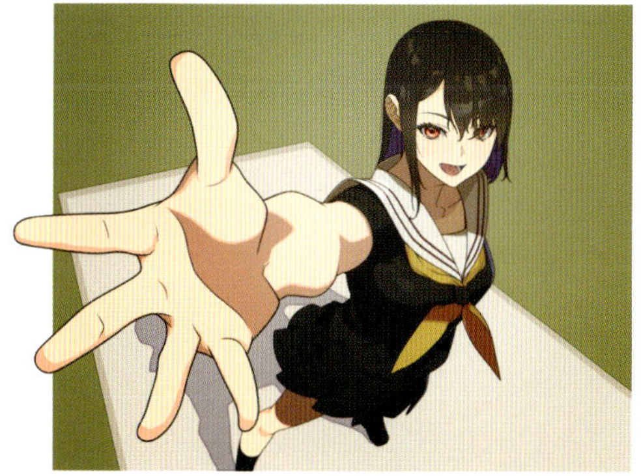

Blending mode: Soft Light

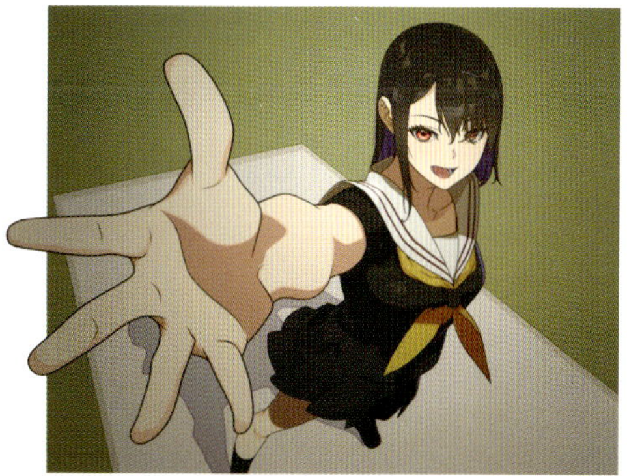

Blending mode: Multiply

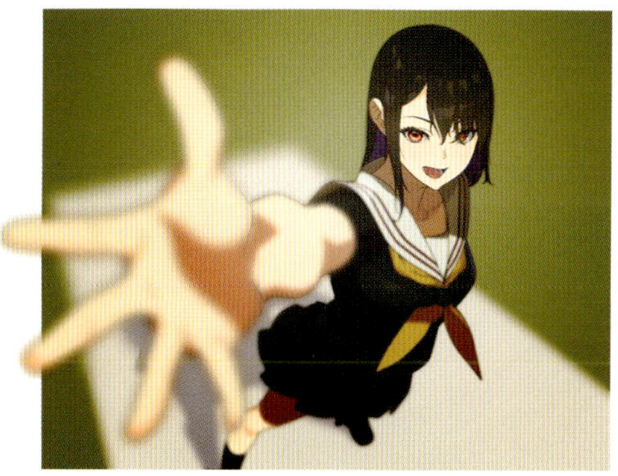

Combining depth of field with vignette effects.

## "Artistic" Toy Camera Effect

The toy camera effect mainly emphasizes the strong orange and blue tones, combined with vignette processing, to make the image look artistic, similar to photographs. The effect mimics the unique color tones often seen in cameras produced in the late 1980s in the former Soviet Union. These Soviet-era cameras frequently had design and manufacturing flaws, resulting in unique photo colorations. These flaws were eventually appreciated for their charm.

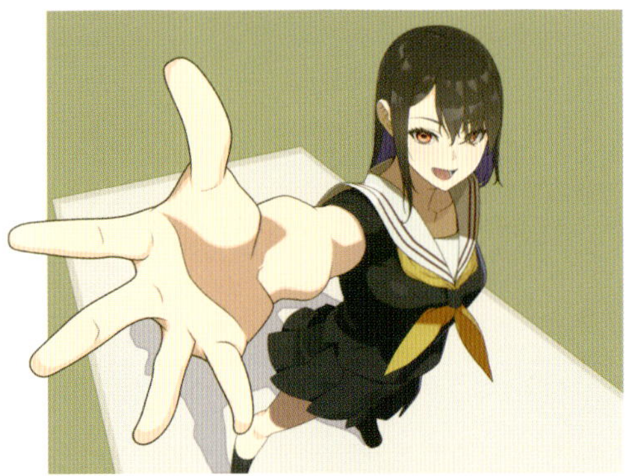



The process is simple. Duplicate the finished illustration, overlay it with a gradient layer, and change the blending modes.

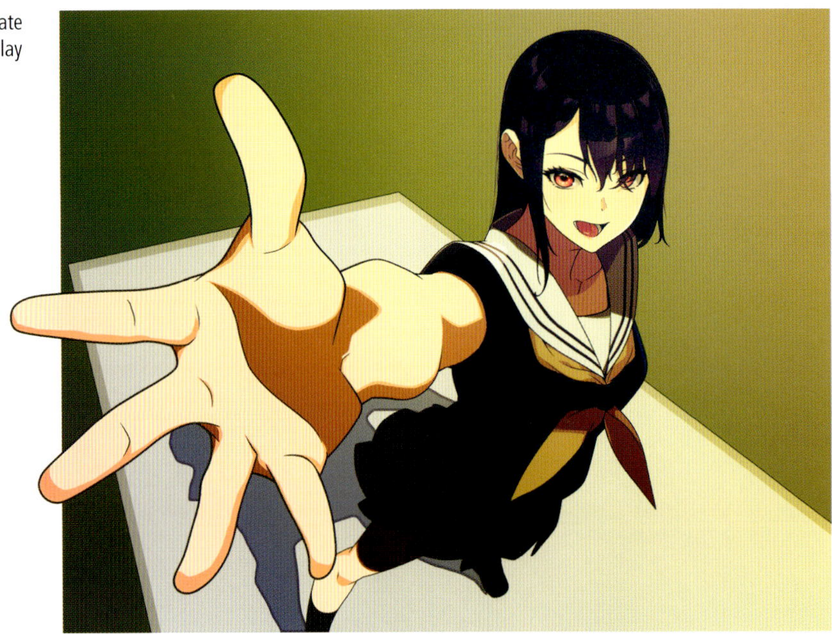

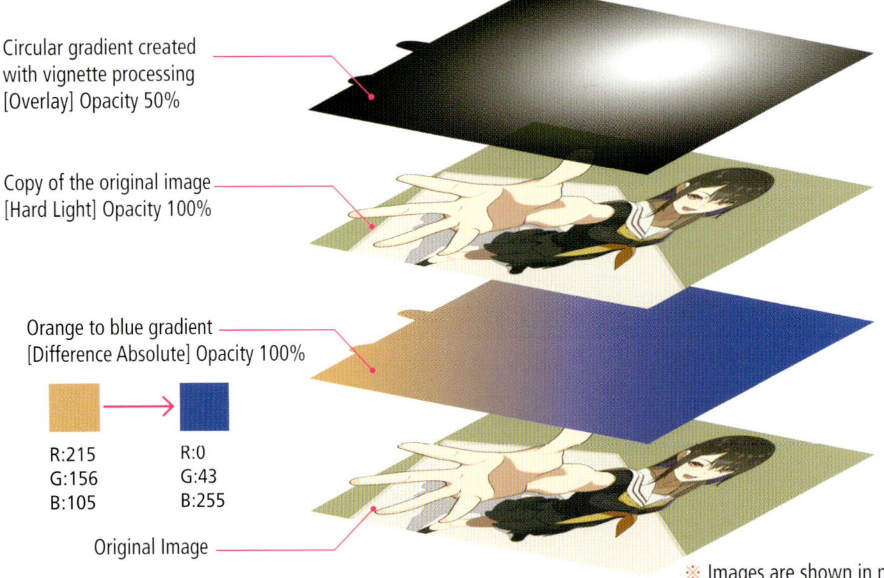



※ Images are shown in normal mode for clarity.

# Color Processing Using Gradients

On page 90, we looked at the method of unifying colors using overlay. Now let's take a look at color processing using the gradient map function. The gradient map replaces colors based on their intensity. This is explained on page 128, so here we'll introduce some variations in processing.

Create a [Gradient Map] on the finished illustration, set the blending mode to [Multiply] and the opacity to around 20%. Feel free to experiment with blending modes and opacity to suit your preference.

### Example using the [Sepia] effect
Gives a retro sepia tone impression.

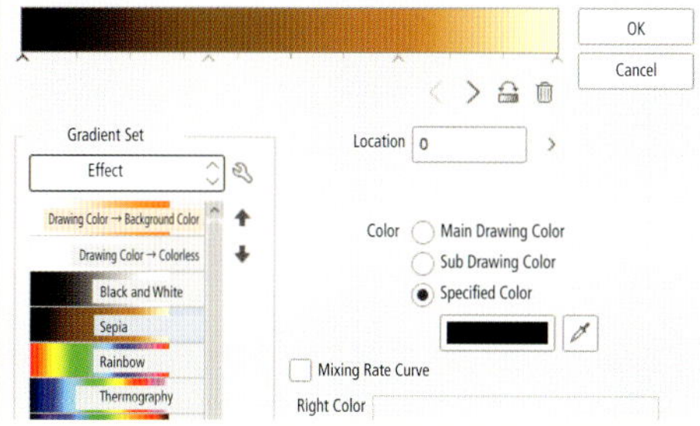

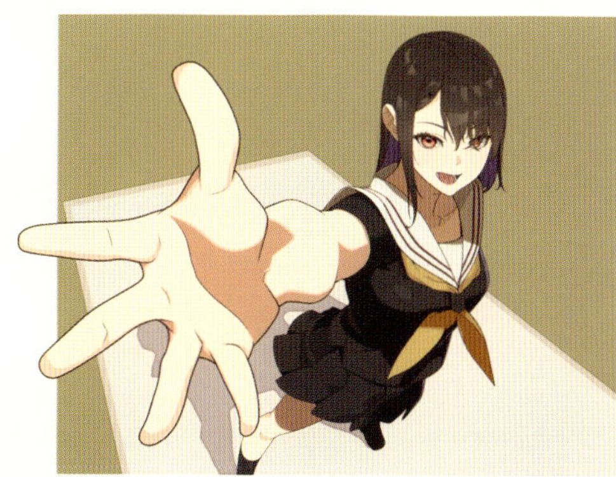

### Example using [Dusky Shadows] with [Dusky Shadows <Purple>]
Enhances the complexion, giving a look often seen in certain video games.

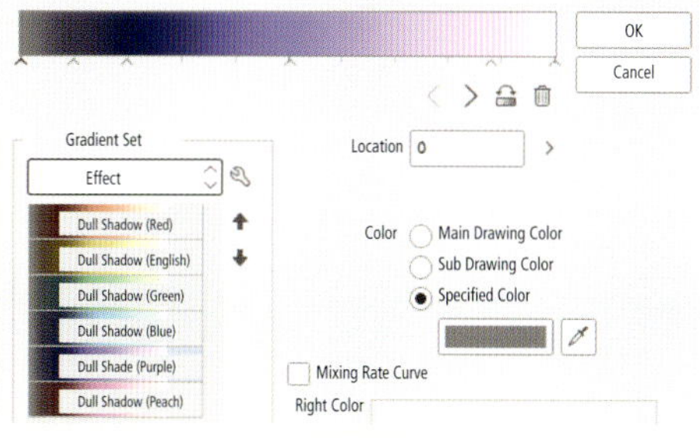

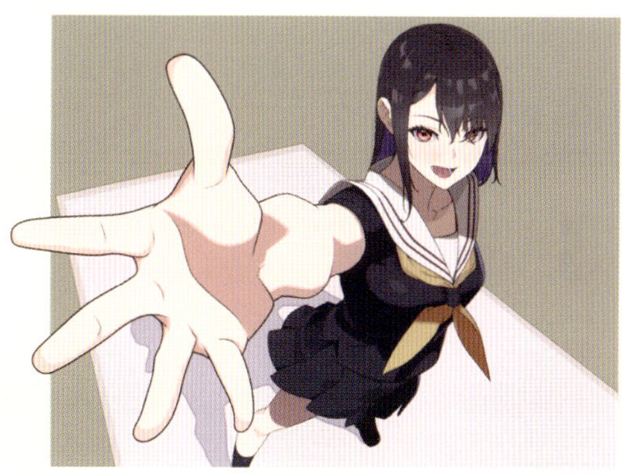

### Example using [Sky] with [Blue Sky]
Summarizes the image with blue tones, giving a refreshing impression.

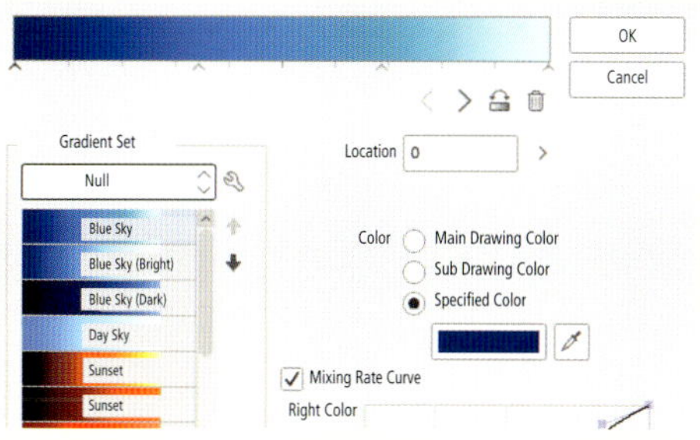

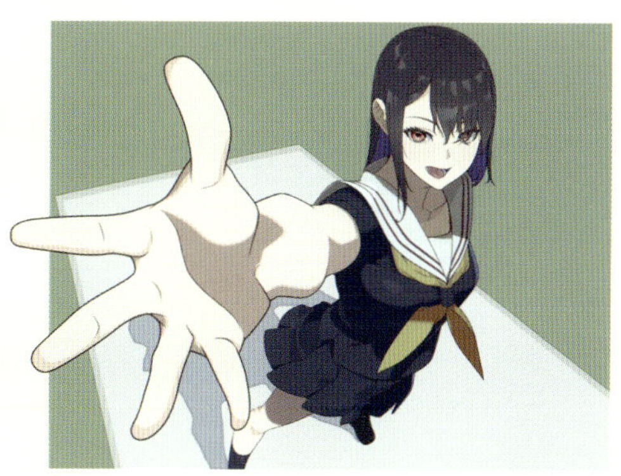

# Blending for a Softer Look

## Which one looks softer?

Doesn't **A** appear softer than **B**? The difference is that in **A**, the line art is colored, while in **B**, the line art remains black. Here, we'll take a closer look at a technique to adjust the line art to make the finished drawing look softer.

**A**
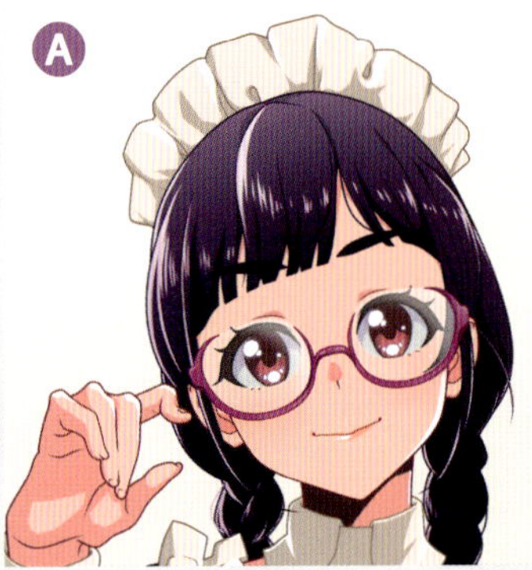

**B**
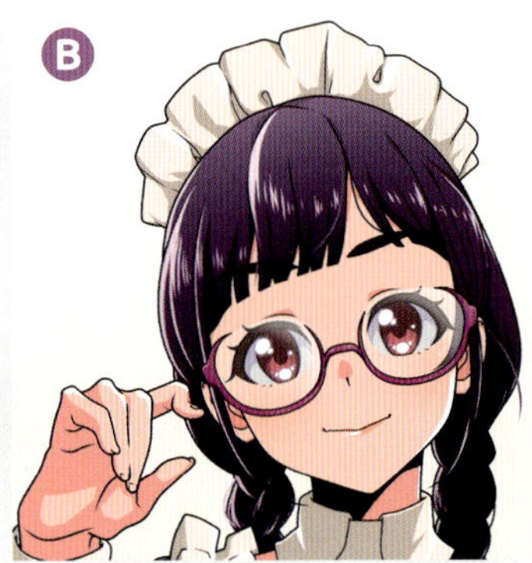

## Color Tracing

1. The illustration is complete, but the line art looks too sharp and somewhat stiff. Let's try color tracing this illustration.

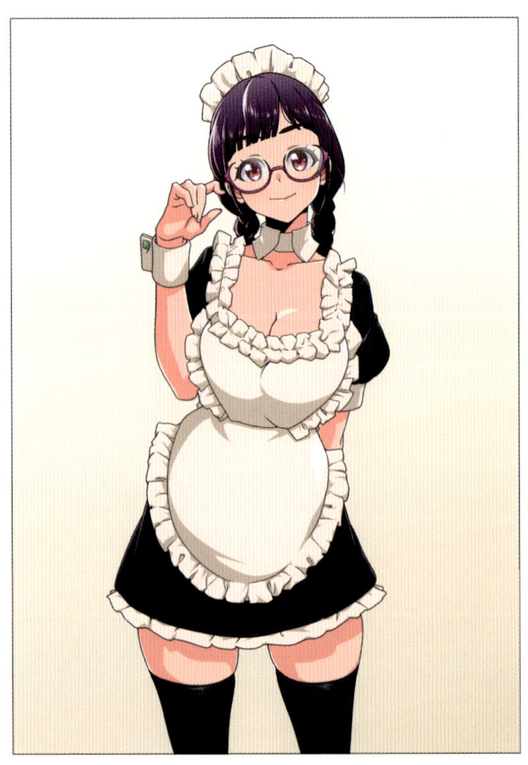

(2) Create a new layer above the line art layer (line art folder) and clip it to the layer below. Use the eyedropper tool to pick up the shadow colors of the parts near the line art, adjust the brightness and saturation, and paint over the line art with these colors.

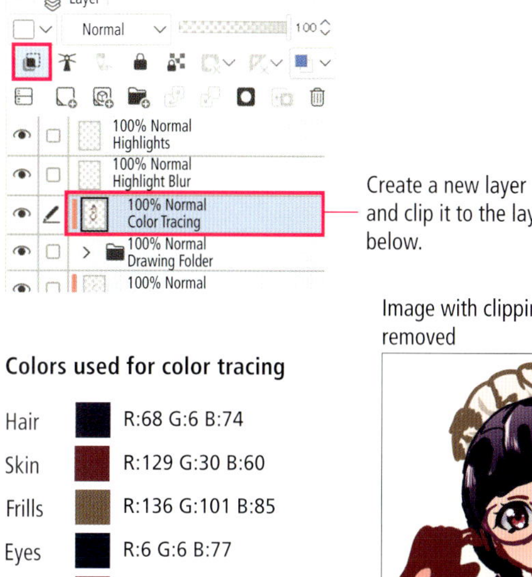

Create a new layer and clip it to the layer below.

### Colors used for color tracing

| Part | Color |
| --- | --- |
| Hair | R:68 G:6 B:74 |
| Skin | R:129 G:30 B:60 |
| Frills | R:136 G:101 B:85 |
| Eyes | R:6 G:6 B:77 |
| Glasses | R:125 G:6 B:89 |
| Cuffs | R:18 G:105 B:73 |

Image with clipping removed

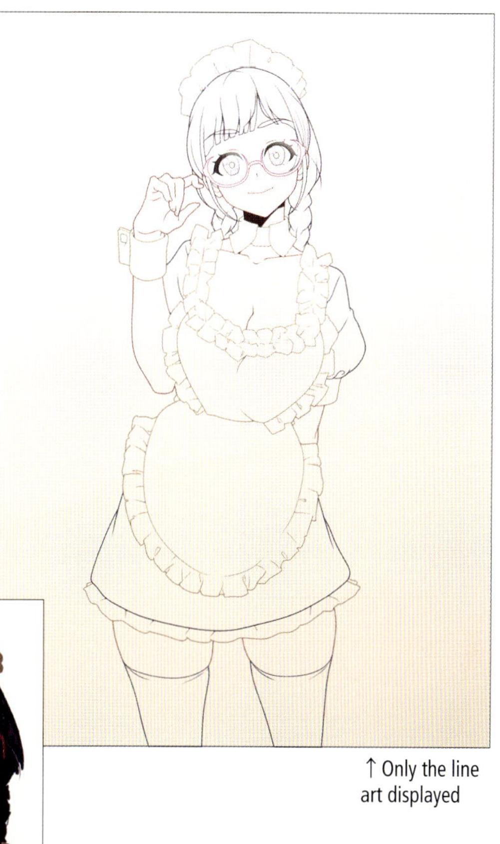

↑ Only the line art displayed

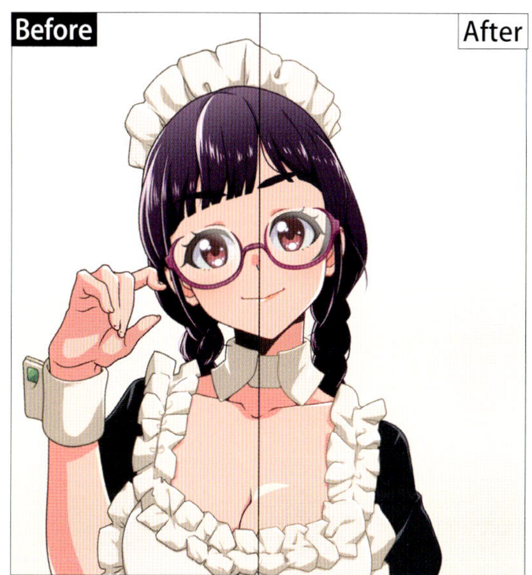



(3) By comparing, you can see that the overall finish looks much softer.

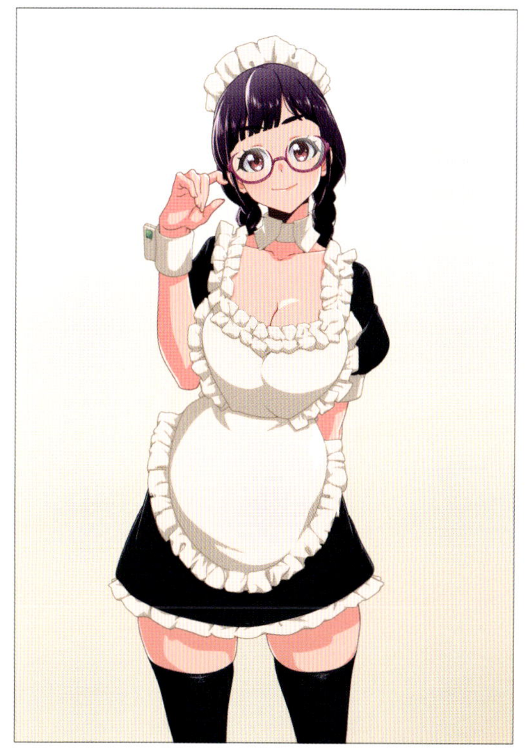

# Simpler Color Tracing

On page 114, we looked at selecting colors for color tracing. Now it's time for an even simpler method! Besides color tracing, you can increase the brightness of the line art (to make it gray) or draw the line art in dark brown or purple from the beginning. Try different methods to suit your particular style.

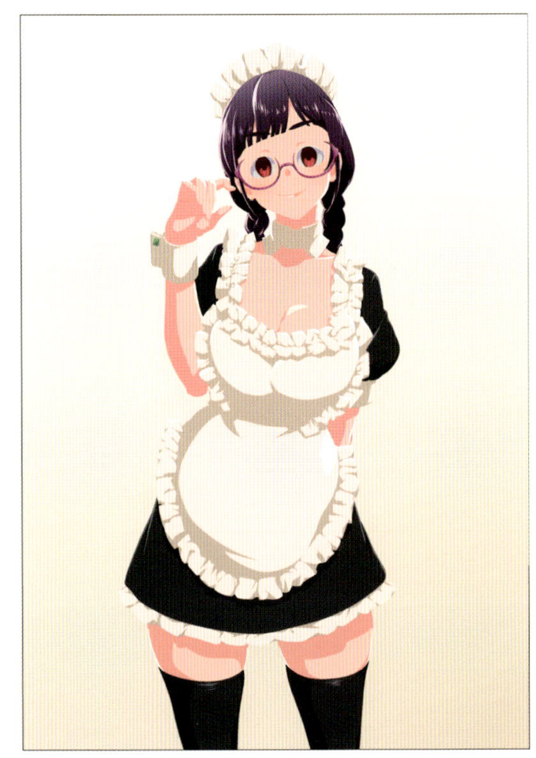

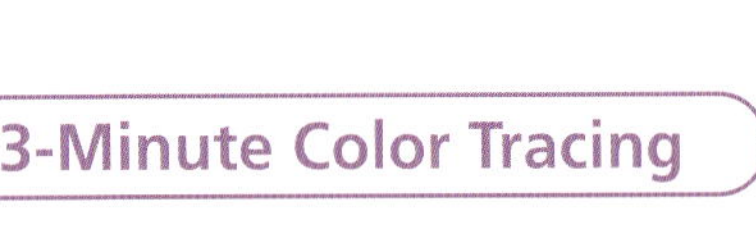



This is a simple method for color tracing using only the colored parts of the finished illustration.

① Duplicate the finished illustration and merge only the colored parts. It's easier if you separate the coloring into a layer folder.

② Select the duplicated and merged coloring layer, go to [Edit] → [Tone Correction] → [Level Correction], and adjust the colors.

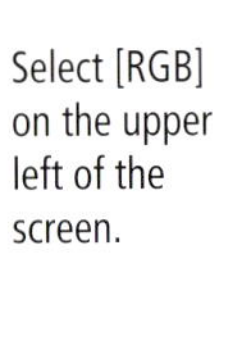

Select [RGB] on the upper left of the screen.

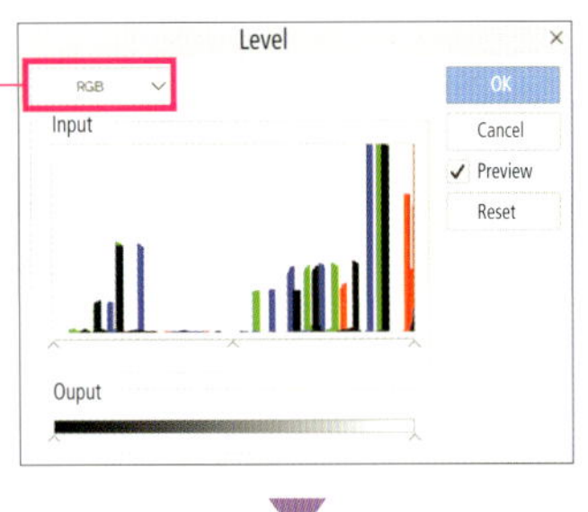


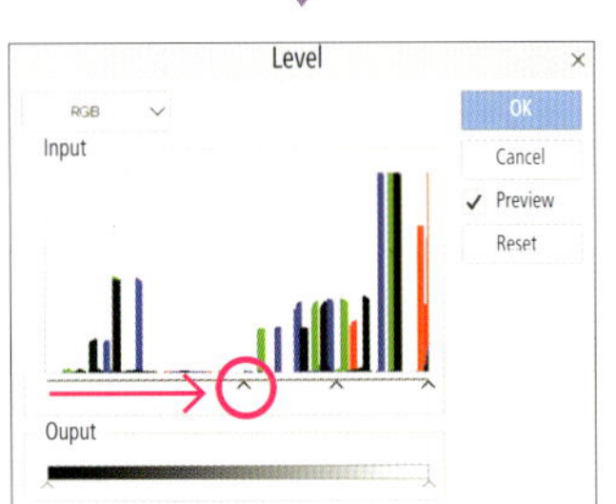


Move the control point in the red circle to the right.

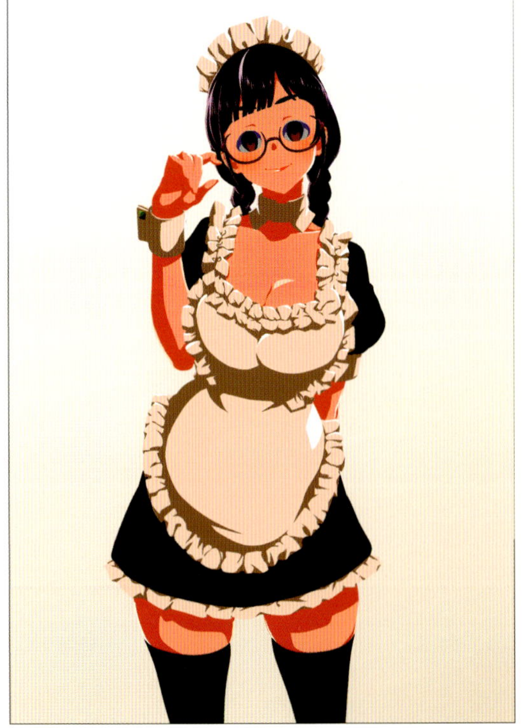

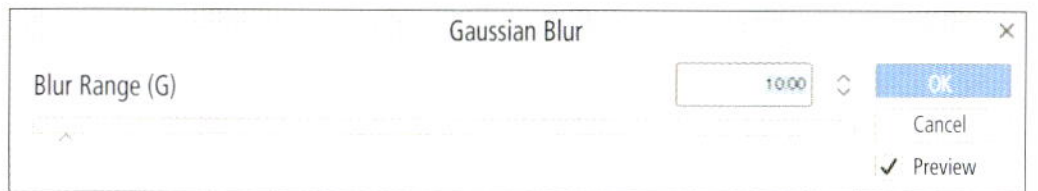

③ Then apply [Filter] → [Blur] → [Gaussian Blur]. In this case, a value of about 10 is used.



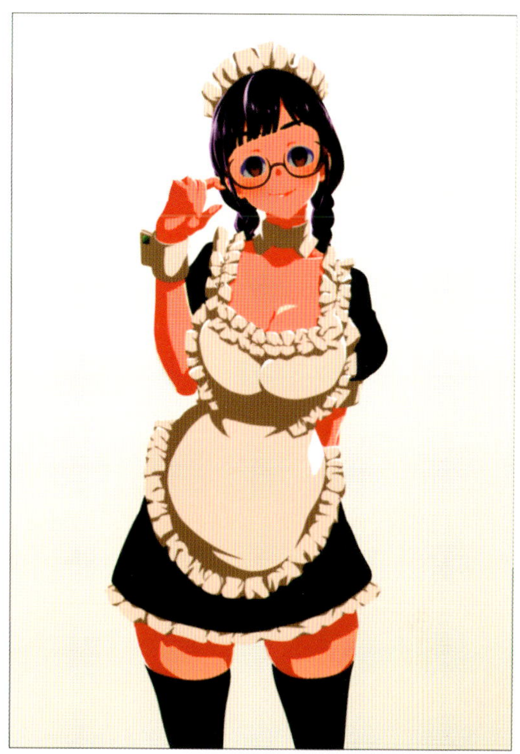

④ Place the processed layer above the line art layer (line art folder), clip it to the layer below and set the blending mode to [Screen]. To prevent the lines from blending too much, set the opacity to 50%. Adjust the opacity as needed for your illustration.

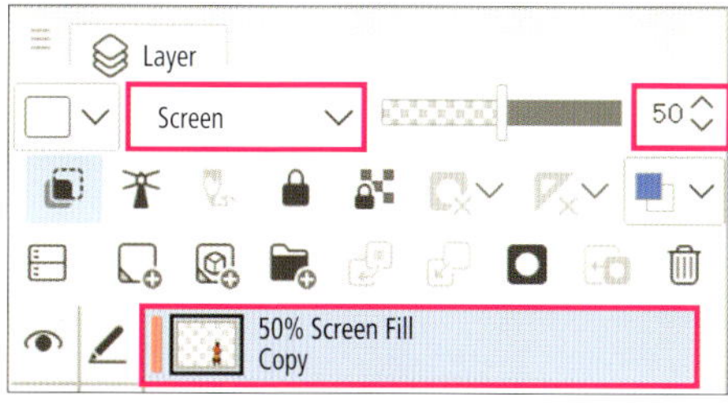



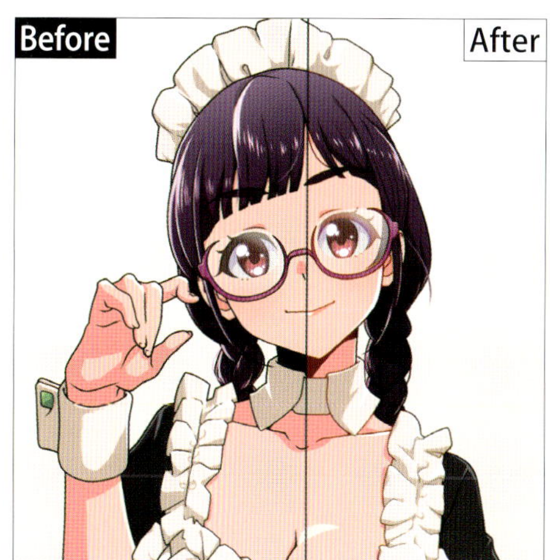



Comparing the images, you can see that the line art is now colored.

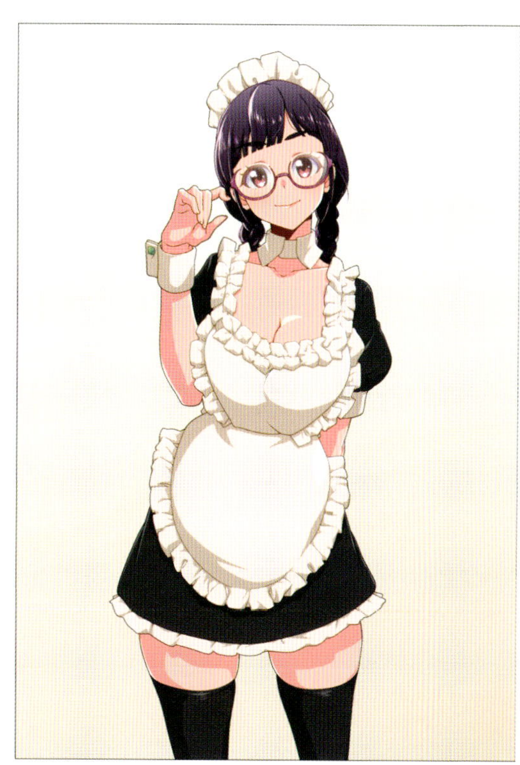

# Blending Line Art

The reason line art doesn't blend well is due to the contrast difference between the line art and the color scheme. By adjusting to eliminate contrast differences, you can blend the line art better. Besides color tracing, there are several other methods to blend your line art.

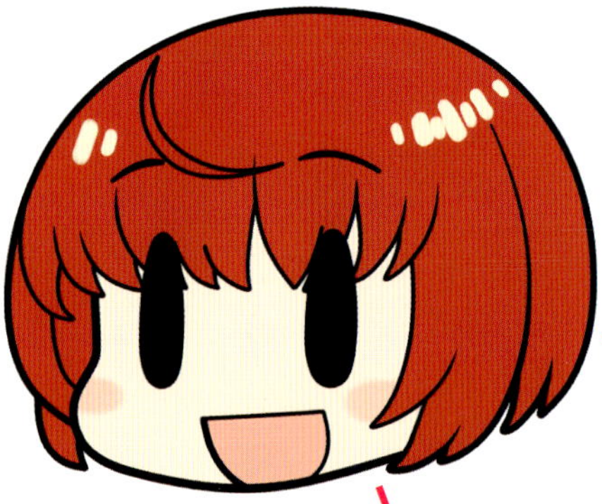

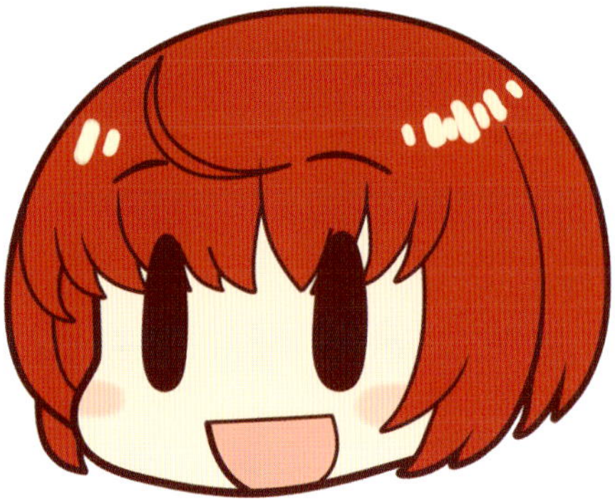

**Color Tracing**
A method where the color of the line art is adjusted to match the surrounding colors.

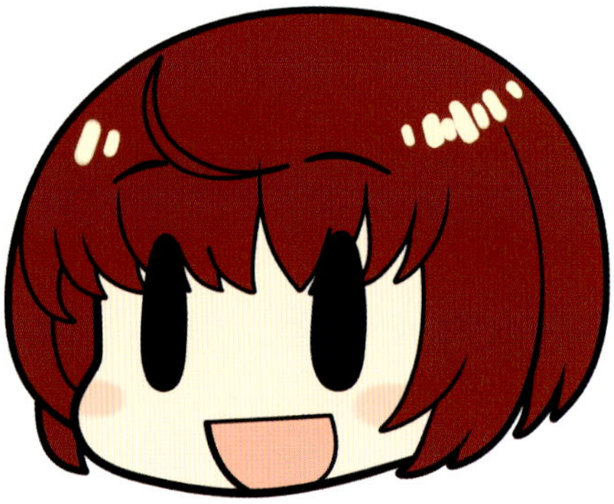

**Adjusting Color Scheme**
Changing the contrast of the color scheme.

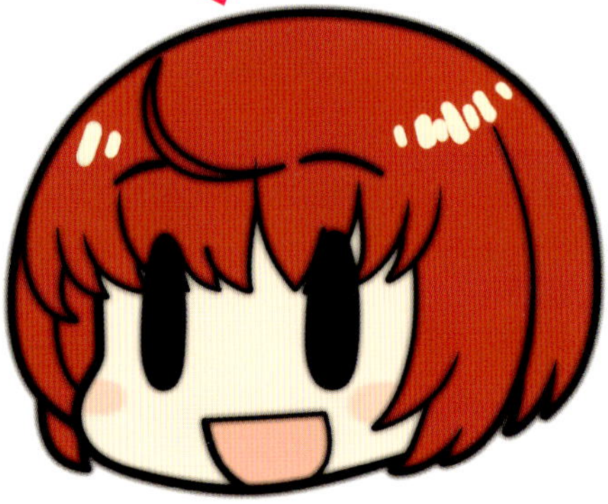

**Blurring Line Art**
A method where the line art is slightly blurred to blend it better.



## WHY BLURRING LINE ART WORKS

One reason line art doesn't blend is the high contrast between the black line art and the white background. Blurring creates intermediate colors, resulting in a softer impression. Be cautious not to overdo it, as it can make the line art look blurry; but it's a useful option to have at your disposal.

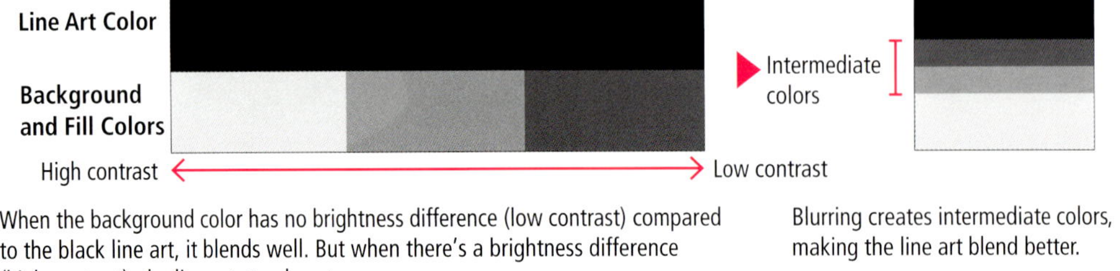


When the background color has no brightness difference (low contrast) compared to the black line art, it blends well. But when there's a brightness difference (high contrast), the line art stands out.

Blurring creates intermediate colors, making the line art blend better.

# Blending with the Background

Sometimes, when you draw a background, the illustration can look unnaturally composed. When that happens, lightly overlay the background on the character to blend them. This technique is used in special-effects-heavy movies, where even a single-color or gradient layer is overlaid, changing the blend mode or adjusting the opacity to achieve a significant blending effect. Other methods include the toy camera effect discussed on page 112 or the orange and teal unification method on page 81, so try whatever approach or technique suits you best.

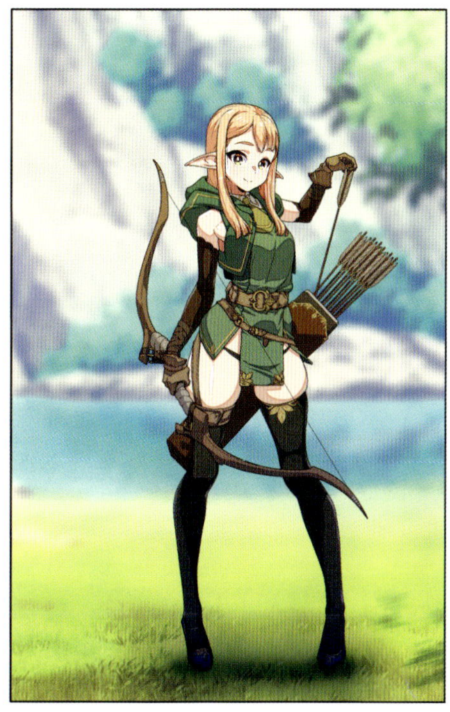

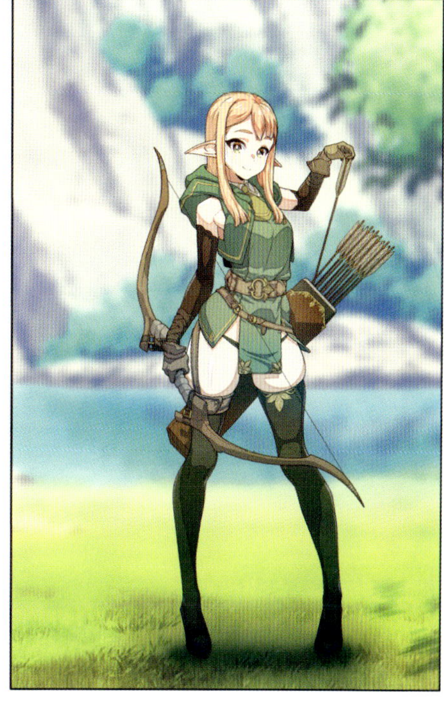

① Duplicate the background layer and heavily blur it with [Gaussian Blur].

② Place it over the character and clip it to the layer below.

③ Set the blend mode to [Soft Light] and the opacity to 70%, and you're done.

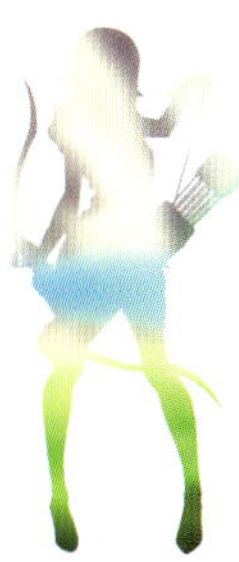

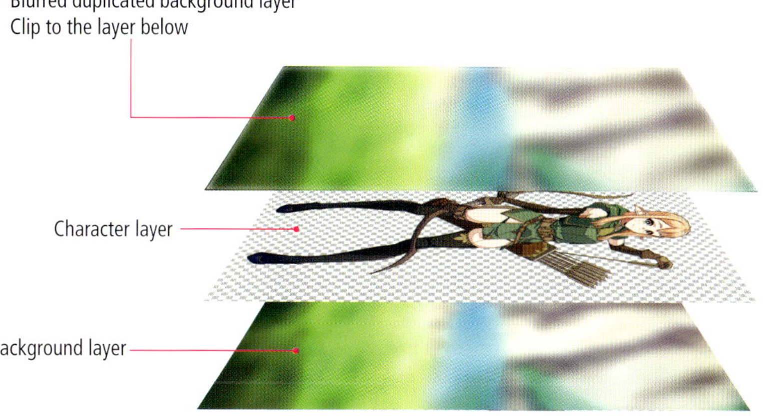


If simply placing the character over the background doesn't blend well, try this method to create a unified look. Essentially, it's like applying the same "atmosphere" to both the background and the character.

# What to Do When You're Stuck

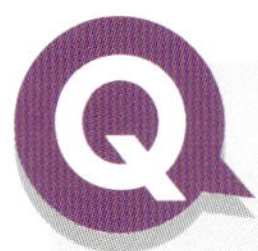

## Which one looks softer?

Look at the diagram on the right. Doesn't **A** seem somewhat unnatural? This is because, unlike **B**, all the shadow boundaries are blurred. This makes it look more like a pattern than actual shadows. This chapter presents tips and methods to troubleshoot these common shadow and coloration issues.

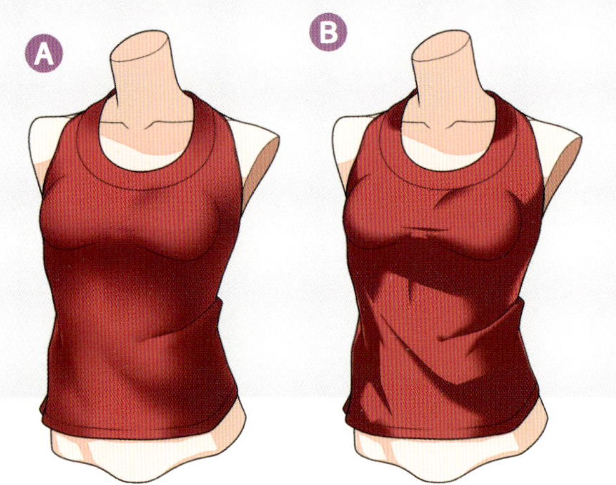


## Method 1: Apply Blurring Effects with Surface Awareness

In the case of the human body, surfaces curve at various angles. The curves become sharper near the edges of the body, softer and less defined toward the center of the torso. Use blurred shadows on gradual curves and avoid blurring on sharp curves or near-angular areas to create contrasting shadows. This technique can be tricky to master, so practice and develop your sense of it initially.

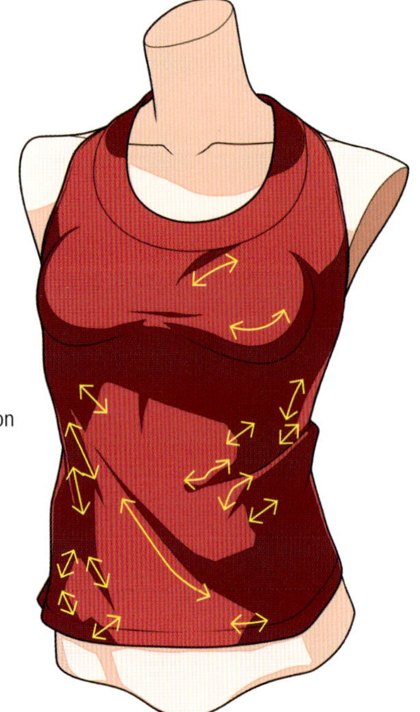

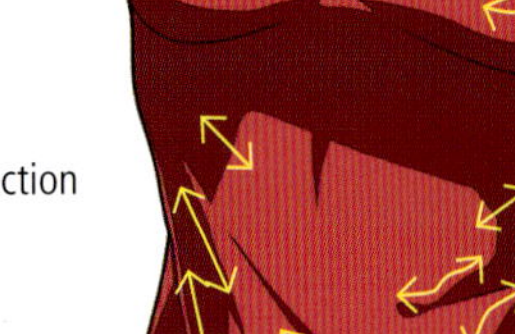
Blur in the direction of the arrows.

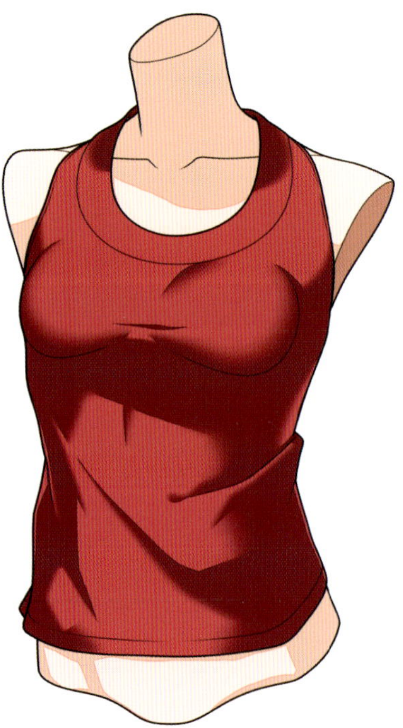

# Method 2: Blurring Shadow Principles

The method and degree of blurring need to change depending on the curvature as well as the particular effect you're after. Sharp curves have defined edges, so don't blur them. Gradual curves, however, should be blurred, so pay particular attention to these areas.

## Principle 1

For sharp curves, trace the shadow boundary with a blur effect to keep the edge defined. For gradual curves, blur against the shadow boundary to create a softer impression. In CLIP STUDIO PAINT, use tools like the [Blend] → [Blur] brush.

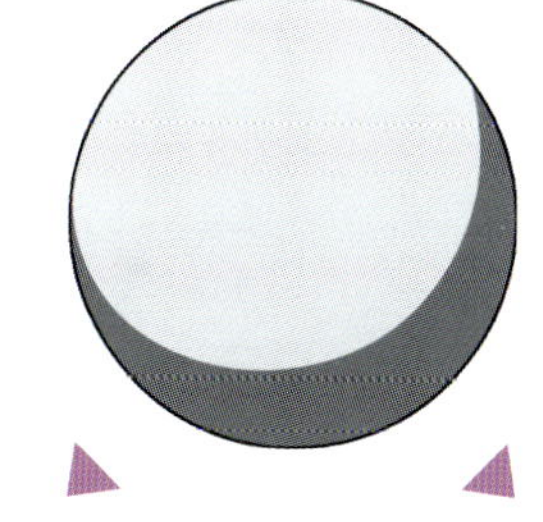

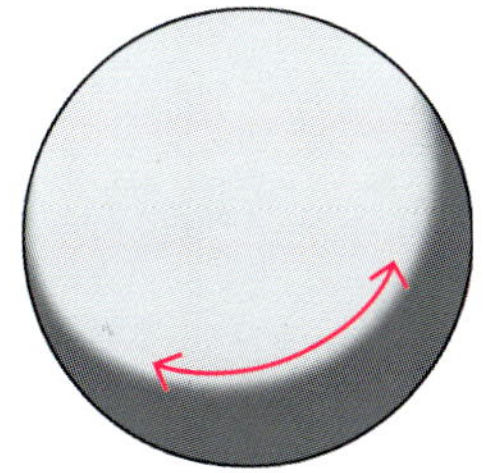

Blurring by tracing the shadow boundary keeps the edge defined.

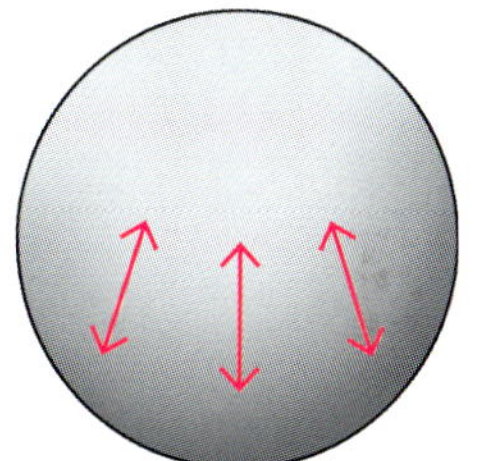

Blurring against the shadow boundary makes the edge ambiguous and less sharp.

## Principle 2

In V-shaped areas, blur against the shape to create soft shadows.

Blur and blend the V-shaped areas.

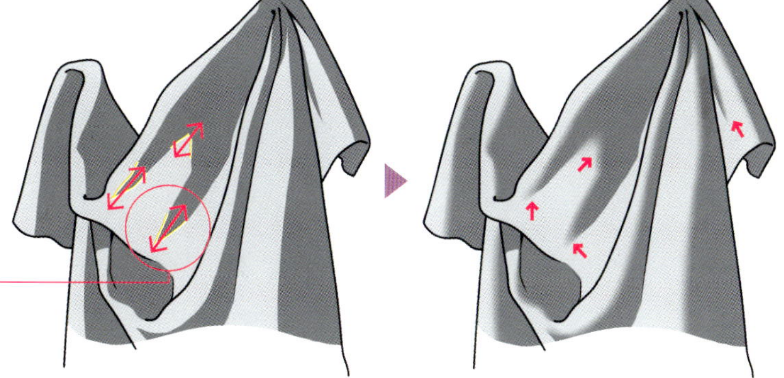

## Principle 3

For round or cylindrical areas without sharp edges, blur against the boundary. For areas with even a slight edge, trace the boundary with blurring.

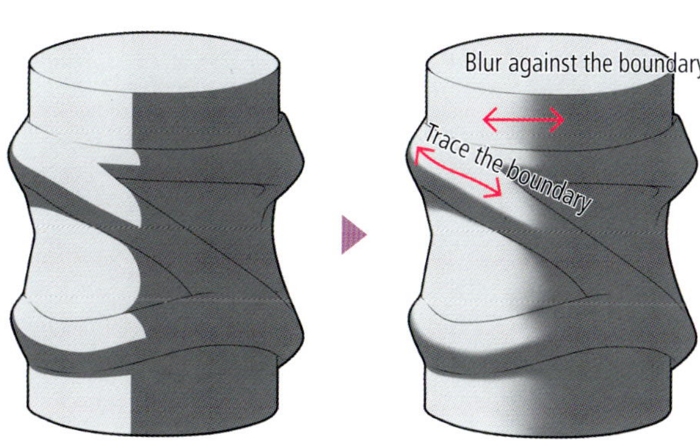

# Method 3: Review the Color Value

Color value is a term that refers to the overall balance of hue, brightness and saturation. Whether the color value is balanced or not is an important aspect and a key technique for finalizing colors.

To create an illustration with balanced color value, it's important to decide on the number of colors used for each hue during the coloring process. Additionally, deciding on the brightness, saturation and hue of the colors used for each category will help reduce any undue difficulties at the final stage. Creating a color sample chart for the character or making a "color rough" during the rough-sketch stage before inking can also help unify the color value.

## Not Ideal

The book's color is too vivid, creating a sense of imbalance and discord. This is an example of an unbalanced color value.

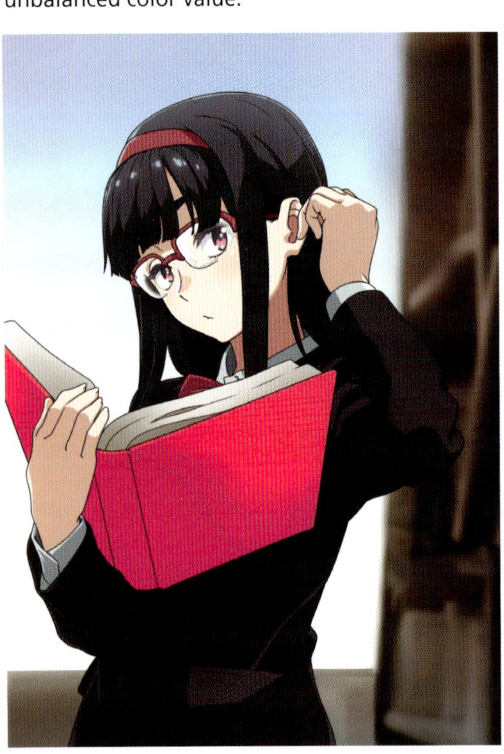

## Do It This Way

The book's color matches the overall tone, making the color value appear balanced and cohesive.

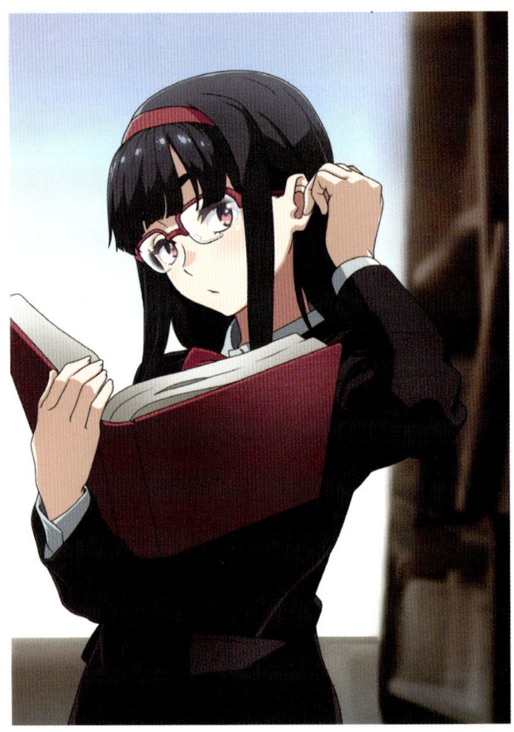

In the real world, it wouldn't be unusual to see a book with a vivid cover. So let's look at an actual photo. There's a person in a red outfit in the center. From the perspective of color value, this is unbalanced. However, in the world of painting and illustration, it's good to remember the technique of balancing color value for overall harmony. While mastering things like deciding the number of colors and matching brightness and saturation can be challenging initially, it's enough to just be aware of the concept of color value. Page 124 introduces processing techniques to balance color value.

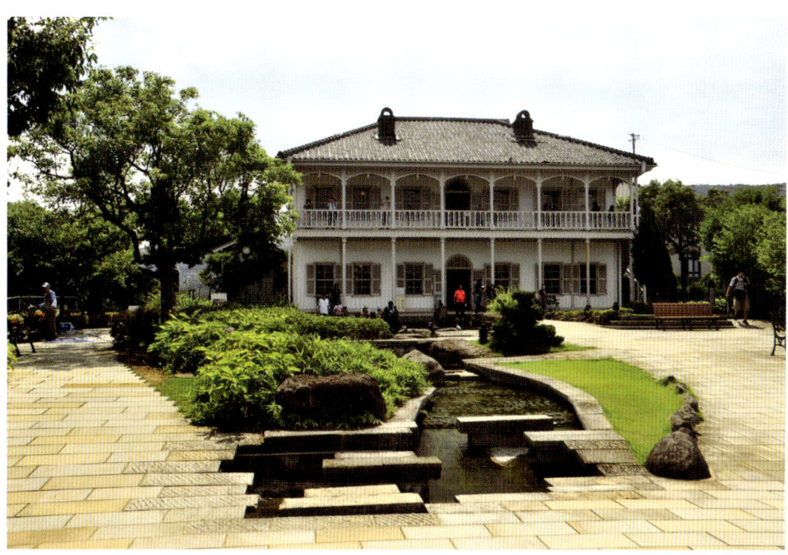

---



## Viewing Issues on Different Screens

Have you ever experienced an illustration that looks beautiful on your computer or iPad but appears lackluster when viewed on your smartphone? While page 24 discussed color changes during printing, let's look at why such phenomena occur on displays. This topic is a bit complex. Computers and smartphones represent data like text, video and audio using only two electrical signals, allowing displays to show about 16.77 million colors. However, as shown in the following diagram, the colors that can be displayed are often limited for various reasons. Additionally, the color display capability varies by device model, functionality and manufacturing period, and colors can change over time with long use. Although display colors can be adjusted with device functions and apps, using a device called a calibrator can precisely adjust colors for accurate color management and control.

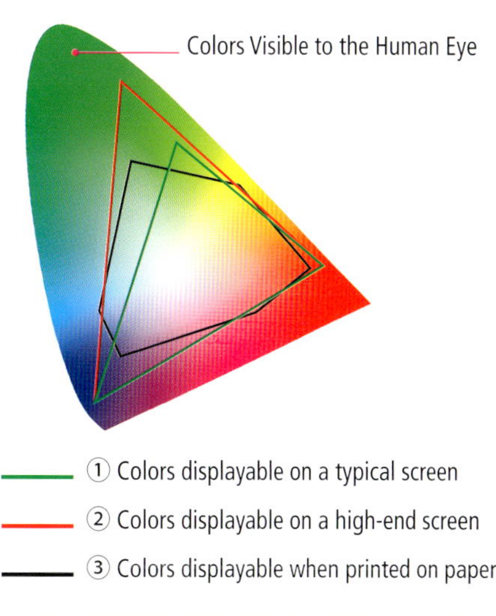

# Method 4: Enhancing Quality Using Color Value

These two illustrations utilized different finishing processes. The major difference lies in the environmental color value. This represents the atmosphere or how light appears at different times of the day, the shifting interplay of environmental light and shadow. If the time of day is noon, yellow represents environmental light and blue represents environmental shadow. By effectively applying these two colors to the light and shadow areas, you can process the illustration to match the time and atmosphere. The difference between the two illustrations lies in whether the environmental color value is considered.

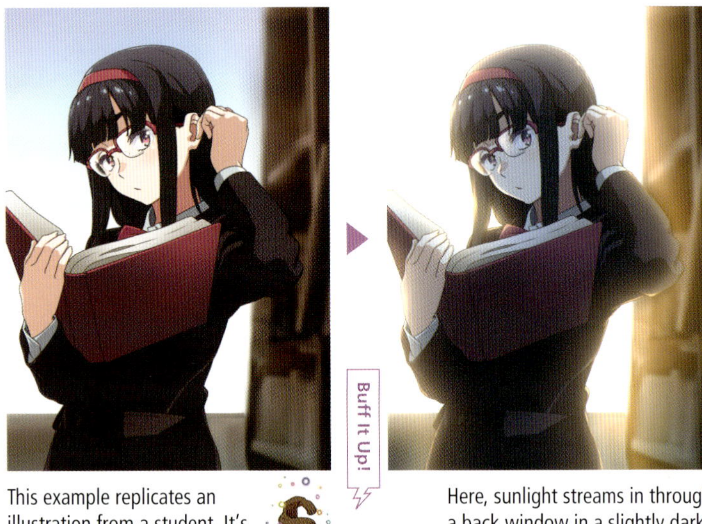

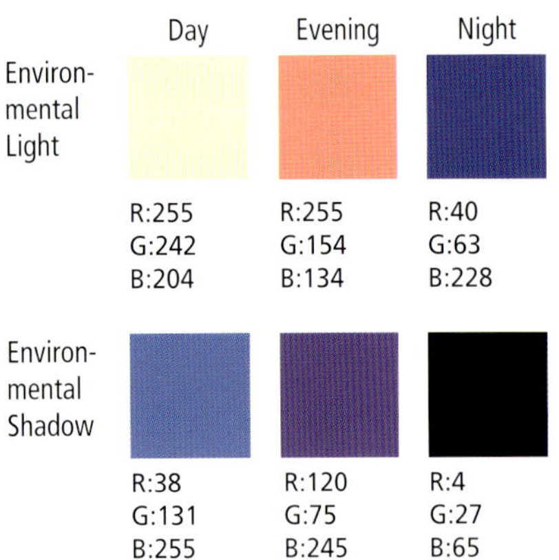


This example replicates an illustration from a student. It's acceptable as it is, but it feels a bit lacking. This is where finishing processing becomes important.

Here, sunlight streams in through a back window in a slightly dark room during the day. This adds various effects to the illustration, similar to applying a buff in a game.

# Method 5: Color-Processing Expressions Based on Time of Day

By applying the concept of color value, different times of day can be captured or suggested: day, evening and night. The color of light and shadow changes depending on the time of day: a reddish tint in the evening or a dark blue tint at night. Determine the colors for the light and shadow present at each time period, and simply layer those colors. This allows you to add expressions for the time of day while balancing the color value. The basic technique involves overlaying solid color layers and changing the blending mode.

|  | Day | Evening | Night |
|---|---|---|---|
| Environmental Light | R:255 G:242 B:204 | R:255 G:154 B:134 | R:40 G:63 B:228 |
| Environmental Shadow | R:38 G:131 B:255 | R:120 G:75 B:245 | R:4 G:27 B:65 |

It's important to note that environmental color value is intuitive and can be difficult to explain theoretically. The methods introduced here are just examples, so feel free to experiment to match the atmosphere of your illustration.

In the diagrams below, the environmental light and shadow for the day are overlaid on pale and dark colors with 50% opacity in multiply mode.

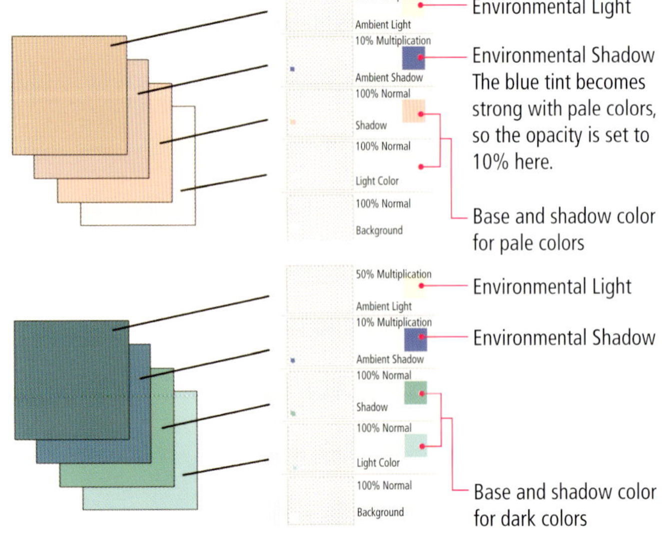

Even with the same illustration, adding a few
layers can change the suggested time of day.
Do you see the difference in the two examples?

## Evening (Indoors)

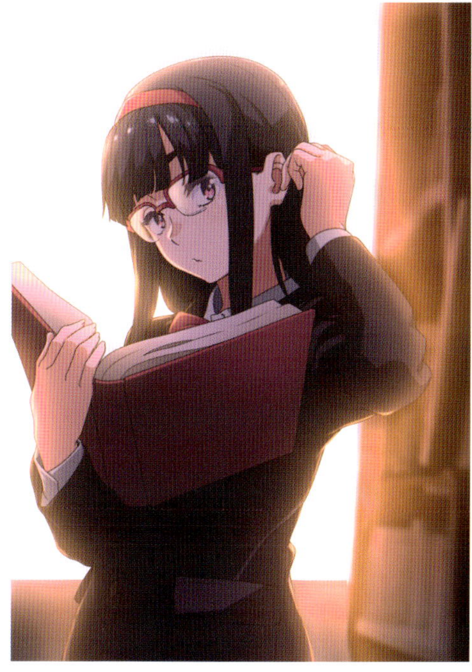

## Night (Indoors)

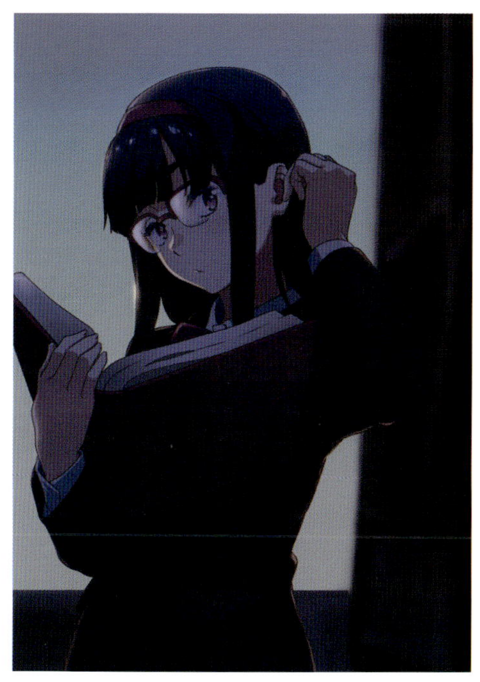

**Layer Configuration**

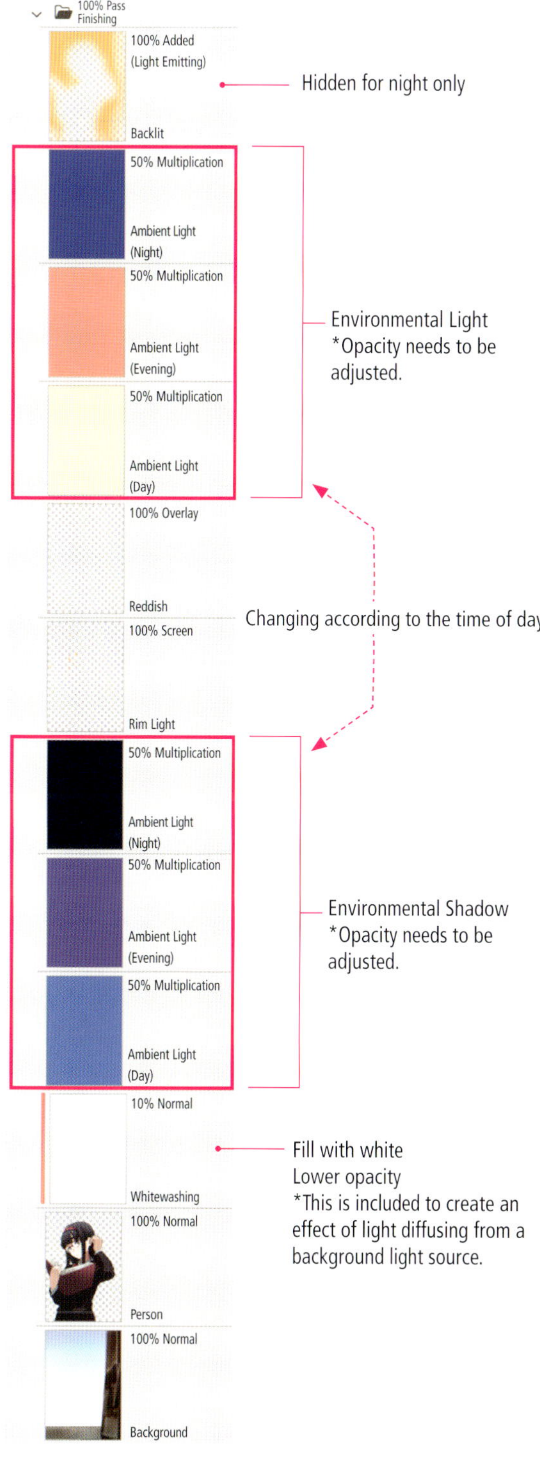


Hidden for night only

Environmental Light
*Opacity needs to be
adjusted.

Changing according to the time of day

Environmental Shadow
*Opacity needs to be
adjusted.

Fill with white
Lower opacity
*This is included to create an
effect of light diffusing from a
background light source.

# Method 6: Simplified Color Value Expression

You can save revision time by using a simplified version of the color value method. This approach is less complex than the method explained on page 124. It involves placing a layer filled with a specific color or gradient on top of the finished illustration. The blending mode can be Overlay, Add (Glow), Multiply or others, and you can choose the settings, including opacity, that you prefer. While this may seem quite rough at first glance, the technique can help unify the color tone and atmosphere of the finished illustration to a certain degree.

## Day (Indoors)

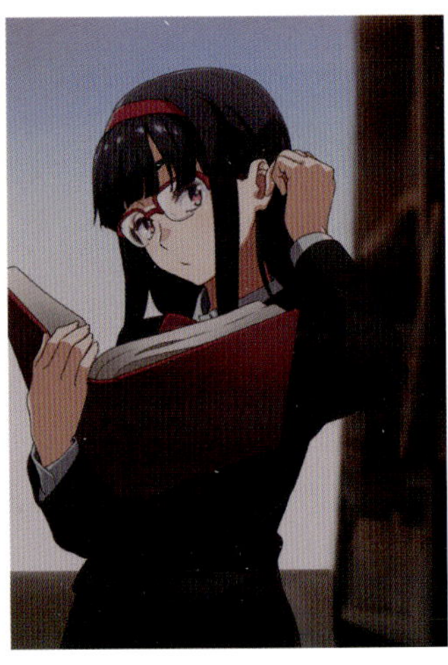

*Displayed at normal 100% opacity

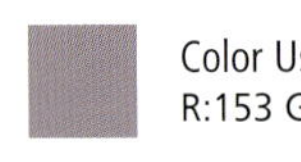
Color Used
R:153 G:136 B:162

**Layer Structure**

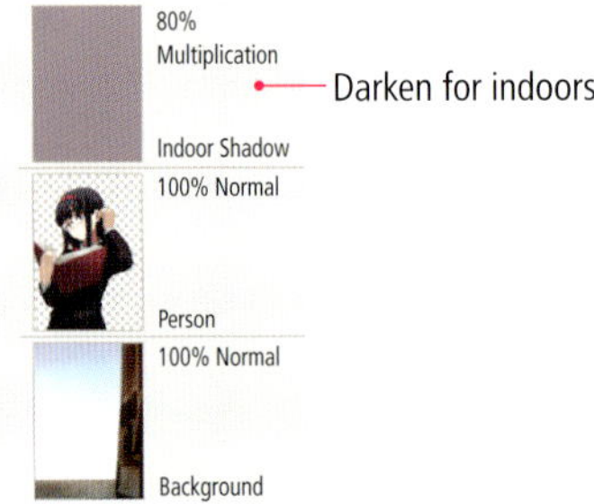


① To express the darkness of the interior, create a layer in Multiply mode and fill it with blue-purple. Set the opacity to 80%.

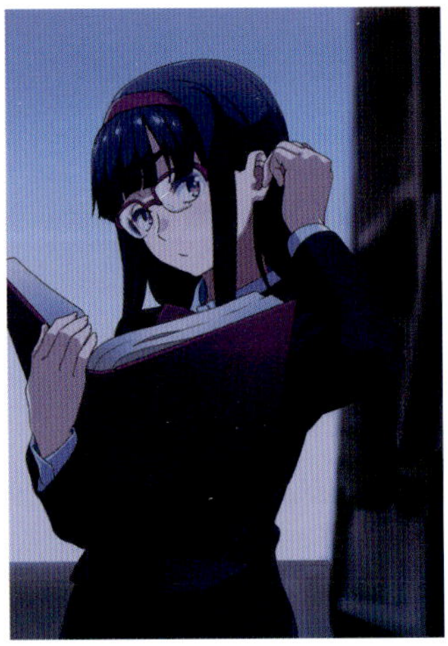

*Displayed at normal 100% opacity

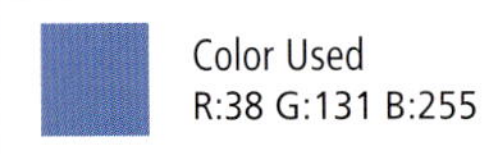
Color Used
R:38 G:131 B:255

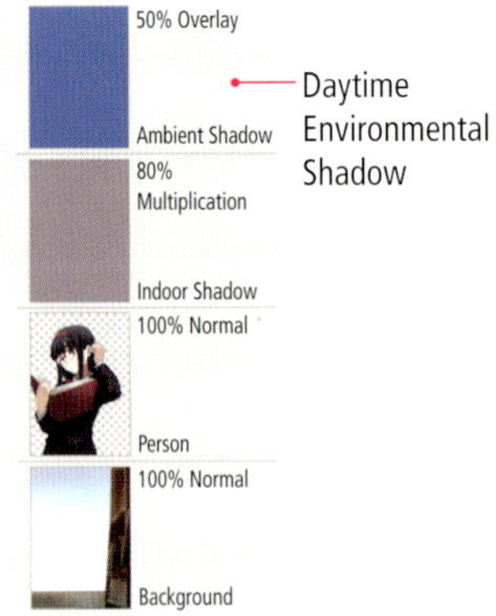


② Create an Overlay layer on top of layer ① and fill it with the daytime environmental shadow color. Set the opacity to 50%.

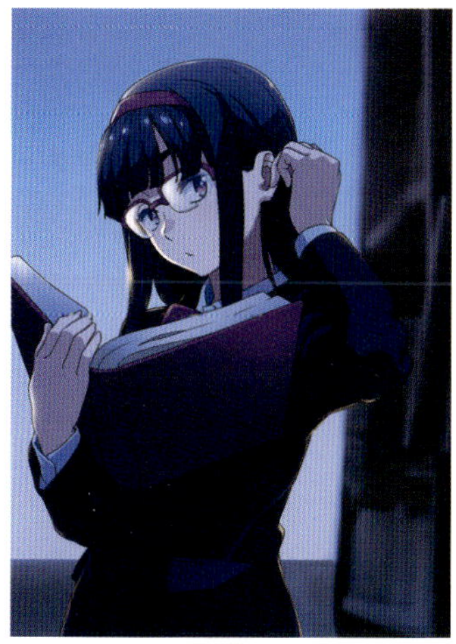 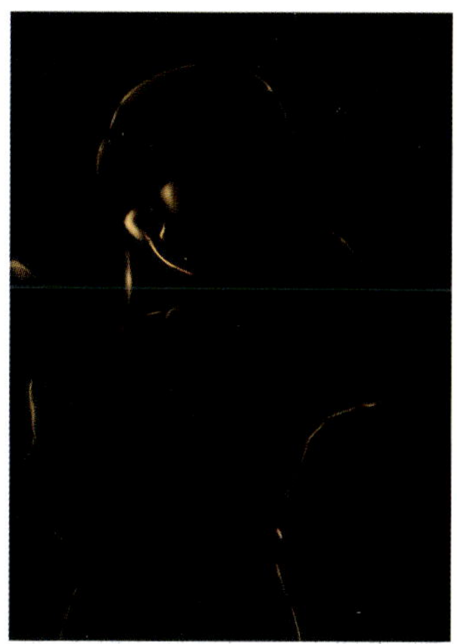 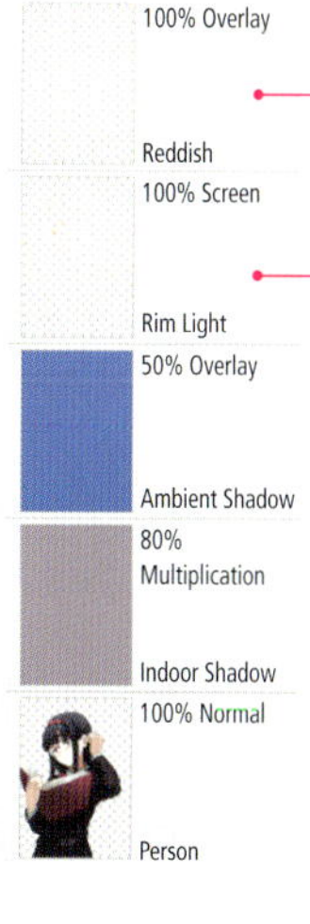

Add a red tint to the light boundary.

Add light

③ Create a Screen layer on top of layer ② and add light effects. Additionally, create an Overlay layer and add a red tint to the light boundaries to increase the sense of depth.

Layers (for ③):
- 100% Overlay — Reddish
- 100% Screen — Rim Light
- 50% Overlay — Ambient Shadow
- 80% Multiplication — Indoor Shadow
- 100% Normal — Person

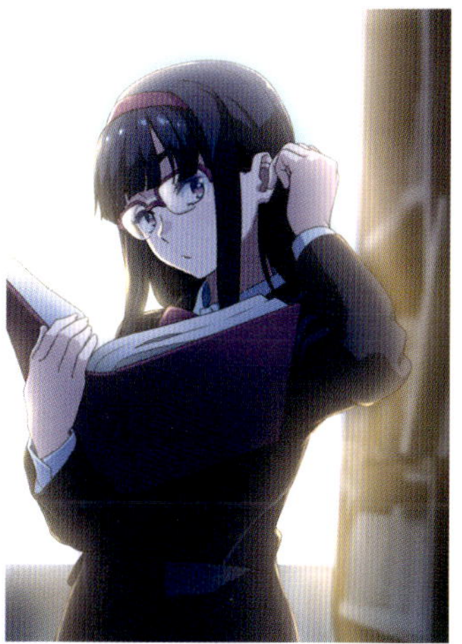 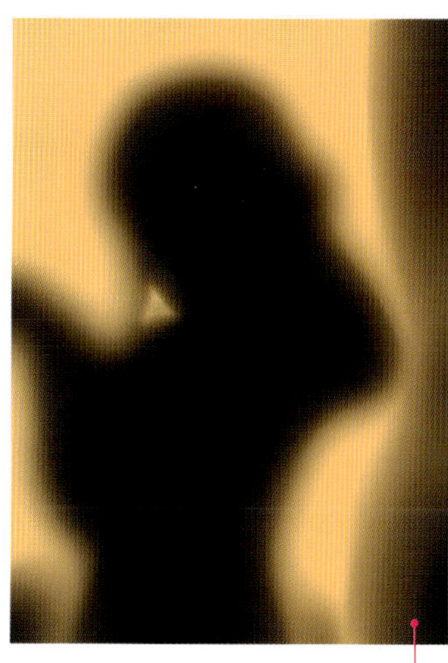

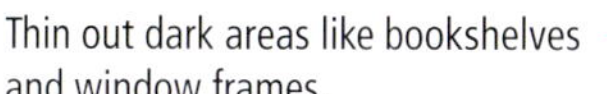
Thin out dark areas like bookshelves and window frames.

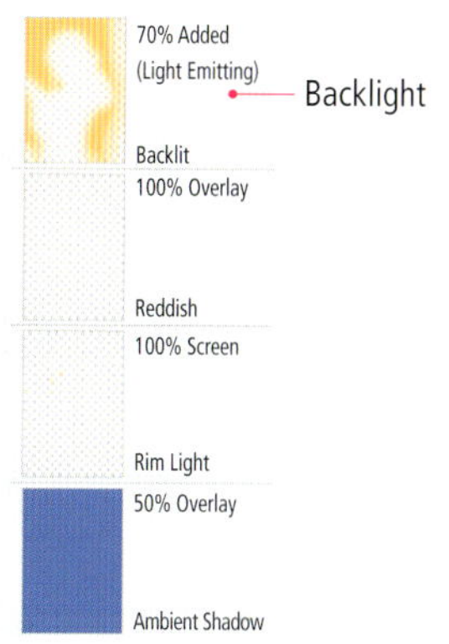

Backlight

Layers (for ④):
- 70% Added (Light Emitting) — Backlit
- 100% Overlay — Reddish
- 100% Screen — Rim Light
- 50% Overlay — Ambient Shadow

④ Select the area outside the character and create a layer in Add (Glow) mode. Fill it with the light color, then apply Gaussian Blur to add the backlight effect.

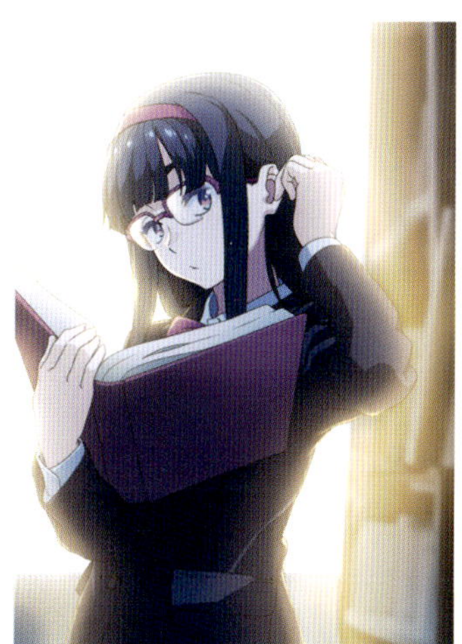 

*Displayed at normal 100% opacity

| | Color Used<br>R:255 G:241 B:201 |
| --- | --- |

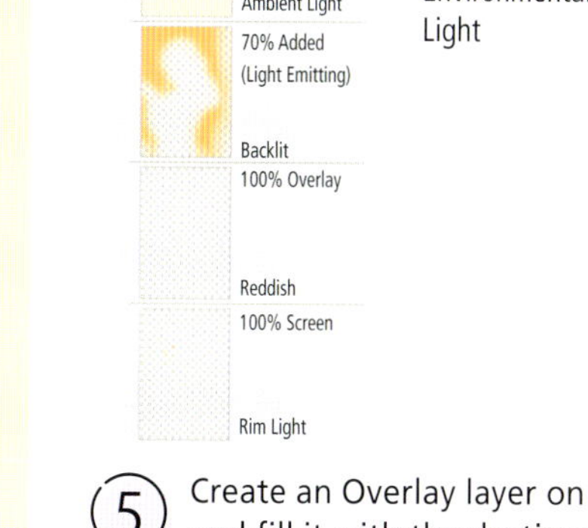

100% Pass
Finishing (simple version)

← Daytime Environmental Light

Layers (for ⑤):
- 50% Overlay — Ambient Light
- 70% Added (Light Emitting) — Backlit
- 100% Overlay — Reddish
- 100% Screen — Rim Light

⑤ Create an Overlay layer on top and fill it with the daytime environmental light color. Set the opacity to 35% to complete.

# Method 7: Coloring Using Gradient Maps

Since the 2010s, a technique called grisaille painting has become popular. This method involves painting only with shades of gray, without considering colors, and then layering other colors on top. Many people attempt this method because it seems simple, requiring only the consideration of light and dark. However, it's often more difficult than expected. The main reason is a lack of understanding of layer blending modes, such as overlay.

Here, we'll look a little more closely at the pitfalls of blending modes and how to use gradient maps to solve these issues.

## Blending Modes

As shown in the diagram on the right, a gray gradient layer is overlaid with a red layer filled with red, changing the blending mode of the red layer.

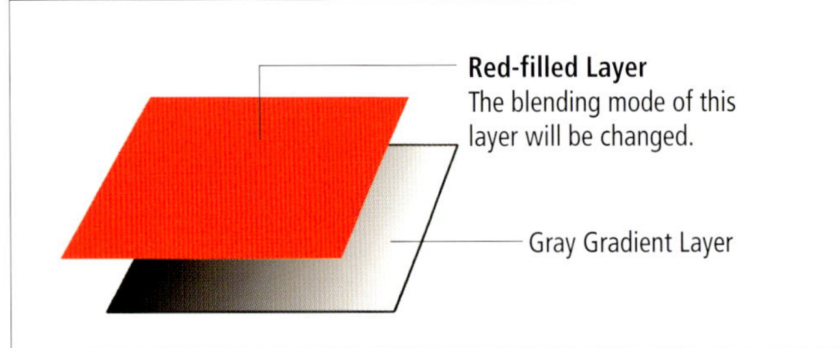


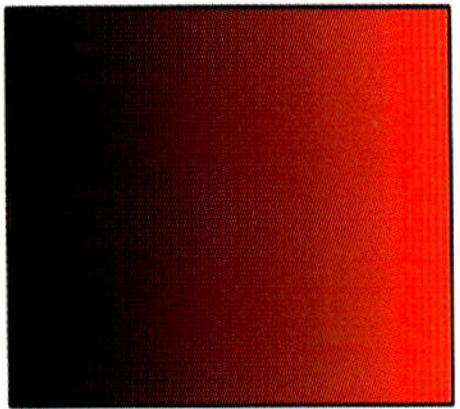

**Multiply**
A mode that blends by multiplying colors together. Colors become darker, eventually turning black.

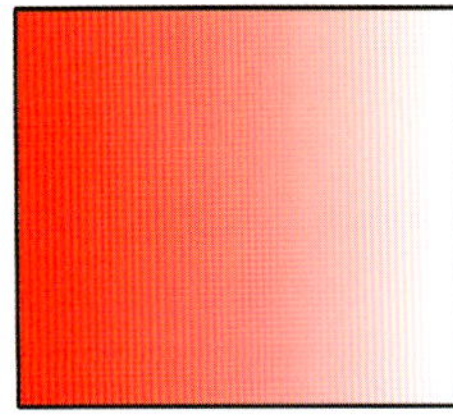

**Screen**
A mode that blends by lightening colors. The darker the underlying color, the more the blended color appears.

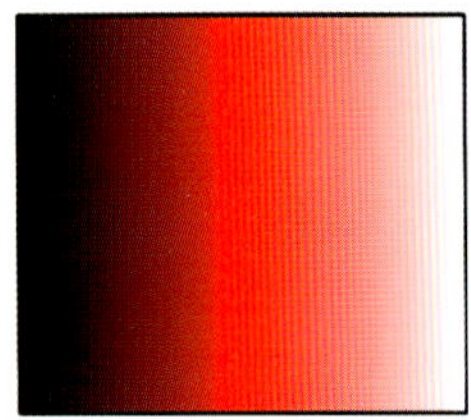

**Overlay**
A mode that applies screen effects to parts lighter than 50% gray and multiply effects to parts darker than 50% gray. Darker areas become darker, while lighter areas become lighter.

When using overlay in grisaille painting, colors can become muddy and dark. This happens because overlay isn't applied correctly over areas lighter than 50% gray. Thus, in grisaille painting, you must center your light and dark on 50% gray. Beginners often find this difficult because they don't fully understand the properties of overlay. On the next page, we'll learn a technique using gradient maps in CLIP STUDIO PAINT or adapt the approach to your chosen digital design software.

**Gradient Map**
Using a gradient map to overlay colors prevents them from becoming too dark, muddy or extremely bright, making the result more viewer-friendly.

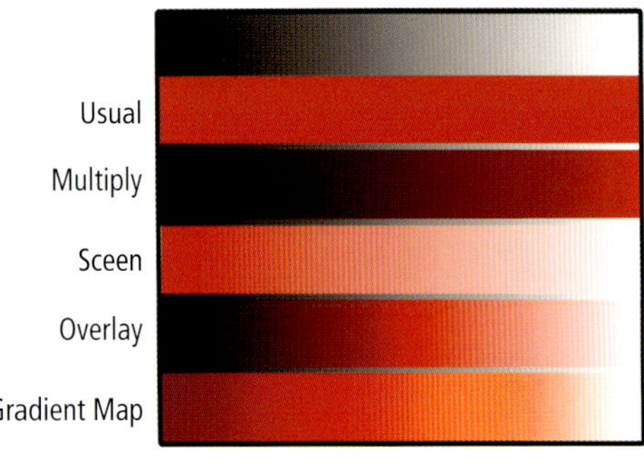


Comparison of Multiply, Screen, Overlay and Gradient Map

# Method 8: How to Use Gradient Maps

Open the gradient map dialog in CLIP STUDIO PAINT via [Layer] → [New Correction Layer] → [Gradient Map].

The window opens with black at 100% on the left and white at 100% on the right.

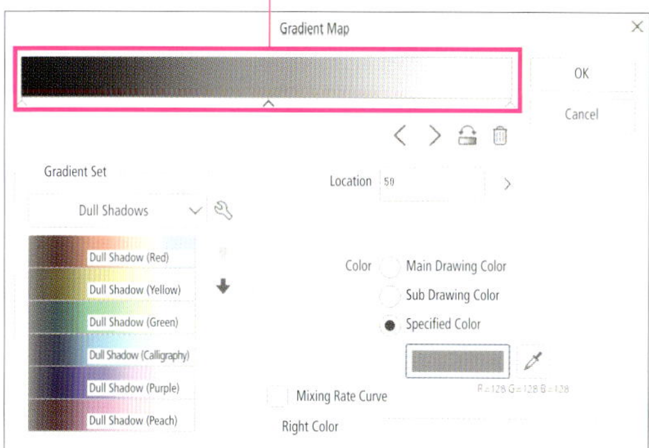

Clicking anywhere on the color bar will add a node mark, allowing you to add colors. For example, if you select red, the area will change from black to red, and from red to white, creating a gradient.

① Click to add a node.

③ Red is added

② Select red

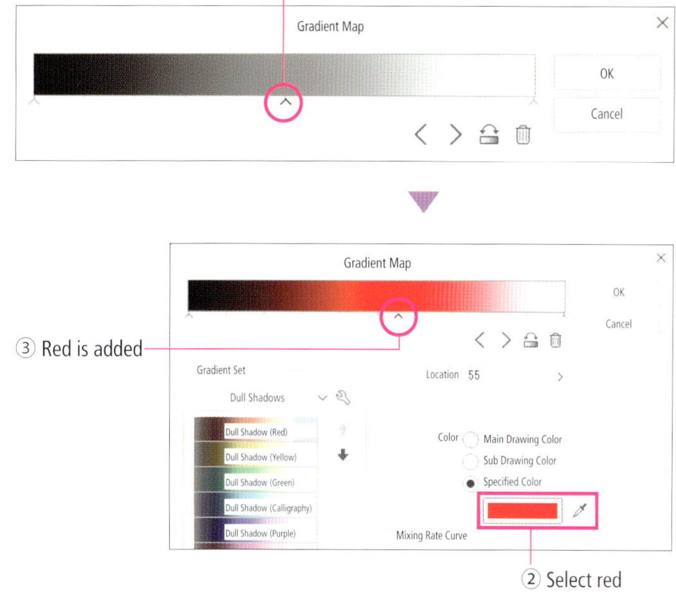

With this gradient, black is too intense. Click the triangle (black) at the far left of the color bar and change it from black to a dark red. This adjust-ment can correct areas that were too dark when using the overlay method in grisaille painting.

To make further adjustments, double-click the layer mark to open the dialog and make

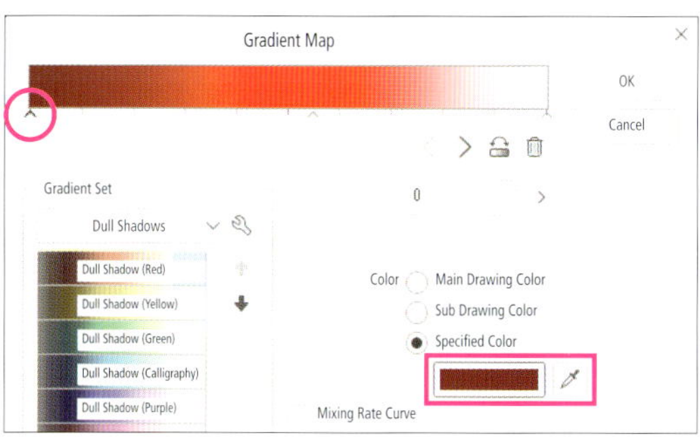

# Method 9: Let's Paint with Gradient Maps

Now let's actually paint using gradients. First, complete the illustration using only grayscale for light
and dark. At this stage, separate the layers for the different parts, such as the skin, hair and clothing.

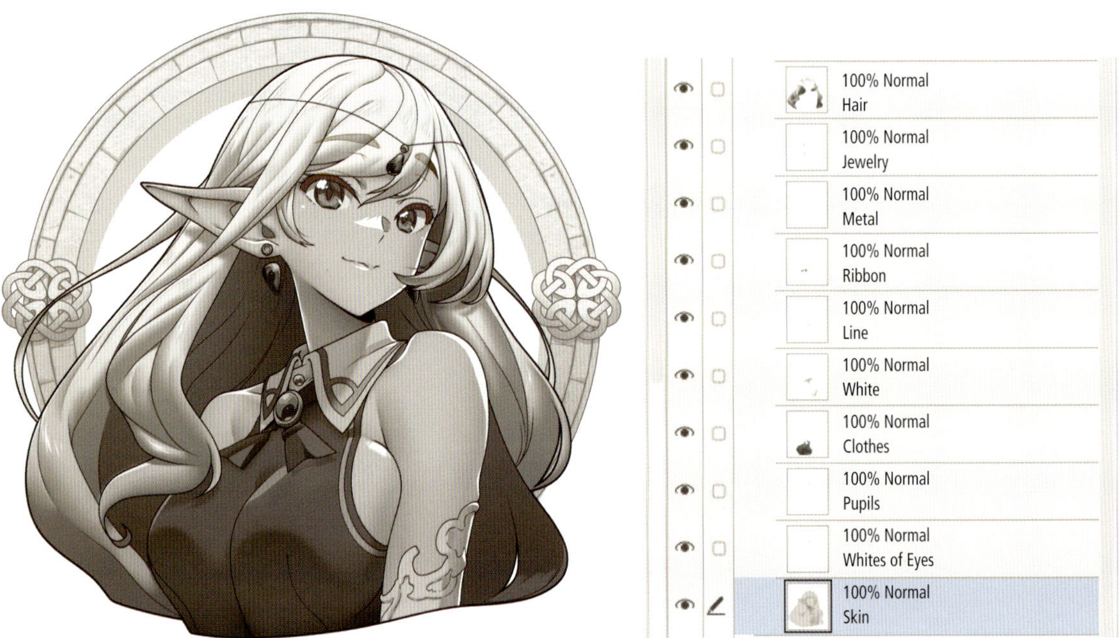

① Complete the grayscale painting.

② Move on to painting the skin. Create a gradient
map correction layer on top of the layer where
you painted the skin, following the previous steps.

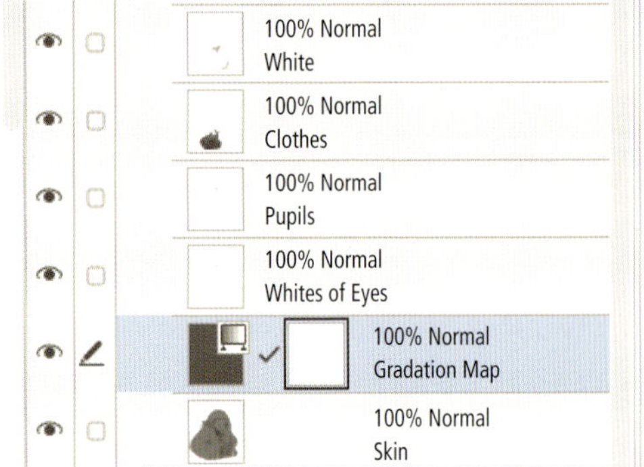

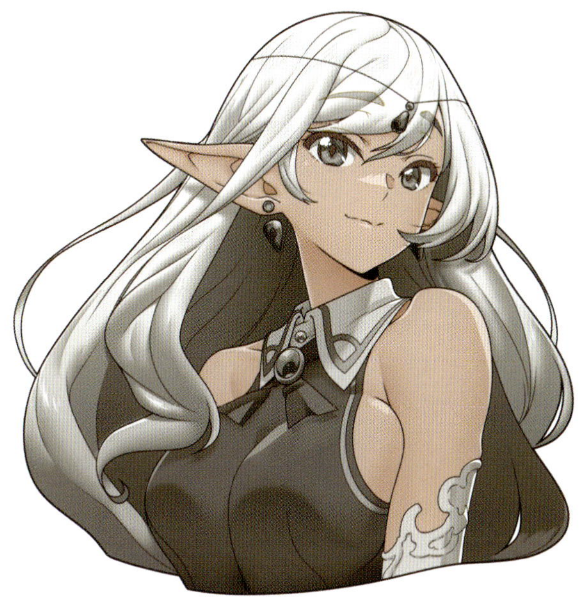
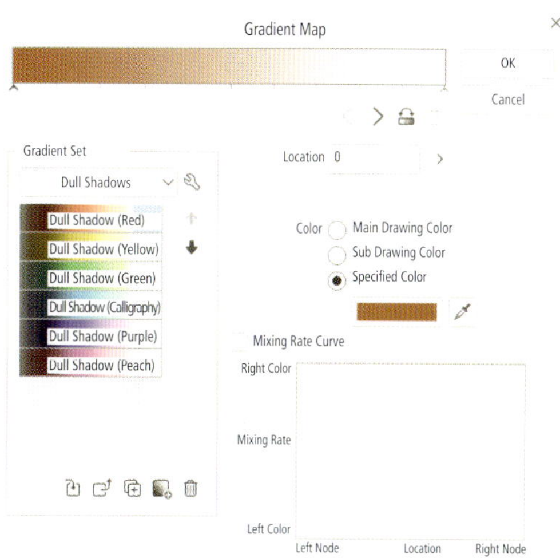


③ Create a gradient map to your liking. This allows you to paint according to the grayscale gradient. In the case of using the overlay method in grisaille painting, you had to be mindful of the 50% brightness to avoid muddy colors. However, using a gradient map, you can paint without the risk of the colors becoming too muddy.

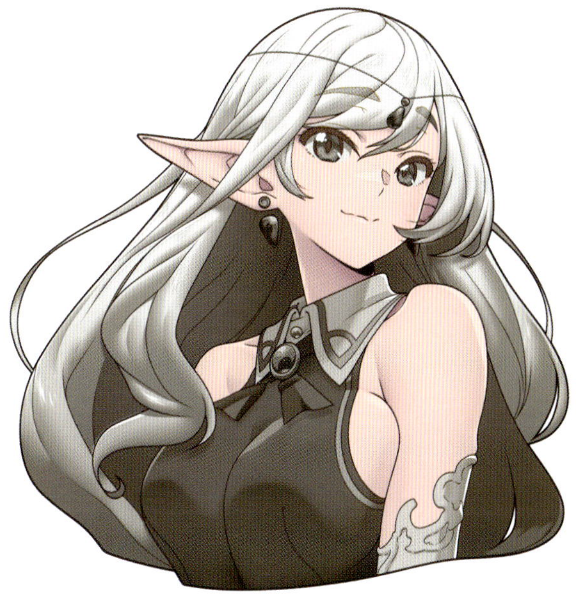
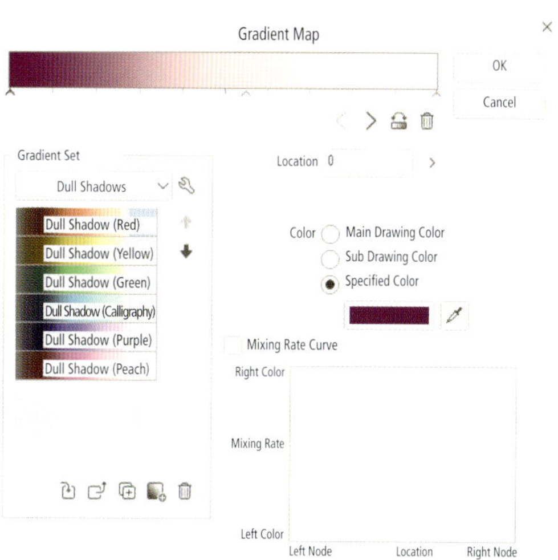


④ By simply adjusting the gradient map later, you can change the colors. If you save the gradient map you created, you can easily change the skin color. For clarity, here the skin tone was adjusted to a slightly purplish color.

# Method 10: Check in Grayscale

Have you ever felt that something is missing from your almost-finished drawing? In these cases, try converting the illustration to grayscale and check it without any colors present. This step will reveal areas with weak brightness contrast, which you can then adjust with stronger colors to create a resulting drawing with higher contrast.

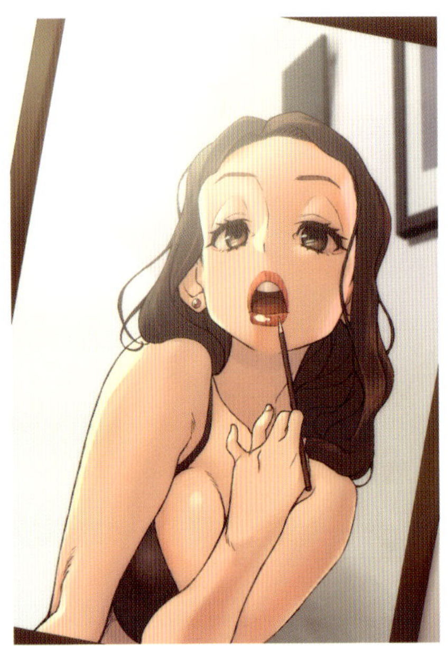

When you're almost finished, you might feel that the color scheme is correct, but something about the image still seems weak.

Grayscale Conversion

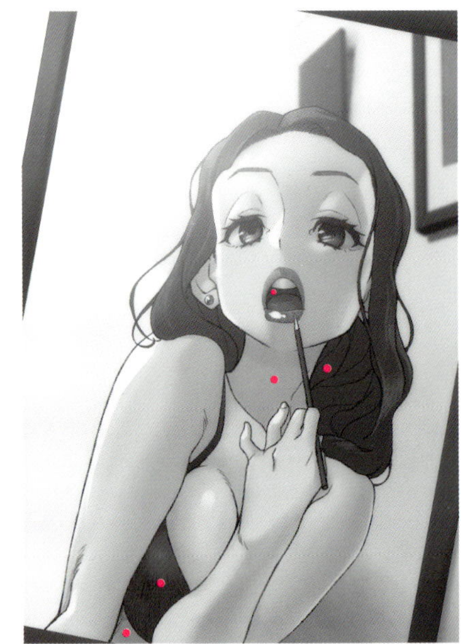

When you convert to grayscale, you may notice that areas such as the mouth interior, parts of the hair, under the neck, the underwear and the torso are not dark enough.

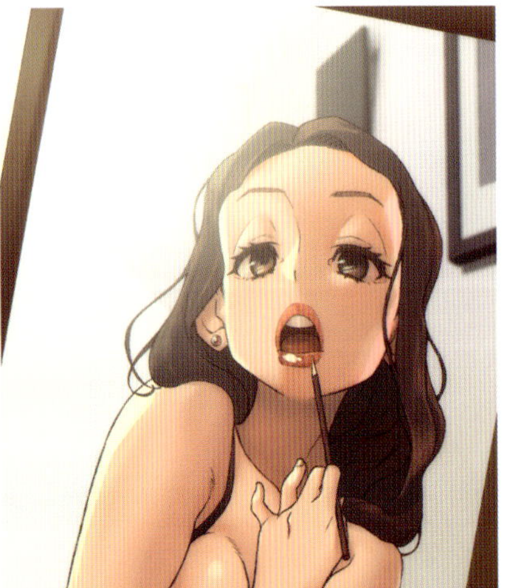

Convert to grayscale.

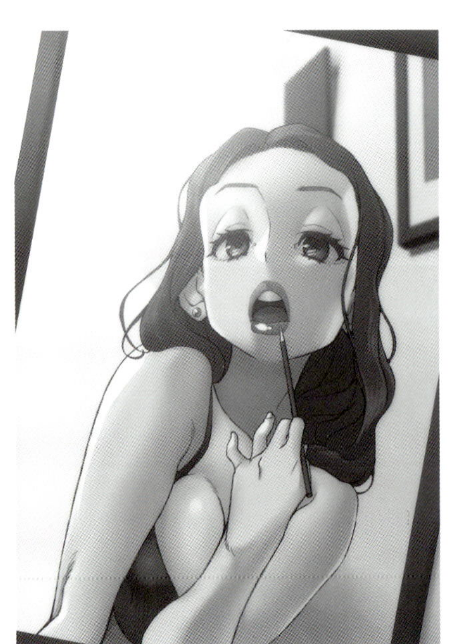

Here, the areas that stood out were darkened, but if you still feel the overall contrast is lacking, increasing the contrast can add more definition to the image.

# Method 11: Adjust Saturation and Contrast

Sometimes, a finished illustration may still appear too vibrant even if you've paid attention to the hue, brightness and saturation. There can be various reasons for this, but in such cases, adjusting the saturation and brightness can soften the colors. In this example, the overall saturation is too high, so the saturation of each individual color was lowered for a more sub-dued look.

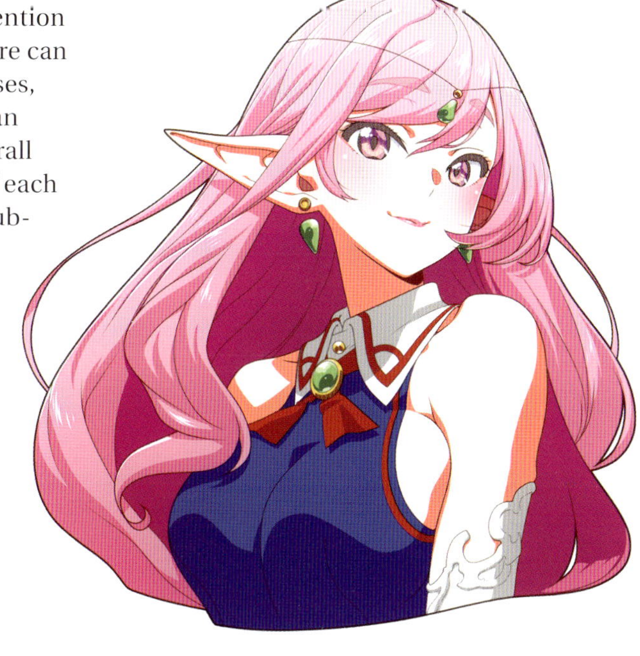

This is an example of coloring by a beginner. Many beginners tend to use high saturation and strong contrast, resulting in colors that clash and strain the eyes. Let's adjust this illustration using color correction.

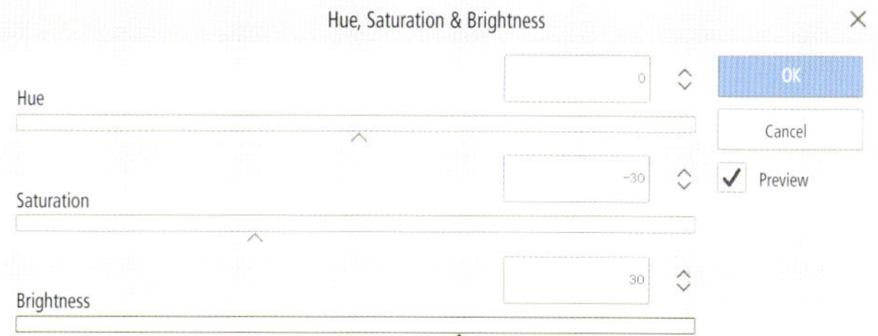


To adjust the overall coloring, select the merged coloring layer, then go to [Edit] → [Tone Correction] → [Hue/Saturation/Brightness] and adjust the settings in the dialog to Saturation -30 and Brightness +30.

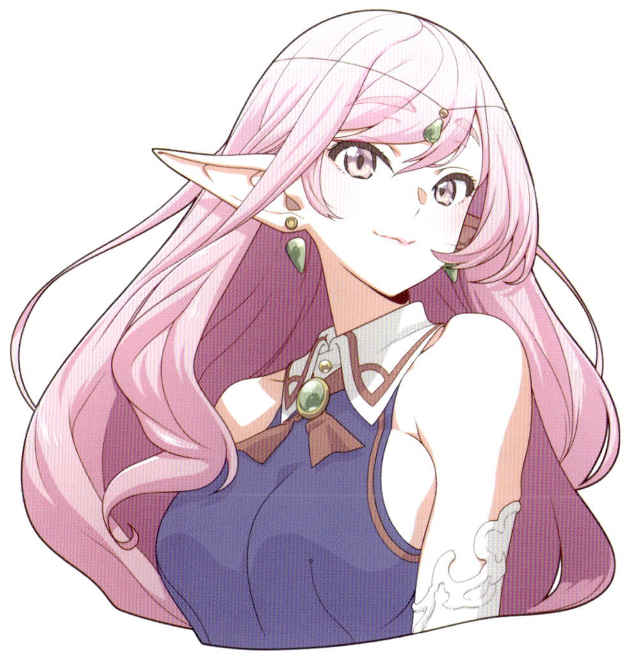

The adjustment should have made the image appear much softer. However, since this illustration was adjusted as a whole, you can also fine-tune individual areas. Specifically, the blue and purple might still appear too intense, so further adjustments might be necessary.

# Why Do We See Colors?

TEXT BY KOJI OSATO

## The Reason We See Colors

Humans can see objects because light strikes the object and the reflected light enters our eyes. For example, a red mailbox absorbs all colors except red and then reflects the red light. This reflected red light enters our eyes, and we're able to perceive the mailbox as red.

Each object absorbs and reflects different wavelengths of light, and these differences determine their colors.

White objects reflect most of the light, while black objects absorb most of it. Glass allows most of the light to pass through, making it transparent.

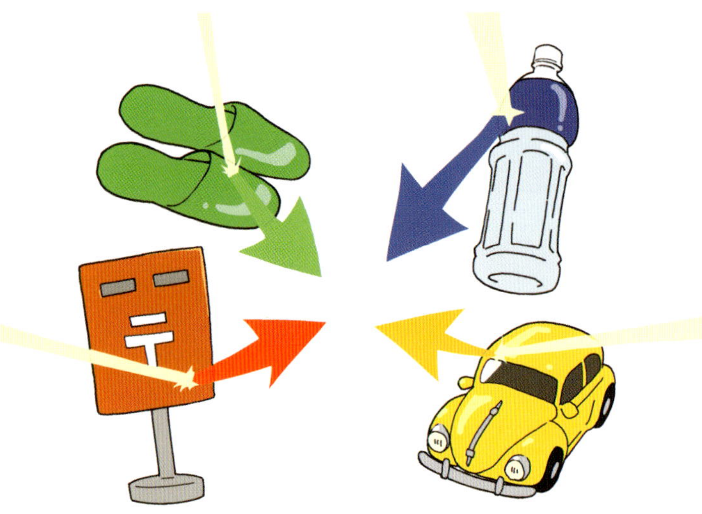

A red mailbox reflects red light, so the light entering our eyes is red. Objects that absorb the most light appear black, and those that reflect the most light appear white.

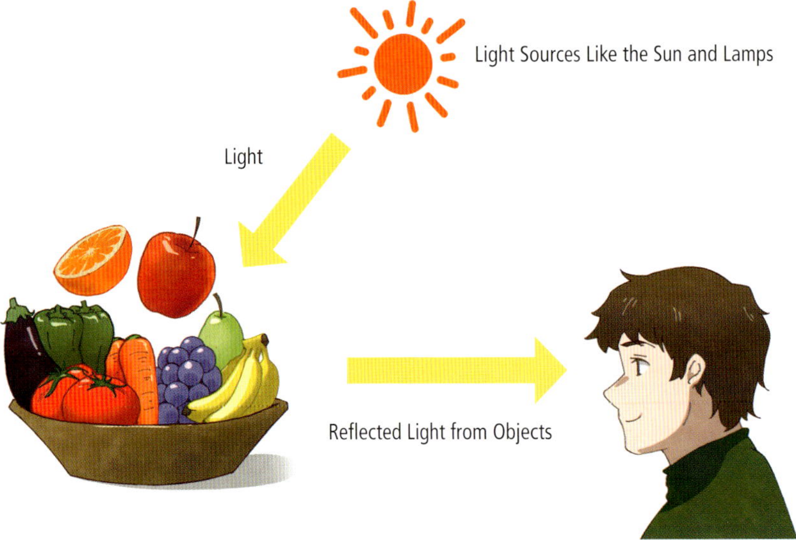

# The Range of Visible Colors

Among the rays of light emitted from the sun, wavelengths between 380 nm (nanometers) and 780 nm are considered visible light. Longer wavelengths appear red, shorter wavelengths appear blue-violet, with various colors in between. When all wavelengths mix, they form colorless, transparent light (white light), which, when separated, reveals its various component colors. A prism used in science experiments shows how white light can be broken down. Similarly, raindrops in the atmosphere act as natural prisms, creating rainbows.

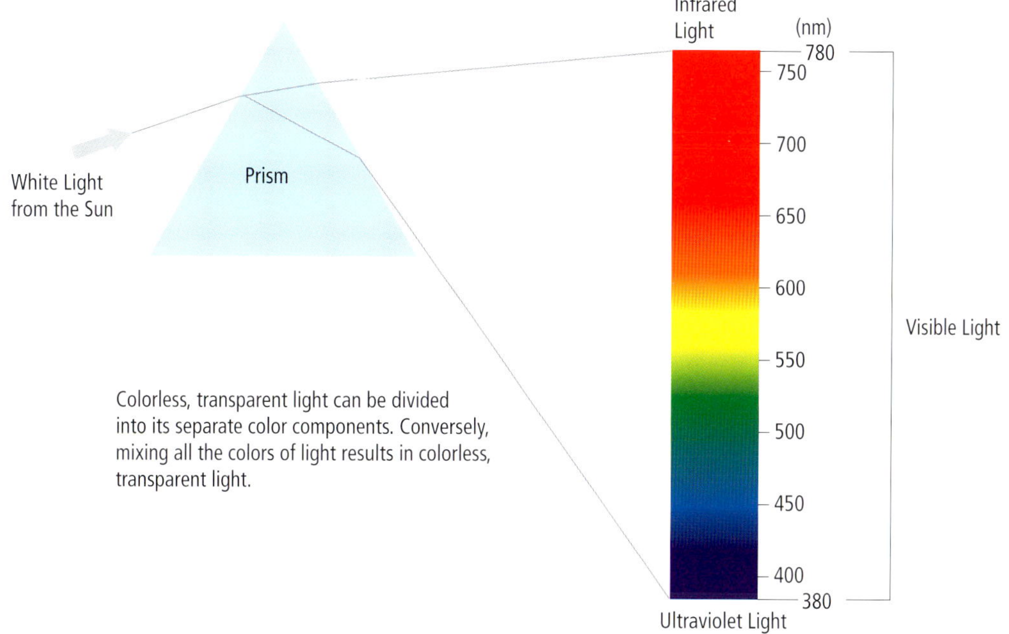


Colorless, transparent light can be divided into its separate color components. Conversely, mixing all the colors of light results in colorless, transparent light.

# How Many Colors Are in a Rainbow?

How many colors are in a rainbow? Many Japanese people would say seven, but as you can see from the wavelength chart above, a rainbow is a gradient, so it doesn't have a fixed number of colors. In the United States, it is said to have six colors, while in Germany, it's five. The perception varies by culture, so keep this in mind when drawing rainbows.

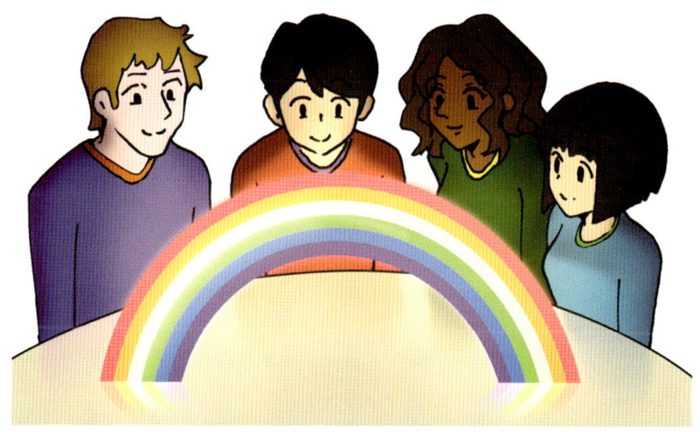

Even when looking at the same rainbow, people in different locations perceive a different number of colors.

# Color Attributes

## Color Solid

The spatial representation of the mutual relationships between hue, saturation and brightness is called a color solid.

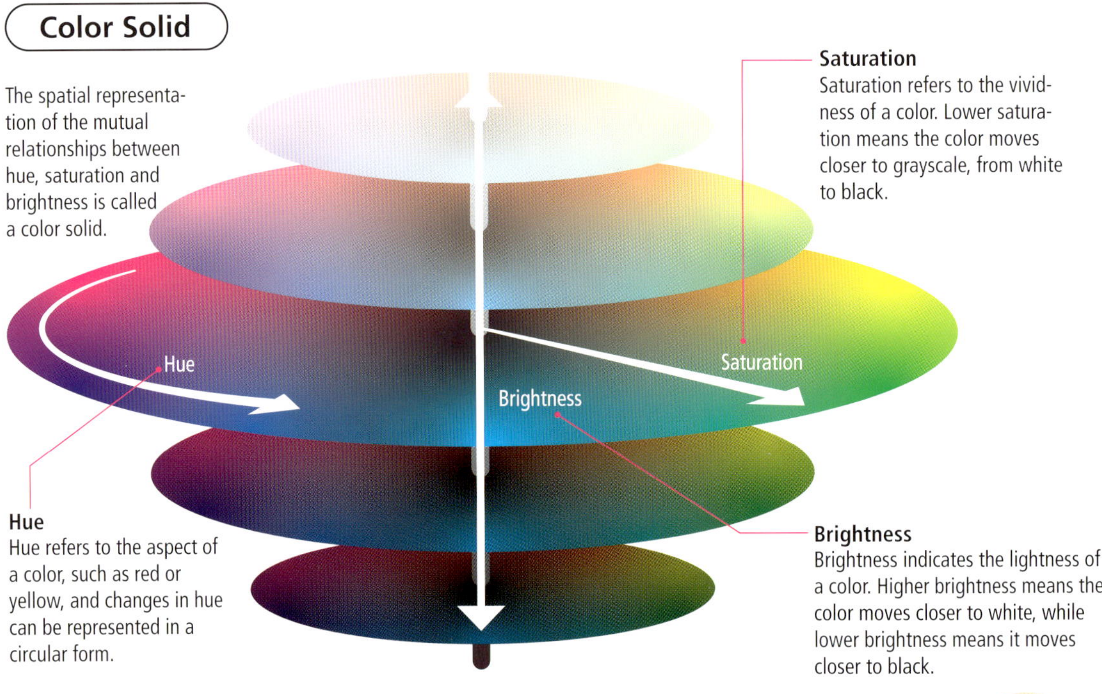


**Saturation**
Saturation refers to the vividness of a color. Lower saturation means the color moves closer to grayscale, from white to black.

**Hue**
Hue refers to the aspect of a color, such as red or yellow, and changes in hue can be represented in a circular form.

**Brightness**
Brightness indicates the lightness of a color. Higher brightness means the color moves closer to white, while lower brightness means it moves closer to black.

## Hue, Saturation and Brightness

Color has three attributes: hue, saturation and brightness. These can be represented in a three-dimensional form known as a color solid. Hue represents changes in color, showing various colors in a circular manner, like a rainbow. The center axis of the solid transitions from white at the top to black at the bottom. This transition is called brightness. Moving outward from the central axis, colors become more vivid, with the outermost part of the solid representing the most vivid colors. This change in vividness is called saturation.



## CHROMATIC COLORS AND ACHROMATIC COLORS

**Colors like red and blue that we perceive are called chromatic colors. The axis from white to black at the center of the color solid lacks hue, meaning it has no saturation and is therefore called achromatic.**

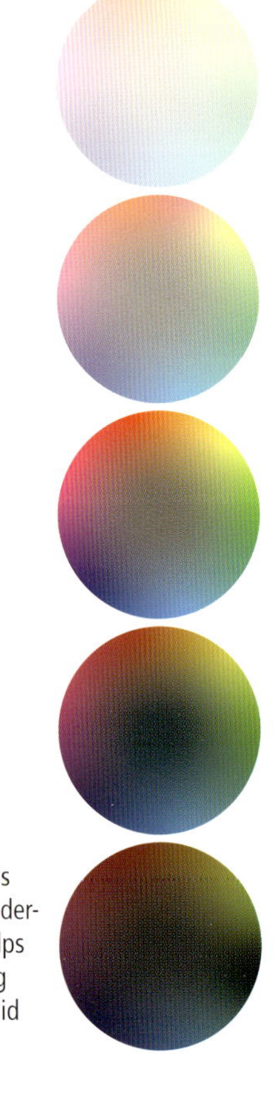

This diagram shows a circular disk viewed from above, with brightness decreasing from top to bottom. Understanding the position of a color helps eliminate confusion when choosing your palette. Visualize the color solid in your mind.

# What Are Complementary and Similar Colors?

## Complementary Colors

The opposite sides of the color wheel represent complementary colors.

The most saturated colors arranged in a donut shape from the left page form the diagram on the right. This is called a color wheel. Colors directly opposite each other on the color wheel are called complementary colors.

Using complementary colors can result in combinations that are visually striking or create strong contrasts.

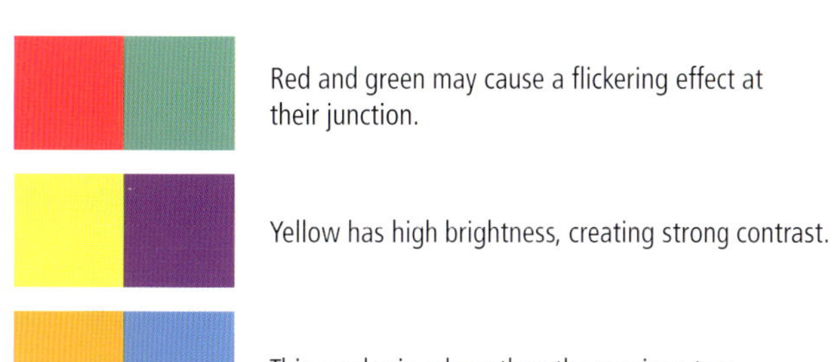

Red and green may cause a flickering effect at their junction.

Yellow has high brightness, creating strong contrast.

This combo is calmer than the previous two.

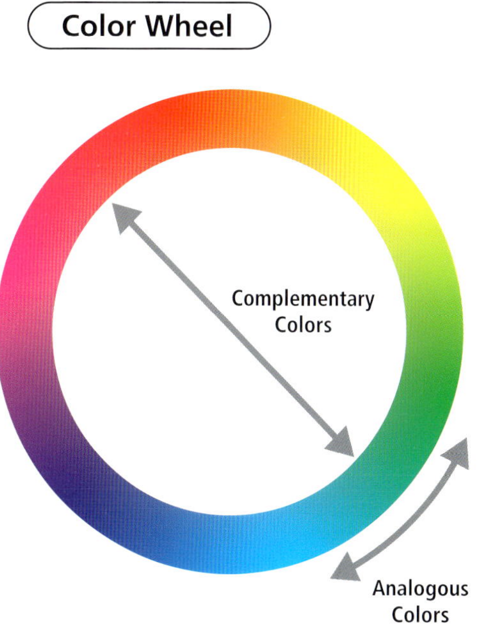


## Colors on the Same Side of the Color Wheel are Analogous

Analogous colors not only include nearby hues on the color wheel but also the areas moving toward the center of the color solid with lower saturation (Diagram A). Changes in brightness, as shown by a vertical cut of the color solid (Diagram B), are also included.

Analogous colors encompass hues close to the base color, including all variations in brightness and saturation. The combination of brightness and saturation is referred to as tone.

Diagram A

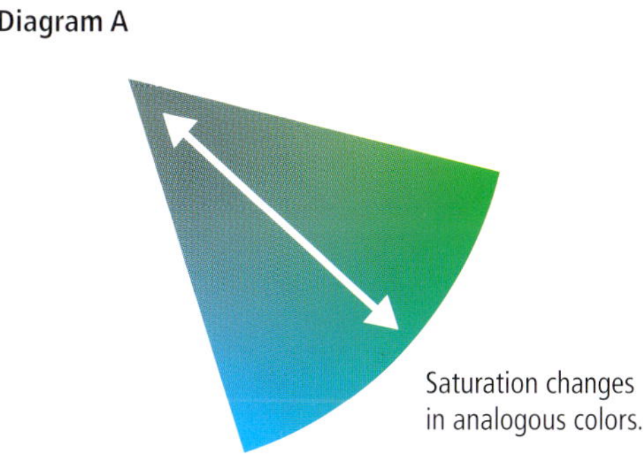


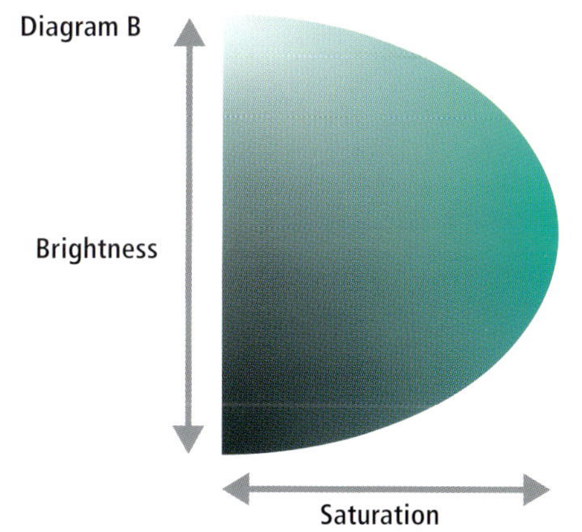


Changes in brightness and saturation (tone) for a selected color.

# Color Imagery

## The Various Effects of Warm and Cool Colors

Colors on the red side of the color wheel are called warm colors, while those on the blue side are called cool colors. As their names suggest, warm colors evoke warmth and heat, while cool colors evoke coolness and coldness.

Warm and cool colors also have other characteristics. Warm colors are considered expansive colors, making objects appear larger than they are, while cool colors are contractive colors, making objects appear smaller. For example, using red on a muscular character can make them look even more substantial, whereas using blue on a slim character can give a sharper, more delineated impression.

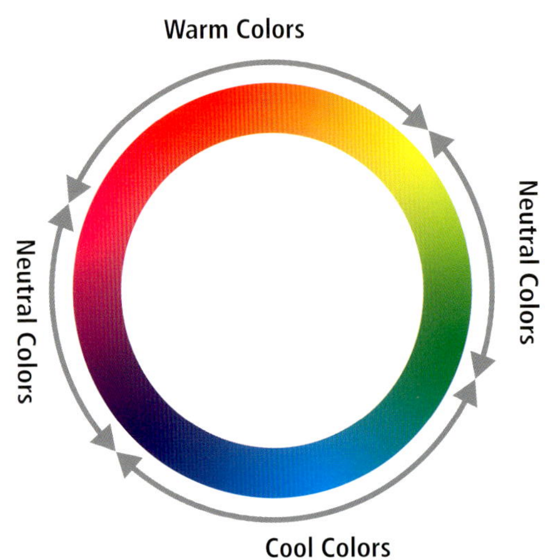


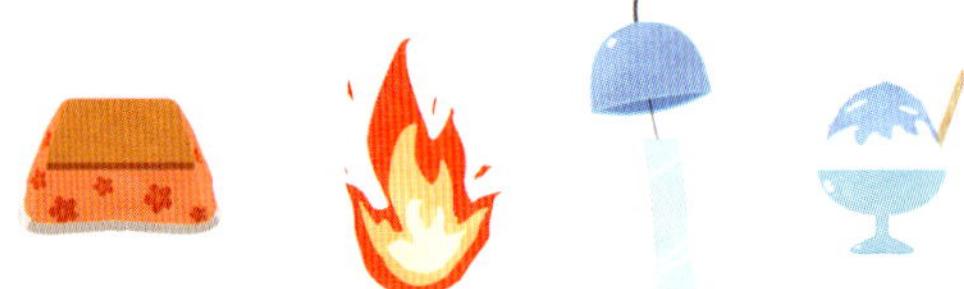

Warm and cool colors are universal and reliable choices for conveying consistent, specific imagery and messaging.

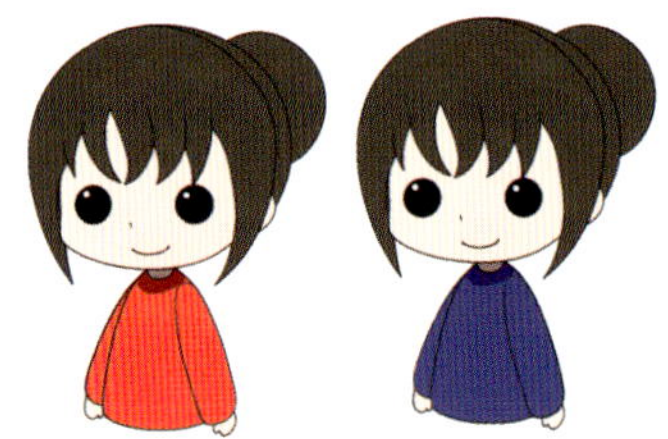

Expansive colors make objects appear larger, while contractive colors make objects appear slimmer.

## Other Expansive and Contractive Colors

Besides warm and cool colors, white and black also exhibit expansive and contractive properties. White, the brightest color, and black, the darkest, have a significant impact on perception. Colors closer to white have higher brightness and tend to appear more expansive, while colors closer to black have lower brightness and tend to contract. Therefore, even cool colors can appear expansive if they're pastel or light, and warm colors can appear contractive if they're dark.

Warm and cool colors also affect the perception of distance. Warm colors are advancing colors that come forward, while cool colors are receding colors that move back. This advancing and receding property has been widely used in the world of painting for creating depth and space in backgrounds.

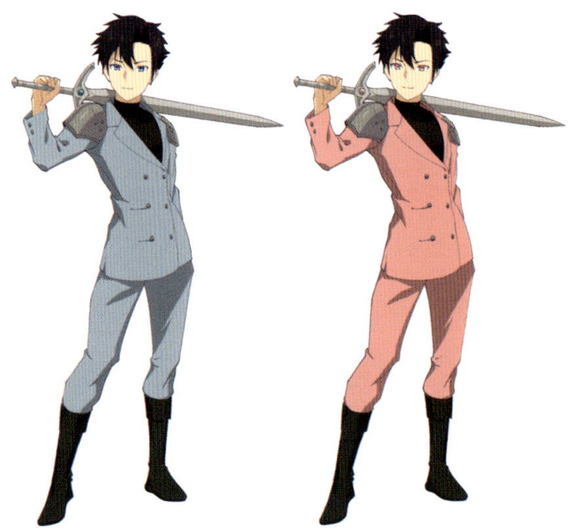

Even cool colors can appear expansive if they have high brightness, and warm colors can appear contractive if they have low brightness.

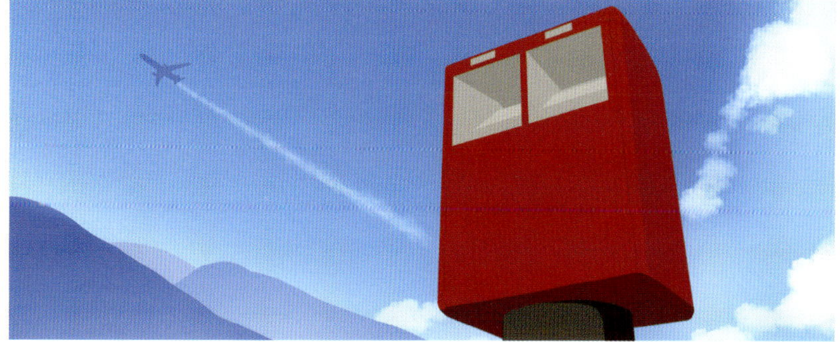

Warm colors are advancing, while cool colors are receding.

## Tone

Tone refers to the combination of brightness and saturation, two of the three attributes of color (hue, brightness and saturation). It describes the color's image in terms of it being light, dark or pale. Let's take a closer look at tone with the diagram below.

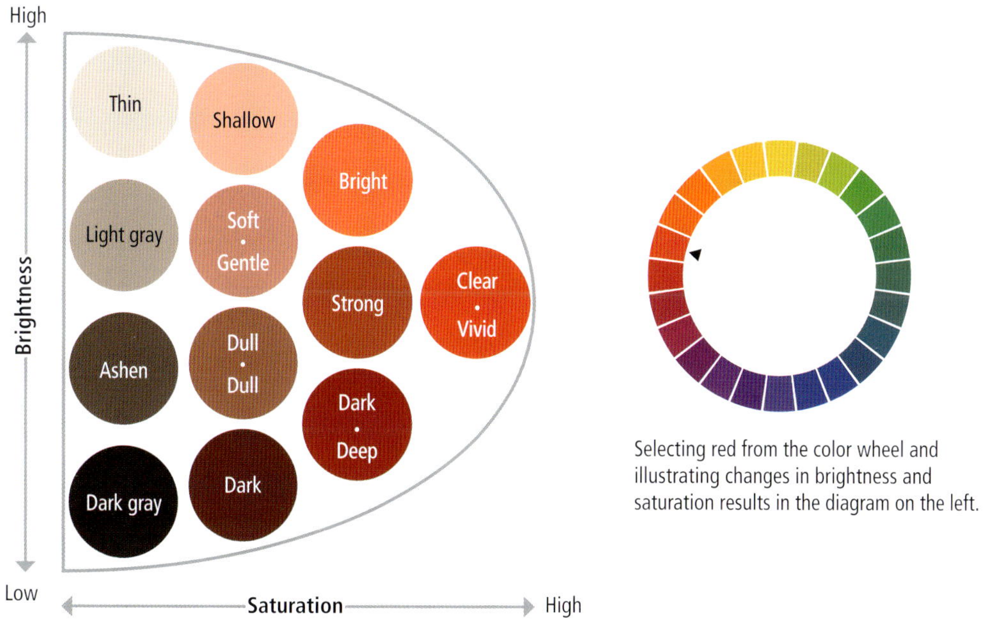



Selecting red from the color wheel and illustrating changes in brightness and saturation results in the diagram on the left.

**24 Hue Tones**

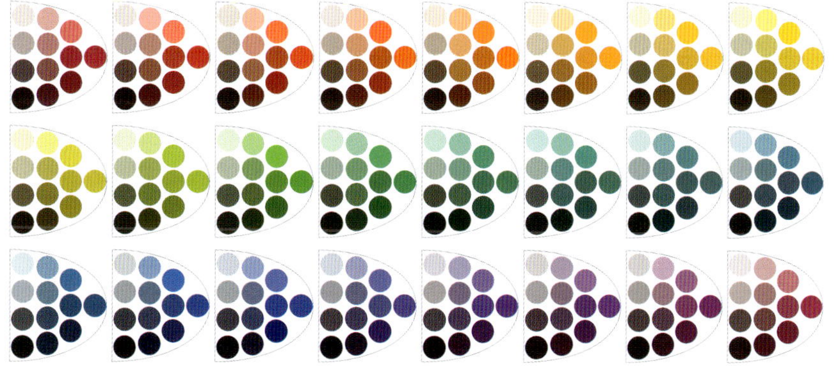

# Conveying Emotions with Colors

Colors can convey emotions beyond just warm and cool tones. For example, in character design, purple can symbolize mystery or magic. Additionally, highly saturated colors can express strong emotions, while softer colors can convey calmer, more subdued feelings.

Colors can convey individual emotions, but combining multiple colors can create nuanced expressions, similar to how chords in music add complexity, resonance and depth to the sound created.

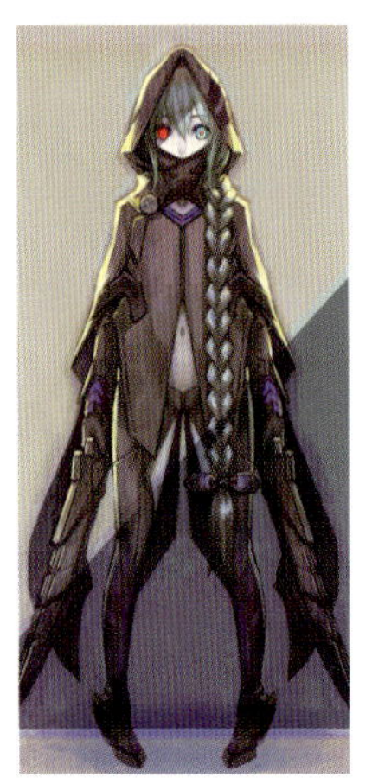

Black Character

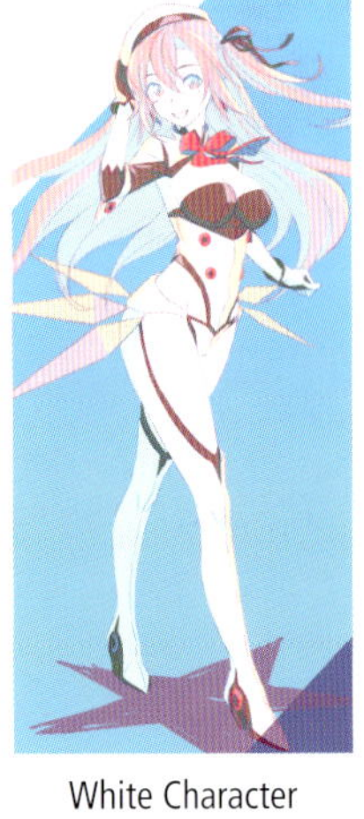

White Character

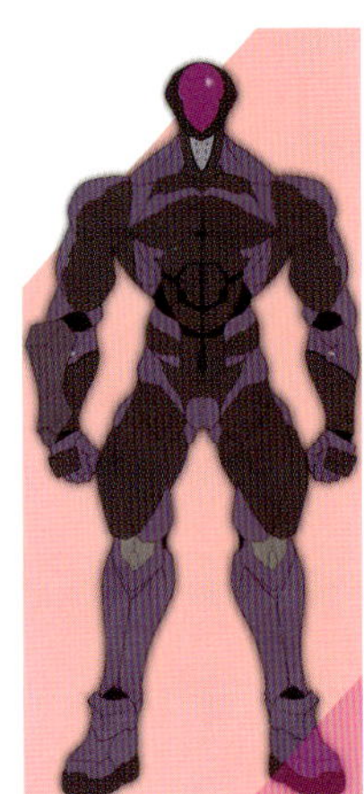

Purple Character

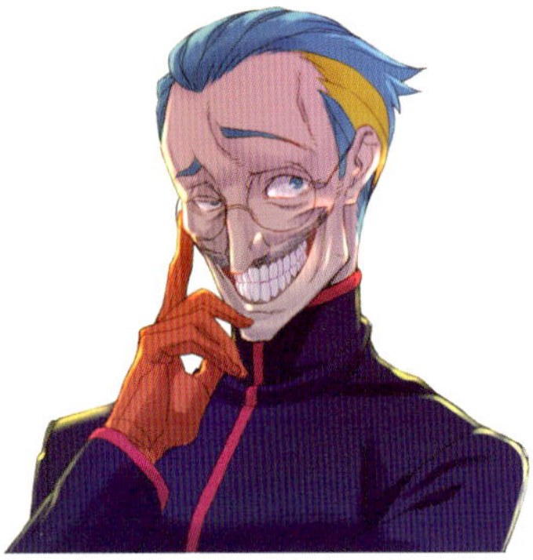

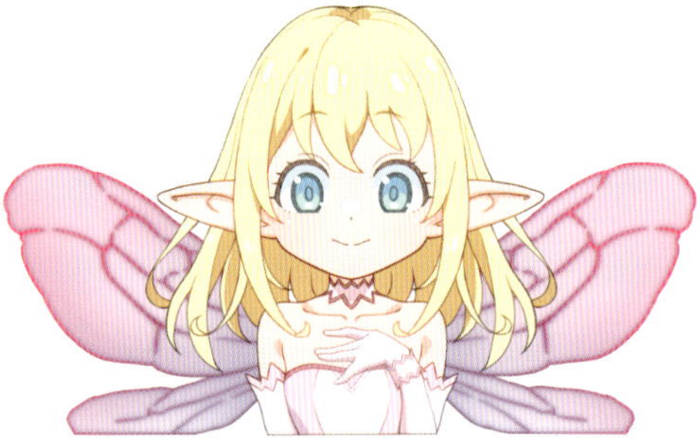

## Changes in Male Image by Age

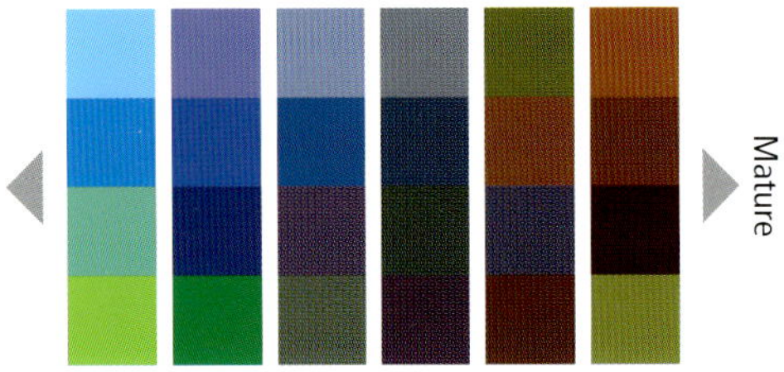

Mature

Urban

Japanese-Style

Spring

## Changes in Female Image by Age

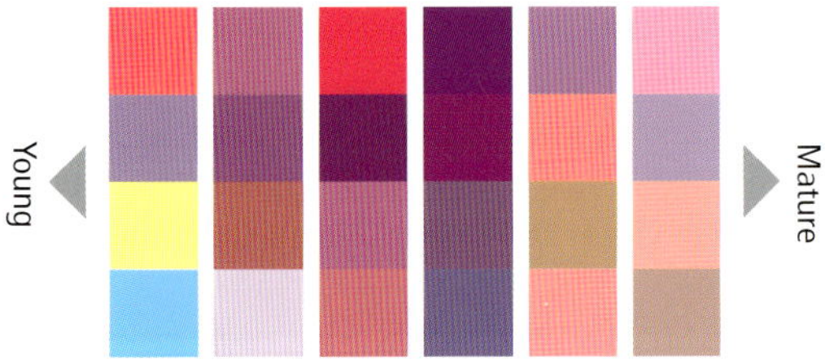

Young

Mature

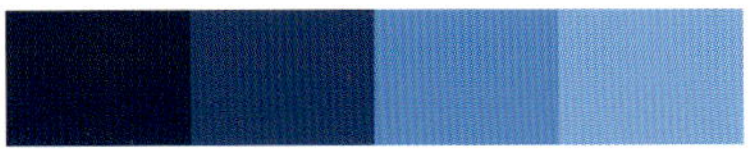

Elegant

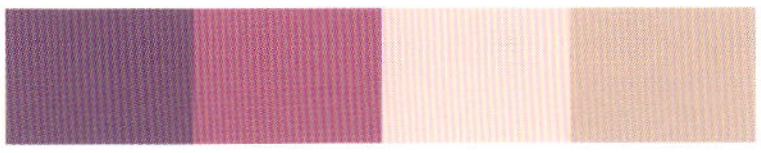

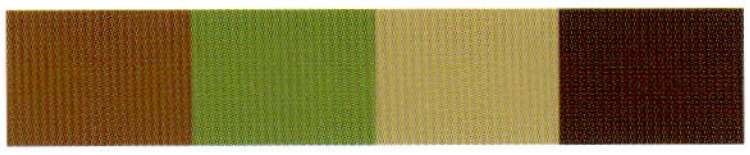

Clean

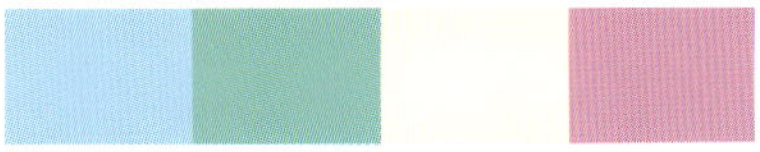

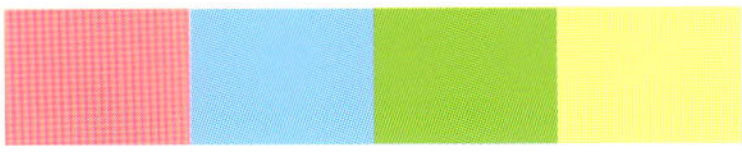

Autumn

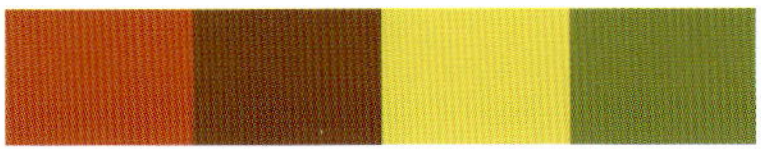

# RGB and CMYK

## Screen RGB, Print CMYK

There are two types of color models: RGB and CMYK. RGB, also known as the primary colors of light, produces colorless, transparent white light when combined. This is called additive color mixing. RGB is used in media such as computer-based and smartphone displays, essentially anything that emits light.

CMYK is used for paints and printed materials, known as the primary pigment colors. When CMY are mixed, they produce black, a process called subtractive color mixing. However, because it's difficult to produce perfect CMY inks, black ink (K) is added, creating CMYK.

The color spaces (the ranges of colors that can be expressed) of RGB and CMYK are not the same. Consequently, converting from RGB to CMYK (or vice versa) often results in significant or noticeable color changes.

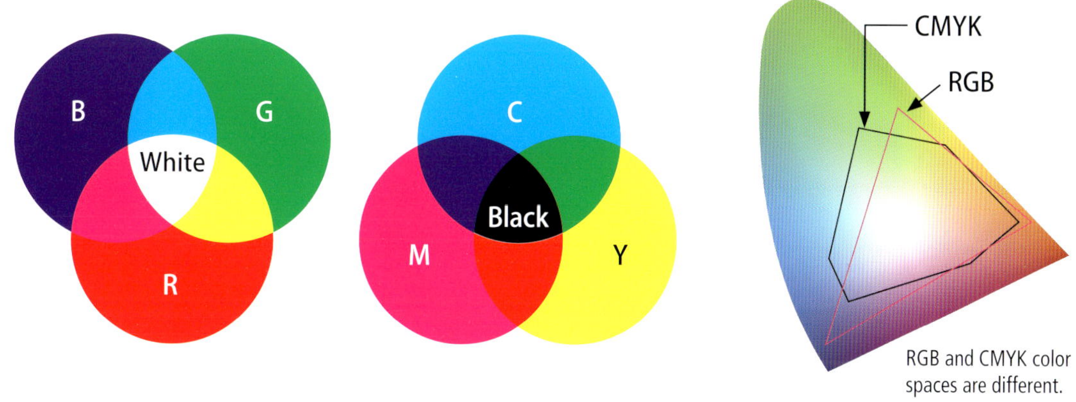


RGB and CMYK color spaces are different.

---

## A CLOSER LOOK

## Clip Studio Paint Color Circle

In its default settings, a square area appears within the color wheel, displaying the tones of the selected hue. The horizontal axis represents saturation, and the vertical axis represents brightness. The most saturated point is at the top right, and the final color selection is made within this area.

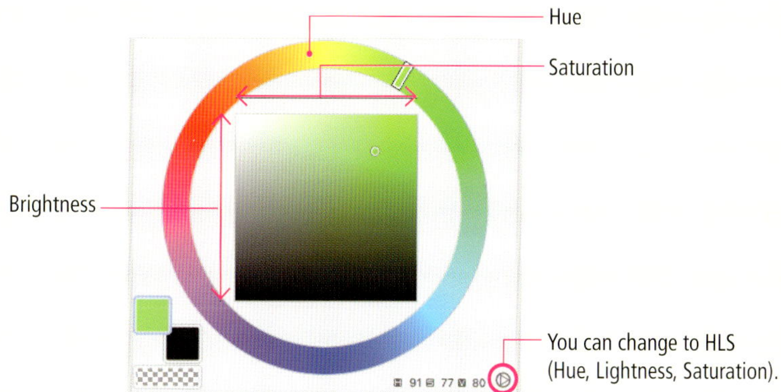

# Various Color Illusions

## Adjacent Colors Influence Each Other

When colors are closely paired or aligned, they can appear different or altered due to their proximity and mutual influence. This phenomenon mainly includes assimilation and contrast. If you don't understand assimilation and contrast, your color scheme might not turn out as intended. Conversely, understanding these phenomena can help you create stronger, more memorable color combinations.

### Assimilation Effect

Assimilation effect occurs when adjacent colors appear closer to each other, creating a specific visual effect or illusion.

### Brightness Assimilation

When the surrounding color influences the inner color, making their brightness appear closer, it's called brightness assimilation.

### Saturation Assimilation

When the surrounding color influences the inner color, making their saturation appear closer, it's called saturation assimilation.

### Hue Assimilation

When the surrounding color influences the inner color, making their hues appear closer, it's called hue assimilation.

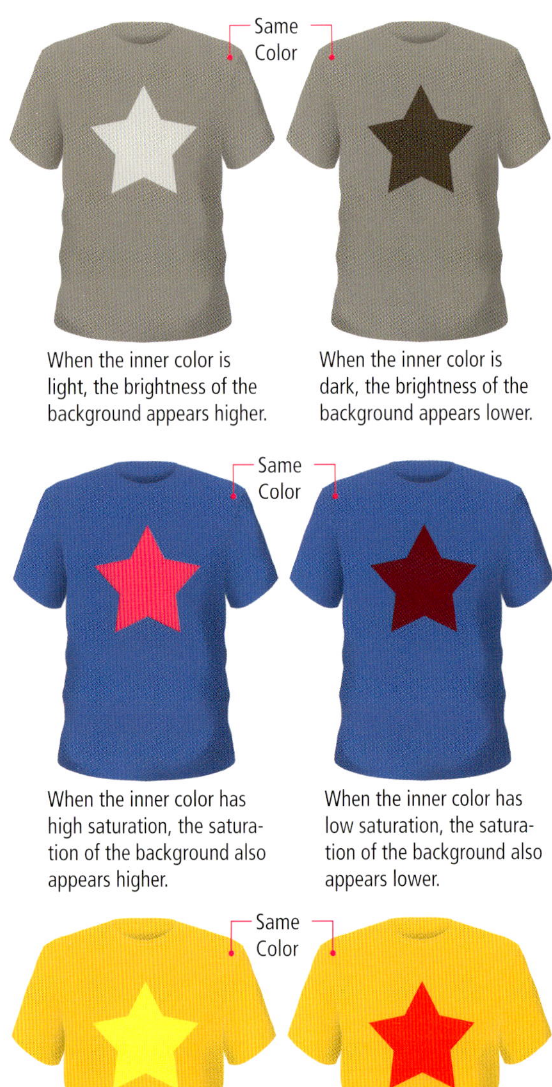


When the inner color is light, the brightness of the background appears higher.

When the inner color is dark, the brightness of the background appears lower.

When the inner color has high saturation, the saturation of the background also appears higher.

When the inner color has low saturation, the saturation of the background also appears lower.

When the inner color is yellow, the hue of the background appears closer to yellow.

When the inner color is red, the hue of the background appears closer to red.

Contrast effects occur when adjacent colors influence each other, causing them to appear different from their actual color.

## Brightness Contrast

When the surrounding color influences the perceived brightness of another color, it's called brightness contrast.

## Saturation Contrast

When the surrounding color influences the perceived saturation of another color, it's called saturation contrast.

## Hue Contrast

When the surrounding color influences the perceived hue of another color, it's called hue contrast.

## Complementary Contrast

When complementary colors are placed next to each other, they appear more saturated. This phenomenon is called complementary contrast.

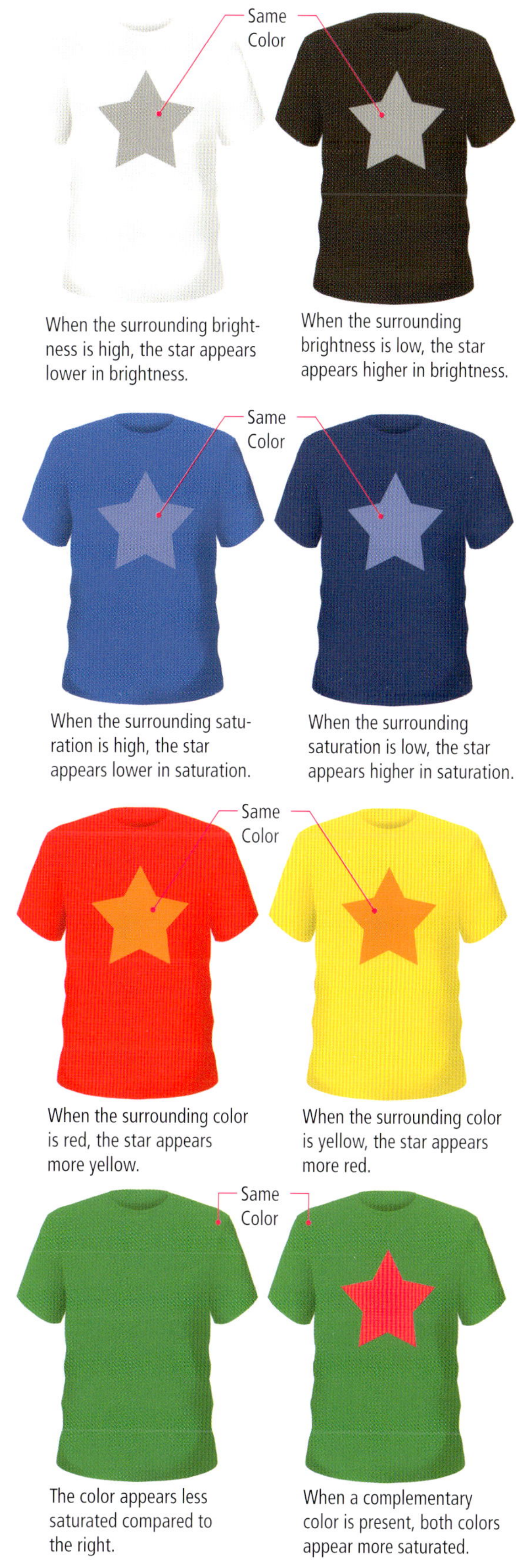


When the surrounding brightness is high, the star appears lower in brightness.

When the surrounding brightness is low, the star appears higher in brightness.

When the surrounding saturation is high, the star appears lower in saturation.

When the surrounding saturation is low, the star appears higher in saturation.

When the surrounding color is red, the star appears more yellow.

When the surrounding color is yellow, the star appears more red.

The color appears less saturated compared to the right.

When a complementary color is present, both colors appear more saturated.

Published by Tuttle Publishing, an imprint of Periplus Editions (HK) Ltd.

**www.tuttlepublishing.com**

ISBN: 978-4-8053-1888-1

Illust Hikari to Shikisai Kaitai Shinsho
© 2022 Naoto Date, Remi-Q
English translation rights arranged with
MyNavi Publishing Corporation Tokyo
through Japan UNI Agency, Inc., Tokyo

English translation © 2025 Periplus Editions (HK) Ltd



27 26 25 24     10 9 8 7 6 5 4 3 2 1

Printed in China     2411EP

Distributed by
**North America, Latin America & Europe**
Tuttle Publishing
364 Innovation Drive
North Clarendon, VT 05759-9436 U.S.A.
Tel: 1 (802) 773-8930
Fax: 1 (802) 773-6993
info@tuttlepublishing.com
www.tuttlepublishing.com

**Japan**
Tuttle Publishing
Yaekari Building, 3rd Floor
5-4-12 Osaki
Shinagawa-ku
Tokyo 141 0032
Tel: (81) 3 5437-0171
Fax: (81) 3 5437-0755
tuttle-sales@gol.com

**Asia Pacific**
Berkeley Books Pte. Ltd.
3 Kallang Sector, #04-01
Singapore 349278
Tel: (65) 67412178
Fax: (65) 67412179
inquiries@periplus.com.sg
www.tuttlepublishing.com